GERMAN SAINTS AT WAR

GERMAN SAINTS AT WAR

Robert C. Freeman

with Jon R. Felt

CFI
Springville, Utah

Those responsible for this volume express sincere thanks to those who have provided images used within. Where individual names are mentioned under photos, such pictures are generally sourced in the Saints at War Collection in the L. Tom Perry Special Collections, Harold B. Lee Library at Brigham Young University in Provo, Utah. Other images are from the Church Archives of The Church of Jesus Christ of Latter-day Saints or from the National Archives.

ISBN: 978-1-59955-224-8

Published by CFI, an imprint of Cedar Fort, Inc., 2373 W. 700 S., Springville, UT, 84663
Distributed by Cedar Fort, Inc., www.cedarfort.com

LIBRARY OF CONGRESS CATALOGING-IN-PUBLICATION DATA

Freeman, Robert C., 1959-
German Saints at war / Robert C. Freeman with Jon R. Felt.
p. cm.
ISBN 978-1-59955-224-8
1. Mormons--Germany--Biography. 2. World War, 1939-1945--Personal narratives, German . 3. World War, 1939-1945--Religious aspects--Church of Jesus Christ of Latter-day Saints. I. Felt, Jon A. II. Title.

BX8693.F73 2008
940.53088'2893--dc22

2008034502

Cover design by Nicole Williams
Cover design © 2008 by Lyle Mortimer
Edited and typeset by Kimiko M. Hammari and Melissa J. Caldwell

Printed in the United States of America

10 9 8 7 6 5 4 3 2 1

Printed on acid-free paper

CONTENTS

Acknowledgments

It is critically important to thank the contributors whose accounts appear herein. We are grateful to each one of those who have shared their ordeal during World War II. We especially appreciate the opportunity to interview President Dieter F. Uchtdorf and F. Enzio Busche about their experiences during and after World War II. President and Sister Uchtdorf and Elder Busche are among the most Christlike individuals I have ever met. Several of our veterans whose stories appear in this volume have passed on. We pay special tribute to them and their families. Furthermore, we realize that there are so many others who want and need to share their stories. We are disappointed that we can't share more accounts in this volume, but want to invite others to come forward and to share with the Saints at War Project at Brigham Young University.

In this book our approach in this book has been to share the accounts of each individual as purely as possible to allow for the volume to be as authentic as possible. We are grateful to Cedar Fort and the vision of their staff, including editors Kimiko Hammari and Melissa Caldwell, for helping this book come to fruition. We are also grateful to Brigham Young University for supporting the Saints at War Project and its goals. Thanks to the several students who have helped on this project. Besides Jon Felt, my co-collaborator on this project, this list includes Jenny Curlee, Nathan Freeman, Tamera Gale, Kaylene McClanahan, Jolyn Metro, Dale Rex, Jason Thompson, and others. We are likewise grateful to LDS Church Archives, Jeff Anderson, Matt Heiss, National Archives, and to our veterans and their families for contributing pictures for this volume.

We are grateful to various others who have continued to partnership with the Saints at War Project in the ongoing effort to discover the Latter-day Saint legacy in wartime. Thanks to my good friend and colleague Dennis Wright, cofounder of the Saints at War Project. Thanks are also extended to Sherman Fleek, Paul Kelly, Don Norton, and others too numerous to mention. Thanks to those donors who help research projects such as Saints at War to flourish at BYU. Without you, we would not be able to do the things that we are doing. Finally, thanks to our wives, Ja Neal and Keriann, and our families for their support as we have worked to access the voices of those whose stories we seek to share. They have been very patient through these years of research and writing.

—Robert Freeman

Preface

When the Saints at War Project started in the year 2000, Directors Robert Freeman and Dennis Wright began their research by focusing on understanding the experiences of Latter-day Saints during World War II. Very soon it became evident that, for Latter-day Saints, the story of the war was more involved than just retelling the American experience during the war such as had been previously done by accomplished authors Tom Brokaw, Stephen Ambrose, and others in their acclaimed works.

For Latter-day Saints, the story of World War II also involved the powerful dynamic of experiences endured by Church members on the other side. While modest in comparison to the number of accounts received from American soldier-saints, the story of German Latter-day Saints was no less compelling. For years we have looked forward to the time when enough German accounts could be brought together to share at least a sampling of these important voices. A couple of those individuals included in this book actually joined the Church after the war, but nonetheless had experiences that we deemed worthy of sharing.

This volume attempts to convey something of the impact of the war on German Saints. While most of the stories in this volume derive from firsthand accounts of Latter-day Saints who fought for German forces, it also provides glimpses into the trials endured by civilian Latter-day Saints who bore such heavy burdens both during and after the war. It becomes clear that the war was horrible for those on both sides. Furthermore, based on the accounts like those that appear in this book, it is apparent that German LDS soldiers were just as inclined to live the Word of Wisdom, pray for protection, and uphold the moral standard as were their American Latter-day Saint brethren. They also sought for and received direction from Heavenly Father in moments of danger just as Latter-day Saints from America and other nations did.

Certainly, the designs of Hitler and his regime were diabolical and evil. War is always complicated, and the human suffering it imposes is often beyond the ability of mortals to fully reconcile with the teachings of the Prince of Peace. Still, war and human conflict has been a consistent part of the experience of God's children since Old Testament times. This book endeavors to commend the faith of German Latter-day Saints who lived through the war and who relied upon their Heavenly Father to see them through this terrible time. In some sense this volume is dedicated to those in any war and on either side who have remained true to their covenants and to the gospel.

INTRODUCTION

Historians generally agree that the seeds for the conflict known as World War II were sown at the end of the Great War, or World War I. The conditions of surrender imposed upon Germany in 1918 by conquering nations created great hardships for the economy and dramatically reduced the national spirit of the citizens of the Fatherland. It also spawned deep resentment born out of a kind of servitude. Ultimately, such desperate conditions created an environment that would be ripe for the radical, new leadership which surfaced in the 1930s in the form of the Third Reich led by Adolf Hitler. Of course, Hitler promised to liberate his fellow countrymen from the shackles of economic bondage to external powers and to restore national pride as well as stimulate industrial growth, employment, and national vitality.[1]

The experience of German Latter-day Saints during this period was not dissimilar from that of their fellow countrymen. They, too, hoped for a better Germany following the hard years of the post–World War I era. Some were clearly persuaded by the sophistry of the charismatic and deceitful personality of Adolf Hitler. Ultimately, the promises of economic and industrial might turned out to simply be a justification for Hitler's drive for power and fame. Many of the challenges of the Church during this period are the subject of a fine master's thesis completed in 1991 by LDS Church Archivist Jeffery L. Anderson.[2]

As Germany's war machine emerged and as Hitler's ambitions became apparent, great concern was felt by leaders at Church headquarters in Utah for the welfare of the German Saints. In 1937, President Heber J. Grant and other leaders conducted a tour of Europe, including Germany, to assess the well-being of the Church and its members. It is important to note that at the end of the 1930s, Church membership in Germany ranked just third behind the United States and Canada. The tour also provided President Grant an opportunity to both express his love for the Saints as well as to warn them that the gathering clouds would make it necessary to have greater self-reliance.

One year later, in September of 1938, a temporary evacuation of missionaries from the region was carried out. While tensions eased and the missionaries were eventually allowed to return, this event turned out to be a dress rehearsal for the 1939 emergency evacuation of approximately 150 missionaries, which was completed almost literally on the eve of Germany's invasion of Poland on September 1, 1939.

Several weeks after the evacuation of missionaries, on September 25, 1939, President Thomas E. McKay, who presided over the Church in Europe throughout most of the war, issued a letter of encouragement to the German members:

"We pray sincerely to our Heavenly Father, that He might protect and bless those that have been called to arms and that He might strengthen those who have remained at home for the additional responsibilities that rest upon your shoulders. Pray, live a pure life, keep the word of wisdom, pay your tithing, visit and participate in all the meetings, keep free from finding fault and bearing false witness, sustain those that have been called to preside and it is our promise that the Lord will guide and lead you in all things and that you, even in the midst of afflictions and difficulties will find joy and satisfaction. Be always mindful that we are engaged in the work of the Lord and that Jesus is the Christ."[3]

In January 1940, local priesthood leaders were called to preside over the missions in Germany and Switzerland to replace the American leaders who had begun returning to the United States. The new leaders included Herbert Klopfer and Christian Heck as acting presidents of the East and West German Missions, respectively. In spite of the hardships of the war, these leaders inspired the members to remain faithful and were vital in keeping the organization of the Church intact during the long isolation from Church headquarters that would follow.

During the years of 1939–45, over four million Germans died, and many cities and towns were utterly destroyed. The tribulations of the war were very heavy for the German members of The Church of Jesus Christ of Latter-day Saints. Hundreds died and thousands were left homeless. Many lost family members, and hunger and hopelessness were everywhere.

It is unknown exactly how many Latter-day Saints served in the German military during the war, but for those who did, military service typically meant isolation from the Church and from family. Many were drafted, and some volunteered for military service out of a sense of patriotism and loyalty to their country. For many, church attendance was impossible, and their spiritual strength came solely from their own personal study, if permitted, and from personal prayer.

Among the most difficult challenges that confronted the Church in Germany were the loss of communications with Church headquarters, which necessitated even more self-reliance. This proved both to be a hardship and a blessing. Additionally, in September 1940, the monthly Church publication *Der Stern,* which had been in publication since 1869, was suspended for the duration of the war. Suspension of the paper came in response to the Nazi government's wartime prohibition against the printing of independent magazines and books.

At the beginning of the war, bolstered by a series of victories, the German government was very confident. The citizenry were upbeat, and the condition of the Church in Germany remained fairly stable. While food and other commodities became increasingly scarce, Church programs generally operated without significant interruption. However, as the war wore on and as German forces began to falter, life for the Saints became increasingly harsh. For those at home, anxiety increased as the war was being waged closer and closer to their hometowns and villages.

Working in the munitions factories by day and on fire crews at night, the members also continued faithful in their Church callings and in ensuring the welfare of those in their congregations. Church leaders endured great sacrifices in personally visiting the various branches throughout the country to encourage and support the members. As the destruction imposed upon Germany intensified, the Saints bonded more tightly together. Additionally, as conditions worsened on the war fronts, additional men, both young and old, were drafted into the military, leaving many of the branches without priesthood leadership.

Those left at home continued to faithfully hold meetings, study the scriptures, and pray for an end to the misery. During the winter of 1944–45, conditions in the branches worsened. As a result of Allied bombing campaigns, tremendous challenges were experienced by the Saints in their efforts to maintain worship practices. The loss of meeting places was a common experience, and by the end of the war, nearly all Latter-day Saint branch facilities were destroyed.

Conditions in Germany were truly desperate. The tide of the war had turned, and Germany's fate seemed clear. As the bombing of key cities in Germany intensified, panic gripped the German people. The endurance and faith of Church members was tried severely. The advancing Russian armies in the East and Allied Forces from the West had caused a mass exodus, and Church leaders struggled to keep track of all of the members forced to flee, many of them widowed mothers with young children. In the city of Dresden alone, tens of thousands of civilians were killed in the space of two days in mid-February 1945.

Finally, after nearly six years of fighting, the conflict in Europe ended with the unconditional surrender of Germany in May 1945. The cessation of hostilities, however, did not mean the end of suffering for the citizens of Germany. In the cities, residents were forced to find shelter within the ruins of their homes.

Within the Church, efforts were undertaken to alleviate the suffering. Local Church leadership arranged for several Latter-day Saint refugee centers to be established in the German cities of Chemnitz, Cottbus, Langen, and Wolfsgruen. Although great challenges confronted those who lived in such settings, the facilities served as safe shelters, places for convalescence, and centers of the Church. Everything from constant shortages of food and other supplies to harassment from local authorities were a part of the experience of the Saints at these locations. Nonetheless, many Saints regained hope and started new lives.

After several months, relief supplies from the Church, including from local congregations in Holland and Norway, began arriving to help alleviate the suffering of the Saints and their neighbors throughout Germany. The needed relief came at a critical time, as many were freezing or were facing starvation from lack of food. Local leaders became known for their efficiency and compassion in dispersing much needed supplies. In a tour of war-ravaged Europe conducted in the spring of 1946, Elder Ezra Taft Benson, then a member of the Quorum of the Twelve Apostles, visited with the Saints in Germany, arranging for their care and opening the way for the needed relief supplies to be delivered. In speaking to the Saints in Karlsruhe, Germany, then Elder Benson spoke concerning all of the German Saints:

"I came here with a heavy heart. As we rode through your green and fruitful land, I saw in every town and hamlet the frightful result of man's disobedience to the laws of God. . . . As I witnessed for the first time the appalling desolation and the almost unbelievable destruction that has taken place, I could not help but project myself and my family into your midst. As I began to contemplate what unspeakable hardships we would have had to endure had we lived in your land these past several years, I began to appreciate what a frightening and heart-sickening experience must have been yours.

"As I looked into your tear-stained eyes and see many of you virtually in rags and at death's door, yet with a smile upon your cracked lips and the light of love and understanding shining in your eyes, I know that you have been true to your covenants, that you have been clean, that you have not permitted hatred and bitterness to fill your hearts. You—many of you—are some of the Lord's choicest witnesses of the fruits of the gospel of Jesus Christ.

"We know something of your terrible hardships. Our hearts have gone out to you in the pure love of God, which is stronger than death. We love you! We are grateful for your devotion, for your faith and your loyalty to the cause of the Master. . . . We have received sufficient records to know that you have done a wonderful work."[4]

By the end of the war, according to Latter-day Saint historian Gilbert Scharffs, almost five hundred Latter-day Saint German soldiers and over one hundred civilians had died, including German Mission presidents Friedrich Biehl and Christian Heck, as well as district presidents Martin Hoppe, Carl Goeckeritz, and Erich Behrndt.[5] Despite such heavy losses, the total number of Latter-day Saints in Germany was approximately twelve thousand, only slightly less than the number of members at the beginning of the war. According to Scharffs, approximately 85 percent of the members were left homeless, and many were unaccounted for, being separated from their families and scattered across the country.

Several trying decades followed the war as Germans experienced many struggles, including nearly fifty years as a divided nation. For many individuals, this meant not seeing their loved ones and families for decades, as one or the other was trapped on the other side of the Iron Curtain. Much of the struggle and faith of Latter-day Saints during this period is recounted in the excellent volume *Behind the Iron Curtain: Recollections of Latter-day Saints in East Germany,* 1945–89.[6]

Through the horror of the war and the difficult aftermath of the conflict, the German Saints remained true to the faith that their fathers had cherished and in the process left their own legacy of faith to their fellow Saints who would follow them. So much of this story remains to be shared, and the effort to present this story has gained momentum in recent years. The present authors commend friend and colleague Dr. Roger Minert, who has undertaken an ambitious effort to document the service and sacrifice of the German Saints during World War II. Publication of his excellent research is anticipated in the near future.

It is important to continue to learn about and to share more of the German Latter-day Saint experience during this very difficult and pivotal period of history. The intent of this publication is to convey something of the sacrifices endured on the other side of the war in a way to complement earlier works from the Saints at War project.

Notes

1. This introduction includes excerpts and modifications from an article by the present author entitled "When the Wicked Rule, the People Mourn: The Experiences of German Saints During World War II," which appeared in the volume *Regional Studies in Latter-day Saint Church History* (Provo, UT: Brigham Young University, 2003).

2. Jeffery L. Anderson, *Mormons and Germany, 1914–1933: A history of The Church of Jesus Christ of Latter-day Saints in Germany and its Relationship with the German Governments From World War I to the Rise of Hitler* (Provo, UT: Brigham Young University, 1991).

3. Justus Ernst, comp., *Highlights from the German-Speaking Latter-day Saints Mission Histories, 1836–60* (Archives, The Church of Jesus Christ of Latter-day Saints, 14 September 1939).

4. Frederick W. Babbel, *On Wings of Faith* (Bookcraft: Salt Lake City, 1972), 37.

5. Gilbert Scharffs, *History of Mormonism in Germany: A History of The Church of Jesus Christ of Latter-day Saints 1840–1970,* (Salt Lake City: Deseret Book, 1970), 116.

6. Garold N. Davis & Norma S. Davis, eds. *Behind the Iron Curtain: Recollections of Latter-day Saints in East Germany, 1945–89* (Provo, UT: Brigham Young University Studies, 2000).

Dieter F. and Harriet Reich Uchtdorf

President Dieter F. Uchtdorf was born November 6, 1940, in then Mährisch-Ostrau, Czechoslovakia. His parents, Karl A. and Hildegard Opelt Uchtdorf, were not members of the Church during the war but were baptized afterward. President Uchtdorf married Harriet in 1962. President Uchtdorf has served as a stake president, as a member of the Quorums of the Seventy, as a member of the Presidency of the Seventy, and as a member of the Quorum of the Twelve Apostles. He was sustained as a member of the First Presidency on April 5, 2008. (Modest portions of this account are drawn from the following article, Jeffrey R. Holland, "Elder Dieter F. Uchtdorf: On to New Horizons," Ensign, *March 2005, 10—15.)*

Our father was a customs officer, stationed at the Czechoslovakian border until the war broke out, and that's why I was born in Czechoslovakia. As the front moved from the east further west, the units of the customs offices were transferred into army service, and my father was then sent to the west front. Some time after my father left, the rest of the family had to leave also because of the approaching war front. My parents had agreed that if they were ever separated, they would go to Zwickau in East Germany, where my mother's family was from.

It took us two weeks by rail to make a trip that would normally take only half a day. I remember this as a very dangerous time, when we were struggling for survival and struggling to stay together as a family. When we arrived in East Germany, the night bombing raids started in our city. As a child I felt it was very threatening; but looking back, I assume that it must have been even more frightening for the adults than for us children, not realizing all the possible consequences. At times I almost thought it was exciting to run from our home to the bomb shelter, seeing the bombers come in with all the lights and the noise, and the bombs beginning to fall.

Not long after we arrived in East Germany, my brother, who was fifteen, was called into the army. It was the last days of the war. He and other young men of his age were assigned to fight the incoming army and protect the city. I remember that we went with my brother to the place of assembly, and that my mother tried to convince the commanding officer to let him go because my father was still serving in the army. I also remember that my brother didn't want to be released, because he felt that he was doing the right thing to protect his country and his people by fighting against the approaching army.

When the war ended, my father, who was in southern Germany, walked all the way to Zwickau to be with us. He had to walk during the night because walking during the day was too risky, and he didn't want to be captured and made a prisoner of war. In fact, out of a group of seven who started the journey, he was the only one who made it all the way safely.

Our family had a special call that was unique to us, a special whistle. I still remember being in our home and hearing that whistle coming from the street, outside on the other side of the wall. A neighbor came up to our door and said, "There is a man out there who says he is your husband and father." My mother went out, and there he was, back from the army. He had reached us healthy and in good condition.

After the war my father could no longer work as a customs officer, so he worked in the mines, even in the uranium mines, to provide for our family. My mother went out into the countryside with the few things we had brought from Czechoslovakia and bartered them in exchange for food. These were very, very difficult times, but our parents provided very well for us children so we really didn't recognize the shortage of things.

One day my grandmother was standing in a line with many others. She might not even have known what was being offered at the front of the line. A wonderful white-haired lady with a kind expression on her face was in the line with her, and they began to talk about religion. My grandmother was a religious person, and she was always interested in the faith of others. So this wonderful lady invited her to come to church, and she went. She came home and asked my parents to go with her. They all decided that the children should not go, because they didn't want to bring four children in to disrupt the meeting. But when they got there, they were surprised to see that the church was full of children. So the next Sunday all of us went, and actually from then on we didn't miss a meeting. It took awhile until we were allowed to be baptized, because we had to prove that we were firm in the faith, but eventually everyone in the family was baptized—except me, because I was only six years old.

So this one wonderful sister, Sister Ewig (*ewig* means "eternal" in German), invited my grandmother to church, and out of this came our conversion. Sister Ewig is truly an eternal friend, family member, and angel. We have pictures of her that someone helped us find not too long ago, and she even looks like an angel. Our children know of her, and our grandchildren know of her. It shows me that one person with a loving, kind, deep, and honest concern for others can make a difference for eternity. She truly is our "Sister Eternal." I'm looking forward to meeting her again after this life. She will always have a special place in our hearts and minds.

HARRIET REICH UCHTDORF

We stayed with my mother's side of the family in Eastern Germany during the war. My grandmother was from Eisenach, so we went to live with her. My father was in the war, even though he was a musician. They trained him to be a Morse code operator, and he was also trained as a truck driver so they could send him where they needed him. He could speak French, so he was stationed in France for a long time.

My first recollections of the war are when I was three and a half years old. I had to always be ready, when Mother called, to jump into a special

ALVIN CARLSON FILE

An American soldier entertains a young girl in Europe.

suit by my bed and get my little bag that Mother had prepared. My little sister was only six months old and slept in a little wicker basket. I was supposed to grab one end of the basket while Mother held the other, as well as her own bag, and together we would walk down the stairs and to the shelter. I remember that we had to sit on benches, and it was a little scary, because everyone was talking about what would happen now and whose homes would be bombarded and were burning. It was scary for a little girl to have the people so excited and scared all around you, and you didn't know what would happen. When the sirens stopped, I was always the first one to run to the door and look for our house, and I would say, "It's still there!" I still remember the wonderful feeling when I saw that our house was still there, that there was no fire, and therefore no more danger.

These were the only times I ever remember being frightened. The other times, I had a lot of family with me. My grandmother was there, my aunts were there, and we always had enough food because we lived in a rural area outside of the city.

After the war we were in Frankfurt, and things were very difficult. Food was very hard to find. One day my mother had taken me into the city, and I was riding in a little handcart. The whole city was busy with people walking around—no cars, just people and soldiers, American soldiers. I still remember an experience I had—it was such a nice experience: I was sitting in my handcart, and all of a sudden a blond, smiling soldier walked up and offered me a piece of chewing gum. I had never seen anything like it. I looked at my mother, and she said it was okay for me to take it. So I had this little piece of chewing gum, and it was wonderful! I just chewed it and chewed it. After a while I said, "You know what, Mom? It's still there!" I had never had chewing gum in my whole life before, so I didn't even know what it was. My mother explained it. I kept this piece of gum for weeks. After chewing it for a while, I always put it back in its nice silver paper and kept it like a treasure. Every so often I would take it out and chew on it a little, but I saved it for a long time.

We recognized that these soldiers were not our enemies but that they were friends of the German people. They spoke a different language, so we could never talk to each other, but I felt that they were friends. This remained with me.

A few years later, when I was twelve years old, two missionaries came to our door, and they were smiling like that soldier. I had such a positive feeling when I saw them, as if I was connecting them with the chewing gum that the very kind and nice American soldier gave to me. So I opened the door. My mother did not want them to come in, but I pled with her to let them in for just a moment.

My father had passed away eight months earlier. When he passed away, there was all of a sudden a big, dark hole in our lives. I still remember that for me this was much harder than the whole war experience, because now there was no father in our life, and my mother was always very sad. But when the missionaries came, they brought light and the gospel. They left us a copy of the Book of Mormon, and my mother began to read it. I couldn't tell you exactly what she read, but I watched her face and noticed something remarkable happening to her countenance. I saw joy returning to her life, and I saw light come back into her eyes. I saw hope find a place in her soul. We were baptized four weeks later.

F. Enzio Busche

Elder F. Enzio Busche was born April 5, 1930, in Dortmund, Germany. His parents were not members of the Church, but they were great examples of honesty, righteousness, and integrity to Enzio and his four sisters. Though occurring during desperate conditions, his childhood was full of love. He was drafted into the German Army at the age of fourteen. The experiences of his early life and the war left in him a deep and burning desire to know the true meaning of life. This desire and yearning only deepened through time. He married his childhood friend Jutta Baum in 1955. But marriage did not solve his dilemma; in fact, it made both his wife and him rather frustrated since it was not all they thought it could be. When American missionaries from The Church of Jesus Christ of Latter-day Saints knocked on his door, he couldn't turn them away. Elder Busche and his wife were baptized in 1958. He was soon called as the Dortmund branch president and later served as a district president and regional representative. He was called as a member of the First Quorum of the Seventy in 1977.

One must understand that in Germany everyone was invested in a new future, a new view of the future. We had an organization; it was called the Hitler Youth. We were educated to believe that we were building a perfect world, that the corruption would be taken away, that all of the promiscuity would be taken away, that the family would be the center of life, and that the people would care for each other.

After World War I, Germany had the feeling that they were not treated right. They didn't feel guiltier for starting the war than any other country; they didn't have a selfish reason for starting it. But the Treaty of Versailles was hitting Germany so hard and unprepared. They had made the agreement to stop fighting, but it was the conditions that came out later that the people thought were not right. Big chunks of German territory were taken away and given to other countries, and many millions of dollars to repay the things that other countries asked them to do. Everything looked like chaos, and then came the chaos of an inexperienced democratic government, with I don't know how many parties, who had all kinds of different opinions. And finally the chaos of hunger came. Eight million people, without any resources, were just walking through the streets shouting for hunger. People turned to corruption and prostitution, and all that was so terrible, and looked so awful. In all of this there was no hope. There was nothing there that they could look forward to, and it was just a disaster without any end. With the inflation that happened, suddenly money had no value anymore. It was very difficult to understand when suddenly a dollar, for instance, was worth seven billion marks. I knew a man who was a doorman at a hotel. He got his tips from American tourists, all in dollars. Because of their value, he was able to buy a farm with his tips. Lots of people knew the situation in Germany and wanted to buy German companies. It seemed that some people knew how to do it, and some did not know how to do it, and therefore there was emotionally a lot of animosity toward the people who had the money. Newspapers were bought, printing companies were bought, steel factories were bought, and suddenly the German people had this feeling that things had gone too far.

People were just looking for something to hold onto, something to look forward to. And there came along an organization that said, "We will build a new society, which will be righteous and honest and decent and it will give you employment and you will have a decent salary so you can feed your family." It was not difficult to understand that people liked the idea to have order and a system back in place. To have clean streets again, to not be fired because there was protection, to have health care, retirement, vacations—this was all very appealing. So it is a very interesting way to think about what was really happening in Germany, and why Adolf Hitler was given the power that the German people gave to him, because he came to power by elections, and not by any kind of coup. He was elected as chancellor of Germany.

We were all united in this same vision that came to us from our leaders. Of course there was only one source of information. I only knew one paper, and that was the paper that came from the party. I knew one radio station, and that came from the government. And the adults believed it also, at least the ones that I was with. There was an enthusiasm, there was a dream. We felt that every individual or good-meaning person in the world would see the same thing, would see the same dream, and would see the same hope. We were told that the majority of people in other places all over Europe would sympathize with what we dreamed of, and they would want to be a part of our dream, and that we would rescue the world with a new world order, and that all of the wars, all of the starvation, and all of the injustice would come to an end.

Therefore, when I was drafted at fourteen years of age, I felt honored! I could do something to protect the Fatherland and to establish this order of righteousness, honesty, and decency. I was ready to go and march and do whatever it took to make it happen. It was the last weeks of the war, and there was a group of about thirty of us, the same age, who had been drafted. Our leader was maybe two years older, but he looked like an adult to us. We got new uniforms, though they were the same as from the youth organization, but we got all the guns and all the ammunition that was all new. We never shot them—we could hardly even carry them, they were so heavy. Then, of course, the reality sank in, because as we left our training, we were chased. We saw the burnings and the destruction and the pain of people dying and people being hurt and the cities being burned. It was chaos, and suddenly we no longer had the same feelings of wanting to defend, but of how we could get out of the mess. I finally saw the whole propaganda machine unraveling, and I could see that things were not exactly how I had dreamed them to be and that the people who were our leaders were sometimes as wicked as anyone else.

At one point I was traveling south in a train. The train was traveling south on the very narrow service tracks because all the other tracks had been destroyed. The train was packed with people, was so full, that we stood like sardines. I remember the experience still today; we were standing crammed and huddling together. We didn't dare breathe for fear that the train would explode. As the train started rolling, I realized that I was standing next to a young couple. They were about seventeen years old. They had such a unique expression, especially considering that time of destruction where most of the cities were destroyed by then and there was so much despair, panic, and hunger. Here were the two young people, standing in a chaste embrace. They didn't kiss or anything, but just stood there smiling at each other with beautiful smiles, looking into each other's eyes with admiration. I realized that all of the others had realized what was happening, and they tried not to interfere with what was going on as it seemed to be something sacred. As the train went on and on, they never changed, always having that same smile, and once in a while a tear rolled down her cheek and then his.

The train was attacked by two fighter planes, and everyone streamed out as soon as it stopped to look for shelter. When the attack was over, after maybe ten minutes, I was the first one to go back onto the train, and I was totally shocked to see those two people still standing there. With all of the screaming and shouting and all of the commotion of the attack, they didn't care. They had found something that is more important: the light of another person's love. I have never forgotten seeing them stand above death. What was death when you had love? From that time on, I had this as my model. I really envied this young man for this obvious match that he had found. I always carried this image with me in my soul—that when you can love, nothing else matters. I was not religious, and I had never heard any religious talk about love, so I didn't know anything about Jesus Christ or religion, but through this I did realize that we are not alone. I realized that there is always a spiritual power trying to reach into our soul and give us understanding and the ability to adapt to all situations.

Especially one thing I have not forgotten. We were marching, always running away. We did not want to be shot at, and we didn't want to shoot, so we were just running. We stayed overnight in a barn in a little village. One of my buddies was not there in the evening. Nobody knew where he was, but we knew his grandmother lived in this same village, and so we thought that he might have escaped to see her.

The next morning I awoke to a terrible scream from a little boy. I will never forget that scream. We found out that it was my buddy who had been hanged from a tree in front of his grandmother's house by the SS for desertion. This cruelty brought me to a state of awakening, and I began to see and understand what was happening. There was such panic in my soul that yes, these things were real, not like a novel or poetry, but were real. I didn't know where my father was. I didn't know what had happened to my mother and my sisters. I was all by myself. I had no money or resources, and I had no idea what my future would be. I was realizing that I needed help, and at this time, though I was not religious, I began to feel like someone was putting his arms around me and helping me make it through another hour and another day. With all of the dangers that came later, with being captured and becoming a prisoner of war, I always had that feeling, not to worry, that everything would be okay.

I was finally captured by Americans, and I could see immediately that I loved the Americans. And this was true of all the Germans; they wanted to be caught by the Americans. They didn't want to be caught by the Russians, or the British, or the French, but they wanted to be caught by the Americans. Some made long detours just to be able to get into an American prison camp. I had always felt, even in my childhood, that America was a different country. I cannot really put my hand on how it happened, because my father did not know too much about America, and he didn't speak overly positive about it, at least no more than he spoke about England or France. But I always had the feeling that Americans were different. I smelled something of agency. I have always had a deep love for agency, for freedom of expression, for freedom from any false influence.

I saw it confirmed with the Americans that took us prisoner.

The first evening in my new role as a prisoner of war, we were in a little firehouse. There was a GI watching us who was so casual and relaxed, almost looking at us like a next-door neighbor. He looked at me and asked if I understood English. I could speak a little English as I had learned some in school, so I was very proud that I could understand what he said. He asked if I was hungry, which I was. He said he couldn't feed us all, but he could feed me, so he told me to come back at ten o'clock to the window and he would bring me something. At ten o'clock he was there, and gave me a whole loaf of bread. It was different bread to me, because bread in Germany is much different than typical American bread. I couldn't believe it. I thought it was cake or something, as it was so light. It was like a delicacy and I of course shared it with the others that were there. He also gave me a tin can of coffee, and I had to be careful not to burn my hands, because it was still so hot. I will never forget the easiness with which he talked to me and that he didn't see me as an enemy or someone that needed to be beaten up or put in jail. He was just happy when I was happy. It was such a comfort to see that and to feel that; it has never left me.

I was in the camp for three weeks, and then they let us come and raise our hand and swear that we would never fight again. We were so ready to swear that. They gave us a sheet of paper as a group of about thirty or forty and told us we could go home. We all had different homes, but we had to stay together as long as we could so we wouldn't be caught without a paper and end up in another camp. My shoes were completely gone. The heel on my right shoe was worn off, and I had to walk on my foot. Since I could speak a little English, I was the spokesman for our group. I asked some American soldiers for help in finding us transportation. They looked at us and told us they would see what they could do. But they were always helping! They stopped a truck driving by and told them to take us on their way. My desire to learn more of their country was growing as I saw their openness, the light, the friendliness, the kindness, and that they had no prejudices against us. They looked at us as human beings as they were themselves. I was interested in learning about the people who had raised them like this. This later was a strong motivation for me when American missionaries came to our door. I could not send them away, because I wanted to learn more from them, from their country. It seemed to me, as they taught, that they told me about the same Utopia that I had learned in Hitler Germany. Therefore, I was very skeptical at the beginning. It took me two years to study this all by myself, taking the time to really learn and understand. When I really got the feeling that it could be true, then the change in my own life began.

—•—

Sometimes we see great heroes, people that stand in great honor, and we admire them and follow their examples. But it seems to me that when I really analyze my first time with the gospel of Jesus Christ, I am most impressed by the examples from those people that were not standing in the limelight. One of these examples was this little woman, Sister Meist, who was absolutely astounding. As I came to the branch on a regular basis, I realized this woman, who seemed very old to me at the time, had to walk two hours every Sunday to get to that meeting place. I don't know exactly how old she was, but she looked very old to me, I being just a young man. I talked to my wife about it and asked if we couldn't rearrange our schedule to make that detour to pick her up. It would only be an extra hour or so. My wife agreed, and we thought we were good Christians to do something like that. When I talked to her about it, she looked at me like I had offended her. She said, "Brother Busche, you can't do that to me." I didn't know what I was doing to her. She said, "I am an old woman and I cannot show the Lord my love and my support like you can. That is the joy of my week, to go on Sunday mornings to show my God that I appreciate the opportunity to go to His Church. Therefore, I get up early in the morning and begin to sing and begin to prepare and to walk. I know all of the windows and who's living behind them. I know all the shrubs, all the flowers, all the kids, and all the dogs. I love them all. I greet them, and I sing with my heart the songs of the hymnbook." I just couldn't understand it. What a remarkable person she was, and I was just beginning to understand her.

Only later, when I knew her a little better, did I understand all the sufferings and difficulties she had experienced in life. She was from East Prussia and had been raped and had her children killed by the enemy. Her husband had been killed in action during the war, and her farmhouse had been burned down. She had walked eight hundred to a thousand kilometers with just a little handcart with the few belongings she had left. She lived in a little shack with no plumbing or running water. But she was happy. She was always happy. She was an example to me. To see the joy from her soul and to see her obedience and how she had engrained into herself to be in the House of God on Sundays has given me strength and understanding of what the gospel can do to individuals, regardless of their circumstances. They can be the happiest people in the world.

When I was a young branch president without any counselors, I had to do everything by myself, including collect the tithing envelopes. She was always the first one to come with her tithing envelop. When I opened it and saw that she had made a very gracious fast offering, I was surprised. I knew her situation and said that she really didn't need to give a fast offering but should take care of herself. She was very upset with me and said, "Brother Busche, you are new in the Church. This is for the poor!" I thought to myself, "If there is anyone that is poorer than you, let me know, because you are the poorest person I have ever seen." This was, however, a tremendous example of commitment, of leadership, and of spirituality because this woman had a testimony.

She still has an influence on my faith to this day. Because of her example and her testimony,

NATIONAL ARCHIVES

Displaced refugees return home.

she has done something that has never left me. Most small branches have different factions that try to prove who's right, and there was always some sort of argument on a Sunday morning about who was right and who was wrong and who was better qualified for this or that. One Sunday, I was thinking to myself, "What am I doing?" I must have looked a little distraught, and as I was standing there in the hallway, she approached me. She came very close, which made me feel uncomfortable, but she came closer than someone normally would and shouted one thing as loud as she could: "Brother Busche, it is true, it is true, it is true!" In German, "*Es ist die Wahrheit, es ist die Wahrheit, es ist die Wahrheit*!" I still feel the screaming of her soul. It's like a rock that has been given me to build on that has never left.

One day she came to me, years later, and said, "Brother Busche, the Lord will permit me to go away from this world."

I said, "Oh Sister Meist, you have a long time left to live."

She said, "You don't understand. The Lord told me that I could go, and so I have prepared everything for the funeral, who should give the opening prayer and so on."

I said again, "Sister Meist, stop that. We don't plan our funerals and we don't know when the end will come."

She looked at me again and said, "You still don't understand, sir. The Lord told me that my time was over and I am permitted to go home."

She gave me money and asked if it would cover the cost of the funeral. It was more than enough. The next Sunday, she did not come to church. She had passed away, smiling in death.

Most of the time we live our life as if we weren't quite alive. We are so distracted by what happens and what we need to take care of. But the essence of life is understood when we face a difficult situation like death. Suddenly you know, and you begin to live. The same happens in war when you have people shooting at you left and right, up and down. You suddenly realize who you really are and how fragile you are. Suddenly the essence of life becomes more visible. Therefore, as strange as it sounds, the hard times and the tough times, I consider as being the best times of my life. This is because I got my foundation of life, my feelings and my trust, and all of that hope and later faith, and even a conversion during these times.

I have seen so many people, so many wonderful members, most of whom are gone now. But they shared with me some of the things they experienced in life. Some participated in the whole war and had to go through all of those things, but were never forced once, in all of this, to shoot at a human being. They felt that this was the greatest thing that could have happened in their lives. I know I could not have shot, either. I was not a member of the Church, but it was completely unthinkable. I was glad I was also not forced to shoot anyone.

A friend of mine was on the island of Crete in the Mediterranean. When it was finally attacked by the British, they had to leave. They were evacuating with airplanes, and he was supposed to go with his group into a specific plane. While he was going up the stairs, a voice told him not to get on the airplane. He was petrified and knew he would be disobeying an order by not going. But the voice told him again not to go. He finally stepped down and said he wouldn't go. They wanted to shoot him on the spot but said that he would be court-martialed and hung when they got out. The plane started and rolled away. It was not quite off the ground when it rolled over and crashed, killing everyone onboard. He was stunned. A voice had told him not to go, and now all that knew he had disobeyed his orders were dead. From that time on, and he wasn't a member at that time either, but he felt that some power was guiding him, preparing him for what would happen later in his life. The same voice also told him that if he kept himself chaste he would be protected and would come out of the war whole. He was protected, which he shared with me with tears in his eyes. He said, "I know that there is a living God that watches over us, and no matter where we are, in which country we are, or on which side we are, whatever happens, we are not alone, we are cared for, we are loved."

For more information on the life, conversion, and service of this remarkable leader and disciple of Christ, see Yearning for the Living God *by F. Enzio Busche (Deseret Book, 2004).*

Ethelgard von Seydlitz Koska Hoelzer

Ethelgard von Seydlitz was born October 12, 1908, in Zukowken, West Prussia, to Wilhelm Kurt von Seydlitz and Elizabeth Laura Hager. Her parents were wealthy and lived on an estate, raising Arabian horses. Her father was a high-ranking officer in the Prussian Army, and the family name was well known in the aristocratic circles of Prussia. Ethelgard's mother came from central Germany, where her parents owned coal mines. The years of growing up were some of Ethelgard's fondest, riding horses, playing with her father's hounds, and receiving her education from German and French governesses. Religion was also an important part of growing up. Ethelgard's mother was a strong Protestant woman who taught her children at a young age to pray often and rely on the Lord.

During the First World War, I had the misfortune of losing my father. One night in 1918, the district magistrate telephoned Mother and requested her to leave our estate as soon as possible because plundering Polish robber bands were drawing near along the newly formed borders. All our valuables were quickly packed. Hurriedly we were taken out of our beds and dressed. In a carriage drawn by a six span of horses, we abandoned our beautiful estate toward the West to my grandparents' home in Dresden. Three hours after our departure, we learned the Polish bandits had burned our castle to the ground.

I will never forget the weeks we spent with my grandmother. In her home, every day began with a morning devotional in which the personnel also took part. Each evening, at twilight, was devoted to the children, during which she retold the experiences she and grandfather had as Lutheran missionaries to India, Borneo, and Sumatra. Then she took us by the hand and led us through pearl curtains into the huge Indian room of her home. A fairyland appeared before our very eyes. In one corner stood the mummy of an Indian princess. On the opposite wall was a full-sized crocodile skin stretched out. Grandfather had had an encounter with this creature as he went to administer the last rights to a dying person. There were many kinds of poison arrows, lances, and also the headdress of a cannibal and the apron of a cannibal girl. One could see a great variety of stuffed snakes which were displayed in a glass case and the most wonderful Oriental birds. The most precious Indian rugs covered the floors and lying on small tables one could see genuine Indian pearls as well as real elephant tusks. Every piece in this room had a label on which the time and place were marked.

After these unforgettable weeks with my grandmother, I went to a boarding school in Breslau, a junior college. After finishing junior college, I went to a boarding school in Lausanne, France; and after a two-year stay in Lausanne, I attended the University of Breslau in Germany to study law.

In 1925 I became acquainted with a missionary of our church. I introduced him to my mother, and when she learned he was a missionary, she engaged him in deep religious conversation. As the missionary related that God had revealed himself from heaven about a hundred years ago to the Prophet Joseph Smith on the American continent, she took him into her arms and said, "I have been waiting my entire life for your message." She knew immediately she had heard the truth. On the same evening we went to a meeting at the branch house with the missionary, and six months later we were baptized.

From then on our lives took an entirely different course. My mother was very happy that she had found the true gospel. She felt it her duty to share it with all her friends and acquaintances. The most distinguished of her friends avoided her, as they believed Mother had been ruined by religious insanity and felt sorry for her. Nevertheless, my mother was very happy in the gospel. Inasmuch as she was an educated and cultured woman, she understood perseverance. She vigorously studied the Church books and was not only a hearer of the word but also a doer, in every deed. Our mother was always an example to us; with real zeal she began to search for her ancestors to have the temple work done for them. She always believed her mother and father were yearning for it.

Mother was the youngest of nine children and the only one in the Church. Four of her sisters were married to Protestant pastors. Naturally they attempted by all means to reconvert her to the Protestant Church but with no success. Often she gave her last piece of bread to some hungry soul, but the biggest blessings were not found wanting. She possessed a strong testimony of the existence of God, and she was a vigorous searcher of truth. My dear brothers and sisters, it is a great blessing for children to claim such a deeply religious mother as your very own.

—•—

In 1931, I married a young man from our branch, Ernst Koska, and we settled in Breslau. My seven children were born from this marriage. Because my husband was of the opinion that an educated woman contributed little to a marriage, I put an end to my study of law. He was drafted into the army early in the war. During the winter of 1944, his unit was assigned to travel through an area near our home. He was able to have some craftsmen in the neighboring town make wonderful handmade wooden toys for the children. They were delivered on Christmas Eve, and even though he was not able to be there, his efforts brought back rays of happiness that had not been felt in some time. He was killed a short time later.

On the twenty-third of January 1945, two of my daughters had gone to the market to get milk for the family. While they waited, they heard over the radio that the Russians were approaching our city. They left the milk container in the store and ran home to tell me. I immediately informed our local neighborhood commander of what the children had heard. He told me that the Russians were not moving forward and that I should

NATIONAL ARCHIVES

German refugees flee their bombed village.

go home and quiet the children. I informed him that I believed my children, as I had taught them never to lie. Later that evening as I prepared the children for bed, we were informed that all of the families with children were to leave the next morning, because the advancing Russian Army was about to arrive in the city. I was requested by the Political Labor Party to be ready the following morning at 7:00 AM in front of our home with my family. We were to take food and clothing to last six weeks. This was already expected because for days many people fleeing the East were streaming through our city, and the day before, the bridges to the east had been destroyed. No one can imagine what this meant to a mother with seven children. I took all of our valuables, including scriptures, hymnbooks, photo albums, and important documents and locked them in a large oak wardrobe.

I put my children to bed early, and then I fell on my knees and asked the Lord for wisdom and His protection, for I had to be both father and mother. At that time my oldest child was thirteen years and the youngest was two.

At 5:00 AM I awoke the children and gave them a good breakfast, allowing them to eat whatever they wished from our well-stocked food storage. I carefully dressed them, and then together on our knees we asked the Lord to go with us on our way. I went through all the rooms of my home once more before bidding farewell to everything that had been so dear to me, for I knew I would never see my home again. The children were already calling, and I had to give my attention to more important things.

All the homeowners of our street stood in front of their homes with their families and a few pieces of luggage. At 7:00 AM the district leader came and gave his orders. We all formed groups and began to move forward. Naturally we had to go by foot; there were no vehicles available. Our block leader was also our transportation director. We marched in the direction of Jauer. On this day it was below zero with a sharp east wind blowing. After two hours the children were already tired, and we had to leave our luggage on the side of the road; we simply could not carry it further. The roads were congested with refugees, and those who couldn't go any further remained lying and the oncoming climbed over them. One hour before we arrived in Jauer, low-flying English planes fired their machine guns. Where could we go to escape? Those who were hit fell and remained lying without any help being extended them. Everyone thought only of himself.

During the evening we arrived in Jauer, where the local citizens gave us a bowl of soup. Each group was housed in a huge room. Our group spent the night in a closed-out dance hall. Dead tired, the children fell on the straw-strewn floor. At 2:00 AM we were awakened, and at 3:00 AM we were transferred to open-freight cars. There were so many people in one car that you couldn't even move. It was agonizing for the children because the adults had no consideration for them. All my thoughts were one continual prayer—all I could think of was, "Lord, help us; Lord, have mercy on us." After several hours of travel, the train stopped and we were able to get out. We were in Leipzig. In a short time it began to rain in torrents. There were nine hundred people in the railroad station platform. We looked for our transportation leader, but he was nowhere to be found. He had disappeared, apparently staying behind in Jauer. What was to happen to us—no one from our group to meet us, everything in ruins, the beautiful Leipzig Railway Station with its twenty-eight tracks was just a pile of ruins. The heavy rain, the desperate mood of the refugees all contributed to a scene of despair. Something had to be done.

I asked an elderly married couple to watch my children. I climbed over the piles of rubble as fast as my feet would carry me to find some person in authority. I finally found an SA uniformed director and told him that over in the depot on track twenty-one a unit of nine hundred refugees had arrived and asked him where we should go. He shrugged his shoulders, so I grabbed him by the arm and pulled him with me until we reached our group. We had scarcely arrived when we heard an air-raid alarm. A frightful panic gripped the group, and they ran in all directions to escape from the depot. The SA director showed us to the nearest air raid shelter, and as the door closed on the last one in, the first bombs began to fall. Terrible minutes of suspense followed. The bunker was already overfilled with refugees who were waiting for transportation possibilities. Several times I came across an elderly gentleman with a nurse. I found an opportunity to enter into a conversation with her. She related that she and Professor Steinberg were from Dresden. Only through a miracle were they able to flee from destruction. After the terrifying bomb raid on Dresden, wild animals were frightened by the flashes of fire. One lion had attacked Professor Steinberg, which caused him to almost lose his mind. She quickly left me to look for the patient, the professor.

In the meantime, trains were brought in to haul the gathered masses of people further. One of the trains took our group, but we didn't know where we were going—only toward the west. On the way our train was attacked by planes. In thirty seconds the train was abandoned, and everyone threw himself on the ground and pressed his face deep into the dirt. During these few terrible moments one could only think, "Lord, help us; Lord, save us." The dead and wounded remained—no one could be bothered with them, and everyone ran to save his own life. The conductor said there remained only thirty seconds to reboard the train. The elderly who could not stand the exertion died. Babies were born and died soon after because their mothers had no nourishment for them. Many were lost. After a few hours our train stopped. Open trucks took us further towards the west.

On the way our train was attacked by planes. In thirty seconds the train was abandoned, and everyone threw himself on the ground and pressed his face deep into the dirt. During these few terrible moments one could only think, "Lord, help us; Lord, save us."

On February 28, we passed over a bridge, and suddenly six Russian panzer units stood in a semicircle before us. Their commander, a Russian general, ordered the driver to stop, and we all had to get out and as captives were taken to an empty schoolhouse. Two elderly couples and my family were put in one room. We were all dead tired and were happy for the prospects of a good night's rest. But we could not to think of sleep. During the entire night doors were slamming; young girls and women screamed who were being dragged from their rooms by the Russian soldiers. I will never forget that night—every time the footsteps neared our door, I feared, "Will you be the next?"

The following morning I knew I had to do something. I could not endure another night like that. I went from room to room asking for someone to go with me to speak with the general concerning the previous night. But no one found courage; they were all full of fear. They all asked me to drop my intentions so as not to make our situation worse. But in our deepest need, indignation grew in me. My father and forefathers before had died for Germany and freedom, and I, one of their daughters, could not watch and do nothing while the barbaric Russians violated my sisters! I couldn't stand it—the soldier blood of my fathers was too strong in me. I thought of a German quotation: "Fear God, but no one else in the world." And then I thought of the words of my successful father: "God helps the courageous; with courage the battle is half won." I decided to go to the General by myself. I asked the post guard to take me to him. The two elderly couples tried to discourage me. Before I left the room, I spoke aloud a prayer with my children. I asked the Lord to put the words into my mouth that would end this shameful behavior.

On the way over to the general's quarters, I still didn't know what to say, and before I knew it, I stood before him. He looked at me from top to bottom with grim, surveying eyes. I introduced myself with my maiden name and asked if he understood German. He said yes. He invited me to take a seat. I asked him if he was aware of last night's happenings, and he asked why. I told him that I had talked with many people during the last few days who believed the Russians to be uncultured, even barbaric. I had not wanted to believe it because during the First World War we had seen Russian prisoners in our town that included several fine youth. But after last night it was hard to believe the Russians weren't barbarians. I stood up and looked him squarely in the eyes and said, "General Zukoff, my father was also a high officer in the First World War, but if I thought he had allowed his soldiers the privileges that occurred last night with your soldiers, then for the remainder of my life I would have to be ashamed of him. I just can't stand this."

The general sprang to his feet, took me by the arm, and led me back to my room. He courteously bowed and left without saying a word. My nerves were tensed to the limit. I couldn't sleep during the approaching night although I was dead tired. I listened for any noise in the corridor, but nothing happened; only the regular footsteps of the guard could be heard. During the night I thought back on many things and thanked the Lord for His guidance and direction. I was thankful to my parents for my good upbringing. I was thankful that early in my youth I was able to accept the true gospel. I recognized its great blessing in time of need; when it was touch and go, it helped us to hold fast. I knew my Heavenly Father was watching over me and had held me by the hand. Yes, there were times when I was so close to Him I needed only to call on Him and I knew He would help me. Only in times of need do we lose all pretense and only what we really are remains. In all these great dangers, God protected us in a wonderful way.

The next morning there was a knock on the door, and it was torn open and there stood the general. With a courteous nod of the head, he said he had been transferred and was setting us free. Again he gave a courteous nod and turned away. I called happily to him, "May I thank you, General." He turned sharply and left. We were free.

ETHELGARD HOELZER FILE

The Hoelzer family, Breslau, 1941.

We attempted again either by train or truck to reach the West. For three hours I stood with my children and other refugees in a pouring rain, seeing no end to our troubles. New and difficult problems had to be solved. In a southern Bavarian city, we were picked up by three waiting buses and taken into the country. The scenery was a welcome sight after all the excitement of the past days; the quiet of the fir forest was peaceful to the soul. At a beautifully located resort the bus stopped in front of a large inn. The mayor of the town welcomed us, and then we registered. We were told there were 315 inhabitants; 35 bombed-out people from the Saar district were already there, and now there were 365 new refugees that had to be taken in. The mayor talked to us in stirring words. He said it was a poor village and he literally did not know how all could be accommodated, but he would do his best.

My family was assigned to a farmhouse up on a hill, about twenty minutes from the village. The house was large, but the occupants totally impoverished. One woman worked the farm—the men were all drafted—no electric lights, no water in the house. As we waited in front of the house, we could hear the mayor and the woman screaming at each other. Though we could not understand their dialect, we knew she did not want us there. We were told to go inside and that the woman would calm down in the morning. She led us into a huge room in which we were to live. With the help of the children, we set up four bed frames. A small stove, on which we were also to cook, stood in the middle of the room. As the room had six windows and was very large, it was quite cold. We had to place the beds around the stove. In the evening a neighbor brought some straw which we put on the beds. There was no bed linen or covers. During the evening, I asked for a cooking pan and then the fireworks began. She screamed, "We don't have anything ourselves. What was the mayor thinking when he brought eight people to my house." She then threw me a pan, and as I tried to get some water from the well, it all ran out—it had three holes. As I told the farmer woman the pan was full of holes she said, "I have no other; you will have to stuff rags in them." She had to do the same with her utensils. You can imagine how I felt.

Brothers and sisters, we were all so tired after all the daily exertions but I just couldn't sleep. I kept thinking, how is all this going to turn out? After midnight two of the children fell through the bed. Three days later it rained during the night and leaked through the roof onto the children's beds, and there my daughter contracted her rheumatism. I waited for the oncoming morning, and at 8:00 AM I was at the mayor's office. I related our conditions to him, and he said he was very sorry he could be of no help; every household had taken in five or six people. Then I asked for a cooking pan, which he also refused. There was nothing I could do but to become a little more aggressive, and they were soon to learn another side of me. I said, "If I don't have a cooking utensil in my possession by evening, my seven children and I will be right here in the morning and we will remain here until you get us accommodations worthy of human habitation. We also have a right to life. There are cooking utensils in the display windows, but they are only to look at. That's my last word."

That evening I had a brand-new saucepan. The next problems were no soap, nothing to eat, one loaf of bread per week that lasted only one day, no clothes, no bed linen. The children were sick; the wheat straw pricked their tender bodies, so I asked for the doctor to come to us. As he saw the lacerated bodies of the children, he had tears in his eyes. We consulted to see what he could do, but there was no help to be expected from anywhere.

On his way home, the doctor went to the Catholic priest and described our situation to him. On the same evening the priest went to his friends to ask for help. The next day we received four blankets and five pieces of soap for which we were very thankful. But still we had no bed linen, which was so important. On the same day the postman, an old man, came to our farm, and as he saw the wounds of the children, he began to weep. He then told me he knew exactly where there was a store with linen, but they would only exchange for food. In the course of our conversation he said that in the neighboring village the SS had set up their quarters. That was terrible for the whole area; it meant they planned to fight to the last man.

During the night a rescuing thought occurred to me. It was a matter of life and death. I looked for the troops in the neighboring village. The officer was a fine young first lieutenant—Joachim Von Schlichting. I told him of our emergency, and he was beside himself and immediately prepared to help us. With two other SS troopers, we rode in an army car back over to our little village. He asked me to go home, and after two hours a car drove up to our farm. The two SS troopers brought huge packages with three wonderful new blankets, four complete sets of linen for our beds, and two new saucepans and a new bathtub for the children. The young officer was so happy that he couldn't help himself, and he took the children on his lap. He encouraged them to be brave to endure the difficult times ahead. I never saw this young officer again, as he and his group fought to the last man.

There was a great famine for four weeks before Germany capitulated. The children were so hungry they couldn't sleep nights. I was desperate. Then the capitulation followed. American tank units occupied our little village. More weeks of starvation followed. Months later my youngest child became very sick with a high fever; he could hardly swallow. As the doctor came, he said, "Quickly isolate the rest of the children." I asked him where, as we only had one room. He was amazed that the others had not been attacked; it was diptheria, a life and death disease. We all kneeled in prayer around my son's bed after the doctor left, and I blessed him and asked our Father in Heaven to preserve him. I had lost everything else; would He spare my children? Soon he opened his eyes and recognized us all. The next day as the doctor called again, he was astonished at the young boy sitting in his bed. He had not believed he would survive the disease. I knew, though, who his Helper was. I often thought of Job, who lost everything—his possessions, his children, even his wife; also his friends and his health were taken from him. On his sick bed, forsaken by everyone, yet he could still say, "I know my Redeemer lives." When my need was the greatest, He was the closest.

Weeks later after the awful war was over, I wrote to the Red Cross requesting information concerning the whereabouts of my mother, sister, and family. They had stayed behind as they had no children and were not required to leave. Fearful weeks of waiting finally brought a postcard from the Red Cross with the signatures of my relatives. They were now in Poland and reported that all the homes had been plundered and then burned to the ground during the bombing raids. But I had the assurance they were all alive. Another additional blessing—I knew there was a branch house nearby. As I stood before the former building, I saw just a pile of ruins. I inquired of the police who the branch head was; he gave me his name and address, but I could not reach him so I wrote him. He informed me that we belonged to the Nurnberg District. I wrote to the Nurnberg branch president, and he answered us immediately and welcomed us into his district.

A loud voice said to me, "Don't take this train." I then went toward the train to get my children, who had partially climbed aboard, and called them back. The children looked at me completely bewildered, for the rain was just pouring down. A week later we found out that this first train was going to Czechoslovakia where a rebellion against the German people was in progress.

It was possible for me to visit the fall conference in Munich. The Swiss Mission president, Max Zimmer, stood before us with tears running down his sweet, friendly face. He was moved, and his voice trembled as he said, "My dear brothers and sisters. What can I say? Nothing. But one thing I would like to tell you. You have come closer to the Lord in this difficult time. Many never reach this state; others only after many years. But you, in such a short time, have gotten so close to Him, and for that we are grateful. Though I do not have much to give you, I was able to bring white kerchiefs over the border with me. I explained to the border authority I had hay fever as he saw so many." Thereupon he distributed them from his pockets. President Zimmer closed the meeting by sending a beautiful prayer to heaven. I learned to know a wonderful woman in Sister Louise Zimmer. Her soft, peaceful way gave me so much comfort. I had to tell her everything and how we had been taken care of. With new hope I rode back to our miserable quarters.

Three weeks later we received three big packages from the Swiss Mission. President Zimmer had packed them himself. In them we found a warm coat for every child, which was another reason to be thankful to the Lord.

Fourteen days before Christmas we received an invitation from the president of the Nurnberg Relief Society to spend Christmas and New Year's with her husband and her. Two days later she sent us the railroad fare which she had collected in Relief Society meeting. You can hardly imagine, brothers and sisters, what that means to a family to live again under normal circumstances.

In the meantime, the first donation from the Lutheran Church arrived, and we received a down quilt and two pillows. We each traded a night in the feather bed so that each could have a good rest occasionally. Then we received our first ration card—one card for each family. We asked for a pair of shoes since no one had any. We received one pair of wooden shoes, but what would one pair be for eight people? We decided the oldest would get the shoes, and anyone who had to go to the village could wear them.

Among the refugees there was a former school principal, and as soon as the opportunity presented itself, I wished to send the children two hours a day to school by train. I was excited for my children to receive an education, and we waited for a train to come. Finally one did arrive. My children immediately began boarding it, and as I tried to follow, someone pulled my shoulder back. Frightened, I turned around, but I could see no one there. Then a loud voice said to me, "Don't take this train." I then went toward the train to get my children, who had partially climbed aboard, and called them back. We no sooner got off, then the train pulled out. The children looked at me completely bewildered, for the rain was just pouring down; and then my daughter asked why we could not have ridden on that train—then we would not have to stand in the rain. A week later we found out that this first train was going to Czechoslovakia where a rebellion against the German people was in progress. The next train came two hours later, and that one took us to Bavaria and therewith to safety.

During the winter months, food was especially scarce as most everything was covered with snow. But during the summer we often went to the forest to pick blueberries and raspberries and wild mushrooms. These we could sell and earn a little money to buy needed supplies. The keeping of the law of tithing was a foregone conclusion in my family. I felt sorry that it could only be pennies which we acquired through the sale of berries and mushrooms. Still the blessings of the Lord were many.

Since it was very cold during the winter, all refugees were directed to the acting forest ranger to apply for wood. I remember very vividly the morning when all refugees were ordered to the upper forest. To get there, one had to climb mountains for five hours. The ranger showed us the trees that he had marked to be cut down. I stood by the big trees but didn't know how to begin and neither did the others. Two days later my whole family walked into the forest armed with a saw, ax, and rope. We had never done this type of work before; we had never seen how a tree is cut down. But in time of need one has to learn everything. My oldest son was eleven years old. He showed us that time that he was quite a boy. After the third falling, a tree was no longer a problem for us. Every tree was sawed into lengths of about forty inches and stacked. Later a truck brought the wood down for us.

When Christmas 1945 came upon us, it was a wonderful experience for us to spend Christmas with our brothers and sisters of the Nurnberg branch. Their love did us so much good. After a wonderful celebration, we were led into a big room nearby where a table had been set up filled with a variety of household items. It was a present from the Nurnberg branch to us. I didn't know what to say. They offered us too much of their love. Two days later we received an invitation to our district president, Brother Weiss's, home. He had a special surprise for us. A shipment from our Church here in America had arrived. It was directed to relieve those in greatest need. Every person received eight cans; that was sixty-four for our family. It was so hard to believe that all this belonged to us. I expressed gratitude to our branch president and especially thanks to the members in America with all my heart, especially to our Father in Heaven. As my daughter Jutta (she was six years old at the time) was to pray that evening, she said, "Dear Father in Heaven: We thank Thee for all the groceries which have been given to us. Now we don't have to go out into the forest to pick berries. But how will we get all this home? Please help us to take everything with us. We thank Thee also, dear Lord, for the light to not have to do things in the dark, that we have here, even though it does hurt our eyes, but it is wonderful to not have to do things in the dark. Please give us a light like that soon." The child's prayer was heard. We found many helping hands which made it possible to take everything safely home. The spirit of the gospel and the love of the Saints renewed our strength to carry our heavy burden.

Having also received Church materials, Ethalgard and her family immediately organized a weekly Sunday

School upon returning home. Soon they had gathered a group of eighteen who met regularly to hear the word of God. With the number of refugees in Bavaria soaring, a special committee was organized in the state to help deal with the problem. In many villages and cities the numbers of refugees had far outgrown the number of residents. Each community elected a housing representative, whose responsibility it was to petition the government for needed supplies. After the first few representatives failed, the refugees in Ethalgard's village called another meeting to choose a new delegate.

The selection fell upon me. Quickly I went to see the magistrate. His secretary greeted me with the usual excuse and wanted to dismiss me with, "The Magistrate is not here; he is in a meeting." I pushed her aside and went directly into his office. He sat at his desk and asked excitedly, "Who are you? How did you get in here?" I introduced myself and said that I was a regional delegate of Bogen and that I walked in through the door. We were soon engaged in a very earnest conversation. He was sorry he was unable to help me, but directed me to speak with higher government officials when they met. He would advise me when the next gathering would be. It would then be necessary, as a delegate, to be there.

In the meantime I traveled to all the villages of the region. Everywhere the same misery existed. In one little place of ninety inhabitants, who were all poor people and had only the bare necessities, they had taken in sixty-seven refugees, thirty-eight of whom were living in a former dance hall. For months they lay next to one another in the same clothes on a straw-strewn floor. With inadequate, unsanitary conditions and poor food, any day an epidemic could break out. Immediate help was necessary here and in many other places.

Armed with the necessary information, I went back to my own pitiful quarters. The very next week the government met in a special meeting. An American occupation officer took me to Regensburg in an army car. The prayers of the refugees accompanied me. Promptly I appeared in the government meeting and presented all that I had observed, saying it was the last cry for help from a desperate people. I told them that no one would survive if one more hour was procrastinated. We could not help ourselves as we had no resources, and they were our only source for help. I requested immediate discussion. Many of the government officials had to wipe a tear from their eye. The government quickly went into a closed meeting, and twenty minutes later fifty thousand marks were allotted for the aid of our little rural district. The administrative president came to me after the meeting, shook my hand, and said, "The District of Bogen could not have sent a more powerful and qualified representative." He asked that I keep them informed and that when I returned I should give his best wishes to the refugees. As I spoke to him, I could not help but to feel grateful once more that the Lord had helped me to speak what I had to. That evening with my children, I thanked the Lord with all my heart for His guidance and direction, and with a feeling of happiness and contentment for serving my fellow man, I fell asleep.

Though conditions remained difficult for some time, Ethelgard became an effective representative for the many hundreds of refugees under her care. To help her family, she taught her children how to use many of the things they found in the forest to make crafts that could be sold for their support. On one occasion they were informed that clothing donations had arrived from the Church in America and that they should travel to Nurnberg to collect their share. Without the money for travel, she gathered the children and prayed for help to pay their way. Not long after they were hired by one of the most influential families in the area to make wreaths for an important relative's funeral. The money was enough to allow them to make the trip. Slowly conditions improved, and the family began to prosper. Ethalgard met and married Heinrich Hoelzer, and in time, with the help of relatives, they immigrated to the United States and settled in Salt Lake City.

Eugene and Brigitte Dautel

Escaping from Breslau with her mother and six siblings was a harrowing experience for Brigitte. Though her mother worked hard to make their flight and time as refugees as comfortable as possible, it was a frightening time for the children. During the food harvest season, the children would glean the fields for food. Three or four of the children would go to the potato fields after the harvest and dig deeper into the ground to find the precious potatoes. Often they would find so many that the other refuges would complain that they were robbing them. Their mother would tell those who objected to the children's harvest that there were eight in the family to feed and that what the little children could find and bring home was scarcely enough to keep the family alive.

They were allowed to go to the village each day for two hours of schooling. Their shoes were worn out, and their mother had begged one pair of wooden shoes from the village government. Each child would go to the school alone, walk home through the snow with freezing feet in those wooden shoes, and then give them to the next child to wear. Often the children would cry that they didn't want to go to school, because the blisters on their feet hurt so much, but their mother realized the importance of education and wanted her children to move forward in life. So off the next child would go, often sliding the shoes through the snow to keep them on their little feet.

Their mother would go to the village to borrow books from the Catholic school library. Then the children would gather around and listen to her and take turns reading. They learned of other countries and cultures and allowed their imaginations to carry them off to better lands and better times. Through their mother's devoted hours of reading, as the seven children sat around her chair, they all became lovers of learning. Through all these dark days, Brigitte followed her mother's outstanding example of a pure Latter-day Saint, and followed her counsel and stayed close to the Lord and the teachings of the restored church. The children always knew that the Lord was watching over them and that somehow their lives would improve.

—•—

Eugene was raised in the western part of Germany. In 1944, at nineteen he was drafted into a medical unit of the German Army, but as the war drew near, he was transferred into an infantry unit. He was given a blessing by a member of the Church, wherein he was promised that he would neither spill enemy blood nor have his blood spilt in the war.

The officer looked at him and said, "You look very pale. You had better drop out and return to your unit." He returned to his medical unit and soon learned that every member of the infantry unit had been killed or severely wounded in the next day's battle. His blessing had been answered.

He received his inoculation shots just prior to the infantry unit moving to the western front. The day after the shots he was feeling rather sick. He informed the army doctor of his condition but was told that all were suffering and that he would be leaving immediately with his unit to the front. The next day the unit was standing in review for their new commanding officer, just prior to their departure to the front. Eugene was standing in the second row of his company as the commander was quickly walking past the troops with a rather distant attitude, when he suddenly stopped in front of Eugene. The officer looked at him for a moment and then said, "You look very pale. You had better drop out and return to your unit." He returned to his medical unit and soon learned that every member of the infantry unit had been killed or severely wounded in the next day's battle. His blessing had been answered.

Some time later his unit passed by his hometown. He had a deep desire to know if his parents were still alive. This was just days before Hitler ended his life, and the Nazi leader had given orders to the German Army to burn all of Germany in front of the enemy advance and to execute any soldier who stepped back from his position in the ranks. Many soldiers were deserting and heading for the Black Forest, which was the area that Eugene was now in. All deserters that could be found were being shot on the spot.

Eugene threw caution to the wind and left his unit to see if his parents were still alive. He soon found that four German officers were living in the apartments that were part of his family home, so he was unable to enter the home and see his parents. As he passed by the home, a shell exploded just ten feet from him. The shell threw shrapnel all over the area, with a close pattern of fragments being thrown against the wall of the home by which he was standing. The only place on the wall of any size that was not hit by shrapnel was the place where he was standing. Again, his life had been spared and the blessing he had received had been answered.

He felt that he must return to his medical unit but needed an officer's authorization for his transportation. As he addressed an officer to obtain permission, the officer asked him where his hometown was. When he learned that Eugene lived in the town they were in, he told him that because he had deserted his unit to come home, he would be shot. A long moment passed as the two stared into each others eyes and the officer held Eugene's life in his hands. Finally the officer lowered his head, stamped the paper, and Eugene was on his way back to his unit. Once more the blessing was answered.

After the war, Brigitte and Eugene met while Eugene served as branch president over the Bietigheim Branch in the Stuttgart District. They were married in 1950 and immigrated to America in 1952.

Herbert K. Ludwig

The oldest child of Kurt and Ida Ludwig, Herbert K. Ludwig was born June 5, 1921, in Bellmansdorf, Schlesien, Germany. Herbert was born into the Church, and his parents were strong members of their local branch. Faced with persecution from an early age, he gained a strong testimony of the gospel while young, which served well later in life. The family moved often, as Kurt, a dairy manager, secured positions larger and better within his field. Herbert excelled in school, which surprised many, since he was from the country. For the Ludwig family, education was very important, and Herbert soon was able to see and understand a great deal of what was occurring around him.

The winds of change were blowing very hard on the political scene, and it is difficult to understand how a change in government can affect a boy in grade school. But the wind changed to hurricane force, and a weak and struggling "democracy" was finally toppled. One name had come into focus, had risen over the horizon and with lots of struggle—often violent—always very cunning. Adolf Hitler came into power. How had the individual, the child, the mother, the father, the community, the whole country been affected by this change? Let me try to show some of the things I saw and experienced. At school you did not have a teaching job, unless you had become an active party member or some functionary. Some resented it, others jumped on the bandwagon. The "resenters" either played along or faded off the scene. In education, history was changed. I remember sitting in school, dreaming, when the teacher asked what had started some war in the eighteenth century. Not knowing the answer, I told him the Jews, knowing it was wrong. Looking at the teacher, I saw him cringe at my answer, but then heard him admit that I was not very far off. Was "wrong" right, or "right" wrong? The lesson and answer to it was more like this: play the game and you will survive, and to the day of infamous shame many millions played it. My experience was slightly different. My father's influence was there, and it was a counter, sometimes subtle and sometimes strong. I admit to "playing" sometimes, and it was definitely "playing," when I raised my hand to the "Heil Hitler" salute, because my heart was not there; or when I took the oath in the army, and my mouth would not speak the words with the rest of them. I would testify to you that sometimes you can live with them, without being a part thereof.

One day a friend of mine and I were walking down the street, and two women were coming in the opposite direction. We of course ignored them. They called us back, asking us why we did not greet them. My friend saluted, "Heil Hitler." I told them that I did not know them. Slam—it hit right in my face. I should have held my tongue. As it turned out they were some of my teachers' wives—they would report me. Nothing I or my parents could have done against it.

The church in Görlitz had a Boy Scout troop. I was one of them. We met Saturday afternoon. Our last meeting went like this: The leader of the scouts speaking welcomed us and then informed us that this was our last meeting as Boy Scouts. From now on we would belong to the Hitler Youth. Make note—not dissolved but taken over. What a way to recruit members; and so it happened to any organization, youth or other. One by one they were taken over, taken into. How well it was organized showed the following Monday when the leader of my Hitler Youth troop waited for me after school, informed me as to where, when, and how we would meet. I saw trouble ahead when I replied that I was not aware of joining the club. Well, trouble came. The day of Ascension is a holiday in Germany. Here was my fearless leader—about seventeen years old—telling me I had to participate on a camping trip. When I excused myself, since my family had other plans, his reply was, "We will see." We did see a few evenings later. There was a rap at the door. Who was there? In he came, not being asked to enter. Father asked him what he wanted. He stated, "Camping." Father told him "no." He gave a snappy answer. Father gave him three seconds to leave. He gave another snouty answer. Father got up and he took off. After that, there were no more "molestations" from the "Fearless Leader." Was it laid to rest? Certainly not, as now there was a black mark on the Ludwig roster.

Of course Father also had problems. He would not join the party, so clouds started to gather. In school I was the constant target of harassment. Whenever there was some punishment, half the class was gathered up in order to get me. Then all were dismissed with a little stroke, and I was singled out to receive the wrath by bending down and getting whipped over the behind. Did it hurt? You bet! Sometimes it was hard to sit down. Did I show it? Not on my life. One day in school I looked over at a fellow and he made a face. I laughed and got caught by the teacher. The *Ohrfeige*, or slap in the face, left his finger marks on my face, even after five hours of school. On the way home I rubbed it red so my parents would not suspect anything.

Life did go on, even though things had changed. The last year in school I took a course only for Protestants, given by their priest to prepare them for confirmation, which meant becoming a full-fledged member of it. Father felt it would not do me any harm. It did not, but I learned different views and teachings. Plus I had to behave like a gentleman. Therefore, Herbert earned high praise from his pastor.

After graduating from school, I would have liked to have studied electrical engineering, but money was not available and scholarships, which were provided by the state, did not come even with written recommendations from some of my better teachers. The reason was, I was not a member of Hitler Youth. So it was decided I should go to business school, which was private and within the means of my parents. I took it for one year. It was not for me, everyone there were snobs—students and teachers—where did I fit in? Other avenues were discussed and rejected, with the end result for me—"Do what Father does." So I became a member of his team. The Church was still very much alive. My father had been called as first counselor in the district presidency, Brother Larish being the president. That meant visiting a lot of branches. Father's motorcycle took him and

Brother Larish on many trips. On one of those they had to visit a small branch. There, two of the brethren were doing the same work father was. One was ready to retire, so father applied for the job, and the Lord took us away from Burkersdorf to a place about a hundred miles away, which left the shadows of the clouds where they belonged and gave us a new place in the sun. Nössige was the place. It was a small farming community. In order to have enough work for our family, we also had to take over a pig farm, which was alright. Getting up at 2:30 AM like in Burkersdorf was out; now it was more like 5:00 AM, and even work during the day was quite a bit less. In other words, we were not killing ourselves with work. Father and I were doing it almost all alone, except for milking time. We also had a branch of the Church in the village. The meeting place was our kitchen. It was big enough for the thirty-plus members to meet. We had taken over an old piano from the previous owner but had no player. Yes, you guessed it; Herbert was elected by his father to take lessons. Where did we find a teacher? Almost ten miles away, at the other end of Meissen, which was the county seat and also the birthplace of Karl G. Maeser. It did not take too long to play some hymns with one hand, and within a year I did quite a few with both hands. All in all it was about two years of lessons I took, and a master I was not. Brother Ludwig (Father) became branch president; Brother Waechtler, first counselor; and Brother Rudolph, second counselor. All of their families plus a few other ones constituted the Nöessige Branch.

HERBERT LUDWIG FILE

Herbert Ludwig in Africa, ca. 1943.

Hitler was in firm command after some half-hearted tries to topple him. He finally had murdered all opposition. He did do many things for the working people, some of the benefits we still don't enjoy in America. Most of the people loved him as the "Fuehrer"; some of them hated him, but to survive they played the game. Undeniable prosperity had come to the nation as a whole. Work was for everyone; the Ludwigs had two motorcycles, and then the Volkswagen was born. For a thousand marks you were put on the list with your number. Everyone could save some money monthly, and after you had paid and your number would come up, the VW would be ready and you were supposed to get one. No one ever did get one. Now, how did my father know these things? I heard him say many times (to friends only) that they would not see them, that there would be war first, and there they would roll. How true that was almost to the letter of the word. How could a whole nation, except for a few, not see what was going on? The Rhineland had been taken back, the Saargebiet had been taken from the French, and Austria had been incorporated in the Reich. The Sudetenland was wrestled away from Czechoslovakia, and finally all of Czechoslovakia was taken over, and all that without a great deal of opposition from the Allies. Germany was great, the people were in a frenzie, the "Master Race" had been born, and so were concentration camps, except that the nation hardly knew anything about them. The Jews sure knew, and some of the very undesirables of the "Master Race," too. But for most of the German people, Hitler was the Fuehrer, and for most of the youth he was everything, superseding Christ and God! Somewhere there came some words in my mind which go like this: "He who soweth the wind will reap the whirlwind and destruction." But—"*Deutschland—Deutschland über Alles*" was the national anthem and it "was sung with fervor and conviction of a master race."

In school we had been taught to trace our ancestors back for four generations, to see whether we were worthy of being one of the Aryan race. Here I have to break in a bit to show what it meant to the LDS Church and genealogy. To do genealogy work had been very difficult in Germany. All records were in the hands of the different churches. Only with money and some luck could anyone obtain information from those people; and if and when anyone found out you did it as a Mormon, out you went. One order from the Fuehrer and all archives were open. The Lord works in mysterious ways!

This and many other things happened during my time in Nössige. So the year 1939 dawned. At the beginning it did not look much different than the others; the "Millennium of Great Germany" was rolling in its sixth year on winds of boisterous bragging, but oh, what a rude awakening we were in for. How fervently I remember the big noise on the iron gate of the *Hof* or inner court where we lived. About two o'clock in the morning, two men asked to be let in. They were delivering a letter to my father from the government. What was it? A call to arms and orders to report at a given time in Meissen. Actually it was a *Secret Mobilmachung*, or an alarm to prepare for war. About a week later, Father had to report, and what a surprise it was. They had everything very well planned. Men with their cars, motorcycles, horses were simply drafted at once. Everything was evaluated at a fair price. You got paid, and two days later every vehicle was sprayed gray, everyone was put in a unit, and an army was ready. The army was about one-third regulars, one-third recruits, one-third World War I men. Two weeks' training and they were ready.

Having lost Father, the workload was on the women and me. Strange, they had not missed Father's motorcycle but had missed my motorcycle and me. But they found me just a few weeks later. Same noise, two men—same order for Herbert and Ms. Motorcycle. So I also had to report, but what saved me at the time from the draft was that I was needed at home on the farm. I had a certain "priority job." The motorcycle, of course, I lost. It would never have done me any good anyhow since civilians were not getting any gasoline unless you needed it to get to work. And so, before the Allies realized it, German forces swept across the Polish border and made sauerkraut out of the Polish Army, which was no match against the German tanks. Within a few weeks Poland was overrun. Russia had come to help and "divided" the cake with Germany. My father was in it and my soon to be brother-in-law, Walter Rudolph, also. But not all went well; there was a declaration of war hanging over Germany's head from France and England. All was quiet in the East and West at the moment, Germany celebrating and regrouping to the West, with France and some of the British troops hiding behind the big impenetrable "Maginot Line"; at least so they thought. The year 1940 came on the horizon, with uncertain wondering as to what some people were going to do with it. Father eventually released himself from the army by falsifying some signatures, which was a big risk, but it worked. For a while we were united again. Then like lightning breaks from the clouds, so did the German Army and Air Force. The bunkers of the Maginot Line were smashed by the German *Stuka*, or dive bombers. They opened up a break and Germany was on its way into France, at the same time going around on the north by walking over Belgium and Holland. France was finished, and how the British made it back to England is history. There was only one force which saved their hide—the Lord. Germany went hysteric. Every man on the street just knew that the war would be over by next summer. We would go to England and smash them in no time flat; that was everyone's opinion. I knew of at least one man who did not believe it—my father—and even though I could not see or understand his reasoning for thinking that way, I began to believe it too. Well, summer turned into fall and fall into winter. Germany increased its bombing of Great Britain, and history knows the outcome. In the Ludwig home was a radio; of course, all listening on "foreign" news was forbidden and getting caught could mean going to a concentration camp. Yet almost every night at eleven, with the lights turned off and the radio turned down, we heard the "voice of Great Britain." We knew about liberty ships and liberator bombers, which the German propaganda minister called American-made sewing machines. So, our picture of the world looked quite different, yet we could not tell anyone, for in that game there was no friends!

But then one night this all changed—the noise at the gate, the two men with a letter for Herbert Ludwig, the notification of the draft for me. We had already experienced it more than once. This time it was the "it" for me. It stated time, place, day, and hour when I would have the great honor to join the "mighty and victorious army of the Fuehrer," and how proud I could be to put my life in the service of my Fatherland. Now, I guess under normal conditions in peacetime or at a time where for some reason the land needed to be defended, the feeling would have been different. How did I feel? I can't describe it, being torn between being anxious to see the world, which I did see to a great extent, and knowing that all was wrong and had to end in disaster. It did not make for big enthusiasm! As I remember, I had about a month to prepare myself. During that time the mood at home was not very happy. We hardly ever spoke about my departure. At last the day arrived. A foggy, cold, and dreary winter day it was; the road was slick and icy. I had to walk four miles to the railroad station, and my sister was going with me to see me off. One last hug with Father and embrace with Mother, and off we went. How can you describe the feelings? And you were called to put more fuel on it, not to extinguish it. You knew within yourself it was all wrong. You should not support the government, but the government was not a democracy. You could not object—on top of it there was the article of faith again, and let's quote it: "We believe in being subject to kings, presidents, rulers and magistrates, in obeying, honoring, and sustaining the law." Could a Mormon do different, even if he would have been willing to die for refusing to go? Immeasurable damage would have been done to the Church as a whole in Germany and the brothers and sisters individually. So, off I went—one last look and waving of hand for good-bye, but what I saw did not help much to get my feelings up, with my mother standing there with Father, weeping hard, trying to control it, and giving me a last smile. That's the last time I saw my family for the next two and a half years. How Father and Mother felt, I do not know. Father was probably confident for my return. Mother, on the other hand, had just sent her only son away to where destination and return were not assured at all! Millions must have felt that way and worse, when the message eventually came—died in action.

At last we arrived at the station. The train arrived and I got on it. Once more the tears of my sister and I started rolling. What occurred to me during the next seven years in uniform I could fit in one sentence: "With the help of the Lord I was preserved and returned home." However, I will try—and I mean *try*—to give a glimpse of what I went through, what I saw, and what I felt, although I know there is no way for me to portray it even close to reality. I just don't have the words in my command to do so. But you, my family, are entitled to know and hear, and marvel along with me at what the Lord can do for us: you, or anyone who believes in Him.

The next stop of the train was Meissen, the gathering place for a transport of recruits. Arriving at the barracks, my papers were checked and I was ordered to Zug 3, which was my unit, and off we went to boot camp. Well, at least I was not alone in this—some conciliation, it took us until the next evening, until our *Sonderzug*, or "special train," arrived in the little Slowakian city, close to the Austrian border. We had some time on the train to get to know a few of us. Being young, most of us were very high in spirit for the honor to serve; there was singing, joking, and some loose talk. Had everyone known at the time how much of the train would be needed to bring us home, I am sure the mood would have been vastly different. On arrival, we were organized and put in troops, or "Zugs" and companies. Our troop consisted of twelve, me, and a leader, or *Unteroffizier*. The Zugs had a sergeant and a lieutenant, the sergeant doing all the work. The company leader was a *Hauptmann*, or captain. Ours happened to be an Austrian, a fine soldier and a just man. Our company was a mix of one-third Austrian, one-third Saxonians, and one-third Prussians. The Austrians and Prussians did not work well together; therefore they put us, the Saxonians, with them. We were to pacify and preserve peace in the unit, and that was not always easy. The next morning, after being awakened at 6:00 AM, started with *Ein-kleiden*—that meant receiving your uniforms. We received three sortments, for work, for training, and for out on the town. Your uniforms were fired at you like a football; you had one chance to exchange later in the day. You were shown how to fold it and put it away, how to make your bed, and you were yelled at like a dog. The first session was to learn the signs on the uniforms so you could distinguish between the "dogs" and the lower and higher staff; not saluting them was a very serious offense! From then on it was fun, hell, or in-between for us. We got roughed up, received punishment or training, according to the mood of the Herr Unteroffizier! Most of us were able to cope with it, but a few committed suicide. I did quite well, having been used to hard work. It took me about two weeks to catch up physically, but from then on there was no punishment in it for me. I remember about two months down the boot camp, I beat the champion obstacle course. That made me the hero of the whole battalion. In weapons we were trained as a tank support unit, which were the troops that followed the tanks to protect them and to mop up after them. Not a pleasant job, but there are no pleasant jobs in the army. After about three months we apparently had graduated to the point that we were ready to go. We had even learned the "parade-march" or goose-step. So the swearing-in ceremony could begin, and it did. With all pomp, music, parade, and talks, we finally raised our hands and repeated the oath of loyalty to the death. How did I feel? Awful. My lips moved, yet no words came out. My heart was empty; I felt helpless and forlorn! That afternoon, we got our first leave on the town. I stayed in the room.

Being young, most of us were very high in spirit for the honor to serve; there was singing, joking, and some loose talk. Had everyone known at the time how much of the train would be needed to bring us home, I am sure the mood would have been vastly different.

Shortly after that I got in serious trouble. We trained physically hard from early morning till 1:00 PM with a piece of bread, some jam or sausage, cereal, and coffee. You came back very exhausted. You had two hours to eat, clean yourself, your uniform and weapon; no time left to relax or rest. Usually then the sergeants came and picked someone they did not like to clean up their room, and boots, too. One day I got picked; I did my best to please them. Then I came back to my room. There were twenty bunk beds with straw mattresses in it. The master sergeant had inspected the room and found one straw under one bed. For that he got the urge and virtually dumped all the mattresses and blankets on the floor; that picture my eyes beheld when I came back from cleaning. I exploded and was telling my buddies the sergeant's mess they had caused and wished them all practically to hell. While I was thus doing so, I all of a sudden saw all eyes going in one direction. Turning around, there was the Herr Sergeant standing in the door frame. He had heard; the situation was ice. Normally someone would yell, "Attention," and report the room and its doing. No one did and all I could hear from him sneering at me, "You will hear from me!" My heart fell; charges could range all the way to open rebellion, which would mean a minimum of two years in the can. I needed help; there was only one power which could help: the Lord. And help he did. Nothing happened all week until Saturday at 2:00 PM when the final parade and mail call and passes for the town were given out, and those who received weekend punishment or watch were called up. My name was called as the last one to report to the master sergeant. He happened to also be a Saxonian; he always had liked me and favored me slightly. After a good lecture of the seriousness of the crime, and an apology from me and a ruined weekend, I had to clean and scrub several of their rooms, and things went back to normal after that. A close call; Herbert was much more careful from then on.

In weapons and all other areas, I was one of the best. I beat everyone in the company in time used blindfolded, to take apart and put together my machine gun. My uniform was always tip top, except twice part of my leather equipment ended up on the pile during inspection. Only after *weinering*, or shining, it for two hours—which I never did—it worked just as well and was found perfect in the reinspection.

—•—

Summer came and the German Army started war with Russia. We were not needed immediately, so I got an assignment to go to Vienna for a course in driving tanks. After two weeks in Vienna and no openings in the course, ten of us were sent to an Austrian village to help the farmers. What a beautiful summer vacation that was. Our contingent was sent to a small Austrian village, and there our leader, or corporal, sent nine of us to a different farmer. I was left; no one wanted another one. While he and I were still deliberating what to do, one of the fellows came back telling us the farmer did not want him because he did not know anything about farming. The corporal, turning to me, not knowing anything about me, just told me to go and try. After close inspection of the old farmer, his wife, son, and daughter, I "passed" and was invited to stay; the strange thing was they did not know anything about my farming background. Two days of hard tests followed; of cleaning barns, chopping wood, and relocating the manure pile. They decided I was good, and since I did not go after work to the local pub I was invited to stay with them after mealtime. But the big surprise for them came when I out-milked, out-worked, and out-guessed every one of the family in farming. I must have been an inspector or manager of a farm, they thought, and Hansy, the good-looking daughter, had dreams in her eyes. Too bad, I did not!

When the time came to say good-bye, tears came freely; even the old one squeezed some out. We had been called back after three weeks of farm work to our home base. The time had come to be shipped to the front lines. With much barking and yelling orders, and a last falling in line and attention plus reports from all units to the Colonel, who rendered a patriotic speech and a concluding *Sieg Heil*, we were off, marching with full load to the train station, where a Sonderzug or "special train" was waiting, to swallow a whole battalion. Our coaches consisted of big freight cars.

For eight days those freighters were our home, rolling north and east. Somewhere in Poland on a river we were put on the side tracks for two days; up ahead, tracks had to be repaired that had been blown up by the Russians. We enjoyed the warm summer days and the "freedom" of marching. Drill, barking orders, and getting insulted beyond human integrity had stopped. Our torturers stayed behind to receive another load of human souls for the three reasons: to train them, to toughen them up, and to make them feel miserable. And I must admit, in general they were quite successful. When the order came to board the train again, we found out that things were getting more serious; two empty cars were in front of the steam engine in case of mines. Behind the engine was a flat car with a twin twenty millimeter gun, and one at the end also; and all of us received live ammunition to be ready, just in case. Well, we kept lustily rolling east through seemingly endless forests and open stretches, once in a while passing through a city with mostly chimneys and no houses; the ravages of the war began to show. Our journey, however, did not get interrupted by any violence from straying partisans; and on a beautiful late August day we arrived at our destination—a side track. We were the first *Ersatz*, or replacement, from home, since the war with Russia began. The first order was, "Take all your equipment and line up according to size"; and now let me tell all those who are less than "tall." What a blessing it was for me, that the Lord had decreed that five feet eight inches was tall enough for me, and endowed me with enough bone, flesh, and muscle plus brain to make up for it. For what happened in the next hour had surely a profound aftertaste, which no one would ever believe or care to believe even after the war; those who muscled in and stood extra tall would regret it for the rest of their natural lives. After all the discussing, gesturing, arguing, and conferencing was over, the first half of our battalion was assigned to the feared SS-Division. The rest of us were taken by the tenth tank division. I don't know of any other regular army unit which was hated more by the enemy than the SS. They were ruthless, which is true, and all were supposed to be volunteers, yet from that day on, they were not and I feel sorry for those who were assigned to them; for after your number had been tattooed on your underarm, you were marked for life, even after the war. Only losing the arm could erase the mark; cutting the number out still left a scar for the few who survived. Hate, disgust, and rejection will follow them all the days of their lives, and their deeds were to a large part rotten, ruthless, and cruel; yet some had not asked to be a part of it, so who is to judge?

As for the lucky rest of us, we got put on trucks and arrived after a short trip at our final destination on the outskirts of a little Russian village. War seemed to have missed it completely, except for all the young men, who were missing. The people were very friendly to us, and we were also in return. Visiting with them and being in their houses was not allowed, fraternization was punishable. We were housed in a barn; no effort was made to hide trucks and equipment, obviously there was no threat from the air. The unit was in rest as they had been heavily engaged. There were losses, and we were the "chosen ones," to fill up the ranks. A few more days of rest and getting to know each other were given us. Except for watch and preparing weapons and equipment for top shape, there was nothing much going on. Our whole division was motorized. Walking only occurred in attack or going back; we were one of the crack divisions aimed in a direct line to Moscow. Of course it was war, and we were not there to get fat and lazy! Therefore, one night it had to happen, and 80 percent of the time it always happens at night. Alarm, grab your stuff, hit the truck; the corporal gave account for his unit, and we were ready to roll. As for the officers and sergeants, I must say they were kind of a different breed than the ones we got to know so well in the boot camp. While complete discipline was expected and enforced, they were human. Perhaps most of them knew by now, death was not a respecter of rank, nor was injury of particular choice; and one human needed the other in spite of environment, religion or politics, or different opinions. After all, what I saw and experienced, one would risk his life for anyone in need; it was a great comfort in the midst of all the suspicion, bloodshed, and terrifying moments of war. How do you write down your feelings about the first real encounter with the enemy? I simply can't.

At last we started rolling and undercover of night we were brought as close to the front lines as possible. There in the darkness we embarked. Every so often we could hear the rumbling of artillery, saw flashes of firing guns, or the shine of flares against the sky—nothing personal yet. The mood showed in every face; very sober, no jokes, hardly any talking, each with his own thoughts. What will the morrow bring? It was the hour and day all of us knew would eventually come; most of us did not want it—yet could not avoid it! Would it be our end or would we be taken away from it all by being wounded, or would it mean we'd have to carry on for another one? We soon would know. The order came to march, and for some time we did. The noise of war came closer, our lines were extended, the distance between you and your next buddy became longer, just in case of stray shells; then the order—no light, no cigarettes, and finally, halt. We had arrived several hundred yards behind the front lines of infantry; by dawn, we were told, the assault would begin with a force of 240 tanks and us with them, to break through the Russian lines and make a push of about twenty miles into their territory. Well, dawn came at last. If we were surprised where all the tanks came from, the Russians must have been as well. Somehow they were there—perhaps brought in earlier. When the fury let go, I was not able to make out at first our fire from theirs. Did I ever learn fast! When the first Russian shells hit our neighborhood, I must have been one of the fastest divers around, much to the smiles of the veterans, who always could tell whether they were close or not. Don't ever believe movies! The real sound is much more frightening and sometimes bone-shaking and nerve rattling than a movie ever will be able to portray.

As the crescendo of battle heightened, we got the order to march; the tanks and our first line of men had broken through; our job was to mop up and clear the land of living enemy soldiers. A dirty job it was. Every dead man was shot again; every little mound or bunker, or pile of hay or straw was turned over or worked over with bullets or hand grenades. Too many of our men had been shot in the back. I saw no prisoners; my assignment was to cover the investigators. No need for me to use my weapon; there were no Russian survivors. How does anyone understand a nineteen-year-old boy who never met violence before in his life—what he felt, when the first enemy was encountered with one-third of his head missing, or the next one with half his chest ripped open and the shoulder missing, only to be shot again? What had their crime been? Opposing the conqueror? How does a nineteen-year-old feel when he sees his own buddy dead or carried away profusely bleeding from mouth and nose and chest, because he was shot through the lung? What was he or I doing there in the first place?

But much time to think or feel was not given. Survival was the word and alertness could mean life rather than death or being crippled. After the first fierce opposition had broken down and mopping up was completed, the tanks started rolling again, and what was there to stop them? The day was hot, late August, the fields dusty, the thirst almost unbearable. We were not allowed to drink out of the wells of the villages we went through, just in case of poisoning. When we finally reached our destination in a ravine, we found a little pond of stale water and we drank, until we discovered a lot of living bugs in there and even that did not stop us altogether. Our tally of the day was all accounted for, none killed or wounded out of our group of twelve and their leader. Not everyone had been that lucky. Digging in was the order, so we did for the night on top of the ravine, in kind of a ring fashion for protection. No disturbance during the night. Food reached us before nightfall, and all slept well like the foxes in their holes, except of course for the watch. The next day we were moved in front of a village to secure and straighten our lines; it was up to the infantry to widen the break and protect our flanks, and that would mean several days for us to wait. No enemy contact was made in our section, although to the right and left of us there were some occasional fireworks or skirmishes. The Russians had some tactic to keep us from getting a night's rest. Two, three, or four would crawl or sneak up to our lines somehow during the cover of night close, throw hand grenades, and let a few bursts of fire go, and then disappear the way they came. It hardly ever did any harm to us, although some of theirs were not always so lucky.

—•—

September was here and we were still far away from Moscow; and if that was the goal of the Fuehrer, to get there before winter, we better get rolling, and this we did. The usual thing, one night infantry took over our position, and we marched about an hour to where our trucks were waiting for us. We had all the next day to wash ourselves, put on clean underwear, shave, get the weapons in order, and do nothing, and so was the next day, and the next. But no good thing lasts forever, nor did this one. I suppose it takes some time to move thousands of troops with all that goes with it, into position; but one evening in September the order came—"Get on your trucks, final count, report to the company staff, company to battalion, battalion to division headquarters,"—and the "all clear" came. We started rolling, and if I thought it was a *Blitzkrieg* when we overran the Russian lines, I was in for a surprise. The big push East had started, the goal was Minsk and some other city, Smolevici—I can't pronounce the name. Can you picture an army rolling, rolling, and rolling for six days and nights? We never got off the truck more than thirty minutes on any day. The havoc we raised in the Russian Army was unbelievable. I guess after the first break we made, the Russians had been trying for two weeks to pour reinforcements in, to establish a new line to try and hold back the German push toward Moscow. But then came the Blitz. Words cannot describe what happened. We were so fast that the Russian MP kept directing traffic at one intersection with us rolling East, and some Russian trucks going west. We had no time to get involved. A company of our tanks was ahead of us and we had to keep up with them and take care of big obstacles, the small business we left to those behind us.

One night we ran into a small Russian village which was occupied by a Russian unit. A small battle ensued. After our tanks and we were through, there was nothing—not one house left, and I do not think any of the occupants escaped. The next night we ran into a column of trucks. Hell lasted about a half hour and all was over; but the worst destruction I saw two mornings later. We had been stalled for about two hours, while the fireworks had been going on ahead and slightly to the north of us. When we hit the scene in the morning, devastation or destruction are not the words to describe it; massacre fits better. Picture a mile-wide valley with a small river meandering through the pasture, the road running along it, forest on both sides from three hundred to five hundred yards away from the road, when two almost identical columns of vehicles met up with each other. Ours consisting of twin and four barrel automatic twenty-millimeter guns, and theirs of heavy machine guns two and four barrel mounted on trucks, and when they had rolled up the full lengths, ours being on full alarm stations. Someone on our side gave the order to fire and the Russians never had a chance—destruction was total, bodies strewn all over trying to escape, some hanging out the truck windows with the trucks still on fire, others with the doors open had just fallen out, others on the way to the woods mowed down. Some trucks tried to escape but were caught in the crossfire and were still burning, their ammunition exploding, while some were ripped apart along with the people inside; a total destruction, and ours? Went on their way after the bloody work was done. We had to go off the road to go around, going, going, going. Was someone still alive? Who cared—the ones after us will finish up.

On the sixth or seventh day we approached the city of "Smolev," for short, our goal. It was early in the morning and the road was littered with Russian trucks. Our tanks had surprised a supply convoy. Some trucks were burning; we had stopped to regroup for the final assault on the city. What a bonus those trucks were for us; bread, cheese, sausage, and other goodies we were able to pull from the still-burning trucks, even sacks of candies. The people must have faded into the woods; we rarely saw any victims. Then the order came: "Off the truck with equipment, and then move." When we at last saw the city, we realized that it had to be a key city. There was a pretty big railroad yard with some trains sitting there; one heavy ammunition train was on fire with shells exploding, throwing their fragments all over the place. We had to detour for a half mile to avoid getting hit. Our assignment was "Move as fast as you can to the north side of the city and guard the railroad bridge," while tanks and half-trucks plus the rest of our battalion cleared the city. So we dug in close to the river, the city behind us above on some low hills. It was one of the worst positions we could have. Although we had encircled a Russian Army of more than 200,000 and a never ending stream of humans kept crossing the bridge to surrender, there were constantly snipers harassing us. So all day long you could not stick your head out of the foxhole.

It had turned cold, and wet snow was falling, making matters worse. At night some of us had to go up the hill to receive food and whatever was needed. Needless to say, after being in that situation for almost two weeks, your feet had grown into your wet boots. When everything was finally all mopped up and we were pulled out one morning to march on the other side of the city where our trucks were camping, the pain in my feet was so intense, I could hardly hobble along. Tears were running down my unshaven, unwashed face like little rivlets; of course, others had the same trouble. Being pulled back to the truck, in most cases, meant rest, cleaning up, etc. So we started the fires. On went the buckets with water, but oh, how wrong we were. Alarm! Can you picture this? Three weeks without washing, shaving, or changing underwear? There was the hot water. Would you abandon it? Well, we did not; and if the Russians ever thought that the German soldiers were crazy, that must have been the day! While our convoy was moving through the city in thirty degrees Fahrenheit, you could see naked figures up there trying to scrub each other and even shave. All in all it was a very refreshing situation with at least partially good results.

The main thrust continued east, the direct highway from Minsk to Moscow. While it seemed in the beginning that all was clear, we became increasingly aware of more and more resistance and slow downs. So we thrust ahead twenty miles to the next city, only to find the bridges over the river totally destroyed; and while the railroad tracks had never been touched before, and all our engineers had to do was to adjust them to our spur width, now every single piece of rail was blown up. Furthermore, as we were going further east, extending the supply lines, it was much harder to protect them against partisans.

In one of those situations, we on the west side of the river were waiting for our forces to establish a beach head and a crossing. There were some destroyed vehicles laying around, among them an old tank sitting conspicuously on a hill overlooking our doings and unit. We had taken up ground around an old Masonry church. Our tanks were in a valley hidden from sight of the enemy; yet consistently artillery fire followed them wherever they went, and we had the same problem until some of us went exploring. Some of our men investigated the tank. There was nothing left of it, just a shell—strange. But by sheer luck someone looking underneath had discovered the forward Russian artillery informant. Off he went for interrogation. The enemy fire became quite aimless after that, although still irritating.

For some reason I got an order against all rules; I was to go to the cemetery, find a good position, and cover the flank for the night, all alone. As crazy as it was, it turned out to be a blessing for me. I dug a hole in the middle of a bush and while artillery salvos raised a ruckus, with one death and two wounded in my group, I had a very good night, with no shells falling on the cemetery. I guess the Russians had some respect and were not about to dig out their own dead. So for the remainder of the day the rest of my group joined me for peace and rest in the cemetery.

I wonder if I will ever know how many were deflected by my guardian angel and how many times I was found in another place when there was no time for him to meddle with bullets. Some of them I noticed, and I will surely testify to it. Yes, the Lord lives even in the atrocities and the slaughter and horror of war.

But late in the afternoon we were ready to move again across the newly built bridge to reinforce the bridge head and enlarge it in preparation for another thrust. The next day we rolled, or I should say walked. Since quite heavy resistance was expected, it was our turn to go with the tanks into battle. To our disappointment the Russians had withdrawn or vanished in the woods. So we got on the tanks to progress faster. That almost proved fatal for me. From somewhere out of the woods we were drawing machine gun fire; we had some wounded and one dead. My "close one" was when a bullet hit the tank's turret, somehow glanced off, and in so doing hit my right shoulder taking with it the epaulette button. Needless to say, my dive was one of the faster ones, and the Lord had made sure that Herbert was all right. I wonder if I will ever know how many were deflected by my guardian angel and how many times I was found in another place when there was no time for him to meddle with bullets. Some of them I noticed, and I will surely testify to it.

In all my activities, frustrations, and suffering by the hands of the enemy, I will say this: I never had the desire to kill for revenge or punish the enemy, and whenever a direct confrontation or situation arose, the Lord showed forth his hand and I did not have to squeeze the trigger, him of course knowing the desire of my heart and seeing the hesitation of my trigger finger. Yes, the Lord lives even in the atrocities and the slaughter and horror of war.

As we pushed forward day after day, we of course sustained losses in tanks and equipment; but what hurt most was the loss of men, your closest friends or buddies. We lost five out of twelve, but replacements came up and filled their places. The tally was two dead, three wounded. One day we had overrun a town, but there was resistance at the outskirts, so we were sent to clean up. It was always a dirty and dangerous game. Behind any door, tree, or in any hole, or bunker, the loaded gun lurked or waited for you. Well, on this day I hit upon a bunker all by myself. Somehow, something told me there were people in it, so my approach was very careful; but not careful enough—for when I was standing there, ready with my gun yelling the equivalent in Russian "Hands up—out," I saw the muzzle, the flame, and felt the powder particles in my face—missed! I was whole, and while I switched positions, slowly loosening my two hand grenades, hating what I must do, and did not want to do, two of my buddies came up to me. After warning them, needless to say, they did the ugly job; two hand grenades rolled in, a rumbling explosion, lots of dust but no sound, and not even moaning followed. Had the Lord sustained me and stayed my hand? I believe so.

On we went straight east, following the highway to Moscow. A day or two afterward I was a witness of great courage along the highway on a crucial point, where going around was quite difficult. The Russians had dug in three of their best tanks covered with good machine gun positions. We had gotten fairly close, as a matter of fact; a slight miscalculation brought our own artillery shells on us, wounding two. Then our dive bombers came, and only on their way down did they see our flares, flattened out and reassessed their positions, and finally let their fury go on the enemy. But we were just not able to destroy or dislodge the tanks. After a two-hour lull we heard a rumbling, and what I witnessed seemed impossible. Up the road came a half truck roaring with an 88-millimeter gun, which was one of the most universal weapons we had—and before anyone of us realized what was going on, the gun was uncoupled and in position, and when the first tank showed up with his turret, the young officer was giving orders loud and clear and the fire obliterated number one, and then number two, and finally number three of the Russian tanks. Then calmly as if nothing had happened the crew hooked up the gun and disappeared. Even I felt proud at the moment, and the hurrah that followed them came with admiration. Well, before nightfall the little town was ours. Skirmish after skirmish, assault after assault. The road to Moscow, still far away as it was, got rougher by the day. Winter was also looming ahead, and the High Command must have had their worries. Smolesk was taken; it probably was, at some time, a fairly nice city for its size. When we went through it, no inner city existed; just some chimneys left standing.

October was here and the cold and the snow or mud were attempting to annoy us. Why we ever took off the highway, I will never know but a week later we found us quite a bit north of it and stalled. While we dug in to defend a forward village, the power saws went day and night on the left of us to build or lay a road through a kind of light swampy forest, made up entirely of tree trunks. It lasted two weeks—what a loss of time. There was so much harassment from the Russians there. We were dug in on the left of the village on a slight incline. The Russians used their old method sneaking up to us during the night, throwing hand grenades, and firing their guns. One night there was frost and light snow on the ground when the attack came on the village; it was a surprise and they succeeded in getting part of the village. Then they tried to roll up our front lines and almost found success. As the drama unfolded before our eyes, we were not sure who was friend or enemy. The steamroller was finally brought to a halt in front of our machine guns. Some of our troops had panicked; one light machine gun was left about eighty yards on the right of us, you could see its outline against the snow. Several times the enemy had tried to capture it but our fire denied them the privilege. Then I was called to report to the company headquarters, which had withdrawn from the village.

When I mentioned the machine gun out in the field, I got the order to get it—even after telling the Herr officer the impossibility of doing so. "Get it," was the order. He might as well have given me the order to commit suicide. Well, I made it safely back to my group leader and told him about the order. His reply was, "That crazy horse is he drunk?"—and some of the words he used I refuse to write—and then the miracle happened, which seemed impossible. That man told me or ordered me not to try to go out there. It was, however, recovered later in the afternoon that day. With that behind us, the order came to cut our group in half, and send one half to the Herr officer to organize a counter attack, still during the dark hours to recover our lost territory. If you think an attack during the day is bad, try it at night. Which houses were still ours? Where was the enemy? With all the shooting, shouting, and yelling for help, two of us had entered a house—dark with no sound. While my buddy was covering the door against surprise of hand grenades, I got in the second room and sensed someone there. I had entered stooping very low, but hard as you tried you made some noise, and so did he. I jumped up and bumped right into him. I bet each of us wished he would have had a pistol instead of a clumsy rifle. I had a faster fist and it landed somewhere on his head or chest, enough to throw him off balance. The dash to the door was swift for me and him too, in the opposite direction I believe, for the hand grenades we threw showed no results. If you ask me why the fellow did not open fire when he heard me enter, I have no answer. Then someone had an idea and used a torch on some houses; up they went in flames, and we had the advantage that night and gained what we lost.

Hard frost hit a few days after and we rolled again right over the *Knüppeldamm*, or highway of trees. But we got stopped again for a few days. Our assignment was "Dig in on the hill and guard the village a half mile off." Dig in? What a beautiful job in frozen ground; but dig we did, for we knew better, and what a surprise came up for us. During the night we found "company" had arrived on the other side, hidden in the woods, of course. When at the beginning of daylight the first man stuck his head out of the foxhole, it said "zing" and his helmet rolled down the hill. One sacrificed his life to warn us all; but before it was all over, our company had lost twelve men shot through the head. I saw one of our sergeants getting up out of the hole looking through his binoculars trying to pinpoint where the fire was coming from. If he saw where they were, he did not have a chance to tell us. "Zing!" it said—his helmet was ripped off, and the spirit world received him. Clearly there was no time for heroes like that.

Even in a situation like that we had some fun. Sometime during the night we collected some old helmets. Every so often we would stick one on a stick of wood and lift it slightly over the little mound of dirt in front of us. For comfort we learned not to tangle that way with Siberian sharp shooters. While most of the time we would get our warm meal in the late afternoon, here we were served at two in the afternoon. Now picture this; since no one could get close to us and we couldn't get close to them, we threw our canteens down the hill; there they were filled and put down about thirty to forty yards from our foxhole. That's army planning! We could almost smell the aroma, and we longed for the food. Why such a torture? But need brings inventors; so for an hour's time no helmets went up, no other movement. Then a jump and a rollover, a whistling of some bullets slightly above you, and you were sitting behind the hill eating a cold lunch in the snow. One problem, however, we could not solve right away—how would you get back into the foxhole? One of us tried surprise and succeeded with the bullet hitting the dirt in front of him and ricocheting, but slowed down enough to hit his belly and not do him any harm—a nice "souvenir." It was too risky, so we at last dug a little ditch and slid down and up on our belly. After a few days of "fun," our artillery began to work over that part of the forest to our lasting relief. Of course, we marched on the next day.

The closer we came to the capital city, the worse the winter was. Any houses were welcome to us now, and with that body lice and bed bugs became our friends, or rather we became theirs. There was really no way for us to get rid of them; we had no effective medicine against them. One night we had stopped at a village and my troop and others had taken quarters in a house. Most village houses were just better log cabins with a huge adobe brick fireplace on one side, built like a huge tunnel with the chimney in the back. In the winter the family, or part of it, would sleep on top. Inside the tunnel, which had no doors in front, all the cooking was done with open kettles. Huge wooden logs would fit in them. I had found quite a comfortable place in an outside corner of the room; but for some reason I had to go to the truck. When I came back two other guys had crammed into my place, and there was no way to get it back. I ended up in the hall, much to my dismay, which, however, did not last long, for the answer arrived about fifteen minutes later when a shell hit the corner of the house, where my place had been, with disastrous results. Both fellows got hurt quite bad; one had a fragment go through his hip, the other through his leg. Herbert was not there. "Thank you, Lord."

Another day and on we went. Every so often we got acquainted with a new weapon, the Stalin organ, or the mounted rockets on trucks was one; it was crude and hard to aim precisely, but very frightening. If it was quiet, you could hear their rumbling when they fired—eight hanging on some rail on a truck, usually they came in sixteen, twenty-four, thirty-two, or forty-eight salvos, and when they hit all around you at once, it was nerve-wracking! One day, four of us were carrying a wounded officer of ours back under sniper fire, but we made it safely; yet on the way to our unit all four of us got surprised by Stalin's organ—no warning, explosions, hell all around us. The result was one of us ended up with his heel ripped off, and we had to take him back. A new contingent of replacements arrived, and the push kept going and the losses, of course, as well. One day our troop leader got it quite bad, but he would live. There were even tears in our eyes when we put him on the canvas to be carried away. He was a veteran, Poland, France, and up to the proximity of Moscow. He was a lucky one too; his wound was bad enough that it precluded rejoining us. On one of those days when we advanced toward a village, spread far apart because of artillery fire. I was running with shells hitting unpredictably to the left and to the right when I felt a big slam at my right side. Pain—yes, but no blood. When I, after taking and securing the village, finally had time to investigate, I found that I had been hit by a good sized fragment of a shell. Where did it hit? It hit my spade where the metal covers the handle all around; penetrating the metal, the wood handle, and part of the side close to my body—only to come to a halt on the last bit of metal. "Thanks again, Lord."

I found that I had been hit by a good sized fragment of a shell. Where did it hit? It hit my spade where the metal covers the handle all around; penetrating the metal, the wood handle and part of the side close to my body—only to come to a halt on the last bit of metal. "Thanks again, Lord."

But east, east we went; Moscow could not be too far off. At night when our bombers roared over us, we could see the anti-aircraft fire from the city; but it got tougher, and it got colder and more miserable, too. Once more reinforcements bolstered our thinned out lines. Five of the twelve originally starting out with me were left. "Good rumors" came to us too, telling us that to the north our army was almost east of the city; too bad for us, for "almost" is not quite. We had moved up about eight to ten miles from Moscow. Some of the big industrial chimneys on the outskirts could be seen from the flat hills.

It was time for the Lord to put a halt to all this, a time for Him to humiliate Germany and extend His hand of judgment over the master race; and oh, how well his angels executed his order! December had arrived. We were in the woods; ahead of us was a nice peaceful-looking village. The night before I had watched Fred looking at some pictures of his wife and two children; he seemed depressed, so I went over to him to talk to him. What he said shook me. His words came somewhat like this: "That was the last time I saw them. Tomorrow I will be dead." I tried to talk him out of it with no success. Needless to say, on next morning, the first casualty was Fred. But the Lord's order was apparently to get the German war machine on its knees, and no Russians, British, or Americans could have done what the Lord did.

It started snowing, and we got the order to move. It snowed harder, the wind blew hard right in our face, and we should not have proceeded. I was carrying a machine gun for some time now; we received some rifle fire, which was not a good omen for us, but six to eight hundred yards was not too bad to cover, or so we thought. We made it to the village. I was put in position with two other men to cover the left flank. One hundred yards down I could not see our own men because of flying snow; all seemed to go well, when we heard or sensed that something was wrong. First the "hurray" was heard swelling more and more in Russian, and then the dark figures of our men rushing toward us, running for their lives. Panic—all of us, officers and men, trying to get back to the woods for safety; but oh, how bad it was! I picked up a young officer lying in the snow crying like a child. I was running toward the woods, seeing the bullets hit the snow and raking it with disastrous results. We had never learned to withdraw. The wounded that made it on their own were safe; it was amazing how some made it. I saw one running with his hands holding his protruding guts; the rest had no hope. After hours of waiting for some tanks and going out under their cover to find wounded and dead, we found thirty-two dead; one wounded in the head was still alive, but his last penetrating words were, "You are some buddies." And as we had received a blow like that, it seemed the whole middle front was in trouble. General winter had come to aid the Russians and words like "straighten and shorten the front" showed up more and more. Although no withdrawal was ever mentioned, from that fatal day our direction was more west than east. First we tried to hold and dig in; then to fall back and then to hold on for any price. Often we were counterattacking; the struggle was very, very bitter and deadly on either side. We knew what giving up ground meant to us.

In this entire horrible struggle one message hit me like a sledge hammer: Pearl Harbor. Most were jubilant. Had they lost all their senses or was it just a glimmer of hope that the war might be just a little bit shortened? As far as I was concerned I had the feeling that we had just received the death blow, and knowing fairly well the Hitler regime and listening to their propaganda for a total war—win or lose—opened some window in my soul to see the things to come. So Christmas found us somewhere out in the cold and snow. We were on highest alarm, but even the Russians honored the birth of the Savior and the message he gave to earth through the angel chorus of "peace on earth, good will toward men," and the voices of those tired, cold, and ragged men trying to sing "Silent Night, Holy Night," melted many a heart, and tears were flowing freely, a very sobering occasion for all. I believe that all the common men of both forces would have accepted an offer of peace, which of course could not come forth because of wicked leaders with revenge as their cry.

Right after Christmas we were pulled back to rest and clean up a bit, so New Year's Eve saw us twenty miles behind the lines with lots of booze and a depressed mood. By midnight most of the men were more or less drunk, except for Herbert of course. Two o'clock it happened, alarm, and by about 4:30 AM we were ready to roll with quite a few drunk drivers. How we made it, or most of us made it, to the front lines is a story by itself, but by daylight we had entered the woods and were looking on a village a mile ahead of us. We were told to attack and recapture it; it had been taken by the Russians the day before, and we had lost two 10.5-cm guns which still were there. All day we had been sitting, walking, and standing in about two feet of snow; no fires, no foxholes, nothing. The snow was slipping into our boots, and as for me it made it down to the ankles, thawed a bit, and then froze in there. What saved me from frostbite were my long johns and socks, which went up to the knees. We learned to cope with this particular problem by putting our pants over our boots and tying them with strings, so the snow could not push up and fall into the boots. About 3:00 PM some tanks arrived and we started rolling. We took the village and the guns, and after everything had been secured the order came: "Withdraw, destroy houses, straw, wood, burn everything, total destruction." I can only guess what the purpose was, but by withdrawing and straightening our lines it put us in more easily defended positions. A policy in the German command had been born, to leave about fifty to eighty miles of totally devastated ground or burned earth. What a horrible thing to do; one must have seen the heartrending scenes of the poor Russian civilians, seeing their only abode going up in flames with everything in it. Village after village, day after day, every little village we came to went up into flames, every barn, shed, even woodpile. At night you could trace the line of the Germans falling back by the red horizon to the south and north. One day our unit got the assignment to burn. I can't describe my feelings as two fellows with gasoline and matches, and one with a gun just in case went to work. I had the gun. As one house after the other on our side went up in flames, we ran into trouble. In one house two very old women would not leave. None of us had the heart to burn them alive, so of course our side was slow. We took too much time and the officer who saw it, came busting in yelling at us to speed up. We pointed at the women. "Throw them out," was his order, so I dragged them out with the "match fellow." There was an old bunker there, and that's where we put them—and on the burning went. But if someone had thought it would slow down the Russians, how wrong they were. We were menaced all the way back to where we made a 180 degree turn and dug in, and a new and different war started for us.

On our way toward Moscow some pretty bad mistakes had been made which now became a bad pain in the neck, and literally in our backs. On our swift push eastward we never took time for a full cleanup of leftover Russian units, too much hurry to reach Moscow. What a headache we had left behind us. Those forlorn units or splinters of them had to survive somehow; it was not too hard during warm times extracting food from villages, fading into the woods before German units, but with winter coming, times got harder and food shorter, so they started raiding the German lifelines to the front, and a serious problem began for us. Another mistake was that many prisoners taken by us, particularly by the Waffen SS, were just told to dig their hole somewhere close to the woods, and then were shot. Lots of them tried to run, some made it back to those leftover stray units, and what followed was simply this: no surrender, fight to the death; indeed very bad for us. While before, surrender was the thing, now it was being hacked to death rather than surrender, so holding and cleaning up was the order for us. It went something like that—one to two weeks at the front at different places, of course, and one week rest, which meant two cleanup operations. The front was "cake" compared to the cleanup. Oh, and no new replacements for us anymore either. So as the units shrunk, one was made out of two and so on. Even the music bands got weapons instead of playing marches; but let's start at the beginning: At our New Year's episode General Winter gave us a bad blow. After burning the village we withdrew all the way to the next village, probably ten miles back. We all were very tired; it was very cold, somewhere below zero. The alcohol had its work cut out to make most of the men unaware of the cold. Lots of them got on top of the tanks to ride. Herbert walked and arrived about two in the next morning in the village. The picture was dismaying: one was helping the other to get the boots off his feet. Most of them had frostbite. We lost one third of the men, none through the enemy. Even I had second degree frostbite, resulting in eventually losing the skin and nails off my first three toes on each foot, but the others had to have amputations of heels, toes, even feet, and that with no bullets fired by the enemy. Surely, the Lord could stop armies.

At last we did arrive at our destination of a little village. The line had been dug just in front of the village; everything had been prepared for us, foxholes, some bunkers, which were square holes about six by six with some lumber across and straw on top, were only a protection against the cold. In the village behind us, a few tanks of ours were supporting us. The first week was quiet; on the second it happened. Some Russian tanks had been rumbling around all morning in the woods, when all of a sudden they broke into the open, coming right at us. Our weapons—machine guns, hand grenades and rifles, our tanks in the village—had they seen us? We held our fire. Where was their infantry? There was none. I gave a prayer of thanks. We all stayed tucked in our holes, except one crew had to abandon theirs, the tank rolled right over their hole, not noticing the running men. Ours was passed up about eight feet away. Not one shot had been fired. What were they up to? All eight Russian tanks kept rolling toward our village. I can still see our tanks lurking behind houses waiting in position, it was a one-sided battle. Eight Russian tanks destroyed, none of ours. If there had been infantry, the situation would have been quite different for us, I think they simply did not know we were there; we were not always that lucky! I remember another situation when two T34s broke through our lines and chased six of our smaller tanks around houses, until ours had maneuvered into position to get them from behind without losing one of ours.

After less than two weeks we were rotated. Back we went to rest; what a beautiful word, and

BLITZKRIEG

The German *Blitzkrieg*, or Lightning War, was a term first applied to the quick Nazi victories over Poland, France, Belgium, and Holland. Though only the invasion of France actually utilized the military strategy that was named Blitzkrieg, the other victories, including the initial invasion of Russia, were grouped under this heading because of their quick suppression of hostile forces.

WILHELM KRISCH FILE

German troops advance through a village on the Russian Front.

The theory behind Blitzkrieg was based on the centralized use of motorized units to quickly outflank enemy units, who would then be "mopped up" by following infantry. With the Treaty of Versailles having drastically limited the operational size of the German Army, military leaders struggled to find a solution to their own defense. In 1920, German officers studying military tactics in Russia saw the emerging strategy of tank warfare and developed the idea of fast mechanized units spearheading military operations rather than maintaining support roles as had been their assignment to that point.

Initial theories surrounding Blitzkrieg were tested and proven effective during the German involvement and support of the Spanish Civil War. Though the invasion of Poland in 1939 was quick and decisive, it did not utilize the theories of Blitzkrieg. With the great success in conquering France, Hitler ordered for the use of the Blitzkrieg strategy to be utilized in the invasion of Russia. Though initially the invasion was greatly successful, the vast terrain, Russian emphasis on artillery, and guerrilla support soon exposed the weaknesses in Lightning War as German troops found themselves cut off from desperately needed supply lines and facing enemies both in front and behind them.

Source: *World War II in Europe an Encyclopedia* (Volume 2: 1175-1177); *Simon and Schuster Encyclopedia of World War II* (68)

what a lie it was. Rest meant hunting partisans. That's what the Russians operating behind the lines were called. Someone had organized them pretty well by now and they were a force to be reckoned with. Our first assignment was a sweep through the woods. How frustrating it was. You could see all the footprints in the snow but nothing else, except trees, and yet you knew they were there, and all of a sudden the fireworks started and some were wounded. We started firing too, but we couldn't ever see them. After several repeats we pulled back with three wounded on our side, the other side having vanished. Before we could go back to our front lines, we had one more expedition—a village behind the lines, somewhere on the Russian plains. As we approached, we received fire and got pinned down, so we split. All of a sudden their sporadic fire stopped. As we entered the village everyone assured us they were friends, but we knew the enemy had to be there.

Well, back to the front—more snow and more cold, the thermometer plunged to fifty-two below zero. Everything came to a halt, the machine gun giving one shot and then jamming. My cheeks and nose got white while walking, my breath almost freezing in an instant. I couldn't touch my weapon with my bare hands, or they would freeze to it. I robbed a dead Russian of his felt boots and fur cap.

Slowly the temperature returned to "normal"—five to twenty below zero, almost "warm." This time something bigger was in store for our rest. While we had lots of walking to do, because of great difficulty with vehicles and the snow and cold, this time we did have transportation. As we finally got off and walked some more until we got to the staging area, we saw a lot of men, a whole battalion plus tanks. We were told it was going to be a nice little Sunday walk. Now let me explain the "Sunday walk." Ahead of us were ten tanks, behind them our company and our troops were right behind the tanks, and behind our company, two more companies. Why such a load on one lonely road? We were soon to find out about the walk.

First of all, picture this—snow four feet and more; no tank could make it off the road. One road leads into the village from where we were coming, the village, itself, we couldn't see; it was located behind a soft, long stretch of the hill. The road ran on the other side of the hill parallel to the village, perhaps a half mile apart, and then swung to the east through a little dent in the hill toward the village. Everybody stopped, last instructions were given, the tanks and our group got to go first. There was no room to spread out. Our tanks started roaring around the bend toward the village, how easy it was for us—four tanks and about forty men—to reach the village, where we spread out and took up positions to the left and right, giving room and security for the rest to come in and take possession of the village. Or so we planned! But where were the rest?

There was not all that much shooting going on. What no one told us was that there was a battery of Russian artillery somewhere hidden in the village. It was so cleverly set that it covered the incoming road, so after the first surprise their fire covered that road coming in so not a mouse got in or out. Four tanks had given their lives trying to make it, and lots of wounded and some dead were out there. The rest were helpless sitting on the road behind the hill, there was no help at all for us. Our leader, realizing the situation, put us in strategic places for defense. With four tanks on our side we felt pretty good, but oh, what a disappointment. Communication was real bad between us and the tanks, and we had none to the outside. So the first of our tanks rolled from behind the house to get in better position. Wham! The end of him. The second tried a different way—Wham! Two down, two more to go. We finally drew fire as well—snipers. Our toll was increasing; the wounded collected in the corner house which was the only brick building. Messengers were sent out, none made it. One tank tried to make a run for it, but never made it. By afternoon the situation got critical. We could see the Russians jumping from house to house trying to close in, not without a price though, as we had some experience in the game too. But when the last tally came in, everybody was wounded except Herbert and one other fellow; even the officer got shot through the hand. Then he gave me and my buddy the order to try to get out. Suicide? Perhaps, but so was staying. We plotted our route, the road being out. The fields had four to five feet of snow, but we decided to try it. We left everything except for a pistol. For one half hour we did not move, hiding in the shadow of our house, and then we jumped up and ran and slithered across the street followed by a hail of bullets; but the surprise worked. We passed the house on the other side of the street, there were some bushes and the top of some fence posts. Our journey began foot by foot over the snow, sometimes finding support for our feet. We finally made it to our unit but our report was devastating. A day later, to my surprise, I meet up with our lieutenant who had sent us out; he made it too, following our tracks, and got another shot through the arm. What a fiasco!

> ***One sniper had done the damage; unobserved he had crawled during the assault closer to the hole, and as one replaced the other, he shot them, making it possible for the Russians to reach our hole. You guessed it, the first shot through the head would have been mine, yet I was not there even though I should have been! "Thank you, Lord!"***

For some reason their heavy weapons were always outside the villages. I am sure it was safer that way for them. One day we were in progress of overrunning one village. From the point where I was, I could see lots of people fleeing from us: they were partly covered by a fence showing the upper part of the chest, shoulders and head. Most of my unit was standing there taking aim with their rifles and let go. I was standing there, my gun in my hands, watching the incredible; they were actually aiming at humans as if they were stray dogs! When all of a sudden I got yelled at and sworn at by my corporal because I was not shooting. I raised my rifle and aimed very careful two feet over their heads and let go; it was fun, for he could not know what I was doing. Did I ever receive an answer and lesson that day! We had taken the village, but outside were still some big guns sitting, ready to blast us. My buddy and I were standing on the corner of a barn with a thatched straw roof, our heads almost touching the roof, when it happened. We must have been looking straight in the muzzle of the gun when it fired a flash, a shadow for less than a split second, and a swoosh two feet above us through the roof. There was no time to act, but at the same moment an impression came, or you could say a voice, which let me know for the rest of my life—"Just as you had aimed!" Nothing more, but what a lesson. "Thank you, Lord!" Had this shell hit a piece of lumber going through the roof, our lives would have ended there; and the last senior, for that's what I was by now, would have found his rest! How can I forget such a lesson? All the days of my life it rings, "Do unto others as you want them to do unto you." Even if I feel justified to act, I still ask, "Would you want them to do it to you?"

It was time to return to the front lines. This time we sure got thrown into a hot spot; a wide valley about four to five miles wide, woods on both sides and in front, where the road went through the woods. About six miles to the west, an old Russian unit was sitting on a frozen swamp, with the regular Russian units trying very hard to connect with them, and then roll our lines up from behind. However, the reed and woods were blocked by crack German troops, the SS directly on the road, and the rest of the tenth tank division to the left, and infantry to the right. Our wise leader of the company had made a very smart decision; instead of putting us on the edge of the woods to flank the road, he pulled us about a hundred yards out in front of the woods. We dug new positions, just holes in the snow, with a piece of lumber in front as a steady pad for the weapons. The holes were positioned in a triangle with one hole farthest in front, and me being the machine gunner, occupying this hole. Our holes and the back were connected with ditches through the snow. When we moved in we were told by those from whom we took over, what hell it was. We soon found out for ourselves. We were under attack every day, often four to five times during day or night, then one fatal morning, it still being dark, the customary hurray could be heard; but we couldn't see anything yet. Our trigger fingers got itchy when we finally saw the shadows and opened fire. "Boom!" it said, and my machine gun jammed. Not being able for some reason to correct it in a hurry, I sent word back for a new machine gun. Instead a whole crew came with the order for me to leave. I went back about 150 yards into a big crater, where I took the whole gun apart to dislodge the shell. When I was thrown into battle again and our front lines, which had been taken by the Russians, were cleared again, I found that three men of ours had met death in my hole, shot through the head. One sniper had done the damage; unobserved he had crawled during the assault closer to the hole, and as one replaced the other, he shot them, making it possible for the Russians to reach our hole. You guessed it, the first shot through the head would have been mine, yet I was not there even though I should have been! "Thank you, Lord!"

On another day, still being in the same position where we sometimes got bombarded with very heavy guns; the holes which they ripped in the deep frozen ground were big enough to accommodate six to eight people. We would sit in them and have a little fire going to warm us up. All the shells were going into the woods, obviously our holes had not been discovered yet; you see the wisdom to be out front? One day, still being in the same position, still being attacked with bodies piling up down the range, being used by their own as shields, some game began. The Russians had thrown up some snow walls with holes in them so they could stand up and stretch. What they did not know was that we could see when their holes showed dark spots of their uniforms. We sent a burst of machine gun fire through and if it was fatal you could wait for the body to be thrown over the wall to be used for catching our bullets.

Obviously they were not making any headway, so their commander decided to send a light airplane over the field to take some pictures. Unfortunately this course was right toward Herb's hole, with Herb being alert so that when the plane was just right in the sight, I fired just for fun. He made it over our hole before the "sput, sput" started, and the engine quit. I had hit it—a sharp, banking turn and to our astonishment the thing landed on its skis between our lines. Before we recovered from our surprise, two guys got out and stumbled for their lives to the Russian lines. Our artillery did the rest to the plane, and I got chewed out for not immediately reporting it to the battalion. The artillery beat us to it and got the credit. So what!

Six of us were sitting in one of those craters dozing at one time. My head was resting on the shoulder of my buddy when a mortar shell hit the branch of a tree next to us and exploded. The reaction was the same for all of us—your body gives a big jerk and you doze off again, until the time came when I was to go and get our warm meal—a three-mile walk through the woods. My buddy still seemed asleep while I was looking for his canteen. I could not find it, so I took his shoulder and shook him and down came his head—he was dead. One of those little wicked pieces of the mortar shell had hit him in the back of the head, missing mine by inches, and his canteen, which had hung on a branch, showed several holes. Off I went for food; artillery was strafing the woods. When one shell came in real close, I tried to throw myself down, but in falling my head was jerked back. After I hit the snow I stayed for awhile, carefully taking inventory. Had I been hit? No, but my fur cap had been

NATIONAL ARCHIVES

A German paratrooper advances during the final German offensive.

ripped open by a fragment of the shell all along the right side of my head. "Thank you, Lord!" At last replacements came, and that part of hell was over.

On we went for rest; it really was rest this time. The trucks took us a long way; we saw warm quarters, a bath, and some beautiful rest. We had time for cleaning and getting equipment up-to-date. On the way back we came through a little village, where in the middle of it a dozen people were hanging from poles; a sign had been placed around their necks saying, "I was plundering food." Some were women, one a kid twelve to thirteen years old. What a shame on the German troops, or those who were in charge there.

However, good times do end and one day we were rolling toward the front again. On the way there a little side trip had to be made—a village had to be retaken. As I was walking down the street, suddenly a shell hit about three feet in front of me. Strange, how fast your spirit works—you freeze, no time to go down, the earth swells up, and your mind says, "That's it." There was the swoosh, the ground rocking coming up; but where was the rest. The explosion blowing me to pieces? At last I realized there was none; I was shaken, but alive. "Thank you, Lord!" While the battle was still raging, someone from our unit picked up a stray cow. "Ludwig, you are from the country. Slaughter it and give it to the kitchen tonight." "Sure, Herr Sergeant, it's easier to kill a cow than people, at least for me anyway." So, with the help of a buddy we got the poor creature in a barn; my shot went in the head, out the neck, and through the door of the barn. Have you ever peeled and cleaned a cow with a pocket knife? Try it, it's "fun"; but for reward we confiscated the heart and liver and for two weeks we had some very good tasting soups!

We took up positions for a while in the village. The days were getting warmer, mostly above zero, suggesting that spring was in the air. Our outfit had taken two prisoners, and they had been with us several days. One day I walked in the room of the Herr Commander. He called me over and gave me the order to take the two Russians out and shoot them. Wow, what a confrontation. Could I refuse? Certainly not, but I sure could bungle the job. While I was marching them out into the field, I ran across an incoming patrol. The patrol leader asked me what I was doing with the two; about hearing the story he just said, "Let me have them." He got them alright, and of course he got them on his conscience too. Why the Lord gave them into his hands to die, while they might have lived in mine, I do not have an answer. Was it because of possible investigation or embarrassment? I don't know, but what I do know is I did not have to shed innocent blood. "Thank you, Lord!"

We were taken to another sector of the front. As we were walking through the woods toward our destination, I could see signs of terrible struggles; trees blown to pieces and dead Russians all over. Then came the halt; we were about a hundred yards from our lines and had to wait until nightfall to get there and take over. We were told to be very alert; the Russians were only sixty to eighty yards away. Someone would start the fireworks, and in seconds the whole section of the front was blazing away. The next morning revealed our situation. The front apparently was meant to run along a river, which made a big bend like a "U" in our sector. So, one day when the ice was thick enough, the Russians attacked unexpectedly and broke through the lines. Our counterattack developed into fierce hand to hand combat, and the Russians were pushed back, but held the "U" on our side of the river. Everyone had dug in; for the first time in this war, we had real bunkers. Since the soil was sandy, it had not been too hard to dig; the top was two layers of tree trunks, plus ground and branches. Nice and snug, even a little wood burning stove was in it. The Russians must have had about the same set up—a peaceful yet odd picture during the day. You could see the smoke curl up during the day on the Russian side and ours too. In that jungle of mowed down trees, the lines were so close, their artillery did not try to bother us out of fear of hitting their own lines; but oh, it was hell during the night. Can you picture a real dense forest, mowed down by bullets between our lines? Some trees up to three feet in diameter were fallen and splintered by thousands and thousands of bullets. Some tree trunks were standing up like a naked monument, pointing to the sky! But spring was coming; a thaw was in the air. A little ditch was running behind our bunker about thirty yards away. We had been getting water for drinking and other purposes from there, until the receding snow showed parts of Russian soldiers left in there to rot. I guess the reason we did not get into trouble was that they had remained frozen.

April came and with April, Easter, and I admire the numbskulls of some German commanders. Our engineers had been blasting some rather big holes behind, in the woods, and as it turned out, they were going to be mass graves for the Russians; and furthermore Easter Sunday was the day for burial. One half of our unit was pulled out in the morning and assigned to collect bodies. Try to imagine, if you can, dragging and carrying dead bodies all day; standing on top of one in the grave, pulling the other one straight, some already starting to decay. I remember wrapping a rifle band around one's leg and throwing the band over my shoulder and starting to pull. I looked around, and all I had was one leg. Then the assignment in the hole—bodies, bodies, bodies; some getting soft, others so frozen you had to pull them in line to get enough bodies in the hole, standing on four to five layers of human flesh—what an Easter! The reward from our numbskulls was two hundred grams, about eight ounces, of chocolate. None of us wanted a meal or any chocolate after ten hours of this; most of our stomachs had turned inside out. Only mine, however, held. Had I been getting used to this business, or was it a blessing and favor of the Lord?

In the night, down at the river, one of our men stepped on a mine. After the explosion, all quiet, and then the ear-piercing cries for help that sent goose pimples down your spine. Another game began; because of the thaw, the ice on the river became thinner, and in order to cross the river the Russians built a small pontoon bridge over it, to hold their position. Every day our artillery destroyed it, every night the Russians rebuilt it, until one night our sector was very quiet and there was no bridge in the morning. They had withdrawn over the river, and just in time. A few days later the ice broke again. We of course took up new positions along the river.

Rumors started to fly about being pulled out and sent back home. Could it be true? Yes, it was. One day late in April, we pulled out of there—marching, wading up to our ankles in mud, sliding, falling on patches of wet ice; did we care? We were going back. Rumors still, but they were telling us about going home, and the rumors did come true. After two weeks of organizing, brain washing, and preparing, we were taken to a train station where the once proud 10th tank division, or at least the remaining men, were loaded on our beloved freight cars to take us west—and west we rolled: Russia, Poland, Germany, Belgium into France, to be rebuilt for more action. How did I feel? Jubilant? No—is there a word for it? I felt warmness in my heart, sunshine in my soul, thankfulness in every fiber. I had gone through hell and deep freeze at the same time; had lost all my original buddies and had been preserved by the hand of the Lord so many times, only He knows! I had been given a new chance, sustained by Him who lives to bless.

How do you stay sane? How do you keep integrity? How do you keep the Word of Wisdom, or the commandments? Well, you just do. You make up your mind and you don't care about peer pressure or the opinion of your superiors. You will have plenty of opportunities to prove that you are loyal, dependable, physically better, and mentally more alert. You will be hated, admired, and commended for your guts. But above all, you will walk ten feet taller—not stuck-up, but for joy in knowing that you are sustained by the Lord. So why worry about what the rest of the world thinks? How do you pray? For me, I prayed very seldomly aloud; but short and to the point. You feel closer than ever to Him. Yet sometimes you have time to meditate and to renew, so you do, always trying to stay human, to be passionate, never trying to destroy life; if you must, you do, but only as a last resort. How can you lose? Remember you are a child of God, so act like one.

For a while I had a sergeant who was a wild one; he had been a soldier for fourteen years; he loved killing. When we needed a prisoner, he always volunteered to get one, and almost always he brought one back with his handpicked men. He drank, swore, and went after any loose girl; stealing from the Russians was his hobby. He got promoted and demoted three times a year, and he hated me. I would not participate in his wild parties, I would not accept his drinks or cigarettes. Oh, he made no secret of his feelings toward me, yet in battle he knew he could depend on me. But one day he thought he saw a chance to humiliate me. The division was planning to create a new unit; they needed experienced, loyal, alert, and physically well people. It was going to be a unit which would filter through the Russian lines and sabotage anything of value to the Russians. What it was really going to be was more a "suicide command" than a sabotage team, even though we would operate on skis with all-white weapons and uniforms. If you got caught, you were dead. Well, he volunteered me and my machine gun for it. So, off I went. What an honor. But his hate backfired, justice prevailed—nothing ever came of it. For two weeks we sat around doing hardly anything, drinking hot chocolate—a luxury. When he came by to visit, he almost exploded for envy. Of course he filled out a request for me and got me back, but what a nice two weeks I had, born out of someone's hate! About a month later he got hit by a shell fragment in his head, which blinded him for some time. When I met him again later on in Africa, he was a different man. Sometimes even those people can see the light!

Rolling westbound I can't describe the feeling; rolling through your homeland, people waving at us, talking to us, offering us goodies. Spring was here, some flowers were out; we owned the world! After eight beautiful days of rolling and dreaming with the "clickety-clack" of the railroad tracks, we arrived at our destination somewhere in the boondoggles of Northern France. The next day we unloaded and stood in formation—I was a corporal by now. Name and units were called out and you stepped forward; finally mine came, regiment, battalion, company. One man stepped forward; the call came again, no other response. Herbert was the only one that had survived the front. "Thank you, Lord!" Of course I found some of my buddies when I arrived at my old outfit. They had been wounded and had recovered enough to join us again, and some had been in our support unit, never coming close to the front. Six times my company had received replacements, yet not even a replacement stood at my side on that day in France.

The new assignment in France was a dramatic change for Herbert. Not only was the constant danger and violence of the front lines absent, but all of the men ordering the men in drills and training had never been in combat. For Herbert, it became difficult to comply with orders that he knew would never be practical in real combat situations. This lack of compliance caused problems with his superiors, until he was able to describe where he had been, what he had survived, and what his country had awarded him for his service, including the Iron Cross first class and several other prestigious combat awards. From that time on, his participation on daily drills became that of an advisor and allowed him to share his experience with the new recruits. Though his new situation was a wonderful change from the battlefield, it also brought its own monotony. Herbert was surprised when he was granted several two-week furloughs within a short period of time. The opportunity to see his family once again was a wonderful blessing, though it was once again difficult to part.

Returning from his last furlough brought Herbert the opportunity for a new assignment. With his experience on a motorcycle he was able to excel in all of the proficiency testing for motorcycle courier and attract the attention of a high-ranking officer. Soon he found himself as a personal courier with a great amount of freedom to move and do as he pleased. Over the next few months, a few invasion alarms sent Herbert all across France, finally ending up in Southern France and Italy. Without the chance to see any of the sights, Herbert soon found himself on his way to North Africa.

Two days later, off we went to the airport; our 3-engine airplanes were waiting to take us. What [an] experience it was; sixteen men, my motorcycle, and one extra drum of gasoline, the pilot and navigator, and that's it. Off we went, slowly around Mt. Vesuvius, gaining height; the next stop was Sicilia where we would have a night off; everybody warned us not to play with the girls as the guys were too good with their knives. The next day we boarded our planes again, off to Africa, with Tunis as our destination. We got informed that we had about fifty planes with two fighter planes for protection. If we got attacked by the enemy there were machine guns hanging on the wall—we were informed to stick them through the holes and shoot. Crazy? Yes. As we approached the coastline we were told that as soon as the plane landed, we were to scramble and take off to the West, because enemy bombers had been sighted in the direction of the airfield for a bombing run. So our machine came in and let the engines run while we unloaded; I got on my motorcycle and zipped over the airfield, across a street and found some holes as shelter, while I waited for the rest to arrive. Then the sirens started wailing and the flak started rumbling while most of our planes got or stayed in the air, and the bombs began to fall. The result was two planes damaged and one fellow wounded. He got loaded in the next plane and off they went. It sure was not Russia; that's what I was thinking and what was confirmed that same night. In Russia you hardly ever gave a second thought to look up into the sky; the little bit of movement by Russian planes was not worth mentioning. Here it was about 60 percent of the war.

After the ruckus at the airfield was over, we all got gathered up, taken on by some trucks and driven about twenty miles out of Tunis. Here by a tiny railroad station we put up camp. I counted five houses, two nice ones made out of good brick, the station, and three scattered around made out of a kind of adobe brick. The sea was about a hundred yards away and we had nothing else to do than to explore. Everyone put up their canvas tents and we all went for a swim. What a "vacation" in Africa!

No one told us to dig in or even to watch the air; which was a costly mistake. It was a beautiful day, very warm; it must have been about 10:00 PM, with some of us already asleep, when all of a sudden the fireworks started at the Tunis Harbor. Christmas tree after Christmas tree appeared in the sky—that's the kind of bombs that light up the night for the bombers to make a run. Then the anti-aircraft guns started blazing away, and the bombs started detonating; all this we could see from a safe distance—or so we thought. Oh, we heard one or two airplanes coming from the west straight at us; wondering why, I had an uneasy feeling about them; but such things never happened in Russia. Well, this was Africa, and a different enemy. The answer came a few seconds later, when the whole sky around us lit up with several of those blasted Christmas trees, and before anyone could say a word, we heard the bombs whistle. There wasn't time for anything, just to hit the dirt; and we made it just that far, when dirt, rocks, bushes, and all kinds of debris swashed over us. There was stillness afterward, then some moaning, as someone was wounded. But it was much worse than that; we had sustained six dead and four wounded, one tent had been obliterated, also one of those adobe houses with all their occupants—some introduction! Herbert got away with a handful of thorns and a neck-full of dirt. "Thank you, Lord!"

We moved out at once into the fields where we dug individual holes twenty to thirty feet apart; believe me, we didn't get caught that way a second time. Those bombing runs became a way of life for us, and soon we would sit on top of our hole and watch the bombers come in twelve to forty-eight at a time. We would watch them with our binoculars and estimate whether the bombs were meant for us or not; as far as damage was concerned, for us it was very minimal; I never saw a direct hit again like those on the first night.

The Americans were pressing toward Tunis, only to be stopped by Rommel's veteran troops and some of their tanks. By that time the Tiger tank had been on the scene for a while, and they had given the Americans a very bloody nose about forty miles west of Tunis; that's where we were headed the second day. Since we had no vehicles of our own yet, walking was the order. At 5:00 AM the company started, except for our motorcycles and the command car, everyone walked. The vehicle, myself included, stayed until noon before we drove off. During my time at the airport, while I was waiting for the rest to get across, I had looked at the grove of trees I was in and discovered they were hanging full with lemons; some already yellow. So I harvested a load in my saddle bag. That day when we caught up with our company we found them resting, spread out against air attack, so we stopped too. When I pulled a lemon out of my saddle bag to eat, everyone was on my back. "Let me have one" went the cry, to the extent that my officer came over to find out what was going on; needless to say, he got one. Since my supply was very limited he gave me permission to go back and harvest all I could get. Eventually I became a very popular person and supplier; whenever I made a trip somewhere, I would always bring something back for my buddies, like oranges, lemons, figs, or small pancakes fried in olive oil, which were peddled along the roadside. What a nice thing to drive a motorcycle, especially when my little rat-a-tat was exchanged for a beautiful BMW with a side car and I got a companion rider.

That night our company replaced an old Rommel unit on top of a chain of hills; they must have been there several days, for the line was all dug in with light bunkers in the back of the hill and machine gun stands and foxholes on top, overlooking a large valley with a city in the back, and beyond that mountains, none like I had ever seen. It looked like the landscape of the moon, totally bare; and where was the enemy? Oh, about four to five miles down in the valley; and what kind of war was that? A very serious one for us; but there we were for several weeks obviously waiting for our heavy weapons to arrive; some artillery was backing us from behind, and from our point of view we could see them fire once in a while at the Americans and could also see when they were getting the answer, about ten times as many shells came back. That was about the extent of the opposing forces, which was also a ratio of nine Allied soldiers and equipment to one Axis soldier and equipment. We have a saying in German that

"I WILL GO BEFORE YOUR FACE"

The safe evacuation of all missionaries from Germany and Czechoslovakia at the onset of World War II was a miracle of tremendous proportions. Though plans for the evacuation had been put in place a year earlier and an initial "practice" evacuation had occurred with the German takeover of Czechoslovakia, the final evacuation was not without difficulty. Unlike the previous year, missionaries found themselves unable to find train connections as all passenger trains were full of military personnel and equipment moving east. Furthermore, several neutral countries designated by mission leaders as safe havens for the missionaries began closing their borders as they were inundated with refugees seeking to flee the continent.

CHURCH ARCHIVES

Joseph Fielding Smith

Overseeing the evacuation was Elder Joseph Fielding Smith, who had been touring the European missions. With his inspired counsel and the great leadership of Danish Mission President Mark B. Garff, communication was established with the Dutch and Swiss missions, who were able to account for most of the missing elders and sisters. As the eve of war approached, only a small group of missionaries from Czechoslovakia, including President Wallace Toronto, were unaccounted for. Fearing her husband's safety, Sister Toronto pled with Elder Smith for assurance that all would be well. Turning to her, Elder Smith simply stated, "Sister Toronto, this war will not start until Brother Toronto and those missionaries are safely out of Czechoslovakia and get on Danish soil." Queried further, he again said, "The war will not start until those . . . men are out of the country." In direct fulfillment of his prophecy, President Toronto and the remaining missionaries crossed the border from Germany into Denmark just hours before the invasion of Poland.

A key to the success of the evacuation was the Danish government, who graciously allowed the missionaries to cross its borders and find safe haven. In gratitude, Elder Smith prophesied that Denmark would be spared the same devastation that would afflict other nations who had closed their borders against the Lord's servants. Though occupied by the Germans, Denmark was largely spared the intense destruction experienced by other occupied nations. In the following months, the rest of the European missions were also evacuated under the close supervision of Elder Smith. By Christmas 1939, 697 missionaries, mission presidents, and families had been evacuated to the United States.

Source: *Regional Studies in Latter-day Saints Church History: Europe*,(Brigham Young University, 2003).

goes about like this: "With many hounds are the hares dead," and that came slowly true here; of course we were not dead yet, to the dismay of the enemy of course, for they had many wounds to lick before we were licked. Some days we could see the Americans play baseball way down in the valley, and as soon as they were done they would run to their guns and let us have it. It was very disturbing and too close for comfort, but we did not suffer any losses.

All of a sudden it got pretty nasty; the rainy season had arrived, and what a season it was; it was raining cats and dogs for days without end, but at least it was warm. We got replaced and on the way back my motorcycle got so mired in the mud or rather clay, which packed between tire and fender that the wheel would not turn. So I gave full throttle, and "bang" it said, and all my spokes popped; a blessing for me, for I got the beloved BMW and what a machine it was; four forward gears, drive-on-side car, and three extra gears for rough going, plus one reverse—a beauty! But even with this I got stuck in a big puddle. An Arab with two mules, who came by, was recruited for help. Well, he cooperated, but his mules wouldn't, even his big stick could not convince them to help. Who invented mules anyway? After a time, a halftrack came and pulled me out.

We got a very interesting assignment during that time. Bizerte was a place guarding the Tunis Harbor. On all the surrounding hills were big gun emplacements to ward off any enemy from the sea; there were searchlights, machine gun nests and whole garrisons on those hills, all French soldiers. They were not engaged in any battle, but had they decided against us, we could have been in big trouble. Our order? "Take over." So one day to their surprise, we attacked every hill at the same time and before they knew what was what, we had their weapons. Some French men were still lying in bed and telling us to be glad to be out of the mess, but adding, "If we would have been Italians, they would have fought us with their knives." We stayed there for several days enjoying dry and warm quarters; once in a while firing one of the big guns which were well hidden in the rocks. Several times I visited Tunis with my officer to pick up mail, quite entertaining, particularly what he did after mail pick-up; well, loose girls will be found all over. Of course during that season, not much went on, not in the air nor land; so I guess the Germans succeeded in getting supply ships over and unloaded.

As soon as the rainy season was over, we started rolling and we even had tanks. The first order for us was to push the enemy back west. When our attack came we had good air cover and tanks, plus artillery. We rolled right into their lines and twenty miles beyond. The Americans did not have much experience; with all the equipment we got we could have repelled a division. The nicest discovery we made on that day was their K-rations and C-rations. What a luxury for us! And the worse discovery they made was that their 10.5-mm guns could not penetrate a Tiger tank. We also took quite a few prisoners, but what a gentle treatment they received compared to the Russians. Even the wounded were treated and taken to hospitals, which had been unthinkable in Russia—what a difference. It felt good! At least some degree of sanity was present here! So, while we were pushing the Americans piece by piece back westwards, the English were pushing us also piece by piece toward the west, all the way from Egypt.

Eventually all that was left for us was Tunisia. We, with our tanks, were scattered all over, so I guess someone had decided to give a lesson to the British; we were rolling south, nights only, through desert and bare mountains; the roads were so narrow that our big guns had a difficult time negotiating the winding roads. While we were stopped for a little time one of those big guns tried to pass another one, only to disappear from the road tumbling down the mountain. On we went. In the early morning we reached even ground covered with little sand dunes. For a while we had to stay in line to avoid our own mines which had been laid by us to slow down the British. We attacked, with our lines stretching as far as the eye could see—dust, sand, and movement; but what the British laid on us we could not believe; barrage after barrage of artillery hit us; thanks to the sand the damage was modest. All day the battle raged, and at night we dug in; that night was the darkest night I had ever experienced, it was so dark you literally could not see your hand eight inches in front of your eyes. Some of our guys left their holes to do the necessary thing and could not find their way back. The next day the raging battle continued with no progress. We had one more night and by the next morning the order came to withdraw. I had a feeling we were not winning the war in Africa. Some withdrawal that was, everyone on his own. What a mess, as we converged toward our own minefield; our own troops had to stem the flow with drawn guns to get us filed into the pass. Once we with our motorcycles were in, we ran up the hills and down again to pass our big vehicles. Two of us made it two and one-half hours sooner to the point of assembly than the rest.

A few days later found us engaged against the Americans again. We sure took revenge and blistered them down at Ahfga. There they mounted a counter attack with some tanks; a big fiasco for them. I picked up two from a tank crew. Their tank had been hit by an 88-mm shell, going in one side and out the other; fragments had hurt four of them. I took the two for a ride around their tank, and all they did was shake their heads; then I took them to a first aid station. They offered me all their money, but I did not take a dime. On the way back to the front lines, I came upon a tank in the road totally burned out. When I tried to push the debris aside, I stumbled over two totally burned bodies; they had been literally fried to a crisp leaving ashes two feet tall, almost enough to turn your stomach inside out. We had recaptured a range of mountains; an important road went through a pass there, wide and well-paved, but under constant fire by the Americans. Getting through there was something in and of itself, quite a gamble; you waited somewhere close by for the last shell to explode, then jumped on the motorcycle or truck and took off at high speed trying to beat the next load, which could happen one minute later or fifteen, and on a stretch of six kilometers they could hit anywhere; bad by day, worse by night, and costly for us on material and men. One of our BMWs got caught during a night try; my buddy ran against the side of a halftruck, ripping off a cylinder and losing his left foot. If that wasn't annoying, their airplanes were worse; sometimes they would hunt single men. I got engaged several times with them playing a kind of Russian roulette. You would drive down the road or over the desert and their fighters would be up in the sky looking for prey. All of a sudden one or two would swoop down on you, and just when they thought they had you in their sight, you make a ninety-degree turn and "ha ha," you escape! Their machine guns were mounted in their wings or through the propeller, and they had to aim the whole machine. Of course it was never wise to drive alone, for you had no eyes in the back. The cold had penetrated my bones in Russia, but here it was the heat, 110 degrees up to 120 degrees, but I liked it better than the cold.

One day I got a young officer assigned as a permanent passenger in my side car, except when we were engaged in battle, and then he had to be on the front lines. It did not take too long and we kind of took a liking to each other; he appreciated my experience and would ask many questions. I wondered about him though, as he knew too much of what was going on in Africa to be just a lowly officer. My hunch had not been wrong, for about six weeks later he was transferred as a "specialist" to Rommel's headquarters, and his parting words were, "I'll be back to get you too, just stay alive!" I did not believe him, yet he kept his word.

With the German troops exhausted from constant fighting and withdrawal, Rommel pulled them back to regroup. For Herbert this meant some well needed rest. However, he still had duties as a courier and on one particular mission, almost lost his life. He had been assigned to reach a unit that had mistakenly gotten off course and was traveling unknowingly toward the enemy. In order to get to them in time, he had to drive at dangerous speeds during the night without headlights. He had borrowed a helmet for this particular mission, feeling that he might need it. Along the way he felt to slow down, and as he did, the motorcycle struck the back of a mule-drawn cart of a Bedouin, who was on the road illegally. Because of the helmet and his slower speed, Herbert escaped the crash with only a broken thumb.

VERNON BEELER FILE

A British soldier captures a surrendering German.

After several days of rest and regrouping, Rommel began a push west, away from the British 8th Army and toward the US II Corp. It was his hope to be able to redeploy his forces into a better defensive position to hold off the enemy until reinforcements from Europe could arrive. Initially, his attack was extremely successful and American forces suffered a bitter defeat at the Kasserine Pass.

I had been sitting on a hill overlooking the battlefield, dodging a stray shell once in a while, and writing a letter home. It was still war for me with death and destruction all around, but other than that the Lord had eased my load. I had been writing about the happenings and telling them at home how mad I was at the Americans for trying to run over us on a Sunday. Did I ever have a wise father. His reply was a beautiful letter, and his great lesson was something like this, "I can understand that you can get mad; however, I hope your madness is not like that of your friend Hans, for he was willing to kill anyone who would come into his sights; you see, he will never come home." For my own good I could assure him that such thinking had never entered my mind!

Knowing he had just destroyed a division of the enemy, Rommel did not hesitate to pursue his advantage. What I did not know was that those forbidding mountains in the West concealed the Katherine (Kasserine) Pass and the way to Algiers. Needless to say, the next night found us at the foot of those mountains; and all that held us up were mines in the road, which had been placed in haste, and a few machine gun nests. Our Tiger tanks came to the rescue; somehow they found that the mines were not strong enough to rip the Tiger tracks apart, so they filed one by one up the road, and we followed at a respectful distance. The morning found us through the pass on a high plateau; we advanced about another twenty miles that day; then Rommel came himself right to our front lines. I heard him talk about securing the flanks. So we halted for several days; our unit was assigned to guard the road. I am sure that stop for several days turned the tide of the battle of Katherine Pass.

The other side had time to regroup and put new units on the line. Artillery activity had very much increased. Their fighter bombers became pretty bold, although some of them had to pay with their lives. And when we wanted to roll again, we found a fresh crack British unit opposing us. We did make slight progress, but it was costly. So the decision to withdraw must have been pure agony to Rommel, for he must have known as well as I did, we could not win this war—just prolong it. While we were waiting in our shortened lines for the enemy to make his move, my officer friend showed up one day and told me to gather my things. He had come to get me and my motorcycle, as his personal driver. I laughed at him, telling him to quit making jokes; however, it was real. Twenty minutes later I had a new assignment—at Rommel's headquarters, it was a miracle! Henceforth I never had to dig a foxhole anymore, put up a tent, or go through air attacks; we were so beautifully concealed, we just could not be spotted. Once a day we had to take secret orders which were only given by mouth to my officer for our Division Headquarters, and bring reports back. Sometimes, when we brought the moving orders at two in the morning, we could see them scrambling for their trucks while we were going back to our "nest." It was some life, one I had never known could exist; sometimes I even felt guilty! They must have given me some security clearance, because I could not help picking up enough information that would have been of great importance to the enemy—like our total amount of tanks, or where reinforcements were sent to, or where some artillery was concealed, etc. Whenever my own company officers and sergeants wanted to know things, I would just give them the answer, "Sorry, it's classified."

But soon it became clear to me that the fate of the Africa Corps was sealed; it was just a matter of time and grinding down of our forces. There was almost no way to get heavy equipment or reinforcements; the sea lanes were cut off and Italy had been a disappointment with their fleet and troops. Then one day General Rommel was transferred to France. It still took a long time to wear us down. Bombs rained down on our units every day, as the air had been taken over by the Allies, our airforce being transferred to Italy.

May 11 dawned and we were called together at Headquarters and told the truth: "Tomorrow we will surrender—each of us is to join his former unit." So we said good-bye to each other; my last trip was to bury the officer's diary, then I joined my old unit. We decided to surrender to the British; and they in turn let us somehow know not to destroy our trucks, or we would have to walk all over Africa. They kept their word; whenever we got moved, they used our trucks. We pushed our motorcycles together, opened the gas lines and were ready to throw a hand grenade on them, when the order reached me to get the motorcycle and make a run to the Regiment. On my arrival at the Regiment I found everyone drunk. I left my orders and was told to stay, but late at night at the height of their drunkenness, I got on the motorcycle and hit the road to my unit and my buddies. They were all drunk too and most of the equipment was destroyed; what a picture of dismay and defeat—couldn't anyone take this with dignity? At noon the next day some British officers arrived to take us to our camp. Every vehicle was to put a white flag on and we were on the move. On the way through the British lines a British soldier jumped onto my sidecar to take possession of my motorcycle, but before he got a good grip I made a swift turn, and he slid off. I was sure glad that I did not understand his language at that time. According to his face and gestures he must not have been very complimentary to me. When we arrived at the camp, I was quickly disowned of my motorcycle. The camp consisted of a big open field with rolls of barbed wire around us. Strange though, we never got searched by the British, which was a great gesture of gentlemanness, even in a time of war. So far it looked like war and bloodshed had come to an end for me; but losing your entire freedom and being at the mercy of your enemy was not all happy hours either. My feelings? "Thank you, Lord, for letting me survive." But I wondered how it would all end. As it turned out, it was a long road and a few years of more lessons and experience for me, but by the end, all was well.

Treatment of the prisoners by the British was decent. The men felt as if they were real men. They had not been stripped of their belongings and valuables, and were given great freedom in governing themselves. Some became quite proficient at fashioning clocks and stoves, as well as sculptures and toys from the many discarded tin cans that were available. After a few weeks, Herbert and the majority of the POWs were transferred into American custody. The treatment was much different. The Americans themselves were very untrusting and would not allow the POWs much freedom. Additionally, much of the guarding was done by French Moroccans or Algerians, who were quick to remove anything valuable from the soldiers. Eventually the POWs ended up in Casablanca, where they remained for several months.

After travel in packed box cars, and a cramped passage on a ship, the POWs' opinion of their American captors was not very high. This soon changed as they were greeted in Norfolk, Virginia, by comfortable train cars, and more food than they could eat.

After arrival at an internment camp in Illinois, the men felt they had arrived in paradise. There was more food than any could eat, and aside from daily work details, they were allowed great freedom in pursuing hobbies or studying what they wished. Herbert was eventually transferred to Wisconsin, where he worked in a canning plant.

And then came the great day when Germany capitulated. How did we feel? For most of us it was disappointment mixed with hope; for some there did not seem to be a future, they had lost loved ones, home, and country. For me it was inner joy and happiness, for as far as I knew, my family had been preserved, and I had a place to go among my family, even if it was in the Russian zone. Sooner or later we would be going home. Unfortunately, it was later rather than sooner!

The news that reached us was good for most of us, except those who were waiting for the Nazis' secret weapon to get into action and turn the war. Germany was simply losing; to me it was as clear as a summer morning—just a matter of time. We also had been allowed to write one letter and one postcard a month to Germany; it was on special paper to make it easier for the censors to work it over. Some of the letters I received from home had a lot blackened out, but we were communicating and that's what counted. Life was not bad in the "golden cage," yet most of us would have traded it for freedom and some degree of misery! I guess that was when I really learned the value of free agency on this planet; it is a priceless gift but not without restraint and responsibility.

One day I got called into the office. Some strange officer was sitting there who spoke German very well. I think he was a German Jew. I was asked a lot of strange questions like, what town in Germany I was from, had I been writing letters home, did I have relatives in Switzerland, and a lot more about me. What in the world was going on? Did I have relatives in the USA? How many? Where were they living? Did I know their addresses? After an hour or so he seemed to be satisfied with my answers, and handed me a package which had been sent by Aunt Francis from Salt Lake City. How had she found out about me? On a hunch she had inquired from Washington about the German POWs in this country and received the answer of where I was. She also tried to keep me here after the war.

A bit later I was called in again and to my surprise Uncle Herbert and Uncle Willie had come to visit me, and one day even the bishop from Milwaukee, Bishop Fred Busselburg, came along to see me. Speaking about special privileges—I had them! Of course for every visit they had to write to Washington, DC, to get permission. We were never left alone, which did not matter to us.

And then came the great day when Germany capitulated. How did we feel? For most of us it was disappointment mixed with hope. For some there did not seem to be a future—they had lost loved ones, home, and country. For me it was inner joy and happiness, for as far as I knew, my family had been preserved, and I had a place to go among my family, even if it was in the Russian zone. Sooner or later we would be going home. Unfortunately, it was later rather than sooner! From the newspapers and from the people we heard stories of German POWs being sent to France and turned over to them to help build up their country; bad news for us we knew. There was lots of anxiety even to the point of uproar; something had to be done to calm us down. So, one day all of us were called out to be confronted by an American colonel, who gave us quite a pep talk, giving us his word as an American officer that we would not have to go to France, but that we would be taken to Frankfurt and from there released to our homes. Until today I am still leery about American promises, and I understand why the European Nations have their doubts sometimes. This "word of honor" never did come true and it created much disappointment, even hate. Well, let's leave it there; mistakes are made by the best, and it is still America which saved the world from total slavery with the help of the Lord.

Finally, the day came when we were told to pack, and we could send one big package home. The day of good-bye came and off we went to Mitchell Field, Milwaukee. About a week later we were handed our envelope with our belongings which had been taken from us in the beginning. Much to our surprise, nothing was missing. On the train we went, only to be two days later in New York, to be put on a fine troop transporter with the name of *General Sherman*. As we were sailing out of New York Harbor I saw, for the first time in my life, the Statue of Liberty. A tear came to my eye, all had gone well so far. "Thank you, Lord." The Eastward trip over the ocean was pleasant except for a storm we ran into, which put about 90 percent of us on our cots—not me, however, and I enjoyed every moment of it on the lee side of the deck, watching the big waves wash over the bow. The storm delayed our trip a day and a half; but then one day we arrived in Cherbourg, Europe, at last, closer to home—and yet so far away; only I did not know it at the time. The next day we got put on a train, and soon started rolling. Anxious, we watched for signs of direction, but no one really knew where we were going.

After a day and a half we came to a stop at our destination. It sure did not look like Frankfurt; it was a big tent camp on an abandoned airfield in France. It was February, cold and wet, and no heat in the tents, and the inside of the camp was governed by Germans. What a rude awakening; here we were in the old army—only worse! First of all, we were searched by our own and anything of value was taken by them. My chess figures, which I had bought in the USA with my saved money, went, along with my soap and a good shirt. It was hard to believe and harder yet not to hate! We were then put in cold, damp tents and finally, to our ultimate humiliation, we were told that the French coal mines had need of good, healthy workers and that we had been selected. Hate against America for bringing us here to France was great, but greater and deeper was to our own for their treatment. The worst I could work up was disgust! The treatment we received from our own was so bad that I thought we had ended up in a concentration camp.

Every morning we had to stomp for two hours through mud up to our ankles, in snow, in wind, or cold for exercise; our tents had stoves, but no wood or coal was delivered. Our clothing was as wet and cold as when we took it off the day before, even our underwear got moldy. The only glimmer of hope was a good, warm meal each day. Then the day came when we were brought before a French doctor to see if we were able to work in their coal mines. We walked into the office and the first question from a German and a French fellow was if we had anything of value for them. If we did, we might have been found not well enough to work, and eventually be sent home. Corruption sure was rampant! The second insult came when we were found O.K. and got sent to the second office. Here we were asked if we wanted to volunteer as a guard for our buddies. For everyone who would volunteer, one of the old guards could go home. I felt like spitting in their face! What they had not figured was that all of us came from the Africa Corps and still had some pride and dignity left, so none of us volunteered.

So came the day when we were brought to our new camp, which was not too far from the German border—a plus for me! The camp consisted of some old but solid four-story brick buildings, with double fence and towers around. The mine was about forty minutes from the camp by foot, part of the route going through the city. The housing was at least dry and warm; eighteen people were crowded in a room designed for six. Six three-story bunk beds had been nailed together, from any lumber available. A straw mattress with a blanket completed the picture. The room was occupied by eighteen POWs and 18,000 bedbugs! What a fight we had on our hands! Of course nothing was done by the French about the conditions; as a matter of fact, what we saw was just sickening! The old POWs who had been taken prisoners by the French, or given to them right after the war by the Allies, could have come out of a concentration camp themselves. They were physically, morally, and in any other way at the end of the road. Malnutrition was showing all over; their skin was pale, their bones were either showing, or their limbs so filled with water that they hardly could walk. A few had really big heads so that if you poked your finger in, the dent would stay. Some had large sores which never did get treated. It was unbelievable! They were supposed to be our liberators!

Of course those poor devils of ours had not one ounce of fight left in them; most of them had been brought down to animal status like sick dogs or worse. We marched in, a picture of health, clean clothing, high morals, a sense of unity and high in spirits, and as long as I was a prisoner there, it was never broken—not that they did not try!

The work in the mine was extremely taxing, and the men were fed very little, and in some cases rotten food. Though escape was on all the prisoners' minds, it meant almost certain death to try. Regardless, the men were desperate to get home, so many attempted to escape anyway. Twelve were executed attempting to escape in the space of a few months. Herbert was also hard at work planning his own escape. With the help of a Polish miner, he was able to hide civilian clothing in the mine as a disguise so he would be able to walk out one day and be mistaken as one of the civilian miners. Before he could try his plan, he became ill.

I think the Lord had another way for me. I was held in camp for about two weeks, and then sent to a farmer. How surprised he was to find such a good worker, and we got along real well. Work was hard, from 5 AM to 9 PM almost every day. Sunday was a bit better. I was living with him, specially locked in, next to his bedroom at night. He had no idea how easy it would have been to get out. One day I got a package from America; don't ask me how it reached me, as I just don't know. Inside were some food and a suit from Aunt Francis. The suit was a little tight but alright. A little later a list was handed to us as a guideline of how France would release POWs. My priority was "zero," meaning I would have to wait another two and a half to three years. Bologna! I had another solution. I did a lot of praying, and one day I was sure. Mister Farmer and wife had gone to a party, and so did I. Wearing my suit, the day of freedom had come; I knew the map in my head. At about 7 AM I approached a little city. Like most cities, all roads led to the center, which is an open place, and the roads fan out from there again. So, there I am walking very confidently toward the center of the city, when a voice, I can't find another word for it, tells me, "Take a right turn!" A right turn, what for? Well, that voice spoke three different times, and three times I knew better—or did I really? Coming to the center of the city I got stopped by two civilians asking me for a pass, even in German. I was caught by secret police and was taken to their car and to a main prison camp, where I was left outside, while they both went in. In the camp I was condemned to a bald head and thirty days of bread and water, and every third day a warm soup.

Had I learned something? I sure did. If you pray for help and you get it, follow the instructions and not your own wisdom. His ways are much more safe, and don't ask questions, just do it! So, where was I? Worse off than before and that just for not being obedient. Here I was in a dark basement with plenty of time to think, and I did, and plan too! After twenty-eight days in a dark basement, in the late afternoon, myself and six others were picked up and taken to a regular camp. The next morning we were taken to work after a fairly good breakfast. Work was in a huge subdivision, where about five hundred houses would be built. I had found a buddy in prison, and we stuck together—both ready to run, if there was a chance. So, all morning we were fencing the compound while working on the side of it. By noon we knew we could try for it. Had the Lord given me another chance? Noon came and we went into camp for lunch. By 1:00 PM we were ready to try for it. Our pant legs had been tied with string at the bottom. I had a piece of towel in them, while he had the shaving tools in his pants, so out we marched. To the right there were lumber piles, houses and all kinds of junk, including piles of dirt, all temptingly close to the woods. We didn't know where the guards were, but our calculations were correct; we figured they could not yet have reached their positions at the woods. We took a plank and carried it to the closest pile by the woods, dropped it, and ran, stumbling over stumps, running from big nettles, always thinking someone was behind us! At last we had to slow down, but kept going until we hit the other end of the woods. It was still daylight so we had to hide, and by looking around we found some old overgrown holes from the war, so we slipped inside.

Hours later we heard them combing the woods. We shrunk and almost stopped breathing, when two of them came within six feet of our hole. Night came, and it was time to move again. We avoided all houses, bridges, cities, and everything else. Never did the North Star look brighter to us than the next three nights. We found one small apricot tree the second night, and when we were through with it, all of the apricots and most of the leaves were missing. After the first night we also found ourselves on the wrong side of a smaller river with a city ahead of us, and the woods to hide in on the other side of the river. We jumped right into the river. Wet to the bone, we made the woods, small planted pine trees only, the rows straight like a line; you could see straight along their trunks when lying down. By now our teeth were chattering from cold and exhaustion. Then some dogs started barking and the noise came closer. As it turned out, and we could see from below through the rows of trees, it was some hunters. How the dogs missed us, I don't know—or do I? On the second night we were very hungry, frustrated, and walking wet through the fields. The morning found us at a good place to rest among big pine trees. The third night we arrived at dawn on the border of France and Germany. We watched until the border guards changed and slid on our bellies over the border, which did not mean too much, since Saarland and the rest around was also occupied by the French. However, it gave us a clear advantage—people spoke German, were Germans, and were very helpful. By now we were totally exhausted, so we decided to travel by day, very carefully of course.

First thing we ran into a road crew. They took one look at us and knew; the foreman told us to clean up and shave in his shack; someone shared a half sandwich with us, our first "real food" after three and a half days. Then they gave us good pointers, not to use the bridge over the Saar River because of guards, and then they told us where to find a man with a boat, who would take us across. We made it, but climbing up the steep incline from the river was almost too much for us. Eventually we found a house and begged the lady for a piece of bread and got a good-sized piece. We then hit the railroad tracks and walked north; we were aiming toward British-occupied Germany. We finally hit a railroad shack with a man inside, where we collapsed and slept on the floor until almost next morning. The fellow handed us two train tickets with instructions to look for French police on the train. We boarded the train, the last wagon; my buddy went inside, I stayed on the front platform. When the train started rolling, two French police jumped on the last platform; we jumped off just in time to catch the last crowd going through the checkpoint. We had yet another hurdle to jump over. On the street, more French police were stopping and checking everyone. In just the last moment a big truck with trailer pulled up, and while they stopped it and checked it, we walked by. "Thank you, Lord!"

After a twenty-mile march, we were at the British line. There was no guard in the field so we crossed and the first person we found welcomed us home. I couldn't hold my tears back.

With some help from the Lord and generous friends, Herbert made it safely into the Russian zone and began his journey home.

I arrived in the afternoon. With only one hour to walk, I wanted it to be dark when I got there so I could surprise them, so I started walking slowly. On my way a few times I just sat down and basked in the sun. When I made the final turn I could see our kitchen window with light in it. I could see Father, Mother, and sister, and my head began to swirl. Down the road I went, into the yard, up the outside flight of stairs, and into the hall. I rapped at the door. "Come in," is the call from father, but I couldn't move. The door burst open and my sister looked out, her mouth dropped wide open and she cried out, "Oh no, Herbert?!" Stirred by Ellis's cry, Father and Mother joined us in the embrace.

I was home after five years from my last furlough and seven after the first call to arms. I couldn't believe it was over, that I was home with my loved ones after being halfway around the world, experiencing slaughter, plain murders, losing most of those around me; seeing crippled ones, wounded ones, sick ones, indescribable suffering, corruption, hunger, thirst, and humiliation. But I was home, and I was fine, with nothing missing, and my physical body in good condition. My spiritual being was well balanced, although not ever again the same as when I left. How grateful I am for some great lessons of life I learned; let me not forget them! Again, "Thank you, Lord!"

Dorothea Speth Condie

After leaving Dresden for the West, Dorothea Speth Condie worked as a registered nurse. She served her mission in Stuttgart, where she met her husband, Elder Spencer J. Condie, now of the First Quorum of the Seventy. She has had many callings in the Church, including the recent assignment with her husband as Elder Condie presided over the New Zealand Area Presidency. The following account is taken from "Let's Follow Dad: He Holds the Priesthood," Behind the Iron Curtain: Recollections of Latter-day Saints in East Germany, 1945–1989 *(Provo, Utah: Brigham Young University, 2000), 34–35.*

February 13, 1945, is an unforgettable day in the lives of thousands who were living in Dresden, Germany. World War II was in full fury with armed forces on all sides pushing towards the German borders trying to end this terrible war.

It was 10:30 that February night when we first heard the dreadful sounds of the sirens and the roar of hundreds of planes and the explosions of the first bombs. When my father looked outside, he noticed strange-looking lights in the shape of Christmas trees lighting the dark sky and the darkened city. These were the flares used to guide the bombers.

We lived on the fourth floor of an apartment building and quickly realized that we needed to get downstairs, to the basement, which served as our bomb shelter. The first air raid lasted about forty-five minutes, and many homes in our neighborhood were set ablaze. But the area hardest hit was the inner city, where every building seemed to be engulfed in flames. For the time being, we seemed to be safe, but with the electricity, gas, and all communications cut off, we decided to remain in the basement for the rest of the night.

Around 1:30 AM, we realized that the planes had returned and that bombs were exploding all around us. Would a bomb hit our house? Would only some or any of us still be alive in one minute or ten minutes or when this air raid ended? It was a terrifying experience! But when the silence finally returned, we were all still alive.

We were alive; however, we were all trapped in the basement. One of the first bombs of the second air raid hit our corner house at an angle, setting the ground on fire so the that the building

THE FIREBOMBING OF DRESDEN

During the three-day period from February 13 to 15, 1945, perhaps the deadliest and most destructive bombing raids in history took place over the city of Dresden, in Eastern Germany. Though its main railroad station had been the target of Allied bombing several times during 1944, the city itself had been spared the full-scale attacks from Allied bombers suffered by other German cities in what the Allies had begun to call "area" bombing campaigns.

NATIONAL ARCHIVES

The aftermath of the Dresden attacks.

With the Russian forces making significant advances toward the East German border in the late part of 1944, Allied Air Command began drawing up plans to disrupt communication and transportation lines between the two fronts, and thereby assist the Russians in their advance and hopefully shorten the war. East German cities, such as Berlin, Leipzig, and Dresden, among others, were chosen as major transportation and communication centers and targeted for bombing raids.

Over three days, beginning the night of February 13, the city was subjected to four major bombing raids, with a total of over a thousand aircraft dropping more than 3,900 tons of explosives on the city. While not an extraordinary number of bombs, conditions on the ground in Dresden were just right for the creation of an incredible firestorm that engulfed the entire city in flames. Flame temperatures reached as high as 2,700 degrees Fahrenheit and produced winds over 100 miles per hour. In some areas, air currents were created that either completely removed all the oxygen, causing suffocation, or sucked fleeing people back into the burning buildings they were attempting to evacuate.

The exact number of deaths caused by the bombings is unknown, but estimates range between 25,000 and 35,000. Dresden had become a center for refugees fleeing the advancing Russian armies in the east. At the time of the attacks, the city's population of 600,000 had swelled by 200,000 refugees. Further, information obtained directly by local officials after the attacks was seized and altered by government propagandists under the direction of Joseph Goebbels to help appeal to neutral countries for assistance.

Source: *World War II in Europe an Encyclopedia* (Volume 2: 1457–58); the *Simon and Schuster Encyclopedia of World War II* (163–64)

started burning from the bottom upward. The stairway, our only exit, was already blocked by fire. The only way out was a hole in our basement wall connecting the basement with the house next door. The hole had been made for this very purpose, but it was barely big enough to crawl through. We couldn't take anything with us. Our family and an older couple who lived on our floor managed to escape through this hole.

Most of the homes in our area of the city were now destroyed or burning, and the few remaining would soon be on fire. We all realized that we needed to get away from the burning houses immediately! Walking on the streets looked very dangerous because a firestorm with the force of a hurricane was raging, sending thousands of sparks and burning objects flying through the air, fueling and spreading the fires. In the streets, there were also many huge bomb craters adding to the danger.

Once outside, we gathered as a family and quickly held a council. My family consisted of my parents, my two older sisters, my twin sister, and myself. It was imperative that we not get separated as we set out to reach the Elbe River. The Elbe with its wide banks would be a perfect haven from the fire and the smoke that was starting to sting our eyes.

For the last time, we looked at our house and all that we owned in this life, knowing that the flames would soon reach the upper level. We lived in a very nice wide street leading directly to the river, which was about four blocks from where we stood. For safety, we did not walk together. My father took one of my older sisters and my twin sister and began to lead the way. My mother, my oldest sister, and I were to follow as closely as possible. As my father started walking, he headed towards a narrow side street instead of choosing the wide street which led directly to our goal, to the river. Mother stopped, not wanting to follow down the narrow burning street and began calling Dad to try to persuade him to turn around and take the more direct route along our street, which seemed so much safer and quicker. But due to the firestorm, Dad could not hear her plea, and continued walking along the narrow side street.

With each passing second, the distance between us increased, but Mom was not willing to abandon her plan. I heard my older sister plead with her, "Mom, let's follow Dad; he holds the priesthood!" With this reminder, we started to move quickly, trying to catch up with Dad, who led us safely in a roundabout way down to the river. We followed several other people into an old hospital building where we could finally sit down, rest, wait out the night, and be protected from the firestorm and its terror.

Martha Bauer Duckwitz

Martha Bauer was born in 1920 to Philipp and Luise Kuhn Bauer. Only six of thirteen children in her family survived past early childhood and World War II, and Luise passed away in childbirth. Three years after Luise's death, Philipp discovered a Church pamphlet, and the whole family was baptized on May 16, 1931. Every one of them would remain faithful until death.

Early in her adult life, Martha married Heinz Duckwitz and moved to Stettin, where two children were born to them before they had to flee before the Russian offensive. Heinz was drafted and served to the end of the war. Martha and children rejoined her father in Celle, where the twenty-three members of their family made up the majority of their branch. Their marriage was another casualty of the war. Martha and Heinz divorced in 1951, and in 1956 Martha immigrated to Salt Lake City, Utah. Shortly after her arrival, she suffered a car accident that put her in critical condition, but with the free help of a well-to-do doctor, Russell M. Nelson, she made a full recovery. Later in life she ran the Beehive Delicatessen until she passed away in 1999.

The third day of March 1945 was a sad day in our lives. At that time we were living in Pölitz, Rheinstrasse 29. As of late we had suffered bomb attacks almost every night. Continually we kept running for shelter to the nearest bunker in order to save our lives. Sometimes we stayed there for hours. Since the city contained a large plant that produced gasoline for the front lines, it became a primary target for the Russian Air Force. The Russian Army had already reached the Oder River and was incessantly shelling the city of Stettin, which was only about twenty miles away from Pölitz. As the Russian Army had threatened to cross the river for quite some time, every family had to evacuate immediately, especially those with small children. I packed two suitcases, mostly clothing for the two children. Although my husband, Heinz, had been exempted from military service in the war because of his technical skills in the plant, he was drafted in the last three months of the war. So we left our home, abandoning everything we ever owned and treasured. Nonetheless, the fear of falling into Russian hands was too great a threat and our freedom meant more to us than all the belongings in the world. At that time the trains were still running, and so we went by rail to Stettin. There was no other way to safety than by passing through the midst of warfare itself. We saw dead people lying in the streets, beautiful homes turned into rubble, and many fires burning in many areas of the city. Yet the Russians did not let up their artillery fire.

So we left our home, abandoning everything we ever owned and treasured. Nonetheless, the fear of falling into Russian hands was too great a threat and our freedom meant more to us than all the belongings in the world.

At the railroad station in Stettin we had to transfer. There were thousands of people waiting to leave by train. Chaos reigned. No one was able to purchase tickets anymore. It seems everybody was coming from the east, desperately trying to go west as far away from the Russian Army as possible. Fortunately, however, mothers with small children were given first priority in order that they might bring their children to safety and so to assure the country's future generations. The waiting was especially a frightening experience when we heard the air raid sirens and felt the bombs falling, but could not get out of the city because the train would not depart. Finally it left the depot. Every mile we traveled toward the west we felt a little safer. It felt somehow comforting that the children at least were not able to comprehend fully any of this danger. I cannot remember how long it took to get to Neubrandenburg, but when we did, I breathed a sigh of relief.

Here I visited my sisters and their families and hoped for some respite. My father had already come here from Schneidemühl in East Germany near the Polish border. He was a great support to us. Without his help and guidance we would have never survived. My youngest sister, Anni, was also there, having come from Schneidemühl as well. We all stayed in my sister Wanda's home. Her husband, Bruno, had been drafted long ago. Although her home was somewhat crowded, we got along really well. Occasionally our father even brought fugitives into the home who had nowhere to stay for the night. They slept on the floor and were grateful to have a roof over their head. Some of those people were terribly desperate. My older sisters, - and Emmi, were also residing in the same city with their families.

Since the Russian Army had still not been able to cross the river Oder, and since we were greatly in need of blankets and other things which were not available in stores, I decided one day to go back home to Pölitz to get these items, especially clothes, shoes, and blankets. By a stroke of luck I learned of someone who happened to be driving to Stettin. I went. Pölitz was a ghost town. There was not a soul around anymore. I thought of how ironic it was that we were so crowded in Wanda's home and that mine, still intact, was completely empty. I packed all the items that I had come for. Then I packed other items for storage in the house. I covered the radio and other valuables with heavy featherbedding and blankets, hoping in this way to save them in case the house was not completely destroyed. We thought in vain that when all this turmoil was over we would be able to go back to our home. To leave my home this time was an emotional experience for me. I looked around, went through all the rooms, and cried bitterly. Perhaps I sensed at that time that I would never see my home again. Since the trains were still going westward, I used the train to get back to Neubrandenburg. The venture had succeeded. All turned out well. My family, especially my children, were happy to see me.

For about seven weeks life was a little easier. In the meantime we learned that the Russian soldiers had crossed the river Oder and were coming closer west. Everyone became nervous. My sisters, Emmi and Wanda, had large families. This made

MARTHA BAUER DUCKWITZ FILE

Martha and her husband, Heinz, after the war. Also pictured are the couple's children, Norbert and Margitta.

their decision whether to leave or not a difficult one. Since my father was able to speak and write both the Polish and the Russian language, he was not so much concerned for himself as he was for us, his five daughters, and our families. In the end our father made the decision and said that none of his daughters would fall into Russian hands. So that was that. I prepared for flight again.

By the end of April the Russians had advanced dangerously close. We knew that the English and American soldiers had already occupied large part of the west, and we were hoping that their advance to the east would be rapid and would intercept us in this part of the country as well. No such luck. We therefore obtained our ration cards and bought as much food as possible. That afternoon all electrical power went off; so did the gas and water supply. We learned that the trains had stopped running altogether and that it was impossible to get out by train any more. Quickly my father prepared a handwagon and pulled our luggage to the nearest stop in order to get away by truck. Considering that we were a family of seventeen people with luggage, we had to wait for a rather large truck. All afternoon we waited. Evening came and night passed. There was no sign of a truck. The next day we heard the sounds of war as we waited. The airport had been bombed. Before noon we were in luck. A large empty truck used for transporting telegraph poles and wiring stopped and took all of us along except Micki and Anni. The drivers were allowed to pick up elderly people and mothers with small children. So Micki and Anni were forced to flee to the west on their bikes and later on foot since their bikes were stolen long the way. To our regret the truck only took us to Malchin. At least we were a little further away from the front lines.

Upon our arrival our father went to the Red Cross and asked for some hot food for us, since everyone was very weary and very hungry. He also requested a handwagon for our luggage, which we had left sitting in front of the church where the truck had taken us. We then went to the train station for information about a train. We were told that a train was expected to go to the west, but no one was certain of its arrival time. A little later we were told that there would be no more trains. Such chaotic times. In the meantime we had brought all our children and luggage to the train depot. Our father did not give up hope. He was constantly asking for information. He finally came back with the good news that a train was still coming in the evening. When we heard the train come in, all of us had tears in our eyes. We were so relieved and so happy. However, the train did not go very far and the trip did not last very long. In Güstrow we had to get off. Yet, again we were glad to be further away from the front lines.

We left our baggage by the tracks and waited outside the whole night. It was very cold, but I was very glad that I had gone back to Pölitz to get the blankets. We put our children on the baggage and covered them well. We did not dare to go to sleep, however, for fear that a train might come and we might miss it. It was a long night. No train came. Nor did anyone know if one was coming at all. In the morning we learned that no passenger trains were scheduled to come anymore, but that a Red Cross train would be passing through. Although it was not normal procedure for such a train to accept regular passengers, an exception was made in this case and several boxcars had been added to pick up all the people who were anxiously waiting to flee from the storm of war. Train cars had been added in the front, behind the engine, and in the back. How relieved we were once we sat in the train. Our lives had been preserved.

We learned at that time that Neubrandenburg had been captured. Horrible events had taken place. The Russian soldiers had violated every female they could lay their hands on, no matter how old or tender in years. There was a beautiful lake, a very large body of water, where I spent a lot of my leisure time as a teenager. Scarcely could I have known that this lovely spot would be the scene where over two thousand took their lives in order not to be captured. Many other people went to the nearby woods and hanged themselves there. The whole city was engulfed in flames. There was nothing left, as we later learned, except for a few homes in the outskirts. We saw the fire in the distance before we entered the train. In gratitude we prayed, thankful to our Heavenly Father for preserving our lives. The sacrifice of leaving our homes was not in vain. However, the Russian front lines continued to advance as we continued to progress. Whenever the air raid alarm was heard, the train pulled back into the nearest forest. Not even the Red Cross train was immune as far as the Russian pilots were concerned. They swooped down close to the train well marked by its red cross and easily discerned from above, and fired. Because of the terrible noise of the bullets and in the confusion of the moment, I, along with many others, took my children off the train and went for shelter in the dry ditch at the side of the tracks, keeping the children close to the ground and covering them up with my body. At once others from inside the train yelled at us and said, "Come back into the train. If they realize that refugees are on this train, they'll never let up." Their warning made good sense, but the moment of being shot at in the train was so terrifying that we all thought that this was the end of our lives. This type of attack occurred repeatedly, but we survived the destruction. On the eighth of May, while traveling on the train, we learned that the war was over. No one can imagine how relieved we felt, how happy we were. Tears came streaming down our faces. The war was over.

But we were still in danger.

Once during the train ride, the train had to stop for quite some time. I got off and was just walking towards the front when I saw an open train car. It was the operating room. I looked and saw the doctor amputating a solder's leg. It was terrible to see, but yet quite fascinating. I have never seen anything like that before or since. A week later we arrived across the river from Lubeck.

When we came close to Lubeck, we had another hindrance, which really scared us. We had to cross the River Elbe. The bridge looked still intact, but when we had crossed about half of the bridge, the train stopped. Rumors were going around that the bridge was mined and the train would not go any further. The English had taken the west up to the other side of the river. We knew once we had crossed the rest of the bridge we would be safe. It was unthinkable for us that the Russians might still catch up with us at those last few yards. Our father got off the train onto a narrow plank. We had decided to forget about our last few belongings and try to walk over that plank to the other side. That was easier said than done. We all were tired and weak after those past days and nights. We were scared stiff, but there was no other way. Our father led every one of us over the plank. Our knees were shaky, but we made it. Once we reached the other side we took a deep breath.

—•—

In the meantime the foundation of the bridge was carefully investigated. They found no trace of mines. We were so glad when the train crossed the bridge completely. This way at least we were able to hold on to our baggage. We went back onto the train and stayed on the train for one week, because we had no place to stay. Lubeck was a large beautiful city in Northwest Germany. They transported the wounded soldiers to the hospital, but forgot all about us refugees. We stayed on that train for three more weeks. Not having a seat in those boxcars, we were sitting, eating, and sleeping on the baggage. We were so overtired, hungry, and weak, even though we were well prepared as far as food was concerned, because by now the food was used up, especially since we had helped out some starving babies. But we could only do so much. Some of them I knew just starved to death. Because after the end of the war no one was responsible for the people (refugees), even the Red Cross did not pitch in. It was chaos. There was no service of trains or mail for about three months, so we were not able to get in touch with anyone. A lot of children were lost. A lot of families parted. It took some years for them to find each other. Some never did. We ended up in a refugee camp quartered in a school that was already completely overcrowded. At first we had to stay in the entry hall for about one week, which was cold and drafty. Our situation really had not improved, for we still had to sleep sitting up on our baggage, which we had done all along. Finally we could move into a classroom that already held twenty people. With us we were thirty-seven. There was straw on the floor. At least here we all were able to stretch out at night, and in the morning we had a washroom; that alone was a blessing!

MARTHA BAUER DUCKWITZ FILE

Martha Duckwitz and her husband, Heinz.

We received ration cards again. With a primitive stove our father built outside we could cook our own food. It was much better than the food which was distributed among the other refugees. At that point, however, the physical and emotion strain caught up with us. A lot of our children and I myself took very ill. My sister's youngest, just a baby of ten months old, barely survived. There were times when it seemed hopeless. But we all made it somehow. I am sure our prayers had a lot to do with it, and our Heavenly Father saw our ordeal and saved us. Under these circumstances we lived for almost three months.

The mail still was not intact, but off and on a train was running. My brother Phillip, who was in the army fighting against the Russians, had his wife's relations living in the Celle/Hanover. Just in case, we all had agreed to meet, if necessary, in Celle. So we all decided this was the time. Like always it was a hassle with our baggage, but we were so lucky to have it. Some of it, I am sorry to say, was stolen along the way. Among the missing items were sleeping bags. Most people had much less. Our father was a good organizer. He had a lot of experience in that sort of thing. We had him to thank for a lot of things. We were in the train again, en route to Celle. This time the trip only took a few hours. Now we thought things would start to look up. But there we learned that my sister-in-law's family had been killed in a bomb attack two days before the war ended. We were devastated.

We wanted to stay in Celle, but none of the officials wanted any more refugees, since the whole city was overcrowded with them. But we had two sick people among us: my niece and myself, who had angina with fever. At least our illnesses afforded an excuse for us to put our foot in the door. We were placed in a refugee center. Due to the sick ones, they had to put us in a separate room. This was heaven. For the first time, except for the sick ones who were in the basement of the school hospital in hospital beds, most of the family could sleep in a bed. These were army beds, and we had metal closets for our clothes. It was heavenly. We had shower rooms and indoor toilets again. We did not have a kitchen, however. Our father once again built a stove from a large tin can, and we were able to cook in the entry hall.

Upon our arrival we heard from our two youngest sisters, Miki and Anni. They had endured perhaps worse hardships than we had, because most of the way they had to walk with no shelter at night. Their bikes had been taken away from them. Our brother Philip had just arrived one day before we did. That was good news. He had fled from a Russian prison camp in Eastern Poland and walked all the way through Poland, East Germany, and finally to West Germany. We were all very poor, had lost our homes and belongings, but we had escaped the Russians, were all safe, and had each other for our support. We were thankful to our Father in Heaven and thankful for our freedom.

Wilhelm Krisch

Wilhelm Krisch was born March 29, 1905, in Odoyen, East Prussia. He was the third child of Marie Peoski and Gottlieb Krisch, a carpenter in the village. To provide for the family, Gottlieb spent most of his time working a small piece of land to raise feed for their one cow, a horse, and some pigs. Only in his spare time was he able to work in his trade.

Wilhelm was nine years old when the First World War began in 1914. Because of its location, only thirty kilometers from the Polish border, the war came quickly to the little town of Odoyen.

In a short time, the Russians came to our town. They burned so many towns close to the Polish border. Our relatives that lived close to the border had to come and live with us as refugees. The Kosaren (Cossacks) were the worst, with their red stripes on their pants. Our relatives told us that they murdered people, cut out tongues, and poked out eyes. Those who were captured were shot. By the time they came to our town, a command had come down from the Russian czars that they should not torture the people, so they behaved like humans.

I still remember when two or three Kosaren rode into our yard. They were thirsty and wanted some milk. We had a cellar in our yard, by our house. There was milk in an earthenware pot. My father went into the cellar and brought the milk. He filled the drinking cup with milk for the Kosaren to drink. My father had to drink the milk first, and then the Kosaren would drink. They were under the impression that the milk had been poisoned.

After a few weeks, even more Russians came in, and we did not feel safe. Our town's mayor decided that we should flee to an island in the middle of the Arys Lake, one kilometer away. There were two long islands in the lake that we used for grazing cattle in the summer. We were sent to the islands by boat with enough provisions for a few days. The Russians saw us on the island during the day and came over on a rowboat. We were ordered to return immediately to our homes. We came home to find that our outside cellar had been broken into, and my father and other men from the town could not be found.

The Russians had come to our town during the night and had taken all of the men that they could find with them. After a few days, my father and his neighbor returned home. They kept one man who they thought was a spy, because he had a German newspaper. The Russian officers had taken my father and the other men to a hill. They had to turn away from the officers and thought they might be shot. But then the Russians decided that they could go home.

On the seventh and eighth of September 1914, there was a battle close to Arys. The Russians were scattered. After the fight, we had a battalion of German soldiers remain in our town. In the fall of 1914, the Russians broke through and we had to flee. My father and his neighbor, Steinmann, got the wagon and horses ready and drove to Loetzen, thirty kilometers away, where they sold their pigs. They met us back in town during the night, and we left. I don't remember anymore how many days we drove in the wagon. The wagons with the horses were sold in the city, and we, the refugees, were loaded on a train. We arrived in Latendorf, in the vicinity of Neumuenster, Schleswig-Holstein, Germany.

We, as refugees, were divided up among the farmers who had gone away to the war, so my father had to take care of their animals. Shortly before Easter 1915, the men returned to East Prussia, and we followed a little later. When we returned our house was still there.

Though still standing, their home had suffered some damage from the fighting. As the summer ended, new windows arrived from Germany, and Wilhelm's father set to work to install them. While working in the cold weather of autumn, he caught cold, became sick, and died in the beginning of January 1916. Only a few months later, Wilhelm's oldest sister passed away in a hospital in Koenigsberg, where she had fallen ill while attending school. The deaths were very difficult for the whole family, and young Wilhelm was required to help his older brother, Emil, work their farm and provide for the family. In 1919, his mother remarried a German widower who had lost his wife during the war.

In 1921, Wilhelm and his brother Emil were invited to a meeting held in their neighbor's home. As they listened to the two men, one German and the other American, speak of the restored gospel, they were touched by the Spirit. The two brothers took the tracts that were offered and studied them, comparing them to what was said in the Bible. They continued to meet with the few members in their town, discussing the gospel and this new religion. After fasting for two days, Wilhelm knelt in a forest to ask God if the teachings he had heard were from Him. He received a sure answer to his prayer and knew from that time that he had found the truth. Though his stepfather was very much against the Church, he gave Wilhelm and Emil permission to do what they wanted, and they were both baptized on May 21, 1922.

My wish was to marry in the Church. I had many opportunities to marry outside the Church, but I could not find a wife that had the same beliefs that I had. I became acquainted with Emma Stank, who was a member of the Church, before Christmas 1937. We got married on the twenty-eighth of October, 1938. I was thirty-three years old, and my wife was twenty-three years old. First we were going to get married in September, but because of a motorcycle accident, we had to postpone the wedding for four weeks.

Everyone who got married during Hitler's time had to produce a certificate proving they were of Aryan descent, which meant you needed to have proof that you had no Jewish ancestors. My wife and I had to have all our documents, so we could receive a "marriage" type of qualified loan from the government consisting of five hundred German marks. We were required to pay back five marks each month, without interest. With the birth of the first child, you did not need to pay anything for a year, and so one hundred marks were subtracted from the loan. If someone had several children, the money became a gift. (The government made these loans available to newlyweds to encourage them to have more children.)

We lived in Selbongen close to the branch, from January 1939 until August 1939. At that time when my work was not far away, I came home every day. When my work was too far away, I stayed at the job site the entire week and only came home for Sunday. The last four weeks before I had to go to the army, I had service duty. I worked as a carpenter in the vicinity of the city of

Memel, close to the East Sea. We built protection bunkers that were used in World War II.

On Saturday I came home from Memel, and the next week I was to be inducted into the army with my motorcycle. I was a courier, with my motorcycle, assigned to a munitions company. The munitions company had horses and wagons. There were twenty men in the munitions company about my age (I was thirty-four years old at that time). Most of the others had fought in World War I.

The war with the Poles started in the beginning of September 1939. We went to Poland as a munitions company. The war in Poland lasted only eighteen days. When it was over, we came back to a small city named Suwalki, not too far from the German border. From there I was allowed to come home on furlough for Sunday. Our stay in Suwalki was not very long. We arrived in Rheinland, Germany, shortly before Christmas 1939. There, we received military training and instruction from men who had fought in World War I. The instructions were very limited, as we were to receive more extensive training in the Muenster facilities in Germany.

After Christmas, in 1940, I received a furlough. I was to report to my company in Hamireln after fourteen days. When I returned from furlough, until March, there were forty of us there. Then all the munitions soldiers that belonged to that regiment were transferred on a train to Muenster Lager at Lueneburger Heide.

In Muenster Lager, the people from the munitions company were added on to other troops. Three other men and I were assigned to Company 14 of the armored tanks and were activated. We had been added to an outfit that had previous training. It was very difficult for me, without previous training, to perform my duty with the armored tanks, but as time went by I figured things out.

At the end of May, we were ready to go to battle. The war with France was to begin any moment. I received another fourteen-day furlough. I had all my gear with me, and we were to be told when the troops would leave Muenster Lager and when we were to rejoin our troops.

WILHELM KRISCH FILE

Wilhelm Krisch

The war with France started when I was at home on furlough. Every hour I waited for a telegram telling me to rejoin my unit. I was able to stay home, as our outfit was not one of the first troops that went to France. I wanted to stay home for Pfingsten (Ascension), a holiday, so I stayed home a day longer than I should have.

I arrived in Bremen and could not make a train connection. I did not return on time but was a few hours late. The military police wrote my name down. I reported to the reconnaissance company. Naturally, I should have reported for duty in the morning, but I arrived about noon. I receive a "good talking to" that was not very pleasant. We stayed approximately fourteen days in Muenster Lager before we were shipped to France.

We first came to Eifel, which was not far from the Belgium border. From there our whole company traveled with military transportation to Belgium. From there we continued on until we reached

France. Upon arriving in France, we were bombed by enemy fliers but did not have any casualties.

Traveling past Paris, we came to the front, where the French shot at us with artillery. We were quartered in a barn that was half damaged from the shooting. There we bandaged the wounded soldiers. One soldier was wounded, and then wounded a second time. How we felt, I can't say. "Today it's my friend, tomorrow I could be dead too." I was carrying on a conversation with this soldier, and then after a few minutes he was dead.

We were in action for only two days and were to be in action again, but France surrendered.

As part of the occupation troops, Wilhelm began working with a French carpenter making beds and tables. The soldiers were allowed to ride the street cars for free, and the best movie theaters were reserved for them. But occupation was still dangerous, and the men were not allowed to be outside after dark, due to the activities of the French Resistance. After six months, Wilhelm and his unit were transferred east.

The war with Russia began at the end of June 1941. We were the first troops to fight against Russia. We crossed the border in a village called Kagnit, East Prussia. We waited there for our orders to begin. Time dragged out slowly because there was not a good reason for the war to begin. From there we crossed over the Memal River and were stationed about seven kilometers from the Lithuanian border. If I am not mistaken, the war with Russia began on a Sunday. They told us we had to be ready to march at nine to ten o'clock at night. It was about midnight when we were given the orders to begin the war with Russia. As we got underway, we could hear the machine guns firing, and as the morning broke, we crossed the border into Lithuania.

Lithuania is a little country where they speak both Lithuanian and Polish. This land had been taken over by Russia shortly before World War II. I was the only man in the company able to understand these people. I asked the people what they thought about communism. They said they did not want to have anything to do with it. They told me how the Russians had desecrated their churches by making them into horse stalls and munitions stores. The whole scene was very sad. One of them begged me to go inside a church and see the damage. It was in terrible condition outside and inside. The floor of the church was torn out and the holy paintings were destroyed. The altar was unrecognizable; everything was broken up. These Godless people had brought this condition upon the Lithuanians.

A Lithuanian told me that the Russians had torn their wives away from them. They did not know where their children were or know of the condition of their wives. I wanted to know the reasons why these families had been torn apart. The reason was that they would not join the communist party and wanted to keep their own religion. The Lithuanians were very happy that we Germans had arrived. As we traveled through the area, they gave us water and food to eat.

Marching through Lithuania for a few days, we did not see any Russian soldiers. All of a sudden we came upon some Russian tanks. They were situated in a camp in a small forest, carefully observing the Germans. I was part of the group that was assigned to defend against tanks. We were trained to use artillery to destroy them. We immediately went into firing positions. Two civilians came to us very excited and offered us vodka (schnapps). I assume that these were Russian soldiers who dressed up in civilian clothes, doing reconnaissance to discover where the German troops were. Consequently, it was not very long before we were fired at in our position. We had to let our cannon down the mountain with ropes because it was impossible for us to get out of there any other way.

We did not come in contact much with the enemy in Lithuania. Occasionally, as we were marching, Russian airplanes flew over us. We were on the march during the day, and there was nowhere to hide, so we suffered casualties. I will never forget how I felt as we crossed the Russian border. Planes flew over us, bombing and machine-gunning us. We were getting set to eat as we were crossing the Russian border. I was running from one position of cover to another, losing half of my mess gear and all of my food on the way. It was then apparent that we were in Russia because we didn't see any people or civilians. It wasn't until we entered farther into Russia that we occasionally saw refugees. Some were heading back to their homes; others were overtaken by German troops.

Russia is a large land with poverty-stricken people, just as the Lithuanians said they were. The farmers had their land taken from them and had to start working on collective farms. They were able to keep one cow and a few acres and were allowed to work this land after completing their assigned jobs. The time in Russia went by very quickly for me. We were on the march a lot until winter arrived, and then we had many local battles.

At one point, we had to attack the Russians. It was about two to three AM when the real battle started. Then, around five to six AM, we approached a small forest from which the Russians were firing artillery. We climbed into our trucks for protection and drove a bit farther. At that time, the enemy began throwing grenades around us. Everyone jumped into a pile. There were soldiers from other units there also. Everyone ran toward the pile, so I began to run toward them also. I only ran a few steps toward the men, when a soft, quiet voice called me by name, telling me that I should go back. When I heard the voice I started to run back. I got thirty to forty steps and threw myself on the ground. Only a few seconds elapsed before a direct hit struck the group in the pile. There were dead and wounded. The only thing that happened to me was a few marks on the stock of my rifle from shrapnel. I immediately ran over to my comrades who were screaming and moaning. I could not see the head of my best comrade. His head and helmet had been ripped from his body, and his body was ripped apart from the shrapnel. All the others were wounded. Heavenly Father warned me with the soft voice. I don't know, perhaps I would have been dead also.

We loaded the dead body in the truck and took it back to the main troop headquarters. In the meantime, a medic from our company told us that we had to drive three to four kilometers to a location where there was a dead motorcycle courier. We had to take these two young dead men to the area medical center. To get there, we had to pass through the combat area, but fortunately it was quiet at the time. We arrived at the location where the man lay that was killed on the motorcycle. He was lying in his blood—it was a terrible sight. The medic had to begin loading the body; no one else wanted to help him. I did not have to do it but helped anyway. We had to work fast, because with an artillery hit, we all could be dead. We loaded up the dead body, and with a full tank of gas, drove to our aid station. We made Russian prisoners of war dig the graves for these two young men.

Sometimes, we spent the night sleeping under our vehicles or sleeping out in the open. During this time, they were dropping bombs on us and machine-gunning us from the air. In the morning, we continued our march. Often, while we were on those marches, our infantry would pass the word to us about battles between our tanks and the enemy tanks. We also had a motorized infantry that had special assignments. One time when we were marching, we came upon a Russian convoy that approached us on a flanking attack. Immediately, we were ordered into fighting position. We placed our artillery in position and were shot at from all sides. A few of the men ran to the vehicles. I was one of the last soldiers to put our weapons into position. It was quite a shoot-out. The Russians were running all around the countryside. The dead and wounded were everywhere. I ran back to our vehicles and found two Russians lying there. I grabbed their hands and made them raise them high. Both of these Russians had a lot of hand grenades hidden under their bodies. One of the Russians said, "Shoot me" in German. He had some hand grenades that he could have thrown at me. They did not want to be taken as prisoners of war; they were so willing to give up their lives.

As I was on my way back to my artillery unit, I met a wounded Russian. I grabbed the Russian

WILHELM KRISCH FILE

German forces struggle through the mud and rain in Russia.

by the arm and took him where the other prisoners of war were held. And what did my comrades say? They said I shouldn't have helped him by supporting him under his arm as we walked along. In other words, they were mad at me and swore at me. I was ruined in their eyes. But, what did Christ say? "Love your enemies. Do good to those who hate and persecute you."

We drove farther down the deserted Russian roads. The roads weren't even covered with cobblestone but were instead dirt country roads. During that time there seldom was a cobblestone road, but instead we struggled on in muck and mud. After the rains came, we encountered colossal mud. Our vehicles got stuck, so we had to chop off branches and bushes and place them on top of the mud. This continued on for days and weeks. Sometimes we fell asleep as we walked along. We had to pull ourselves together and go farther. Whenever we had a slight break, we seized the opportunity to get some sleep.

One day, as evening was approaching, we came to a village. Since we were a motorized unit, we arrived there a few hours before the others. We certainly did not know that we were the very first ones to reach the Russian positions. A few civilians were in the village. In the meantime, I dug a deep hole for myself. If the shooting started, I would have a place to take cover. I was finished digging or at least half finished by the time it became dark. The Russians had shot up the village. The houses were burning so the civilians were trying to douse the fires in their own houses.

During that time, a few of us soldiers went into the village. We were thirsty, so we wanted something to drink. All of a sudden, I saw a Russian woman come out of a wooden bunker. I approached this woman. "I have not seen any German soldiers," she was screaming incoherently. She thought she was approaching her last hour on earth.

The Russian soldiers had told these civilians when the Germans soldiers came, all the civilians would be shot. A Russian asked us if we had some bandages. His daughter had been wounded by the Russians as they had stormed the village. He spoke a bit of German and told us the name of the city in Germany where he had been a prisoner of war during World War I. He had no fear of the Germans.

During the night, I had to stand guard. If something happened, I had to sound the alarm. The barn was full of sleeping soldiers. I saw a person walking toward me. It was already somewhat light as this woman approached. She was very excited. It actually was a Russian soldier wearing women's clothes. "She" wanted to check out our position and further spy on where the German troops were. I knew that the Russian troops were in front of us, and also knew there were no houses in the area where civilians were living. I immediately woke up my comrades. The "woman" ran away a short distance and hid in a field of barley. We were unable to find him.

On the next day, the Russians started firing their artillery at us. Through our binoculars, we could see the Russian soldiers at the edge of the forest. They were sending a reconnaissance group to check us out. We fired back at them with machine guns, and then it became quiet for a while. Occasionally, the Russians fired their artillery at us. I could not relax. I told my comrades that something eventful would happen that day. I ran back and forth through the artillery fire. It was about midday when a fragment from a grenade struck me in the midsection, going through a matchbox in my pocket, and into my belly. My intestines were punctured. Because I was wearing such large underwear and had bands wrapped around my middle with lots of folds, the shrapnel did not do extensive damage. None of my comrades were nearby. No one came and carried me to safety because the Russians were firing their artillery at us. A medic came from a different unit and bandaged me up. Three men carried me through the bushes and undergrowth without using a stretcher. This happened during the end of July or beginning of August 1941. I spent a few days in Russia in a military hospital. Afterwards, I was taken to Lithuania and finally arrived in Allenstein, East Prussia.

Just before we began our march into Russia, I had received a telegram telling me, "Renate was born June 13, 1941." I am very thankful to my Father in Heaven that I was wounded and had not remained long in Russia. After a short time, the man who replaced me in my artillery unit stepped on a land mine and was blown to pieces. They could not find any of his remains. The time had not arrived when I was supposed to die. My testimony was strengthened. Through this experience I learned that the prayers we send to our Father in Heaven are correctly fulfilled. Through these experiences I came nearer to God. In this life a man can either strengthen his testimony or lose it. For me, it was a great lesson. The soft voice always warned me so that I remained alive to fulfill my mission on earth.

From Allenstein, I went on leave to Selbongen, East Prussia. After my leave, I went to Berlin, where I spent the night with my sister-in-law, Martha Stank Kuffner. And then I went on to Hamburg, Luetan, Vorberg, Wandsbek, and Kaserne. That was in the summer of 1941.

I was in Hamburg over a year. There we were trained for only a few days. I was assigned with two other men to the uniform supply command, where we cleaned the uniforms. Some things such as socks and shirts we sent out for mending. Almost every week we had to equip more soldiers with uniforms as they went to the front.

I was not able to attend my Sunday church meetings, as there were many air raids, or we had to peel potatoes. One time while I was assigned to peel potatoes, I went to my church meetings without my officer's permission. I was lucky he did not report me, because otherwise I would have been punished.

Since I was a carpenter by vocation, I had orders in Hamburg to repair the roofs of the buildings that were destroyed by enemy air raids. A few other men and I were assigned to the Hamburg harbor for a course of instruction in first aid for victims of air raids. We were also ordered to complete six-month training in the *Firlingstlak*. That was the artillery used to shoot down airplanes. We had to go through the entire training.

A few of us received orders to go to France, including me. We returned to the barracks in Wandsbek. It took several weeks to get the new division organized, so several of us had to work in the gardens. Where there were open spaces, we spaded the area and seeded it with vegetables.

Before I went to France, I was given a leave. After I returned from my leave, I had to go to Lueneburger Heide (the heathers of Lueneburg), where I had orders to report to the new division. From there we were transferred to the province of Normandy. We were there in the fall and winter, when it rains a lot. We lived in tents, but they were leaky. We also had to be on guard duty during the night. During the day we built bunkers so that we could live and sleep in them. We also were given training concerning Belgian artilleries. We were waiting for the invasion in 1943. The bunkers had water in them during high tide; between high and low tide, the water came up only a hundred meters on the beach.

The invasion took place in June 1944. When the invasion took place, we had been withdrawn a few kilometers. We were quartered at a farmer's house. There we had to build two locations for cannons, and at night we had to stand guard. We erected our tents in the farmer's garden, where we slept. Every two hours we had to change guard. I had my shift in the middle of the night. It was during this night that enemy airplanes lit up the countryside. It looked just like Christmas trees with burning candles falling to the earth. That took place several times, and I was there when the invasion took place. When I saw the parachutes open, I woke the other soldiers up. There were no telephones to warn us ahead of time. A short distance from us, there was a machine gun nest. The corporal came to us and informed us that the invasion was taking place. As the day progressed, we hid in the bushes and watched the parachutes open.

I wanted to follow the captain and his men, but I heard a voice that called me by name, saying, "Willie, don't go!" The voice was so strong that my whole body shook. I thought to myself that I must listen more to God, instead of other men. Then I heard a tank coming.

We found a parachuter who was Canadian. We had a naturalized German from France who spoke French in our group, who was able to converse with the Canadian in the French language. The Canadian's parents had emigrated from France to Canada; therefore, he spoke French. He was a sergeant. He said he came down with a parachute and hurt his foot so he couldn't walk. We captured several of the Canadian parachuters and took them as prisoners of war. We went farther ahead with our artillery, when we met many German soldiers walking. We learned that they couldn't fly their airplanes because there was no gasoline available. We placed our cannon on a high hill not far from the ocean. We were shot at by artillery from a ship, with the shells damaging our artillery, so we became infantrymen.

The next day, it was pretty quiet in the early morning hours. Occasionally we were bombed. Shortly before noon we were attacked with heavy weapons. Everything started. One grenade followed another. I took the door of a house and placed it over a hole, and threw dirt on top of the door to protect myself from the artillery fire. I laid my rifle and bread sack by a stump since there was little room in my hole. I can't say how many hours we were under artillery fire, but one thing I do know: that it lasted several hours. I thought to myself that my last hour had come. The earth was shaking. My hole became smaller, because the earth caved in on all sides. As I sat there in fear, with my whole body shaking, a still soft voice said to me, "Willie, you will live." It was not only once, but several times.

We had to leave our vehicles, as well as our packs and grenades, because of the approaching enemy tanks. A captain of a pioneer company (reconnaissance unit) was there with a few men. (A pioneer company has 120 men.) I asked one of these soldiers where all the others were, but he didn't know. The captain from our unit told one of these men to spy out where the enemy was. The boy was only eighteen to twenty years old, and he trembled from fear. Then the captain took out his pistol and wanted to shoot this young man, but he didn't. Just then it was reported that the enemy tanks were approaching. The captain told me to get some grenades back in the forest, where our vehicles and ammunition were located, and where also our tanks were located for protection. I told my commanding officer I couldn't go there because the tanks were shooting where the ammunition was located. Another soldier was sent instead. I saw this same man a few hours later, dead. I thought it was a man from our unit, but after all the confusion, I knew it was the same man our commanding officer had sent for the grenades. I wanted to follow the captain and his men, but I heard a voice that called me by name, saying, "Willie, don't go!" The voice was so strong that my whole body shook. I thought to myself that I must listen more to God, instead of other men. Then I heard a tank coming. There was lots of excitement. The tank drove right beside me as I was hiding in the bushes. The man driving the tank threw open the hatch and looked around the countryside to see where the Germans were. I watched as my corporal was killed and my sergeant was wounded. After I saw what had happened, I realized all the soldiers from my unit had run away.

Then I heard other tanks coming, so in the excitement I ran away. I came to a wall that was so high that I couldn't climb it, so I ran through the trees down the street where the tanks were coming. I was running down the street when I heard a shot that was so close that I nearly fell from the force of the shell. There was a German tank placed in a position that I did not know about. If I had gone a few seconds earlier, I know one of my own tanks would have shot me with a single round. This tank was on fire. As the tank was trying to fire a second round, the muzzle of the tank's cannon exploded, which seldom happens. The tank couldn't shoot any more rounds. Otherwise, I would have been killed with the second round.

I didn't know where I should go. I was alone, in another division's area. The commander of the artillery wanted to scout out where the enemy was, so I went with him, hoping to find my own outfit. We hadn't gone far when we encountered some machine gun fire, so we returned where we started from. The tank was still burning. One of the crew jumped out of the tank. He was wounded, and died. The other crew members died in the tank fire. A tank burns for several hours because the ammunition and gasoline explode, and the ammunition continues to fire off inside the tank.

I did not know where I should go. During times like this, one doesn't even think about being hungry. He is just grateful to be alive. Just then some soldiers came by carrying a dead soldier. I could see it was our company commander, the one who ordered me to fetch the grenades. If he had lived, he would have shot me, but he was dead. I knew then I had to listen to God more and pay less attention to my superiors. If I had gone to get those grenades, I would be dead now, just like the young man who was sent for them also.

Just then my sergeant came by. He was wounded, so I took him to a first-aid station. We were very hungry. We had some pea soup that we ate from the lid of a garbage can. We had so many casualties that I was transferred to a different officer. We were supposed to move closer to the enemy, but we couldn't find their position. This could have taken place over one or more days. Our supply truck unloaded us, but could not remain standing there for too long because [of] the enemy's airplanes. At that time the only supplies I had were a rifle and gas mask.

I was the first to arrive in our new location, so I had the choice to select the best hole to jump into. These holes were only half finished, and it was very difficult digging because of the root structure of the trees. I found a hole that was completely dug. I jumped in, but it was just as if a voice said to me, "You should not go in that hole, here come the enemy bombers." At first I did not know what I should do. I went in and out of the hole. How many times I went in and out of the hole, I do not know anymore, but I had no peace and had to come out. Two other men went into that hole instead. I had no hole and no place to protect myself from the airplanes and bombs. That night I slept under the trees, but how could I sleep?

When it got light, I dug my own hole. I didn't have a shovel, and the roots of the trees made the digging very difficult. Tears rolled down my unshaven cheeks. I cut away the roots with my bayonet and threw out the dirt with my hands. My fingers were all bloody. Someone from our group went past me, laughed at me, and was surprised that one could even dig a hole with his hands. It took a long time until my hole was ready enough to protect me from bomb fragments.

We might have been there one or more days, I don't know. At sundown the airplanes flew over us dropping bombs. The branches of the trees were scattered all over. I was hit in the back with a big lump of dirt. Then I heard screaming. Our

AN UNLIKELY MISSION

From the account of Benner Hall, Mesa, Arizona

In the winter of 1944, our troops had pretty much pushed the Germans out of Italy, France, Belgium—and all of that area, back across the Rhine River over into Germany. They started a big counterattack in the Ardennes region in Belgium. Well, our platoon was across the river from Saarburg. The Germans were over in Saarburg, and there were two patrols of us. A patrol was ten men. There were two of us in this one town, and my particular patrol was in a house right at the end of a street. The houses weren't very big, but they had about three floors, most of them. They would have a basement and a first floor where the kitchen and living area were, then the second floor where they slept, and then they all had an attic. We could go up in this attic and look out the window, and we could see down the street toward the river. They had a bridge across the river that had been damaged by artillery fire, and our assignment was to just watch the bridge and see if anything came across.

"On the morning of December 23, one of our men took two other men to patrol down by the river to see what they could see of what was happening to the bridge. We had heard a lot of activity down by the bridge during the night, but there was nothing going on during the daytime. They took a side street down to the river, and left myself, Paul, and Herman up in the attic to keep observing the bridge. We saw two German soldiers come across the bridge and start up the street. The snow was quite deep on the ground, and they would go into each house as they came up the street. They would go into each one on one side and then across to the other side of the street. We assumed that they had been sent on a patrol to see if there were any Americans in this town. Well, when they got close to our house, I sent Paul downstairs. I told him that if they started to come into our house that he was to go out and tell them to raise their hands. He, being Pennsylvania Dutch, spoke a little more German than we did, so that's why I sent him.

"He went down the stairs, and they approached the door and he opened it and stepped out with his gun and told them, 'Haende hoch,' which is 'Hands up' in German. Well, one of them immediately dropped his gun and raised his hands. The other started to reach around for his rifle and bring it up, so we shot him. Well, when that happened the other one turned around and started running as fast as he could down the street. I had a thirty caliber carbine, and we didn't want him to get away so they would know where we were. I aimed right between his shoulders and shot. He kept running, and so I shot again and he fell. I thought I'd hit him, but I guess he just slipped in the snow, because he jumped up right away and started running again. The distance was now too far for my carbine, so I reached over and took Herman's M1 rifle, which was better for distance, and fired three more times right in that same spot—right between his shoulders. He kept running toward the bridge and went around behind a house. We went downstairs to see if Paul was all right. He was looking down the street and asked, 'Where did that other guy go?' I said, 'Well, I don't know, but wherever he is he's got about five bullet holes right in the middle of his back.'

"About that time we looked up the street and here came the patrol, with our German friend in front of them with his hands up in the air. One man yelled, 'Hey, Hall! We found a friend of yours down there.' I said, 'What do you mean a friend of mine?' They responded, 'Well, when we found him he was down behind a house on his knees praying, and you're the only guy we've ever seen doing that, so we thought you must know each other.' Well, he was just a young kid. I don't imagine he was over seventeen—if he was that old. We took him in the house and brought an interpreter over to interpret as we questioned him. He told us his name was Wilhelm and he was very cooperative. One of the men jokingly said to the interpreter, 'Tell him that he's really lucky because Hall's Dead Eye Dick, a cowboy from Arizona.' He said, 'Oh, my family has a good friend in Mesa, Arizona—Elder Max Webb. He baptized my family when I was just a boy.' I told him that I knew Max's family. The interpreter knew that I was a Mormon and he told Willie. His eyes brightened up and he grabbed my hand and shook it and said, 'Ah, Bruder Hall!'

"We went outside and I wondered what was wrong with the sites on our guns, so I looked at Herman's rifle, and his sight looked good. I checked my carbine, and it looked all right. Probably a little over fifty feet down the street on the gate post of a house was a fancy little ornament. So I raised my carbine up and shot and hit it right dead center. I had qualified as an expert on both the carbine and the M1 rifle. So I went back in and said, 'Ask him what he was praying for. Was he praying that he wouldn't be killed?' He said, 'Oh no, I prayed for that before we crossed the bridge this morning. When your men found me I was thanking my Father in Heaven that I hadn't been killed when I was running down the street.' "

Source: Saints at War, Interview with Benner Hall

sergeant, who was in my first hole, was our first casualty. When I got there he was dead, and the other man in the hole was dying. Father in Heaven had warned me with a voice that I heard. "Here comes a bomber." I do not know where the voice came from. It was as if someone was telling me, and I did not have any peace.

I had to spy out the enemy with a sergeant. It was nighttime, and there was an awful odor. This was a place where wounded men had their broken limbs placed in casts. We were afoot, so we took these wounded a distance with us. We had no idea that we had been encircled. The man we had picked up was originally from our company, and one of the first to tell us we were to surrender. We went farther because the enemy troops were behind us. One man came to me and told me that the soldiers moving our artillery had been taken prisoners. This man had escaped, so he and I ran to a bunker. But the bunker was already full of soldiers. Positioned on top of the bunker was a piece of artillery. We were well protected in the bunker. The bunker was completely enclosed so the air was very bad. However, we were able to pump fresh air inside, taking turns turning the crank.

We were able to shoot a few rounds from the bunker but could not continue shooting because the turning mechanism was bent, preventing us from turning the gun farther around. So that was the end of the shooting. One of us took a white handkerchief and hung it on the outside of the bunker.

Nearby was another bunker with an officer inside. My comrades told me that this officer telephoned from the other bunker, telling us that we had to pull our white handkerchief inside. I don't know for sure if we pulled it back or not. It was not long before two American soldiers came inside the bunker. We raised our hands over our heads. Afterwards, two American officers came into the bunker. They spoke very good German. I assume that they were Jews who immigrated to America before the war. We had to go out of the bunker and line up outside. Then they searched our pockets. I had a pocket watch, but they did not take it from me. That was the end of the war for me. I was captured on June 30, 1944. Fourteen days later, on July 15, 1944, I had already arrived in Camp Chaffee, Arkansas, USA.

Life as a POW meant a lot of hard work, but the men were well taken care of. Wilhelm found himself harvesting grapes and cotton and even laundering the

BOB JARMAN FILE

A German soldier surrenders in France.

uniforms of the local police force. In the winter, the men were able to attend various classes offered by the government and were even given clothes and musical instruments to form a band and put on plays.

On Sundays, we could attend Sunday church services, but there were very few who actually attended. In the camp there was a Catholic priest who was an officer, so they did not require him to work. But we did not have a Lutheran minister in our camp. However, we had an American Army chaplain who came to us every Sunday. His parents came from Germany, so he spoke very good German. When it was time for the church services to begin, he would play a phonograph record that was heard through the camp loudspeakers. In this way, we could hear the loud bell chimes just like it was in Germany in the Lutheran churches.

I attended the Lutheran church services. (Before I was a member of the LDS Church, I was a Lutheran.) We went to the church services just to get out of the barracks. They did not teach me anything. During the week they taught a Bible study class, so I went to it also. After the class was over, the chaplain told us about German Russians who had emigrated from Russia to America. I found this very interesting.

Often I looked for a place where I could be alone to pray, but I was never able to find such a place. Wherever I went, the camp was full of people, so I just walked back and forth through the camp praying silently to myself. It was not possible to do it any other way.

The Lutheran chaplain gave me a German Bible with the picture of Jesus stamped on the front. The Red Cross gave these Bibles out to all prisoners of war. I read this Bible a great deal on Sundays.

As I was reading the Bible one of those Sundays in the barracks, one of the prisoners ripped the Bible out of my hands and said to me, "Do you believe in these fairy tales?" He then read from the Bible and cursed God. I told this man that it was not a book of fairy tales. I said I did not believe everything that was written in other books, but that I believed 100 percent that the Bible was true and that is where one could find pure truth. There were eighteen men stationed in our barracks, but I don't know if they were all present at the time. There was an outburst of laughter from them because they were Godless men. I was laughed at because I believed in the Bible. I was just a lamb among the wolves.

I fainted and fell to the concrete floor, landing head first on the floor. As I fell to the floor, I saw a guardian angel standing before me. I felt his hands cushion my head as I struck the cement floor, so that I had no pain from the fall. I didn't experience any excruciating pain as I crawled back to bed.

Though heavily persecuted by his comrades, Wilhelm continued to persistently study the Bible. He meticulously underlined and marked those scriptures he considered most important, dealing with prayer, obedience, diligence, and enduring to the end. This time of constant study became a foundation for his life and served to further strengthen his testimony.

After almost two years as a POW in the United States, Wilhelm was told that they were to be sent home. In May 1946, he boarded a ship heading for Europe. Underway, the men were informed that they were to be taken to Scotland.

When we arrived in Liverpool, we were surrounded and held at gunpoint. It took from early morning until late afternoon before we were loaded aboard a train. There was an armed English soldier everywhere we looked, pointing his gun at us. We were not allowed to speak a word. On the train, each prisoner received three pieces of cheese. That was our day's food allowance. During the night we arrived in Scotland. There we had to carry our duffel bags several kilometers until we arrived at the prisoner-of-war camp.

Upon arrival, the first thing they did was thoroughly search our duffel bags. The quilts we had received in America were taken away from us and were replaced by inferior blankets. Other things were confiscated from us also. Then we were crammed together, seventy prisoners in each barrack. We were freezing, as it was a drastic change in climate from Oklahoma to the cold climate of Scotland. There was very little to eat, and it was of poor quality. One of my fellow prisoners told me that his father had been processed as a prisoner of war here during World War I.

The thought of spending a winter in Scotland terrified Wilhelm. The POWs had only been allowed to keep the summer clothing they were wearing. Everything else had been confiscated. For the first few weeks of autumn, the weather remained warm but soon turned bitter cold. Only one barrack was allowed to be heated due to a shortage of wood. Many of the men snuck wood back into camp from their work details but could only make small fires in their own rooms to avoid notice and punishment.

Shortly before Christmas, I was not feeling well at all. On December 24, 1946, I went to work as usual and worked for a few hours. Suddenly I felt so bad, but I pulled myself together and returned to my barracks. When I returned, the barracks were heated and so I felt better. In the camp we ate dinner at 1:00 PM. After I ate I went to take a shower. The hot water gave me additional fortitude. When I returned to the barracks, we were told to prepare for a Christmas party. We all went there, where each of us received a white loaf of bread. That was our Christmas cake. The flour for these loaves of bread was obtained by saving flour each day from our ration. Our Polish officer wished us the best and told us that next Christmas we would be in our own homeland.

After the party we went back to our cold barracks. There was no wood to burn, so we went to bed cold. Then I began to shiver. My comrades told me to go to the doctor. Evening was coming on and I was in no condition to go to the doctor, so one of my comrades took me there. I thought I would be allowed to stay in our hospital barracks, where it was heated. This turned out to be a great disappointment for me, because the doctor said that I was not sick, and he could find nothing wrong with me. So I was forced to go back to my cold barracks. I had to climb up in my top bunk, and then sat on the edge of the bunk. I fainted and fell to the concrete floor, landing head first on the floor. As I fell to the floor, I saw a guardian angel standing before me. I felt his hands cushion my head as I struck the cement floor, so that I had no pain from the fall. I didn't experience any excruciating pain as I crawled back to bed. The camp commander was summoned and the camp doctor came also. The doctor told me that I was healthy and that I was pretending I was sick.

On Christmas Day, I had to go to the doctor, who put me on sick leave for a few days. He also gave me some pills. When I came back from the doctor, I went to bed with a terrible headache. I began fasting even with my hunger-ridden stomach. It would not have been possible for me to fast, if I had not been lying in bed. After the fast, I immediately felt better, and my headaches disappeared. That evening I was able to eat all the food I saved during the day and finally had enough to eat.

I arrived in Soest, West Germany, on October 6, 1947. I found my brother Emil and his wife, Gertrude, living in makeshift living quarters constructed out of the ruins. I had a terrible time convincing the housing officials that there was enough room for the three of us to live together.

I only had the clothes that I brought with me from my prisoner-of-war days. It was in the fall, and the weather was cold, so I received an "under" jacket. That's what I wore to work. I had two pairs of trousers, so I had one pair for work and could wear the other cotton pair on Sundays. The Sunday pair had "P.W." stamped on them. (P.W. meant Prisoner of War.) I tried every conceivable way I knew, but I was unable to remove the P.W. from the trousers, so I had to wear them on Sundays anyway. I wore the light jacket to church also. During a church meeting, a brother from Essen asked me if I had any other clothes. I told him no. He told me that they had received some clothes from the LDS Church from America. Shortly thereafter, I received some clothes, as well as some food.

Shortly before Christmas, in 1949, I was able to get mail from my wife. My wife and children were still living in Selbongen, East Prussia, which was now part of communist Poland. To begin with, I could not send any packages. Later, I could send a two-pound package. Several years elapsed before I could send large packages to them. In Germany I prayed and fasted many days for my family, so that we could be together again.

Even though his family had still not found a way to leave Poland by 1953, Wilhelm felt that he should join Emil in immigrating to the United States. Once in Utah, he was able to visit the temple and receive a patriarchal blessing that promised him that he would be reunited with his family. With great hope, he began preparing a home for their eventual arrival at some unknown future date.

It was an extremely difficult time for Emma and her daughters. Food and clothing were extremely scarce. They treasured the few items from Papa that made it through the censors. The girls received their first oranges from their father, as well as their only books. Renate had only been two years old when her father had last visited on leave, and Christa had never met him. Finally, on August 8, 1957, after fourteen years of separation, Emma and her daughters were able to leave Poland for America to be with Wilhelm. Christa wrote about their reunion,

"As I sat on the plane I was overcome with the reality and finality of our journey. I would actually meet my

'Papa,' after fourteen years. I thought about it on the long bus ride from New York to Salt Lake City. What would it be like to have a father? Our dream had finally become a reality! As we stepped off the bus, mother was in dad's arms. Then Renate and I received a big hug.

"'Papa' was so proud to have two daughters. His face just beamed each time he introduced us to his friends and Ward members. I soon learned how much he loved us. He had saved all of his money, in the event we would be reunited. Within three months we bought our home. I remember dad taking me to the grocery store and showing me all that was available to buy. It was almost beyond comprehension. He said, 'Jetzt wirst du nicht mehr hungrig sein.' 'Now you will never have to be hungry again.'"

After thirteen and a half years of separation, we were together again as a family. That was the greatest joy of my life! I believe for sure that when we try to live the gospel, our patriarchal blessings will be fulfilled. I lived the gospel, as I understood it.

Philipp J. Bauer

Philipp J. Bauer was born January 4, 1915, in the village of Wittkowo, West Prussia. He was the tenth child of Philipp and Luise Bauer. Although Philipp and Luise had thirteen children, only seven lived to reach adulthood. Raised Lutheran, Philipp was well acquainted with religion. He attended Lutheran, Pentacostal, and Baptist meetings throughout his childhood. After the First World War, parts of West Prussia, including Wittkowo, were granted to the Polish. Ensuing tension between the Germans and Poles forced many German-speaking families to move toward Germany. In 1923, the Bauer family moved to Pommern, in northeast Germany, and after several years of moving from village to village in pursuit of work, they settled in Duebzow. In 1928, Philipp's mother died from complications relating to childbirth, and the family moved again to Moelln, in Mecklenburg. It was there that Philipp's sister, while cleaning in the castle of a local nobleman, discovered a pamphlet from a local church in nearby Neubrandenburg. Her father, not recognizing the church, decided to visit their meetings. Philipp, a teenager, was afraid that this new church would be too much like the Pentacostals, not allowing him to listen to modern music and holding long prayer meetings. He was pleasantly surprised by the friendliness of the church members and their short prayers, which were only offered at the beginning and end of their meetings. After meeting for several months with the missionaries, who would bike out to their home in Moelln, the Bauer family was baptized members of The Church of Jesus Christ of Latter-day Saints in the Tolensee on May 16, 1931.

Unable to find work enough to help support the family, Philipp moved away from home to Eichenwalde, near Massow (currently Poland), where he began to train as a cobblestone layer. He was able to attend church meetings at a branch in the city of Stargard, around thirty kilometers away. It was in Stargard, on a branch outing to the village of Schneidemuehl, that Philipp first met Elfriede Ross. They were able to spend three days together and quickly fell in love. On parting they promised to write each other, and Philipp made Elfriede promise to visit him when he knew where he would be stationed for military training after being drafted into the German Army.

It didn't take very long after that that I received my draft note. I was supposed to serve with the 25th Infantry Regiment in Stargard (Kleist Kaserne). I was happy to stay in Stargard. The first thing I did, I wrote to Elfriede to come to Stargard. She was a little scared and reluctant, but she came and we had a joyous reunion. On October 2, we got engaged at the district conference in Stettin.

In October 1938, I started my military service. The first four weeks we didn't get any leave at all. This was the basic training. It was tough, and strict obedience was expected. After that we could go out one evening in the week until ten. I was happy to see Elfriede and go to church meetings again. Later this leave was extended to midnight. How I enjoyed being with Elfriede together in her nice little room at Kuppermanns in Karowstrasse. She fixed and ironed my clothes and watched the clock so I would be back to the barracks on time. Sometimes she even set the clock an hour ahead without me knowing it. When I got to the barracks I was surprised that I had so much time left. It was our desire to be morally clean entering our marriage, and I must say she was strong in pursuing this goal.

In the spring of 1939, our unit left Stargard. We were motorized and went to the south over Breslau to the Czechoslovakian border. We slept on German soil that night and drove into Boehmen the next morning. In our unit not one single shot was fired. As we drove through the northern part of the country, the people were German and were really friendly toward our soldiers. In Slovakia it was different. The people didn't like us, but they didn't have any choice, so they tolerated us, but occasionally there was shooting. That's why Hitler declared the northern part belonging to Germany and the southern part as a protectorate.

We stayed in Czechoslovakia until summer and came back to Stargard, receiving a warm welcome from the local people. Elfriede was really happy to see me back, and so was our little branch. But our happiness didn't last very long, maybe two or three weeks at the most. This time the army had to help farmers harvest their crops. For about six weeks we lived, slept, worked, and ate with the farmers. This was almost like civilian life. After the harvest was in, we went back to our barracks in Stargard, and again we had a joyous reunion, and again it was really short.

When we came home to Stargard again, the international situation had worsened. Our relationship with Poland was tense. Hitler wanted a landway of around fifteen kilometers to get to East Prussia and also wanted Danzig back as a part of Germany.

Again we had to leave. It was a lot harder to part with Elfriede this time. Everybody felt it would come to a war. Our troops, myself included, rushed to the Polish border. Our regiment put their bivouac up in the forest of Schlochau. For one week we didn't do too much except check on our rifles and equipment. We had to keep everything in top shape. Our officers had changed and were a lot friendlier than before. We listened to the news every hour and wrote letters to our loved ones.

Finally when Poland didn't meet Hitler's deadline nor accept his demands, our troops marched into Poland. I remember it very well. Our air force (*Luftwaffe*) struck first and cut out 90 percent of the Polish air power on the ground. In the air we didn't see any Polish planes at all. Along the street we saw bomb craters, dead soldiers and horses, as well as destroyed wagons, supplies, and some motor vehicles. It was my first contact with war and it was cruel. The first six hours we were not involved in the fighting, but it started for us in the afternoon.

It was this afternoon that our company had her first two deaths. Those deaths were caused by guerilla fighting out of the trees while we were getting our dinner. One evening as we camped for the night, we didn't expect any fighting because we were in German occupied land. Most of us dug a hold under or behind our vehicles and went to rest there. Suddenly, as darkness fell, shooting began. It started from a nearby windmill and then came from all around. We had lost a lot of our men before we were really ready to fight back. The fighting didn't stop for many hours, and I didn't think anybody would come out alive. I was scared to death. I thought this would be my end. I prayed to the Lord like I had never prayed before. I promised him that if I would come out of this terrible shooting alive, I would serve Him and do whatever He asked of me all of my life. I never forgot this incident and always remember this promise when I need comfort.

The next morning, we saw that we had paid a high price. One or two deaths had even been caused by our own soldiers. The next day, Hitler visited us. We stood on both sides of the street, of course without rifles, and he saluted us from his jeep. I still remember his serious face. From then on, the fighting was light and in eighteen days the Blitzkrieg was over and I knew what war was like.

We went back to our home base in Stargard again. Ten kilometers before Stargard, our regiment commander, Oberst Huehner, notified us that a big parade awaited us in town. We cleaned up as much as we could and put on our helmets. In Stargard's main street, the city had placed a podium for the commander and his staff and for the regiment's band. The whole city was along the street. They gave us an enthusiastic welcome and a lot of "Heil, Heil, Heil." Many seats on our carriers were vacant, showing those men who hadn't come back. The band played as we saluted and drove by our earnest-looking commander. Elfriede was on the street too, but she didn't recognize me among all the helmeted soldiers.

You can imagine the welcome I received from Elfriede and from the branch. There were a lot of tears and thanksgiving to our Father in Heaven for my safe return. That first night, every soldier was given leave until the morning. Elfriede and I had a lot to talk about—the war and about our future life. But in all those excitements, departures, and reunions, we didn't forget our goals and principles, thanks especially to her strength. Our stay in Stargard only lasted three days. Not even time enough for Elfriede to get all my clothes cleaned and fixed. Again we had to depart, and like before it was not easy.

All our equipment and our troop carrier we put on the train this time and we were rushed to the West. From there I filled out an application for marriage. It had to go to higher ranking officers so it took a while. In the meantime our unit took quarters in Heckholzhausen, Oberlahn. There I was notified that my marriage request had been granted. Because of the political situation, I only received three days leave. I sent a telegram to Elfriede, which stated, "Come tomorrow, wedding." Because I could only use military trains, I had to wait another day. Elfriede, not knowing that, went to the train to pick me up, but I didn't come. Everything was prepared for the wedding, except for the groom who hadn't shown up. One day later I arrived, and after notifying everybody, we were married on November 29, 1939. Nobody had phones so we had to bike around Schneidemuehl. We had a wonderful wedding. We spent our short honeymoon in the home of her parents. Again I said good-bye, not knowing when we would see each other again, as we felt a war was in the making with France.

PHILIPP BAUER FILE

Philipp J. Bauer

The buildup of troops along the Western borders continued for several weeks. The troops trained endlessly for assaults on bunkers, as it was anticipated that a direct attack on the famous French Maginot Line was inevitable. Philipp was selected to train as a truck driver for his division but was not very successful, having never stepped behind the wheel of any type of vehicle before. He was then trained as a motorcycle courier, a position he filled for most of his time in the military. As the tension and expectation of an imminent battle increased, many of the soldiers found various ways to fill their free time.

As a sport activity we played soccer quite often, where I played goalie. Once as we played another company, I got kicked on my left ankle. It swelled up rapidly, and I had to stop playing. I was able to march home, but it hurt very much. I hoped it would be better the next day, but it got worse. I didn't want to, but I had to see the doctor. "Don't walk, and keep your foot up," he said. The next day our company left, but they couldn't take me along. Somebody drove me to the temporary military hospital in Castle Dern. All my comrades, with whom I had been with and shared everything with for two years, were gone. The doctor said, "It will be at least six weeks until you can use your foot, so relax and be patient." When I heard that, I wrote Elfriede and asked her to come and visit me. She did, and when she arrived, I was transferred to a permanent hospital in Bad Ems, not too far away. She came along and rented a little room, and we had the opportunity to see each other, at first not too often, but later quite a lot.

I was only in the hospital three days when we learned of the news that the war with France had broken out. Our division was attacking from the north and had sustained heavy casualties. I understood now, and was thankful to the Lord for my blessings. I know it was through His goodness and love that I could be away from the fighting and was blessed with such a wonderful time. One thing was sure—the war in France was over for me and my life was spared.

Elfriede was in Bad Ems for six weeks before she returned to Schneidemuehl. Though we couldn't live together, we had a wonderful time. Looking back, we always call it our honeymoon. Bad Ems is a beautiful place. It is a health resort on the River Lahn. We were able to sit in beautiful parks and talk and love, like young couples do. Later we went on canoe rides along the Lahn River and saw the beautiful green slopes of the mountains. When I could walk more, we climbed those slopes and had a fine view from the top. The food and care in the hospital was good, and I could eat things I had never eaten in the army before. Only fourteen days after Elfriede left, I was released from the hospital and assigned again to Stargard to instruct and train new recruits.

The winter of 1940 came. I still spent my time in Stargard training and teaching in the army, but as a trainer it was a lot easier, and I almost enjoyed the time. I enjoyed working in the branch also. When 1941 started—it must have been in February—I was transferred to Goerlitz. Goerlitz was a nice city, and I had the same job.

On April 14, Eckhard was born. This brought a lot of joy to our marriage, even though I could not be home for the occasion.

In Goerlitz, the branch members were real nice and many invited me to their homes for dinner. I appreciated it, especially since everything was rationed for them. I participated in their outings and all their functions. Before the fall arrived, the conflict with Russia had started.

I wrote Elfriede and asked her to come to Goerlitz because I had the feeling it wouldn't be long, and I would be on the Russian front. She left her little baby with her mother and came. I am thankful for her mother taking care of Eckhard. We rented an apartment close by the barracks. I even got permission to live with my wife. We saw a circus, walked to the Landeskrone, and even took the train and went to the beautiful spot Oybin. We had a wonderful day there. In a troubled and wartorn time like that, you are thankful to your Heavenly Father for every day you can be together. It is natural that Elfriede thought a lot of Eckhard. After two weeks she wanted to go home, but I talked her into staying six more weeks.

In Russia, our troops advanced quickly at first, but a short rain period came and a lot of our weapons and equipment sunk in the muddy streets. This was not the worst, though, as a strong frost came, four weeks early than other years, and much of our equipment became frozen in the mud. Our soldiers were also not prepared for the hard Russian winter, and we had big losses in manpower. Some died, and many had to be brought back to hospitals for frostbite treatment. The government appealed to all civilians in Germany to give warm clothes to our soldiers in Russia. All the German people gave freely of all they had. I drove around from our unit to collect those clothes, and I admired the people for what they gave.

Christmas of 1941 brought a joyous reunion for Philipp and Elfriede and the opportunity for Philipp to meet his newborn son, Eckhard. Happiness quickly turned to sadness as word came to the family that Philipp's older brother Otto had been killed on the Russian front. The death was a shock for the family. Otto, like Philipp, had married shortly before his deployment, and Philipp and Elfriede were now faced with the reality of Philipp's situation.

In January, the train left Gleiwitz through Poland and into Russia. Anyone could imagine our feelings as we sat in the freight train. What will my fate be? Will I lose my life, too?

New troops were needed in Russia, and I was shipped with other soldiers to Gleiwitz, close to the Polish border. There we were put together for one week, and we received winter clothes and weapons. I even had a chance to visit the branch and attend an operetta with the youth. In January, the train left Gleiwitz through Poland and into Russia. Anyone could imagine our feelings as we sat in the freight train. What will my fate be? Will I lose my life, too? We were crowded together, but it was still cold without a heater. We left the train in Brjansk (Central Russia), quite a ways behind the front line, where we stayed a few days. Here I was transferred to the 4th Tank Division and was sent right to the front line in Mzensk.

Our defenses were scarce. Maybe every seventy-five meters was stationed one soldier. But the area was relatively calm. Once in a while, the artillery fired, especially when our *Gulaschcanone* (field kitchen) brought our dinner. It was really cold, and the wind blew over the snowfields. There were no mountains or trees to act as a barrier to provide even a little protection, but I survived with only a few frostbites on my toes. Not enough to worry about in those days.

The spring came and that was a relief. The government in Germany had passed a law that when a father had lost one or more sons in the war, the last surviving son could be taken out of the combat zone and transferred to the rear. My father wrote such a request and it was granted. My company commander was not too happy about it and revoked my advancement. I said to him, "If my family wants it this way, so do I." So I went back to Orel to a supply company. Our mission was to get ammunition, gasoline, and food from the rear and bring it to the division headquarters, which required a lot of driving. What a difference it was, though, being able to sleep in a school and just patrol the school and our trucks a few hours at night. It was as different as coming from a hut to a mansion. It was a good feeling to know there was not an enemy a hundred meters in front of you.

I had some Church books—the New Testament and the Book of Mormon. Reading those gave me spiritual food. Once in a while we had a religious service behind the lines. You could easily attend Catholic or Protestant services, and once I even attended a Lutheran service. Of course there were no services from the LDS Church.

The older Russian people were friendly to us, but the younger generation, having been indoctrinated by the communists, hated us. They were the ones who caused all kinds of trouble. They became guerrilla fighters, blowing up convoys, bridges, railroad tracks, etc. If we caught them, they were hanged publicly, but it did not help. Later, each German commander in a city or village took ten to twenty hostages and told the people that if the guerrillas killed one German soldier or more, then all the hostages would be shot or hung. That was the only language they understood, and it cut down on the guerilla warfare.

As often as I could, I wrote letters home, and almost all arrived. From our unit we received liquor, candy, and cigarettes. I always exchanged my liquor and cigarettes for canned fish and more candy and sent it home. I know Elfriede enjoyed it. In June 1942, Renate was born. I was so happy to have a boy and a girl. Elfriede sent me a picture of her, and I remember I was a little disappointed because she didn't have any hair. Somehow I thought all babies are born with hair.

Belonging to a tank division, we had to change positions quite often. Every time the enemy broke through our lines, our division had to rush there and push them back. Throughout my military career, I worked as a messenger, mostly on a motorcycle. It was dangerous, especially in Russia, but I liked the challenge. Quite often, guerrillas shot at us, or they mined the roads or did both, but I always managed to escape unharmed. On dangerous rides two always rode together, especially in the wintertime, as the icy roads caused many accidents.

As the time went by and the bombing of Germany continued, it was hard to get new equipment and ammunition. Gasoline was also very hard to find. The Russians received help from the United States. We saw a lot of American tanks, equipment, and canned food. Where manpower was concerned, the Russians outnumbered us ten to one. Although we fought bravely, we still had to retreat. We retreated through Kiev and the Ukraine, went up to the north again, and took position around Libau in Latvia. It was then about Christmas 1944. Here we witnessed a big air battle between our fighter planes and the Russians. It only lasted about fifteen minutes, and one plane after another fell burning on land or in the ocean. We were proud to see our fliers victorious. Many Russian fliers even shot at us while coming down in their parachutes. Air battles were a rare thing on the Eastern Front. The Russians had a slow, small plane at night that dropped bombs hear and there, just to keep us awake and disturb our troops. We called it the *Kaffeemuehle* (coffee grinder).

The war looked gloomy for Germany. American and English troops crossed the channel and moved into Germany. In Africa the allied troops pressed into Italy, and on our front, Russian troops took East Prussia. In so doing, they cut off the escape of our troops there by land. To help those troops in East Prussia, we were shipped from Libau to Gotenhafen and rushed to the battlefront. On our way we were suddenly attacked from the side. I saw some Russian soldiers take position behind a hedge. I took my machine gun and was shooting it for over thirty minutes. The company lost a few trucks but was able to move on, though without me as I hadn't noticed their departure. It took me hours to find my way back to my unit. Our company had given me up as dead already, but they were surprised and happy to see me back again. For my actions I was promoted to the rank of corporal and received the *Eisernes Kreuz Erste Klasse und Zweite Klasse* (Iron Cross, first and second classes). In the beginning of 1945 our division received the newest type of tank, the King Tiger. They were the strongest and fastest ever built. However, without ammunition or gasoline, we could not use them, so we had to blow them up.

We took quarters first in Gotenhafen, later in Danzig-Langfur, both Harbor cities. Danzig was under constant artillery attack. One time as I brought written reports to headquarters, a bomb exploded right in front of me on a bridge. That motorbike was completely destroyed, but luckily I didn't receive a scratch. I am sure the Lord had His hand over me. Many soldiers felt at this time that the war was lost and tried to hide. When the military police found them, they came before a court martial and were sentenced to death. On the street to Danziger Allee, I saw soldiers hanging on every tree with posters on them: "*Ich bin ein Leichenflederer*" ("I am a deserter"). It was cruel to see, and pointless, as it did nothing to stop the desertions.

Later we took quarters in Schivenhorst. Here we stayed until the end of the war. It was relatively calm there. The first night I slept in the front room of a home of German civilians, but afterward we lived in dugouts in a field close by. Many civilians flocked into the city, but there was no clear road out to escape from the Russians, so they tried by sea. They could do so but had to leave their horses and carts behind. They gave us their food that they couldn't take with them. We had plenty to eat, and I even slept on a ham and side of bacon in my little hole. The fields and meadows were filled with cows and horses left behind by the refugees. Many were shot later when it became apparent that the Russians would take over the land.

Here in Schivenhorst we learned that Hitler was killed in the fighting around the Chancelry. We honored him with several minutes of silence and then pledged our oath to our new commander in chief, Admiral Doenitz. A few days after that, our unit was to ship out to Helena and from there take a bigger ship to Denmark. That was the rumor, at least. A staff sergeant, a lieutenant, and I had to stay and arrange the shipping. We were supposed to leave with the last group of our division. It was hard to see all your comrades go to safety and have to stay behind. The last ship never went out of the harbor. In the night of the eighth to the ninth of May 1945, we learned that Doenitz had declared peace. Everybody had to stay and not move from his place. By bringing this message to another company where the Russians were already, I was taken prisoner. The first thing they did was take away my pistol. How can I describe our feelings? Sure we were happy that the war was over, but when we thought of our future, loneliness and emptiness filled our hearts. It was awful being without a rifle, our companion for years. We felt we had given part of ourselves away. Now we knew the enemy could do what they wanted with us.

How can I describe our feelings? Sure we were happy that the war was over, but when we thought of our future, loneliness and emptiness filled our hearts.

I had a prayer for myself, and a still voice came to me: "You served your country. The war is over. You are not obligated to the German government anymore. Go home, go to Celle, and see your family." Those words I heard over and over.

With this spiritual confirmation from the Lord, Philipp's thoughts were now turned toward escape. The only questions were when and how. The prisoners were organized into long columns, closely guarded by Russian soldiers on horseback. As they marched toward Danzig, the guards rode in and out of the column demanding any valuables, and shot any prisoner who did not comply.

I had two wedding bands, my own and another I had traded for cigarettes. I slipped them off my fingers and dropped them in my boots. It worked well for a while, but later the rings hurt so much I had to take off my boot. In the dark I lost my wedding band but was able to save the other. Later, I had Elfriede's and my engagement date engraved on it, and I use that band until this day.

On our way we went through many German villages. Our guards were sparse, so I was able to ask for civilian clothes and receive them without being seen. The guards told us that we were lucky, because the war was over for us. They said we would march to Danzig to be released. I didn't believe a single word. I knew the communists better than that. For me it was sure that from Danzig we would go to Siberia. In a silent prayer, I asked the Lord again what to do. The still voice said to me, "Try to escape before you come to Danzig. After you have been registered and are on your way into Russia, it will be impossible." I persuaded two other soldiers next to me to come along. It was a rainy, warm evening, and we were still far away from Danzig when we were called to halt in the small village of Praust by our guards. They told us we would sleep overnight in the church and go on tomorrow. Around the church was a cemetery surrounded by a stone wall. When we entered the gate I said to my comrades, "Let's go." We three went along the wall to the far corner. There we put on as many civilian clothes as we had and left the others behind. We jumped over the wall into the dark and rainy night, but we were free.

All we knew was that we wanted to go west. My compass helped me to find the general direction. We didn't walk on the road but crossed fields, fenced cow pastures, and ditches. We fell and got up, and sometimes we ran around in circles. We passed one house and said, "These are German people. Let's go in." But when we came closer, we

NATIONAL ARCHIVES

American forces cross a makeshift bridge into a destroyed German village.

could hear a crying for help, and it sounded like Russian soldiers were raping women. I shall never forget that cry. But could we help? Weren't we fugitives ourselves? We had to pass that house. Far away there was a light on the horizon. It looked like a city and must have been Danzig. We must have walked until one or two in the morning until we suddenly came upon a shelter. It was quiet and looked deserted, so we decided to stay there for a few hours to get a little sleep. We surely were tired and slept a little longer than we wanted. When we looked out of the shelter, we saw a Russian bivouac four to five hundred yards in front of us. We got around them without being seen. Walking in the morning hours was much better than it had been at night.

The continued journey was not easy for these young men. Not only were they fleeing for their lives, but they were witnesses to the many atrocities suffered by the German people who were unable to flee. What comfort could be given to young women who had been raped, beaten, and left for dead? Or mothers whose husbands had been executed before their eyes? All these men could offer was small thanks for the food and clothing they received and silent prayers that their own families had been kept safely preserved from the same. Traveling day after day, avoiding any village that looked to be occupied by the Russians, the three soldiers covered a great distance. Approaching western Poland, the men took to the woods to avoid any chance of contact.

Suddenly, there was a big explosion that must have been a land mine. Our first guy had stepped on it and now had an injured leg. We put a bandage around it, but he could walk only on one leg. I was right behind him and was hurt on my left arm. I was in a lot of pain and was unable to lift my hand. I left a lot of my baggage behind, because I couldn't carry it on my back with my wounded arm. We helped our wounded comrade to the nearest road and went in hiding. After a little while we saw people in a horse and buggy pick him up and take him along. We felt a lot better now. I had to think about Schiller, who said in Wallenstein, "*Und setzt ihr nicht das Leben ein, nie wird euch das Leben beschieden sein.*" In English you would say, "If you don't put your whole life forth, never will that life be yours."

We went our way. I still had a lot of pain, but I didn't want to give up. The desire to see my family was stronger than the pain. Suddenly, out of the bushes, three or four men approached us with long beards and said, "You are soldiers, too?"

We did not admit it, but they knew. Then they said, "We have been in hiding for many weeks. Tell us, is the war still going on?"

"It's all over," we answered, "and we are on our way home."

They were happy, as they had lived in fear for weeks of being caught and hung for desertion.

We never admitted that we were soldiers, nor did we give our real names. My name was Willy Bair. I used to run a train from Danzig to Warsaw, and my companion used to work in the shipyard in Danzig. With this explanation, most Russians and Poles were satisfied. Our beards made us look old enough to believe our stories.

As we walked along a forest path uphill in the afternoon, we saw two riders coming toward us. We felt they had seen us, so we did not hide, and walked toward them.

"What are you doing here?"

We told them our story and said we wanted to go home.

"Why do you go through the forests? There are many armed German soldiers in the forest. Use the open road, and there won't be any suspicion." We had never considered this and learned a valuable lesson.

"Come," they said, "we will bring you to our village, and there you can stay overnight."

They locked us in a house, told us not to escape, and that they would let us go in the morning. We knew they had a guard around the house, so we didn't dare try to escape. We spent the whole evening planning what to do and decided we would wait until morning. I did a lot of praying that night and had the feeling that all would be well. Even with all our worry we slept well, and when the next morning came the officer knocked at the door, told us the time, and wished us well on our journey. He reminded us not to use the forest trails anymore. I thanked the Lord, for I saw His hand in it. From now on we always traveled on public roads, singing our songs, and were a lot happier. Our thoughts were quite often with our comrade we had left behind. We were sure he had been taken care of, but we wondered if he would be sent to Siberia when he recovered.

The men found the advice they had received to be effective. Many were afraid to travel, so the roads remained mostly clear. Meetings with soldiers, though terrifying, ended uneventfully as their stories were believed. The further they moved from the front lines, the more help they received from families along the way, even managing to obtain passports from a Polish official.

[At one village] a man came galloping on a horse and confronted us with a pistol. "I am a Polish policeman and the major of this village. Come with me." He checked us for weapons, and we showed him our passports. He looked at them, tore them up, and said, "I have permission from the Russian commander to catch everybody I want for farm help. Go to the town." What could we do? We went to town with the policeman on his horse with the pistol in his hand right behind us. Here we were assigned to sleep and eat at a little farmer's place and work at the big farm called Colchose. I could not do much with one hand, so I had to run the butter machine. The man in charge told us not to escape, but work for eight days, and then they would let us go, so we stayed. Food and treatment were not too bad. When we asked if we could go, after our eight days, he replied to me, "You may go, because you can't do too much with your arm anyway, but I still will keep the others." We didn't like that at all. In the evening, we planned our escape. We packed everything the same night, and when it was dark we hid our luggage behind the house in a big straw heap close to the grain field. Every day we had a two hour lunchtime, so we planned to leave during the break.

That was the way we had planned it, and that was the way we did it. By the time we were missed we were already two hours away. We avoided the roads and slept in the fields. We came closer and closer to my old hometown. We passed by Dramburg, where my dad had been in the hospital after my mother had passed away. How it hurt, to see all of these towns, all the many sweet memories I had, and now after having been away for so many years I couldn't walk those streets for fear of being caught by Polish or Russian authorities. People told us there were plenty of Russian and Polish troops in the area. All along the way, everyone wanted to know if the war was really over and when the American troops would move in. They could not believe that America would leave all their land in the hands of the Russians.

The desire to see his former home was too great, so risking recapture, Phillipp snuck into the village. It was small enough that there were no enemy soldiers garrisoned there, yet their presence could still be felt. Though the reunion with old friends and neighbors was joyous, there was great sadness and despair as the horrors of the depravities inflicted upon the women and children by their captors unfolded.

It was no wonder to me that the people were praying so hard for the American troops to move in, but their hope was in vain.

Before sunrise, we got up, and I went across the street to the cemetery to visit the graves of my mother and sister. Even as a hard, old soldier who had seen many deaths, tears still came to my eyes. How I wished I could talk to my mother. I had been thirteen when she had passed away, and now I was thirty, but still missed her. I could only stay a few minutes, before we had to continue west. On our way to Stargard, we slept in a barn close to the Autobahn. Stargard was so close and there were so many church members there who were close to my heart, but when I heard of the destruction and danger I would encounter, we had to pass it by.

Along the Autobahn we went. On this part of the Autobahn we saw many people going back to the east. When we asked why, they said, "Nobody can cross the River Oder to the west, so we may just as well go back to our homes in Pomerenia or East Prussia." When we came to the bridges we saw the Polish and Russian security forces turning everybody away, and we saw that we had no chance of crossing either bridge. Many people went farther south and tried to swim across. Some made it; many were shot or captured. Not wanting to risk either, I approached one of the drivers of a Russian horse and buggy convoy waiting in line to cross the bridges. With my broken Russian, I told him my story. "The war is over, and I have been separated from my family for so long. They are on the other side of the river. Can't you take us along until we reach the other side?" He looked at us and said, "You know I am not allowed to have civilians in my convoy, but if you promise me you will hide so nobody can find you, I will take you along." We did hide and when we came to the checkpoint our hearts were beating for fear the guards would find us. But we were lucky, as they only counted the number of wagons and let us pass. That was a relief, and we were the happiest people in the world. We drove over both bridges without trouble and thanked the driver and our Heavenly Father for their help.

West of the River Oder was territory under the German government, and we felt we would have an easier time. Our next goal was Berlin. The weather was good and our moods were good. When we arrived in Eberswalde, we learned that freight trains were going from there to Berlin. We jumped on a coal train and had a first class sixty-kilometer ride to Berlin. Here we separated from each other, the other two wanting to go to Saxony and I wishing to remain in Berlin to see my brother's wife. Even after being so close for so many weeks, we never thought of exchanging home addresses. Everyone had only one thought in mind: "What is my family doing? Are they still alive?" So we never saw or heard from each other again. Even their names have slipped my mind.

In Berlin, I saw for the first time what a bombed city looked like. I wanted to cry, and my heart was full of sorrow. It sure was a surprise for Vera to see me, and I was happy for a few days rest and for her hospitality. In the six or seven weeks I stayed with her, I went to the hospital for treatment for my arm. I told the officials that I had come from a military hospital by Magdeburg. That hospital had been dissolved, which was true, and I had been transferred to Berlin for further treatment. There was no way, no telephone or post, to check my story, so they accepted it and gave me good free treatment. I also went to the Church Mission Home and reported that I had returned from the war. President Ranglack said, "You are the first soldier from our mission to come back. Thank you and welcome home." He also gave me a membership card so I could always identify myself. I was advised not to go west right away because the Allies were taking all young and middle-aged men as German soldiers and putting them in prison camps. I went to the city employment office for a job, and the city sent me out to fix the most important things on the streets.

The city was so glad to have me, and I could have stayed there for good, but my desire was to see Elfriede and the children. I attended meetings, and everybody was friendly toward the first soldier back from the war. Most of them knew my brother in the branch very well and liked him. That made me feel good, but I knew I needed to leave for the west. The news spread and many people came to me and asked me to take a letter to their relatives in the west, especially all those who had relatives in and around Celle. I took around sixty letters and received quite a bit of payment for taking the risk to carry their messages. This was the only way those in the west would know that they, in Berlin, were still alive.

Everything was at a standstill. Trains, buses, cars, and even bikes were not available. The only way was to walk, and that was dangerous too. The Allied troops had opened the prisons, and therefore, prisoners were roaming the streets. All civilians, for their safety, had been ordered to remain where they were. The day came for me to leave, and I said good-bye to Vera and her mother, Sister Giehr, who had been so good to me. First I went to Standal. There I had to cross the River Elbe, which was not easy. People had been waiting there for weeks and were turned back by the Russians. Some had tried to swim across in a quiet place, and few had made it. I tried to cross the bridge in the early morning hours when almost everyone was asleep. I was lucky, and the guard let me pass, perhaps because I had been able to converse with him in Russian. On the other side of the river I was able to catch a freight train all the way to Oebisfelde. That was the border town between East and West Germany. The River Aller was the borderline. As I was in no hurry, I delivered two letters in Oebisfelde and of course, the joy of hearing from close relatives was great.

The next day I went to the border station and asked to cross the border. I showed the officer my church papers and explained to him that I wanted to go to my wife and children in Celle. He took the papers and went to a higher-ranking officer. After one hour he came back, gave me my papers, and said no. I expected that, because the people in the city had given me little, if any, hope that I would succeed, but I had to try. I went along the river to take a closer look and saw the Russians patrolling the bank. It was a tight patrol on the Russian side, but on the English side there were no patrols at all. Every hour I saw a jeep driving along the banks of the river. I returned back to the family I had visited and asked the Lord's help in my decision to cross the border illegally, but I had to wait until it was dark to make my attempt. In the evening, I said good-bye to the family, and with their good-luck wishes I was on my way. First, I went through a high grain field. Grain grows man high in Germany, so nobody could see me. The field did not reach all the way to the river, and I would be required to cross a hundred-yard potato field. I waited in the grain field until I saw the silhouettes of two patrolmen going toward each other. They talked to each other for about eight minutes and separated in different directions. When I felt they were far enough apart, I ran across the potato field as fast as I could and jumped into the river, my belongings high over my head. I could not tell if the Russians had noticed or not, as it had happened so fast. I was lucky that the river was not too wide or too deep in this spot. I was able to walk across it without a shot fired or an alarm sounded. I arrived safely at the other side, was soaking wet and shivering, but I felt good. I was on my way to my family. I didn't sleep very well this night, whether from the excitement of the last few hours, or the nervousness of seeing Elfriede and the children, I did not know. One thing was for sure: I was thankful to the Lord that He had guided and protected me while I had crossed the Elbe and Aller Rivers.

The next morning I departed early. I wanted to make it to Celle as soon as possible. I knew I could not take a train, but there was one thing I knew I could do—that was to walk. So I went along the road, and there came a farmer with a horse and cart. I asked him if he would take me along. He did, but not for too long. Then he changed directions, so there I was again on my feet for quite some time. Finally an old truck stopped and asked me if I wanted a ride. I gladly accepted and drove all the way to Celle with him. In Celle, I asked people the whereabouts of Marienstrasse, where my wife's sister lived and where I expected to find my wife. "Marienstrasse?" they said. "There is no Marienstrasse anymore." I wanted to collapse, but I felt that Elfriede and the children were still alive. Then I remembered the address of the Pohlsander family, the home of the branch president. I asked for that street, and when I arrived, the daughter, Ingrid, opened the door. When I told her who I was, she almost fainted but told me where Elfriede and the children were. It was a joyous reunion with Elfriede, with our children, and her mother. Nobody can really describe the feeling—the happiness and joy—we experienced on July 15, 1945. A long journey of hardship, of suffering, but always of hope, had ended. I had finally reached my destination and had made it home. That was the end of my escape. Daily we make decisions, but the decision to escape, I have never regretted in all my life.

After having served seven years in the German Army, my civilian life started, a life without much hope. All around us were bombed cities, destruction, rubble, and hungry, starving faces. That was the result of war. My first job, upon reaching Celle, was to deliver all of my letters, and it brought a lot of joy and tears of thankfulness to many families. My next task was to find a job. It was not hard, without many men around, and I started working for the building contractor, Siegfried Dumon. I worked in the field I had learned in Berlin, laying cobblestone. In the evening I went to Doctor Glaser for treatment to heal the nerves in my arm. After two days, we received a surprise. My father and my sisters, Emma, Wanda, Martha, and their families arrived in Celle. The city put them temporarily in an old inn (Scheutzenhaus). Later they moved to wooden barracks, where they lived for some time and where we held our Sunday School quite often. A few weeks earlier, Anni and Frida had also arrived from the east, so my whole family was together once again. It was a wonderful blessing. My father and all my sisters knew that Elfriede's sister lived in West Germany, in Celle, and that Elfriede would flee there from the Russians. They knew that this would be the only way to find each other. My father, from Schneidemuehl, had stopped in Neubrandenburg and Mecklenburg, took his three daughters and their families, and went to Celle. There always has been a close relationship not only with my sisters, but also with our nieces and nephews. We were blessed, as it took other families years to find or hear from each other.

Horst Kurt Hilbert

Horst Kurt Hilbert was born July 10, 1919, to Paul Gotthold Hilbert and Maria Klein Hilbert, in Leipzig, Germany. Both his parents had been taught and baptized by missionaries tracting in Germany just prior to the outbreak of the First World War. Horst's parents were very active within the Church, and his father served as Leipzig's branch president for eight years until 1937, when the family was forced to move to Berlin to find work. Paul had been outspoken during the early days of the Hitler regime, denouncing Hitler's claims that Germany could easily defeat the United States in a war. His views were not political but strictly logical, citing the fact that American steel production was seven times that of Germany. His views were not received well by his coworkers or employers, and he lost his job. After moving to Berlin, he was called again to serve as branch president there until 1947.

For Horst, growing up was a wonderful experience. He spent a great deal of time with the American missionaries who were working in their area, learning about America and also learning English. The Hilbert home was always full of love and laughter, and Horst's mother always made it a priority to teach all the children the importance of holding to the principles of the gospel. These were valuable lessons that would later save Horst's life.

In 1934, I started an apprenticeship as a bookbinder. A year later, there was a tournament called *Reichs Berufs Wettkampf* (Empire's Work Competition). Every apprentice had to create a work piece and pass a written and oral examination, being graded in all three areas. I worked hard, and I was lucky to be the best of a class of about a hundred boys. The prize could have been a free college education. When I was interviewed, the first question was, are you a member of the Hitler Youth? When I answered no, the man said, "We do not want you for anything; you will never amount to anything in your life." Well, I wonder how he is doing today.

On April 1, 1939, I was drafted to the *Reichs Arbeits Dienst*, a paramilitary organization, for the duration of six months. My job was to build a dike against floodwaters on the Baltic Sea. I was stationed in Karlshagen on Usedom, Pommern. I was also responsible to help the farmers working in their fields. When World War II started on August 26, 1939, I was drafted the same day into the *Wehrmacht*, the German Army. The rest of 1939 I built fortifications on the shores of the Baltic Sea, and toward the end of 1939 I was transferred to the city of Rostock, on the Baltic

Sea, to receive basic training for the service of a 75-mm howitzer. At Christmas 1939, I got a two-week leave, and in this time I was able to meet my future wife, Irene Buchta. I asked for a date and her address, and our courtship began, all by mail; but how I waited for her letters.

In February 1940, I was sent to a field unit on the Western Front. I was stationed alternating two weeks in the city of Saarbruecken and on the heights of Spichern, France. Except for occasional artillery barrages, there was not much war going on. Later after May 10, 1940, my unit went through the famous Maginot Line at St. Avold. The Line was very impressive, but since German troops were already behind the Line, coming from the north (Ardennes) there was not much action from the French. After France surrendered, my division was transferred to Poland in July 1940. We were stationed in the city of Lublin. In October 1940 I got three weeks' leave, and Irene and I were engaged. I returned to Lublin and stayed there till April 1941, when we were moved to the demarcation line between Russia and Germany. We stayed in the little village of Prhorylo. I could see the river Bug, and on the other side I could see the Russian border guards making their rounds. I began to fear about the future. What was the purpose of amassing so many German troops on the border? The Russians and Germans had a treaty, but with open eyes, I could already see how much a promise or treaty was worth to this Adolf Hitler. I remembered my father's observations of the steel production in regards to a war and knew we could not win.

On June 21, 1941, the troops got ready. In the evening an order from Adolf Hitler was read, in which he stated that after long thinking and pondering he had decided to attack Russia the next morning, June 22, 1941, at 3:15. When I heard this, I had the worst foreboding. What did Germany want in Russia? With a population three times as many as Germany, and unfinished business in the West, what were the chances and the outlook for my family?

The next morning at 3:15 AM sharp, the German artillery started to pound the other side. My unit crossed the river Bug into Russia. Climbing up the riverbank on the other side, I looked back and saw many German soldiers moving toward the river. It looked like Germany had already been destroyed and this was a funeral parade.

I said to my buddy, "I just wonder how many of all these men moving toward the river will be going home again?"

But this fellow was either drunk or a fanatic believer, because he said, "You shut up or I will report you."

All the time I expected waves of Russian soldiers to pour from the hills and forests. But they were smarter. They let the Germans penetrate deep into Russia and fought them on their terms; as history reports, a hard lesson Napoleon had learned a long time before the Germans.

About one month into the invasion, it rained every day, and with no paved streets the vehicles sank into the mud to their axles. Everybody had to push, and often the horses died in their harness. After the war, I heard that two million horses died in Russia. Our shoes were in poor condition, and as a consequence so were our feet, but we were driven forward regardless of hardships. In Sumy I was quartered in a house in which an old man lived who had spent twelve years in New York. We talked about America and how we both would like to visit there. The Germans and Russians in that room did not understand what we both were talking about as we spoke in English.

In the area of the city of Tomarowka I came to a village where our officers told us to go into the houses and ask the people to give us oats for our horses. We were supposed to give them a receipt so they could get compensated for it later. When I came into one house, I heard much wailing and weeping. A young woman had tried to start a fire in a big stove, and the flame had struck back and burned the woman's hand. I looked at it and saw the bones of her fingers, the flesh gone. At the wrist the color of the flesh was dark brownish. I asked the man of the house why he did not take her to a doctor. He said, "Sir, we cannot go from one village to the other. We will be suspected to be agents or guerillas and will be shot." I said to him, "I will write a piece of paper that says you are not an agent, and that the woman needs help. If you misuse my trust, I will be shot also." The man promised not to misuse my trust, got his sled ready, put the woman on it, and drove off quickly. My way led me on further east, so I could not hear the result of the woman's treatment, but I hoped she could live out her life.

She got up quickly, woke up my four sisters, and said, "We have to pray fast. Horst is in mortal danger and needs our prayer." The five women knelt down, and my mother pleaded with the Lord to keep His protecting hand over me. After the prayer my mother told my sisters to go back to sleep and be of good cheer: "Horst has been in danger but the Lord has helped him."

In December 1941, it got very cold. My unit had to march to the village of Melichowo, thirty kilometers north of Belgorod, where we had to establish an outpost and hold it. That day, December 6, the temperature dropped to minus 43 degrees Centigrade, which equals about minus 45 degrees Fahrenheit. I did not have any gloves or warm underwear, only a summer coat. Many soldiers were injured by frostbite, or even worse, lost their ears if not their legs. My buddies demanded that I drink alcohol to keep myself from getting sick. I asked for one more day to stay away from the alcohol, and the next day they were sick and I was still healthy. They quite trying to force me to drink, and I did not have to break the Word of Wisdom.

One early morning, the sixth of January 1942, I had to stand guard duty with a buddy, Hans Plank. We were standing beside a little shack, the straw roof covered with snow. A Russian machine gun started to shoot at us. I could see the tracers hitting the ground before my feet, skipping off to the sky. Other rounds hit the straw roof, and I could see the bullets making rows of holes and causing the snow to come down like sugar coming out of a bowl. I was very afraid, and since I was forbidden to leave the post, I wanted to pray. I could feel the power of the destroyer, but I could not utter one word of prayer as my tongue felt paralyzed. To think that the first words in my life were prayers on my mother's lap. All I was able to say was, "If only my mother could pray for me right now, so the Lord might hear the prayer of a righteous woman." With this thought I looked to the east and felt prompted to look north. When I did this and turned, a bullet passed and hit my coat at my stomach. Had I not turned, it would have struck me. Some days later I received a letter from my mother. In this letter she wrote that in the night of January the sixth she woke up hearing me call her Mama. Also she heard the sound of shooting. She got up quickly, woke up my four sisters, and said, "We have to pray fast. Horst is in mortal danger and needs our prayer." The five women knelt down, and my mother pleaded with the Lord to keep His protecting hand over me. After the prayer my mother told my sisters to go back to sleep and be of good cheer: "Horst has been in danger but the Lord has helped him."

In June or July 1942, the Germans started their offensive toward Stalingrad, and my division was the northernmost unit of the ill-fated 6th Army. It started out for me by being loaded on trucks along with a hundred other German soldiers. Then we were driven, by nightfall, thirty kilometers behind the Russian lines. The Russians retreated, and we were supposed to get ahead of them and take them prisoners. By midnight we arrived in a village and dug ourselves in. When I had finished my foxhole and looked at it, I had a feeling like I was looking at my grave. First I tried to shake off that thought, but a fear kept creeping over me and I knew it was a warning. I asked my commanding officer for permission to build another hole fifty feet to the left.

HORST HILBERT FILE

Horst Hilbert and Irene Buchta on their wedding day.

When I had finished the second hole, by 3:00 AM, we could hear the Russians coming. It was a clear night; we could hear their horses, trucks, tanks, and their voices. Then they stopped, warned by the local population of our presence. They shouted in conference as to what to do as they certainly did not want to give up. After some time they decided to explore the situation with three tanks, moving toward us in the early morning dawn. Each tank had a few men sitting on it, ready to jump down and fight. Right at my first foxhole the lead tank got knocked out by an antitank gun. The Russians sitting on it jumped down, and there was a brief hand fight. After it was over, the fellow who occupied my first hole after I had abandoned it was shot in the head and killed. His name was Franz Jadzewski, a very fine young man. I am sorry that I was not aware and did not know that someone else had taken this hole.

Later on we moved to the vicinity of one of the supporting Hungarian armies at Korotoriak on the Don River. We had to establish a beach head across the Don River, which was bloody business. Much confusion reigned, and many German soldiers were captured by the Russians. The evening before we crossed, we watched about forty-five Russian tanks moving along a highway. When this was reported to the regiment commander, he scolded us and said, "You are seeing white mice. They do not have so many tanks." The next day we faced them, and I missed by a tiny hair being taken prisoner and had to run like an Olympic champion to get away. There were only five men left from the original group of twelve. Trying to return, we walked into a trap of fifty Russian soldiers. We had one way to escape, and while running I looked back and saw them standing there like in a shooting gallery, me being the target. I zigzagged and hit the ground so that they could not take aim at me. After I got away, we met German troops this time, and again I found myself in a foxhole, and again a dozen tanks came. It is a feeling of despair and hopelessness to face someone protected by steel plates of four to eight inches thickness that is bent on your destruction. This time I could not run anymore, the tanks were so close. Suddenly a battery of 88-mm antiaircraft guns a half mile away on the west side of the Don River opened up on them, and four or five burst into flames and the rest turned away. The next day, thank goodness, the Germans vacated the bridge head as it had become costlier every day.

In September 1942, I finally got three weeks' leave to return to Berlin. In order to get leave you had to be married, so in April, five months before, I signed our marriage papers in Russia and sent them to Irene to sign in Berlin, which she did on April 27, 1942. This made me eligible to get leave, and on the nineteenth of September 1942, we were married (again) by the district president of the Berlin District. It was a wonderful time, having been so close to death, being so close to my beloved wife, and my family. Only too soon, on October 2, 1942, I had to return to the Russian Front. It was heartbreaking to see the scenes on the railway platform, when all the sons and fathers, husbands, and brothers had to be given up by their families.

I came back to Voronesh in the middle of October and was very disturbed to see fortifications being built at the west end of the city. To me it felt like going inside a mousetrap. Then, while in Voronesh, the tragedy of Stalingrad unfolded, with Hitler's orders to hold it to the last man. Voronesh was next on his agenda. Fortunately, our generals with us in Voronesh gave the order to retreat on their own. At the end of January 1943, we moved away from Voronesh, and from my officers I learned that there were seven German divisions, surrounded by forty-five Russian divisions, plus a few motorized brigades. The retreat had all the trimmings of total defeat, with nothing to eat, out in the cold day and night, and many narrow escapes. The worst was the fate of the wounded soldiers. Not much medical attention was available, and if their unit did not abandon them, they lay on sleds, covered with one or two thin blankets at subzero temperatures. Many died from lack of warmth and care. The Lord was kind to me to spare me injury or capture. After six weeks in the westward moving cauldron, filled with misery, we finally got out of the Russian pincers for the time being.

After getting some new equipment and a thorough delousing, my unit moved to the village of Besdrick, near Sumy. In Besdrick the war was relatively quiet, as the Russians were regrouping and preparing for their next big offensive. We each had to man an observation post for two hours a day in a house outside the village, on a hilltop. An old man was living there who looked like a patriarch: old, with long whiskers and an appearance of noble design. One day he took a Russian printed Bible from a hiding place. It was forbidden for the Russian people to have a Bible in their possession, or at least they would face insult and ridicule from their own people. The old man read in the Bible and came to me, tears in his eyes, and showed a passage to me. I could not read it, but my heart was moved by so much faithfulness. I said to him, "Read the Bible, and the Lord will be with you." Suddenly he knelt down and invited me to kneel down with him. He first prayed in Russian, and then I prayed in German. After this we got up, and after Russian custom he kissed my cheeks and called me brother. Some time after this incident I talked to our interpreter, and he asked me what was going on between the old man and me. The old man went around the village and told the villagers that soldier with the glasses (I was the only one wearing glasses) must have been baptized by immersion, as he had felt it very strongly.

On the evening of August 14, 1943, as we were moving to a new position, we found a wounded Russian soldier by the wayside. One fellow—his name was Hugo Panten—took his machine pistol and held it on the head of this Russian.

I immediately pushed the muzzle aside and said to him, "This man is wounded; we are soldiers and not murderers."

He said to me, "You and your sentimentalities will not win the war for us."

I answered, "You and your senseless cruelty will not win it either." Then I picked up the Russian. He could not speak German, but he understood the meaning of our conversation and clung to me. He begged for water, and I was sad that I did not have a drop with me. We went to the next road crossing where the field kitchens might come by and help him. I said a short prayer for him and told him that I had to go on. I know the Lord saw this event, for two days later I saw His hand in my life.

On the sixteenth of August 1943, I was standing at a somewhat elevated railway track talking with a friend, Otto Becker. Suddenly I saw a big flame to my right about ten feet away. I felt like evil smoke pressed into my mouth and then felt a hard blow on my right side. When I became aware of myself, I found I was lying on the ground with a terrible pain in my head, right arm, shoulder, breast, stomach, and hind parts, all at the same time. I had been hit by a mortar shell, and blood was streaming all over me. Otto Becker got one piece of metal in his neck and was killed instantly. I got about thirty pieces, but I was luckier, but at that moment did not know whether I would die or be a cripple, or if the Germans who were getting ready to give up the position in a hurry would take me with them or leave me. Two buddies put me in a blanket and carried me to a first aid station. There I saw rows of wounded soldiers and figured if they put me at the end of that long line, the Russians will be there before the doctor got there. So I said to the doctor when I was brought in, "Sir, all I need is a tetanus and a morphine shot." He gave me both shots and put me on the next ambulance. It was a bumpy ride and it hurt, but a check on myself and a feeling told me that I would be all right. When I looked around and saw the mangled bodies, I felt grateful that my injuries did not seem that serious.

—•—

After some days in Kiev, I was able to be transported a longer distance and a train took me to Erfurt, Germany. I stayed for about six weeks, and after that I was sent to the home company of my field unit. It was located in the city of Rostock on the Baltic Sea. There the soldiers were kept for only a short time, and every week a group was newly equipped and sent to the Russian Front. Luck smiled at me, as the platoon leader of my combat unit was there and gave a good report of me to the sergeant, who seemed to like me. When the required physical came up, I was on an assignment out of town so I could not be pronounced fit to be sent back to Russia. In January 1944, I was transferred to a noncommissioned officer school as an instructor for howitzers. The school was located in Wloclawek (Leslau), Poland, and I spent one year there seeing the collapse of Germany taking shape. Meanwhile, the Russian steamroller moved closer to Germany, and nobody could stop them anymore. On January 27 or 28, Russian tanks appeared on the outskirts of Wloclawek. We escaped across the Weichsel River and that evening moved westward. The next day some Russian tanks got in our way. I took a bazooka and walked with a buddy, Herbert Schreiter, in the direction of the tanks. At a corner I met my lieutenant, Martin Kruger. He said to me, "Where are you going, Hilbert? If you want to live, drop the bazooka and come with me. If you want to die a cheap hero's death, go where you are going." I turned into the street with Kruger. Herbert Schreiter shot his bazooka at the tank. The bazooka did not damage it, and the tank shot at Schreiter and killed him. Lieutenant Kruger had spoken to me often before that and agreed with my father about the war. He had told me that we had to try to avoid capture by the Russians. If our deaths could prevent what was in store for Germany, we would die gladly, but nothing could change what was in store for our country, not even if whole divisions died.

At the beginning of April 1945, my unit was close to the eastward moving U.S. forces. The sky was congested with American and English planes; the birds, methinks, had to walk. My captain told me to be handy as an interpreter when the need called for it. We had found out that the allied fliers started their war at 9:00 AM sharp, right after breakfast. We wanted to reach a forest in the mountains, so we started out early and reached the forest by 8:55 AM. Five minutes later the sky was alive with planes. A truck which did not make it to the forest got caught by the planes and destroyed. In the evening we moved on, and suddenly my officers were afraid to give up. They told us that shortly a change in German policy was expected, for the better. Of course, from leaflets and broadcasts I had learned that the only thing for Germany was unconditional surrender. Everything else meant death or worse, delivery to the Russians. When we passed through the city of Hettstedt in the Harz Mountains, many people were standing in their doorways watching us march back to the fighting. One man must have seen how troubled I was, for he said to me, "Why do you want to continue this senseless war and bloodshed? Come into my house, have something to eat, sleep here and tomorrow when the Americans come, give yourself up to them." So I stayed overnight, and the next morning, after a delicious vitamin A, B, and C breakfast, the Americans moved in. I let the first ones pass, watching them from an attic window. Some hours later in the afternoon I walked out of the house along the street. A jeep came around the corner with three Yanks on it. They stopped, and I said in my best English, "I am on my way to the next prisoner-gathering place. Can you give me directions?" One said, "Hop in. We'll take you there." They were nice men, coming from Cincinnati, Ohio. After all my years on the Eastern Front, this was a far better ending to the war than I could have expected from the Russians.

Two weeks later I landed in a prisoner camp at the bridge of Remagen, on the Rhine River. It was an assembly of 220,000 German prisoners, and food was very short. In this bad time I was able to get on a work detail as an interpreter. We had to unload trucks loaded with crackers. They came in fivegallon cans, six cans in one box. We had to unwrap the boxes and stack them up for distribution to the different compounds. A dozen American soldiers were supervising us, so we could not take any crackers for ourselves. Meanwhile, we had built a pile of waste paper as high as a house. One of my fellow prisoners poked me in my side and said, "Hey you, it is your turn in the waste pile." So I went into the waste pile and followed a trampled path. At the end of it I found one big can of crackers and another one filled with water. So I ate crackers till they came out of my ears and buttonholes. Then I filled up all of my pockets and walked out again. This continued till everyone had a turn and then we got a second turn. At quitting time the fellows told me to ask the American captain for some pay. He looked at me and smiled: "Say, did you not get your pay in the waste pile? I knew you had to work and you had to eat, but do not ask me for pay now." I went back to the other prisoners and told them that he knew, and they did not want anything else after that.

Because I could speak English, I asked the guard if there were any Mormons in the camp. I was so excited to learn that there was one, and asked if I could speak with him. The GI that I saw coming toward me was smoking a cigarette. I could not believe he was a Mormon and asked him. He replied that he was but was not very active. I learned that there were other Mormons in the camp and that they held a Sunday meeting. I arranged to meet them, and they were able to have me released to attend their small church service. This was the first time I had been able to meet with other members of the Church since leaving home. When I arrived the first Sunday, I was asked if I wanted to assist in passing the sacrament. There I was, in my dirty German uniform passing the sacrament to my American brothers. I knew at that moment, that for me, the war was over. I was so grateful to my Father in Heaven for my membership in the Church and the blessings that were mine that day.

On June 6, 1945, I was turned over to the British, at the camp of Wickrath in the British zone of

HORST HILBERT FILE

Horst Hilbert dressed in his German Army uniform in 1940

occupation. An American sergeant had warned me that all prisoners living in East Germany and Berlin would be turned over to the French. Since I had no desire to get into French hands, I gave a West German address to be released to West Germany.

When I arrived in Berlin, there was a special meeting the next day. Apostle Ezra Taft Benson was there to visit the Saints. When he came to the meetinghouse, the congregation arose and the District choir sang "Let the Mountains Shout for Joy." Elder Benson had tears in his eyes, and in his speech he let us know how big his and the other members of the Council of the Twelve's love was for us.

IRENE BUCHTA HILBERT

When Irene was six months pregnant with Eveline, the Russian troops came into the town where Irene was living. The Russians were raping every woman they could find. Irene managed to dodge them, but one day a Russian soldier caught her and dragged her into a room. Irene fought so fiercely that the Russian soldier could not handle her by himself, so he locked her in the room and went to go get help.

Irene was afraid that if she were raped by a gang of Russians, as they often did, that she would not only lose her life, but she would lose her baby. The room she was locked in was on the second floor, so she went to the window, said a prayer, and jumped. She felt as if she were floating to the ground, and when she landed she only twisted her ankle a little and began running down the street. A neighbor saw her and took her in and hid her for the last three months of her pregnancy until her baby was born.

Eveline Irene Hilbert was born in Berlin on August 30, 1945. Seventy-five percent of the babies born that year died from lack of food, medicine, and doctors. Irene and her grandparents did their utmost to keep the baby alive, with the help of some LDS servicemen. One, Grant Gunnell, from Mesa, Arizona, helped quite a bit with apples, soap, food, and whatever else he and some of his buddies could get.

A MISSION OF MERCY

At the war's conclusion, leaders at Church headquarters were greatly concerned to discover the condition of the members in Europe and to reestablish contact on the continent. The First Presidency assigned Elder Ezra Taft Benson the task of traveling to Europe to reopen the European missions, assess the needs of the Saints, and open the doors for relief supplies from the Church to be distributed. The task was daunting, and Elder Benson sought the help of army chaplain Frederick W. Babbel to assist him in his mission. Departing Salt Lake City in January 1946, the two men embarked on a journey of faith and miracles to bring desperately needed hope and relief to the scattered Saints of Europe.

CHURCH ARCHIVES

Norwegian saints prepare relief supplies to be delivered to Germany.

CHURCH ARCHIVES

Elder Ezra Taft Benson

Though only military and government officials were allowed freedom to travel between the various zones of occupation set up by the allied nations, Elder Benson was able to obtain visas, special passes, and a vehicle to complete their mission. Elder Benson and Brother Babbel traveled to as many places as they could, meeting with the Saints and government officials, and assessing the overall situation of the members in Europe. Missions were reopened in France, Switzerland, Holland, Czechoslovakia, Denmark, Norway, and Sweden. It was found that although many of the Saints were starving and in dire need of clothing and supplies, their spiritual health and well-being had never been stronger. After ten months, and traveling more than sixty thousand miles, Elder Benson returned to Salt Lake City having reestablished the Church on the European continent and having opened the way for hundreds of thousands of pounds of relief supplies to be delivered to the German Saints and those worst affected by the devastation of the war.

Source: Frederick W. Babbel, *On Wings of Faith* (Bookcraft: Salt Lake City, 1972).

John A. Dahl

John A. Dahl was born September 22, 1912, in Karlsruhe, Germany. His parents were both very active in The Church of Jesus Christ of Latter-day Saints. When John was just two years of age, his father was drafted into the German Army during World War I, and was killed in 1915 during fighting in eastern Poland. The family received a letter informing them of his death with a promise for more information to follow, which never came. With this difficult situation, John learned early the value of hard work, often rising early as a young man to pull a small wagon around their city, picking up horse and cattle droppings to be used as manure. After graduating from Hochschule in 1933, he left home to serve as a missionary in the Swiss-German Mission.

By his mission's end, Adolf Hitler was firmly in control of the German government. Having not joined the Nazi Party, John was unable to obtain any employment from the state and therefore chose to enter an apprenticeship as a draftsman for a company in Karlsruhe. Not long after, he married Betty Baier, a member of the Church from Nuernberg, and they moved to southern Germany for better employment. With the birth of their first daughter, Helga, in 1940, the Dahls were hopeful to move away from the bigger city of Munich and begin their own home in the country, when John was called up in the draft.

In December 1940 shortly before Christmas I received a note to report for military service. Betty packed her suitcase for her and Helga to go to Nurnberg, and I did the same for me to go to Augsburg. We said farewell in the train at Augsburg, hoping that it would not be too long before we could be together again. It was hard for all of us to have our family separated, not knowing what the future might bring. We knelt in prayer before we left and asked that Heavenly Father would protect us while we were apart. We had faith and great hope that our prayers would be answered, and they were in many and special ways.

The first six weeks in boot camp we were drilled and instructed in military discipline as soldiers, how to fight, and how to defend ourselves. Also we learned how to handle a gun and other small defense weapons. Then we were trained and taught the rules of military life. It was not easy to get familiar with the military jargon or special terms in the field of telecommunication, and normalcy of military life, such as saluting a superior officer and addressing them, knocking at the door, asking for permission to enter when we were already half way in, etc. All these formalities had to be strictly obeyed, plus dozens more, before you were allowed to leave the barracks with a military pass.

After this basic training had ended, the qualified recruits, me included, were selected and sent to a military school at Halle a. d. Saale, Germany, for further training in telecommunication. Nobody liked the Halle school. But it was an honor to be admitted into this military school for further training both in the telephone as well as in the telegraphing and maintenance sector. Once you went through Halle, you were almost certain not to be assigned to the front line. As a matter of fact, we had a special paragraph in our military pass that no soldier of the FNR, #601 could be transferred into any other unit of the German Army. While in Halle I had the opportunity to attend and be active in the LDS Church each Sunday.

After ending this part of our training, another selection took place. On a snowy day an elite group of the Halle school left early in the morning with backpacks, gun, bayonet, and in full uniform to an unknown destination. I was one of them. We crossed the Rhine near Cologne. After one day and one night traveling we arrived at Brussels, Belgium, where we were divided into two groups, one group for telegraph communication, the other for telephone communication, maintenance, and repair. I was assigned to join the telephone, maintenance, and repair group. We enjoyed the night in Brussels, but we still did not know our final destination until we finally left by train the next morning for Paris, France. This was in March 1941, on a sunny warm spring day. While there we received further training in our special fields but no drill. In our free time we visited Champs Elyse, the Louvre, Notre Dame, Folly Berger, Eglise de Madeleine, Sacre Ceur, Mont Matre, and Moulin Rouge. We were also able to climb up the Eifel Tower, even though the elevators did not function during the war. It was used as a radio observation tower, but the view over Paris was great.

We also went shopping in the Boulevard department stores. My knowledge of French helped me. In Paris our quarters were in Neuvilles, one of the finest sections of Paris, with direct Metro connections to the city center. Some of us went to the horse races in Bois de Boulogne, while others frequented places of entertainment for which Paris is well known. My comrade Heribert Nikolai had an aunt in Paris who owned a hotel, whom we visited several times. Then we would sit down in one of the many sidewalk cafes to enjoy some ice cream with a piece of torte. The days in Paris were like being on leave.

It is a well-known fact that when you are called to serve in the army for your Fatherland, and have pledged allegiance to the flag, that you do follow orders, or assignments or what else it might be. I would rather have stayed on the Western Front for the rest of the war. But it did not happen that way. On one sunny morning in May of 1941, our group received orders to pack and leave eastwards, destination unknown. We passed Brussels and Achen, crossed the Rhine, Weser and Elbe rivers on the way eastward to Berlin, where we spent the night. We were invited to a farewell dinner by friends of one of our troop, which was the last German hot meal we ate for a long time. The next morning we left early, crossing some of Europe's largest waterways like the Oder and Weichsel in West Prussia. Our next stop was Schneidemuhl, where we had lunch. The further east we came the colder it was, and the more miserable the roads were. After passing through West Prussia and entering East Prussia, we still had no idea where we were. We had the most fantastic guesses, whether we would stay in East Germany or would get into Russia to prepare the way to the Middle East. But we were all wrong. The further we moved east, the more monotonous the scenery, as spring had not yet arrived. We ended in Suwalki on the new Polish-Russian border. The roads were even more terrible as we entered Polish territory. Every so often we saw burned-out farm houses. Occasionally a farmer sitting on a wagon, drawn by a

NATIONAL ARCHIVES

Street fighting in Paris.

meager horse, crossed our path. One could only feel pity for these poor people who had endured the German *Blitzkrieg*. Suwalki was a small Polish city with old homes. When we arrived, we rested a few minutes and then unloaded our equipment into a house that looked as if it would fall down any minute. We shared the house with a telegraph unit and the *Geheime Kommando Sache* (Secret Command Matters) who had arrived a few days earlier than we did. By now we had become aware that our coming to Suwalki had nothing to do with the oil fields of Iraq or Iran. Suwalki was located just across the Russian city Augustenburg. German *panzer* (tanks) under General Guderian rattled four days and three nights, moving into position to attack and fight the Bolshevik Army and destroy Communism. This was one of the main goals of Hitler. The other was the final solution, regarding the Jews in Europe, and finally the restoration of a Greater German Empire, as it was before the Treaty of Versailles.

Finally, a few days later, we were informed that the date of the invasion of Russia had been set for June 4 at 3:00 AM. Technically, we were prepared, but not necessarily mentally and physically. However, we trusted God, our air force, and tanks. Our Intelligence found out that the Russians had built bunkers and had their tank troops ready to attack first. Our small detachment had prepared a good dinner in case we should not see daylight again. We had finished our meal exactly at 3:00 AM. Then we went out on a small veranda, where we saw German dive bombers (*Stukas*) releasing fireworks from their planes, to lighten up the night sky together with their bombs. On the ground General Guderian and his tanks started moving deep into Russian territory. Only a few days later we moved to Vilnius, capital city of Lithuania. On the way to Vilnius we saw only a few burned farm houses still smoking.

For perhaps a week we quartered in a hotel in Vilnius. It was in this hotel where a Jew offered us a large sum of money if we would bring him with our car to some secret place in Lithuania. We all felt sorry for this man, but we could not help him. First, we had no car, and second, we could not get gas. Finally, the risk for him and us to lose our lives was too high. He was sadly disappointed, and so were we. The next morning, a security man dressed in a green uniform, came to the hotel, telling us that last night they, the security service, had killed four thousand Jews somewhere outside of Vilnius. They buried them in a mass grave. We were so upset that we asked him to leave us alone. This was the first time in my life that I learned firsthand about the final solution or extermination plan against the Jews and other ethnic groups.

Our stay in the hotel did not last long. We moved into a schoolroom and had to sleep on straw sacks. It was getting cold in the night, so instead [of] removing our clothes when we lay down to sleep, we took every piece of cloth we could find to keep us warm. From our window in the hotel we could oversee the street below where we could observe a Polish girl selling newspapers. One day I went down and bought all the papers she had in her hands. She was young and seemed to be well educated. Besides Polish, she spoke French and German, two languages which I spoke as well. Since she did not want to speak German, we used French. We talked about the war. She did not like the Russians or the Germans, but she hoped that as the war continued, the Americans would come and liberate her homeland. I warned her not to be too optimistic. Unfortunately, I was right. It is true that the USA entered the war, but instead of liberating Poland from German occupation, the Russians came and Poland became a satellite state of the Soviet Union, together with several small eastern European states and parts of Germany, according to the agreement of August 2, 1945.

Being in the signal corp and away from the front line, the soldiers were allowed great freedom to move around and sightsee. The men were often invited to fine dinners and events, as guests of the local aristocracy or officers of the Lithuanian army, who wanted to fight the Russians under their own flag as allies to the Germans, which Hitler would not allow.

You might wonder what we actually did in the army. We had twenty-four-hour shifts during which we had to watch that our equipment functioned properly, and also were responsible for keeping the communication lines in repair. During the cold winter, especially, we had problems keeping the lines intact. When it was cold and the telephone lines snapped, we had to see that the lines were fixed as quickly as possible. That is, we had to find out where the line was interrupted and inform the repair crew where to go. The Russian wires were not very resistant to the cold, so this was a large problem. We also had to ensure that the relays were solidly connected to the relay board; if not, we had to resolder them. To do so was quite an art. We also installed new lines. It was an interesting yet challenging job.

Being with the signal corps had great advantages but could also be dangerous. Once when one of the transformers on a line became disconnected, I started to resolder the line without noticing that the floor was covered with iron plates. I was electrocuted. Immediately I threw away the soldering tool and ran like crazy in a circle around the equipment. I only suffered a light burn wound which healed fast, but I had learned my lesson. An advantage being with the signal corps was that we could call home to our families in Germany. One day I called my wife in Karlsruhe. My call there was handled by a lady operator whom I had never met but became well acquainted with over time (I connected her one day with her husband on the Russian Front). Anyhow, she told me just to wait a minute, because there was an incoming call, and she thought it might be my wife. And indeed it was Betty who called from a telephone box near our home in Karlsruhe to ask the operator if she had heard from me. She told her that I was on the other end of the line. So Betty talked to me for twenty cents from more than 1500 kilometers away in Saparozje. What a wonder! Calls like these were of course taboo.

One evening I tried again to call home. According to our time, it was in the evening. While trying to get through, somebody came onto my line. I asked him to please get off the line, because I was trying to call home. The person who interrupted me was the officer of the night shift. He asked for my name, which I refused to give, so he hung up and within a few minutes he was in my room. Well, to make it short, he forgave me after I had apologized for being so rough with him. He left, and I was able to complete my call to Karlsruhe, while he called his wife somewhere else in Germany on a different line.

Again, I wish to underline that while all this sounds more like a vacation, it was not. We were separated from our loved ones, had no chance to attend church, and most of the time were very lonesome during the night shift, especially those of us who had families at home with their lives endangered by the terrible air war.

While in Saparzje I was hospitalized for about six weeks for malaria. One day, after we had finished our meal, a nurse came to our room and asked if one of us would be willing to donate some blood of a certain type. There were only a few in the room, and I was the only one who had the blood type needed, so I volunteered. The nurse took me to the operating room and placed me on a table next to a soldier whose body was only a torso. He had been brought in from the front at the Caucasus on the Azov See and had lost one arm and both legs. He was unconscious and still so young. His face was as white as fresh fallen snow. The blood transplant went directly from my body into his arm. I donated three quarters of a liter of my blood. As the blood flowed into his body, the color of his face changed into a light red. This gave me hope; however, they took him to his room with little hope for survival. When I saw the nurse the next morning, she told me that they even had to amputate his only arm, but his life could not be saved. What a crime war is!

The blood transplant went directly from my body into his arm. I donated three quarters of a liter of my blood. As the blood flowed into his body, the color of his face changed into a light red. This gave me hope; however, they took him to his room with little hope for survival. When I saw the nurse the next morning, she told me that they even had to amputate his only arm, but his life could not be saved. What a crime war is!

The doctor ordered that I should drink plenty of fruit juice to replace the blood I had donated. The young kitchen nurse, who was from the Burgenland in Rumania, told me that on the kitchen table I should find a bottle of juice. So I went to the kitchen to look for the cherry juice medication, and found a bottle, took it under my arm, and went back to my room. I invited the elderly sergeant who was my roommate to have some of my cherry medication. After we had tasted it, we looked at each other and wondered what we had drunk. At that moment the kitchen nurse came, saw us with that bottle, became quite upset and took the bottle from us, ran into the kitchen, and brought us the right bottle. But no harm was done, for we only had tasted very little red wine.

After I was released, I received the War Service Cross without Swords. This surprised me very, very much, because a few weeks before, after I had passed well in a military training course, I was refused rank advancement because I was a member of the Mormon Church, an American church. This caused suspicion of my being a spy, so they argued. I did not care much about the promotion, yet I felt humiliated, because I was at the top of the class, and the advancement would have meant more money for me and my family at home.

—•—

During Christmas of that year I went to Karlsruhe on my leave and brought with me a large package full of food and other items. It was a Christmas present from Adolf Hitler. Only certain members of special regiments received such welcomed presents. I spent my time with our families in Karlsruhe and Nurnberg. We also visited my aunt Elisabeth in Wirtzburg, Germany, who had lost her son Hans Weber. He had been killed by stepping on a mine in Greece. Her other son, Kurt, was on the northern Russian front, on a very dangerous secret mission behind the Russian lines, from which he returned home unscathed. After a prolonged leave, I was ordered to go to Char'kov to attend the course which I mentioned above.

I left Karlsruhe for Angerburg in East Prussia. The sky over East Prussia was covered with monotonous gray clouds on this sleepy winter day in December. It was raining and very cold. The rooms in the barracks certainly were not much warmer; nevertheless I found it comfortable to be protected with a roof over my head. Down in the boot camp, fresh recruits were drilled. Fully outfitted and in their fatigues, they were chased across and around the yard and trained recklessly by their corporal in combat exercises, like falling on the ground and getting up and running with their rifles. Many of these man were older than their trainers. The shouting of the corporal giving commands and the shrill sound of his whistle did hurt my ears. I did not belong to that unit. My unit had its quarters south in a forest near Rastenburg in East Prussia, located near the headquarters of Hitler, known as the Wolfschanze, which became notable due to an assassination attempt on Hitler, June 20, 1944. Many Germans regretted that the attack by Count Staufenberg failed. But one had to be careful in expressing your feelings. It was the second attempt since the war had started.

Nobody knew me here or bothered me. Indeed I was only a number among millions of soldiers in the army of Great Germany. As far as I was concerned, it appeared as if I would spend the next few weeks somewhere between East Prussia and Char'kow in the Ukraine. My unit was located in Char'kow, and that is where my orders told me to go. I could have left the army; nobody might have ever found me, for I had civilian clothes with me. I thought of my family, far away from here. I had orders to Char'kow to participate on a training course for corporals. The other candidates, transported by trucks, were already there. I was lucky that I could go there by train. I had already traveled once by truck from Allenstein to Krakow in Poland during a terribly cold winter, and that had been enough. Even wearing thirty-eight pieces of clothes, which should have kept me warm, I nearly froze to death. Of course a little private had to obey orders. I had no choice but to follow orders, even if they might have cost me my life. They took their time in the office to write out my marching orders. This gave me time to pack. It was very important to report in best order to my sergeant in Char'kow, when returning from leave. I succeeded in getting a new uniform and was able to leave my rifle and bayonet with the arsenal. This made my traveling lighter. As signal corps soldiers, we really did not need this kind of weaponry. I carried under my arm my violin etui with my violin inside.

The beginning of my trip to the front was surprisingly comfortable. I was in a special courier train, going from Angerburg by way of Brest-Litow, Kiew, capital city of the Ukraine, to Poltawa. Fortunately the train was heated. The weather outside was stormy. Pitifully, a thick cover of fresh fallen clean snow covered the ground of the battlefields of the past months. The white monotony together with the anachronisms of the time caused me depression. I was longing for home, for Betty and Helga. Millions of Russians had been driven from their homes and homeland. Nobody was there to share with in my loneliness. Was I the only person in the train? I offered a silent prayer.

At about 4:00 PM we approached Poltawa. The road to the depot was filled with destroyed tanks and black burned house ruins. As mute witnesses of a senseless war, they offered a cruel picture of destruction. The train crossed, slowly rumbling, over a squeaking emergency bridge, destroyed by the Russians, and reconstructed by German engineer troops.

It was early evening when the train pulled into Poltawa, and the first time in two days that I set my feet on Russian soil, and saw human beings again. The weather was rough, and very cold. Really I should have been thankful to again be among people. Only a few trains without locomotives stood on the tracks outside, but they were all empty. I was told that no train would leave out of Poltawa any more this day in any direction. The waiting room was overcrowded with Ukrainian woman, children, and German soldiers. Thick smoke clouds mixed together with the smell of sweat and cheap perfume nearly took my breath away. The polluted air made breathing hard. Groups of smoking German solders of various army units were standing or sitting on banks or on the floor, talking, or snoring in the half dark room. Among them were soldiers from Italy, Hungary, and Spain. The mixture of languages in Babylon could not have been much greater. The well-nourished and well shaped round faced Ukrainian woman, veiled in dark shawls, some of them with babies in their arms, [were] a picture of piety, love, innocence, and purity in the midst of war and disruption. They steadily chewed their home-grown sunflower seeds. With unbelievable talent they put a handful of them in their mouths, pealed them with their teeth and tongues, chewed them, and then spit out the waste on the dirty floor; without using their hands at all, speaking, and debating, arguing, and gesticulating with each other as if they were alone in the room.

Everybody was going in different directions. Some were headed home, others to the front, others to Africa, or Nark in Norway. It was a wonder that with so many troops moving in so many directions that enough soldiers were available to resist the Red Army steamroller on the Volga front. Many of the local Russians, mostly children, women, and older people, did not know where to go. Their homeland was divided into fronts, occupied by German forces, their families destroyed.

On the street side of the depot large signs had been placed. They provided information of all kinds, even in code form. Information regarding military locations, such as the office of the (German) city commander, cinemas, the registration office, soldier billeting, officer casinos, the army hospital, and delousing and sanitation rooms. Some of these large signs gave distances in kilometers from Poltawa to Berlin, Paris, Stalingrad, Narvik, Char'kow, as well as to most European capital cities, which were occupied by German soldiers. Even Cairo and Tobruck in Africa were listed.

One of the signs mentioned that victory was close. Only the stubborn red Army of Russia, supported by the USA, had to be defeated, and the final solution would become reality. With the help of the signs, I found my way to the home for soldiers. As tired as I was, I threw myself in my uniform on the old straw sack bed. I only had one blanket. I did not dare take off my gas mask from around my neck. My heavy boots, however, I removed. Rolling myself together like a hedgehog, I immediately fell in a deep, dreamless sleep. Neither the ever present cockroaches nor the steady coming and going of comrades could bother me.

Nobody was allowed to stay in the quarters after 8:00 AM. Breakfast could be had at the Soldier's Home. My near-dead body felt very tired. Perhaps a tin pot of hot Ersatz coffee might make me feel better again. To free my hands, I placed my backpack and other things where I could keep an eye on them. More than on anything else I kept watch on my gas mask. In the moment, however, when I received my coffee, I lost sight of my mask. At this critical moment a "good" comrade must have snapped my box with the mask. It is hardly believable what can happen in a few seconds. Returning to my unit in Char'kow without a gas mask was unthinkable. Instead of attending a corporal class, I would have ended up most likely spending several days in isolation with water and bread. Without much hope, I returned to the quarters and questioned the private at the desk as naively as possible whether any one of the comrades had brought in a gas mask. I might as well have asked whether or not one of the "good" comrades had returned a hundred mark bill which he had found on the street. But I was very surprised when he pointed to a blue painted gas mask box standing by the window. My heart started beating faster. Since the container was not painted dark green, I immediately knew it was not my stolen gas mask. But I knew that I could not give up this lucky find. A gas mask is a gas mask, no matter what color of the container. However, I was not cool enough just to claim the mask. So I tried to deal with him on a diplomatic basis to not burden my conscience too heavily. A few packs of cigarettes which I carried with me as a nonsmoker made the deal perfect. I again had a gas mask, and the guard easily entered the number of the gas mask on my army pass. With mixed feelings, I returned with the blue gas mask to the railroad station where the masses moved towards a train, hoping that it would bring them to Char'kow.

After waiting patiently for several hours longer, the train to Char'kow was finally coupled to a locomotive. I entered a compartment and was very surprised that it was nearly fully occupied by Russian women. Their faces reflected grief and worry from Stalin's cruel communistic system of socialism and their loss of freedom which turned them into slaves. The communistic system deprived them of their own thinking. Without hope or faith they lived in the largest concentration camp of the world within their own homeland. Many of their husbands had been killed fighting a murderous and hungry winter war or were kept in open prison camps far away from their loved ones. One day, early in the war, we saw them marching disarmed through Vilnius in the hot summer of 1941, hungry and thirsty. We shared our own small rations with them by throwing food through a window.

The sky was covered with dark clouds and for reasons of security there was no light in the train. Ukraine was the war zone of the southern front of Russia. Any minute partisans could attack the train or block the tracks. Vis-a-vis from me was sitting a young woman. I had the feeling that she was interested in me because of my uniform and wanted to find out which German Army unit I belonged to. I suspected that she could be a Russian agent. She said she was going to Char'kow and asked me where I was going. I told her that this is also where I was headed to. We carried on our conversation partly in Ukainian mixed with German. I was surprised how many Ukrainians or Russians spoke German. She opened a pack of chicken sandwiches and shared them with me. I thanked her, for I had nothing to eat since breakfast. She also offered some to the other women.

I told her about my hometown of Karlsruhe on the Rhine. Then it was quiet in the coup. Most of the passengers fell asleep. The train had reduced speed, most likely because we crossed an emergency bridge. The darkness felt like balsam to those tired souls. I, too, had closed my eyes. Something, however, told me to be watchful. Sweet odor surrounded me. It came from that young woman. Her breathing was lightly irregular. The benches were close together. I felt her hands touching my shoulders; I grabbed them and held them from moving. They were rough working hands, not well cared for woman hands. She did not move and spoke no word. What she wanted was obvious, perhaps because she was lonesome and alone. I gently removed her hands from my shoulders and carefully moved her back into her bench seat and released her hands. Even before the train entered the station of Char'kow, she prepared to exit and leave the train. She avoided looking at the other passengers. Perhaps she was ashamed, or yet perhaps she was a Russian spy who did not want to be recognized. Quickly she got lost in the masses on the still dark station of Char'kow.

I entered the waiting hall. Would somebody pick me up and bring me to my unit? After standing around for a long while, day broke. Then a little, poorly dressed young boy came to me and offered to assist me. I named the street where my unit was quartered. He placed my luggage on a simple sled and we marched up an empty street. The new fallen snow made the sled glide easily. It took us about one hour to get to my company. I gave him a tip of five rubles. After saying an impish *Spassiva,* he turned around and took the same street back to the rail road depot. The company was just assembling for the morning roll call. What a relief it was to be with them and see daylight again.

The next day I joined the training class, which I passed with the best possible grade. But any expected promotion was not granted. I only found out much later in Zaparozje from one of the lieutenants of our regiment the reason why I was not promoted. Here are his own words, as far as I remember them: "Dahl you 'explicit.' Why did you mention in your vitae that you are a member of an American Church? This made you suspect of being an agent for America. There was no need to mention this, and you would have been promoted at least to the rank of corporal." I was bitterly disappointed but gave him no answer. My family suffered more under this intolerant decision, for the promotion would have meant a rise in my pay. Ignorance is the enemy of tolerance!

I did not see much of Char'kow while there. As a matter of fact, I saw nothing of the city. But here again I had an experience typical for military stupidity. Soon after I arrived in Char'kow, the Russians after they won the battle of Stalingrad quickly turned west and were approaching Char'kow again. While making preparations to leave Char'kow, our company commander wanted to appoint me to be in charge of a small rearguard consisting of six men and a machine gun.

I made it very clear that I did not think I could ever accept this assignment. I did not know how to handle a machine gun, nor did I want to end up in a Russian POW camp, or worse, be sent home in a coffin. No further comments were made on either side. I know it was the influence of the Holy Ghost that gave me the strength to act as I did and disobey his order.

There was not much time, for our armies were on the run. We hit the runway (*Rollbahn*) with several trucks, together with other German units in Char'kow. With us, but on foot, fled unnumbered Ukrainians to escape the Red Army. They had enough of Stalin's suppression and concentration camp terrorism, of which the common population of the world knew little or nothing.

The trek seemed to be endless, the sacrifices of those fleeing terribly horrendous. But fortunately there were no Russian airplanes in the air to bomb or pursue the fleeing masses. We made it safely to Vinnitsa in eastern Ukraine and Hitler's headquarters, Amt Irene. This was the place from which Hitler had hoped to pronounce defeat of the Red Army by Christmas 1941 and victory of Germany. An early cold winter in 1941 had contributed to the defeat of the German Army more than anything else.

One day I was ordered to be in charge of the night guard shift, even though I was only a private. Normally this was the job of a corporal. This required that I would have to do night watch and patrolling. Usually there were two or three privates assigned to the corporal to make the rounds. But this night I had to guard the buildings of our communication center far away from our quarters all alone until the next morning. In order to make it during the night, I alternated between lying down on one of the hard benches in a hall of the building and going outside into the fresh night air walking up and down the avenue, with my rifle shouldered. No matter what I did and where I did it, I was scared. I prayed to our Heavenly Father for protection more than once. I came through all right; my prayers had been answered.

Our stay in Vinnitsa was not too long. Together with a few others of my detachment I was sent to Llow (Lemberg) formerly in Poland. A truck took us to the freight railroad station. I do not know what time of the day it was, but it was again dark. After waiting between the tracks out in the cold for a while, a freight train arrived. Luckily we could crawl into a covered freight car, after begging those who already occupied it to let us join them. Most of those inside the car were sleeping on straw. We did not close the car doors completely, in order to get some fresh air. I do not know how many hours had gone by when the train stopped, but it was daylight and the sun was shining. Just where the car stopped were some Ukrainian men. They were friendly and soon we were engaged in a black market trade. I had a brown shirt with me and traded it for some bread; I also had one good army boot with me. The other one I had lost somewhere somehow. Anyhow, I traded it for butter. So with bread and butter, I had something to eat.

The train brought us nearer to Lemberg (Llow); then it stopped and we had to get off the train. Soon another freight train came puffing up the hill. Even though I and the others did not know where this one was headed, we swung ourselves onto it. We could only do so, because the track was going up a long steep hill, and the tempo of the train was slow. With all my baggage, including my violin, I jumped into a little brake cabin of an uncovered freight wagon. Soon it began to snow. The cabin had no door, but a seat inside. A closed glass window was in the direction in which the train traveled. This together with a warm winter coat gave me some protection. My prayers had been answered.

The stay in Llow was quite comfortable. The men, with no equipment, could not work, but were only required to participate in light daily drills. During this time, John was required to provide escort to two Jewish laborers who were contracted to paint the barracks from their concentration camp on the outskirts of the city. He was never allowed to enter the camp, and though he never saw any mistreatment of the Jews, he felt the whole situation unpleasant and was glad when the assignment ended.

I never found out why I was selected to that job. Perhaps it had to do something with my religion again that I was appointed to do this. Fortunately, the job did not last long.

Soon we evacuated Llow and were transferred to Allenstein again. From there I caught a train in Konigsberg. I had to transfer in Frankfurt, Main, but I arrived in Karlsruthe the next day in the evening and was happy to sleep in the arms of my dear Betty again. I was home for about seven days. When I returned my commander informed me that I had orders to go the Crimean island on the Black Sea. I talked to my lieutenant friend, with whom I had been together in the Ukraine, asking him to please change my orders, and instead send me to Munich, Germany. He asked me why I wanted to go to Munich. I told him that I had friends there, and I also could be with my family, and that my wife was expecting. He told me that the order came from the regiment and could not be changed. I explained to him that I had spent nearly four years in Russia and that I had had enough of it and would not go. I recommended sending some of the new recruits who just joined the army to Crimea and that they should send me, an old war veteran, to Munich. Soon he returned with the good news that I too should report to Munich the next morning. I thanked him for his efforts. I was happy that the Lord answered my prayer again. The next morning I was on a train to Munich with one of our corporals, in a second class coupe. We arrived safely in Munich the same day and reported for duty in the German Air Force administration building where our office was located in the basement. I called Betty and told her about my transfer. As soon as I had settled down and recovered from the stress of the last few days, I contacted our LDS friend Hans Thaller in Munchen-Solln, on the outskirts of Munich, and asked him if Betty, Helga, and I could stay with him after I had obtained permission by my commanding officer to do so. It was approved. Hans had evacuated his wife, Thea, and their children to a fairly secure place in Austria not far from Munich, so there would be space for us for quite some time.

Life in Munich was different. While on the front in the Ukraine, we never had any air raids. In Munich we could expect one each day or night. During one of them our building was hit on the

ABBOTT MANLEY FILE

B-17s of the U.S. Air Force bomb a target in Germany.

other end from our office, but life still went on as normal. The trolley and buses were running regularly, stores were open, entertainment, opera, theaters and cinemas, museums and galleries were open, and sport activities continued. Even the October fest on the Wiesen was not interrupted until near the end of the war. We went to church as we did before the war, even on the Sunday afternoon when Munich was taken at the end of the war, and continued to do so after the U.S. 7th Army occupation. The home of the Thallers was near a wide open field. Heavy flak artillery guns had been placed at one end of the field. One day during an air raid, Betty, Helga, and baby Rainer were in Karlsruhe. The flak was busy trying to down the attacking planes while we were finding shelter in the basement of Thallers' home, when all of a sudden we heard the shrill sound of a bomb coming down over the house. We hurried to one corner of the cellar for better protection and prayed. We heard no explosion, and soon it was quiet again. We went upstairs and saw no fire or homes destroyed. The attack, however, had done much damage within the inner city. Some days later we had another air raid, while I was walking to work. When I came to the rail depot, I took shelter in a house. After the worst was over, I went on walking along the trolley tracks, which had been destroyed, some of them bent straight upwards into the sky. The depot and some big buildings were on fire. While the flak (*Flieger Abwehr Kanonen*) brought more of the bombers down than the U.S. Air Force hoped they would be able to do, there were still many of them which made it to their bases in England after they had followed orders to release the rest of their ammunition anywhere possible. It reminded me of Dante's *Inferno*.

After this air raid our group was marked to be transferred to Zagreb (Agram) in Yugoslavia. I explained to those in command that it would be a big mistake to replace us with another group, since we knew the damaged lines and how to get them restored faster. This worked and we remained in Munich until Germany's unconditional surrender a few months later.

Another raid which I shall never forget was a night attack. I was on a short leave in Karlsruhe, my hometown. My train to Munich had left early in the evening. All of a sudden the train stopped and then moved again into a tunnel to find shelter, so we could not be seen and bombarded. It took one hour or more, before the signal was given that we could move on.

Betty and Helga had moved back to Karlsruhe to await our new baby. Traudel Strobel went with them. Before the train could go west, it had to go east towards Austria, because the tracks west were destroyed during an air raid. Betty in her pregnant condition had to crawl through a window to get on the train and find a seat for her, Helga, and Traudel. Rainer was born on August 11, 1944, as a healthy, strong baby. I asked for a short leave to see my newborn son, but this time my request was denied. I had to wait a while before I could take Rainier in my arms when Betty and Helga brought him to Munich. The Thalers had a large basket in which we placed Rainier as his bed. The children nicknamed him Moses. When Thea Thaller returned from her evacuation in Austria, Betty and the children moved back to Nurnberg.

There she experienced one of the most frightful air raids of the war. The area where Betty's parents resided was completely destroyed except the house Schmausengartenstr #5. Betty described the attack:

My sister Anni and I were on our way to go to see a movie. Halfway there, the sirens sounded alarm, signaling an early warning for Nurnberg of an approaching air raid. We returned home immediately. By the time we were running down in the house bomb shelter, we already heard bombs exploding. We ran up to get Helga and also Rainer in his baby carriage and then back to the shelter, which was overcrowded, not only by renters in the house, but also with passersby from the street. After the attack had lasted past midnight and everyone had become very nervous, people of the house who knew my mother as a faithful and religious person begged her to kneel down and pray. She invited everybody in the room to kneel down also, fold their hands, and close their eyes while she was praying. And then she offered a simple prayer asking Heavenly Father that their and other homes would be spared from destruction. By now everybody had their gas mask put on. Rainer was laying in his carriage, covered with a blanket, to protect him from dust and soot. At about six o'clock in the morning, my mother asked me to look after Rainer, and to feed him. She had two bottles prepared for him before they went down into the cellar. I was very doubtful whether or not Rainer was still alive, for he had not moved or made a noise during the attack. Finally I removed the blanket and found him sleeping. What a relief it was for me. At about seven o'clock in the morning the attack was over. Some men went up to the street to see what had happened. They had a hard time opening the doors, but otherwise, the house was still standing, except for some broken windows. Most houses in the neighborhood were either burning or a total loss. The raid had cost the lives of about 1800 people. At about ten o'clock in the morning a squadron of the British Royal Air Force finished up the terror act of that night with another two-hour attack. And such an act it was, for the bombs fell into populated areas, to unnerve the people of the city.

We felt the ground shaking in Munich, caused by the impact of the heavy bombs in Nurnberg on the night of January 2, 1945. Despite these terror attacks, it still took another four months until Germany had no other choice but to surrender.

After the above mentioned air attack, an order was released, stating that mothers with young children had to be evacuated to villages outside the big cities. In Betty's case, Mrs. Paulus, also of Nurnberg, and a member of the LDS Church, thought that she knew a place near Markt Erlbach where Betty and the two children could stay with an elderly lady. So, together they went by train to that lady. It was a cool and dark evening. The lady had only a very small room. Rainer slept in his carriage, and Helga and Betty on a bench around the oven in the small room with no heat. These conditions were unbearable for Betty and the children, so, early next morning Mrs. Paulus with Betty and the children went to the mayor's office and asked for asylum in another home. This time it was a home in Markt Erlbach, large enough for Betty and the children to stay. The lady who owned it was the daughter of a family with a large farm. She also kept many doves and often prepared some of them for dinner. Betty appreciated her hospitality.

It was almost near the end of World War II. One afternoon she took the children for a walk in Markt Erlbach when unexpectedly a pilot in a low flying fighter plane dead aimed towards their direction. After he recognized that they were civilians, he turned upwards and flew out of sight. After staying in Markt Erlbach for nearly four months, the war came to an end. A messenger of the city came to our house with an order that we had to leave the house immediately so the soldiers could use it as their quarters. Betty and the children left the house were she had lived for about five months, but help came in the form of a lady who also was a member of the LDS Church. She had told Betty earlier that she and the children could stay in her home whenever needed. Betty took Rainer and Helga and walked to this lady's home. After a short while, the soldiers came with loaded guns to the sister's home. They were looking for a German soldier hiding somewhere in the house, and they searched but found no soldier anywhere. They where standing in the living room when one of the U.S. soldiers saw a row of pictures on the top of the commode. He asked Betty who the good looking young men in the pictures were. Betty explained to him that they were former American missionaries of the Mormon Church who had served a mission in Germany. He asked if she were a Mormon and she responded yes. The questioner excused himself and asked his commander if she could stay in the house with the children. When he returned he told her that she could stay in the house. In the afternoon he came back to Betty with a pack of cigarettes and offered her a smoke. She thanked him, telling him that she never had smoked in all her life. He patted her on her shoulder and said, "Now I know that you are a good Mormon."

The U.S. 7th Army took Munich, coming from Nurnberg in the North on April 30, 1945. The army reached the outskirts of the city at about midnight. The population had been warned by radio to remain either in their homes or go to a shelter. Many houses, roofs, and windows displayed white flags declaring Munich as a free city. There was no resistance by the German Army, hence no fighting when the troops marched into the city.

As soon as we knew that U.S. Army troops were approaching Munich, we left our office, without destroying any equipment. To do so would have been meaningless. At our last morning call, we were released from duty. Most of our detachment had no civilian clothes, and many of them were most likely made prisoners of war. They knew that I spoke English and asked me to make I.D. cards for them, especially our sergeant. But I declined, explaining to them that it would not help them in any way. I, however, had a street car pass with my name and picture on it. I added some more data and used it as my civilian passport. Thanks to Helga, our daughter who put that passport in my backpack, when I went to Russia the last time. Then I put my civilian clothes on and took my violin. Then our lieutenant and I drove with his car to my apartment. I also had taken some food with me that I had found stored in the air force building, including a large wheel of cheese and some bottles of wine. These, if necessary, could be used on the black market, or for my friends to drink. I instructed my friends in the apartment how to act, when the doorbell rang. I advised my lieutenant, who was still in uniform, to hide in the kitchen cabinet and stay there until the air was clear, as his family lived in Westphalia.

On the morning of the same day at about eleven, as expected, the doorbell rang. I answered the door and welcomed a young short lieutenant of the 7th Army. He was not rough, nor was he friendly, but he had manners. He must have been surprised that I spoke English and asked me why I was not in the army. I briefly explained to him that I was not in the army anymore, which was true, and that the war was over, at the same time showing him my passport with picture. Apparently he could not read German. I asked him to come in, which he did, as he wanted to see the rooms. I took him into the living room. I made it clear to him that this was not my home. He asked who and where the owner was. I explained that the owner was an officer of World War I in the German Army and had moved away when air raids became too heavy. He made some funny remarks regarding the old gentleman. Then he discovered a gun cabinet. He asked me to open it. I told him that I had no keys. He wanted me to break the glass, so I told him if he wanted a gun he must break the glass himself. He looked at me, took his gun, and broke the glass of the door to the gun cabinet and took only one hunting gun. Then he wanted to see the other rooms, but the only other room was locked. In leaving, he said I had better get the key by the time he returned that afternoon. He probably thought there were German solders hiding. He also warned me not to open the window and look down the street. As soon as he had left, I looked for the key and found it, and then I told my German lieutenant to get out of sight. He found a bicycle to ride home. I never heard from him again.

As promised, the Ami returned after lunch. (*Ami* is the German nickname for any American soldier.) As soon as we had entered the bedroom, he saw a table with some drawers. He walked over to it and pulled out one of the drawers. There were small open boxes filled with cheap jewelry. He took a few and left the room and the apartment. We were never bothered again by any other visitors like him.

Because of my good English I found a job inside the building. It was an unpleasant, dirty job, and I hated to accept the offer. A lieutenant invited me into his office, where he wished to talk with me. The red-haired lieutenant, well built, sitting relaxed in a club chair started praising the German soldiers against which his troops had fought in southern Italy. He thought they were well fed and well trained. To this I replied to him that he was wrong regarding being well fed; but he was darn correct about being well trained. At that point in time (1943), Italy had already capitulated. A German soldier or any good soldier would never give up fighting as long as there was one bullet in his gun or a bayonet in his hand. He agreed, and then he changed the subject saying: "I want to ask you to go to each family in this house and tell them to leave their home immediately. They can only take with them what they have on their body. You can stay in your room where you are now, and we will bring you food to your room. We need the homes as billets for our soldiers."

This was a hard assignment, and I thought about it for awhile. I was alone in Munich and without a job. I could have gone back to Karlsruhe to my family, but it was occupied by the French, and I did not want to be sent to the coal mines in southern France. I agreed to the order and went to a few families in the house and delivered the bad news of the American lieutenant. This order, which could have been avoided if the Americans would have used the modern German quarters, just built in the last few years, would have saved much heartache and many hard feelings. After I had followed my orders, I returned into my small room in the basement. A GI had to bring me my daily rations of food to my room. Fortunately, this lieutenant and his company or whatever it was were transferred soon. They left enough food behind so at least I had something to eat and a roof over my head. I immediately went to the U.S. Military Government in Munich, to apply for a job.

The American soldiers were permitted only to fraternize with girls, regardless of nationality. However, since I worked for the U.S. Military Government, I had contact with many fine U.S. officers and soldiers who treated me well and saw to it that I would not starve. Some of them were LDS. Shortly thereafter a Professor Schwarz of a high school in Munich contacted me and offered me a job as an interpreter for an officer of a signal corps. I could stay in my room again, received a nice salary, and was entitled to German food rationing tickets.

One evening, I walked over to my former apartment. Opening the door to get into the house, I was surprised to meet some fellows coming down the stairs, each holding a bottle or two in their hands. They must have assumed that I was an American officer and became confused. In their excitement they nervously excused themselves and told me that the war is over. I told them that I was aware of that and advised them to go to their room and they did.

Another experience was more dangerous. It was late in the evening again, and I was looking out of one of my open windows. I heard some radio news from an open window on the other side of the street. Since I had no radio, I decided to go down to get closer to the window to hear the news. As I came near to the house door, two fellows came running at me each with revolvers. I kept cool but felt somewhat endangered as they placed their guns at my front and back ready to shoot. They asked me what I was doing outside so late in the evening, when nobody was allowed to be out during curfew hours without a passport. I told them who I was and that I had a right to be out at this time of the night. They removed their guns from my body and immediately took off, running as fast as they could back into their house. I could not tell whether they where U.S. GIs or German gangsters. My knowledge of English, together with the protection of my guardian angel, saved my life.

In September 1945 I tried to find transportation to return to my family in Karlsruhe. I was lucky to find a truck which took me and others to Bruchsal, only about nineteen kilometers north of my hometown. From there I took the train to Karlsruhe. Seeing my wife, children, and my mother again, all in good health, ended World

Walter H. Kindt

The second child of Johannes and Frieda Kindt, Walter Kindt was born November 15, 1923, in Schneidemuehl, West Prussia. Early in his adult life, Johannes was called to serve as the district president of the area, and the family was very active in their local branch of the Church in Schneidemuehl. When Walter was only fifteen years old, his mother, Frieda, died of cancer, leaving Johannes alone to raise the five children. Nevertheless, the family grew strong and was never without guidance. After a year, Johannes remarried Maria Bernau, who was a member of their branch, and they had five more children. As the war began, the family was at peace in their knowledge of the gospel.

Our city of Schneidemuehl was only three miles from the Polish border. The city was overcrowded with soldiers who marched into Poland and started World War II on September 1, 1939. Probably because Schneidemuehl was on the major train line from Berlin, we saw a lot of soldiers in our town. At the same time the prophet of our church, Heber J. Grant, withdrew eight hundred missionaries from Europe and sent them back to the States. The same thing happened at the beginning of World War I, when two hundred missionaries returned to the United States. I was only a kid (fifteen years old), but I was amazed how the prophet knew that Hitler would start a war with a surprise attack.

Hitler's march into Poland was indeed a surprise attack. It happened on a Sunday morning. My brother Wilford, my sister Sigrid, and I were all sick at home in bed. This gave me the opportunity to follow the daily newspaper reports of the war against Poland that lasted only eighteen days. Two years later, and again on a Sunday morning, the twenty-second of June 1941, Hitler's troops marched into Russia. My brother Wilford and I went together to church that morning, and I said to Wilford that Germany could never win that war against Russia because Hitler marched into Russia on a holy Sabbath day.

I was then sixteen years old. My father was the district president, in charge of the branches Schneidemuehl, Schoenlanke, Kreuz, Driesen, Landsberg, and Flatow. A week after this he told me that the branch president, Friedrich Birth, my uncle, would like to ordain me to be a priest. But there was a problem. At the time I was not on speaking terms with his daughter, my cousin Irmgard, so I went and embraced her and said I was sorry. Then I was ordained a priest.

RUTH BIRTH FILE

A group of young women fulfilling their required Arbeitsdienst.

Later, when my father addressed the brethren of the priesthood at a stake conference, he said, "Brethren, I enjoy rather to work with a brother who is unable but very willing than with a person who is very able but not willing." Then he continued, "The Lord will bless the willing man in His church with powers and gifts to enable them to do the work of the Lord, just like the boy, the Prophet Joseph Smith."

At age seventeen, in August 1941, I joined the army voluntarily so that I would receive full payment for my government job (surveyor) during the war. The government pay was higher than pay for a soldier. I volunteered because I thought I would be drafted anyway, and at least this way I earned money during the war. Although this seemed like a good idea, at the end of the war my bank account book was stolen from my stepmother as she left with the last train from Schneidemuehl. I had a lot of money in my account which was cleared out by someone.

I started my army life in a work camp (*Arbeitsdienst*), a kind of pre-army training where we built a dam on the Baltic Sea for three months in Pogegen, near the city of Tilsit. We had shovels, not rifles. While there, I prayed to be able to go to church. Soon my prayer was answered. All the soldiers in the work camps in East Prussia were sent overnight to the Russian front, except for my work camp. The other work camps also didn't have military training, so I assume they were sent to support the soldiers on the front. However, many of them were killed while on the front. My particular camp was dispersed, and we were assigned to guard the other camps which were empty now that the soldiers had left to the Russian front. On a Sunday morning, I was sent to Tilsit to guard the camp there. It so happened that in Tilsit there was a branch and I was able to travel by boat and attend the meeting there. This church attendance was an outstanding experience. At my first day of church I made lifelong friends. The members in Tilsit were incredibly kind to me. They had me speak in church and several families fed me after church. During those days there weren't many visitors attending such small branches. They were thrilled to see that there were other good Mormons around. And I was thrilled with the great love which they showed to me. Three weeks later I was also asked to speak at the stake conference in Koenigsberg. My new Mormon friends in Tilsit paid my way to Koenigsberg as I had no money.

After three months of work camp, in October 1941, I went home for a week and then was assigned to begin active military training in Pasewalk, near Stettin where I celebrated my eighteenth birthday. I trained there for seven months, and at the end I was given a two-week furlough, a home pass. Other army training camps only trained for front line duty for six weeks. I went from Pasewalk to Schneidemuehl. On the way back to Pasewalk, I went via Tilsit. When I returned from my furlough, I was surprised because the whole company had been shipped to Russia.

I was sad to have missed this transfer to the Russian front line with my friends with whom I had trained—I was young and didn't have a clear perspective on the war. One day I met my staff sergeant in the washroom and asked him, "How come you didn't call me back from my vacation? You had my address and telephone numbers." He surprisingly did not answer me. He was older and perhaps thought this young soldier did not realize how lucky he was. Finally he said, "In two weeks there will be another transport going to France."

When we arrived in Rouen, I wrote twenty-four letters to all of my army buddies from my seven months stay in Pasewalk. I felt close to them. All twenty-four letters came back to me with the same message on the envelopes: "Died for the fatherland (country)." This woke me up, and I offered a special prayer of thanks to my Heavenly Father for being alive. I realized then that this was the second time that God had spared my life—the first being that my work camp was the only one not shipped to the Russian front. All the months in France I said my prayers, and I sent my tithing to my branch president, R. Jonischus, in Schneidemuehl, and otherwise kept the commandments of the Lord.

We stayed in an army complex in downtown Rouen. One of my responsibilities was to make out the weekly guard duty roster for the office, street, etc. One soldier came to me and looked at the posted assignment chart outside my office. He looked at it and I stood next to him. He said, "You must hate me. I am more on duty than anybody." To which I responded, "Yes, I do." He had some issues. We went to his room and talked things over and wouldn't you know it, he wasn't on guard duty as much going forward.

Later my troop moved to a chateau in Montigny, a suburb maybe five to ten miles from Rouen for better quarters. One day we witnessed a young U.S. captain, a pilot, come floating down in a parachute right next to our chateau. Some of my comrades talked about killing him because they had lost their homes and families in the many bombings in Germany. I asked them, "Are you of the Jewish faith, believing an eye for an eye, or are you a forgiving Christian?" He was taken to Rouen to be questioned at the general headquarters.

At another time, the French underground bombed our soldiers' movie theater in Rouen. It was also here, in the chateau in Montigny, that I

WALTER KINDT FILE

Walter Kindt, 1942

learned, fourteen hours before Hitler did, of the D-Day invasion at Normandy in June 1944. From the office in the chateau where I worked with the staff-sergeant, a door led into a room that was our living quarters for four soldiers. In Pasewalk, I was trained as a telephone lineman, to lay phone lines so the German Army could communicate. But in France I was assigned to the Signal Corps. My duties included office work such as taking notes and preparing letters for the commanders, transfers, transporting commanders, duty rosters, preparing maps, delivering classified mail to various cities that couldn't be shipped through regular mail, and other office duties. I rarely carried a gun.

One day I went for a little snack into my living quarters which were adjacent to the radio room and overheard on the radio that the U.S. planes were flying over France. The Allies had jammed our radio station, which they never had done before. But the jamming did not always work, so I could hear some messages in between the jamming noise. I heard that the airplanes had returned to England, but there was not any report of them having dropped any bombs. Then I knew. They

WALTER KINDT FILE

Walter Kindt and members of his company, 1943.

had dropped their parachute troops and gliders behind our front lines on the coast of Normandy. The Allies had landed in west France about two hundred miles away. For three years we had waited for it, expecting this invasion to come.

A few weeks before the invasion in June 1944, I had a special spiritual experience while stationed in Montigny near Rouen of Normandy, France. One Sunday morning, I prayed in the woods, asking my Heavenly Father to help me find a way to increase my faith and testimony and to always have His Holy Spirit. I was then told by a great impression of the Spirit to "read the Book of Mormon." Immediately, I sent a letter to my parents asking them to send me a copy of the book, and they, of course, sent it to me at once. However, soon study became impossible because the Allies had just landed in France. I didn't get to read hardly a thing in the Book of Mormon and had to bury my Book of Mormon along with other possessions when we pulled out of our quarters.

We were stationed in the northeast of France, but the invasion took place in the northwest. Paratroops captured the general in that western area, and our general was transferred to take his place. From Rouen I drove with my Captain von Tilly through Paris and on to Nantes and many miles thereafter. While we traveled, the airplanes attacked our cars by shooting at us. Before they came, we would hurry to park the car under the trees, but they would still shoot at us until they were able to hit our car. I soon had an idea. I knew that if they did not see smoke, they would come back to finish the job. So after every first attempt of shooting at us, I put a fog hand grenade on top of the car. When they saw the smoke, they thought they had hit us and took off.

As soon as we arrived in Nantes on the west coast of France with the assignment to take care of communications in the division whose general was captured, we were told to turn around immediately because the Allies were only one mile away. So we turned back and eventually landed again in Rouen. In one of the villages on the way back, the villagers had put down metal tacks to flatten the tires, so I had to clear the road of them. Again, in one of the villages as we were returning to Rouen, we checked on the position of the Allied forces and found that at that location, one of the phone lines was cut to General Dietrich, the SS general. I volunteered to go and find and fix the phone line, as I was trained to do so, but my captain said, "Are you nuts? When you get there to where the line is broken, the resistance will be waiting and will shoot you." I never thought of that possibility.

The German field marshal, Manfred von Rommel, came to Rouen to help us. I was assigned to make an eight-by-twelve-foot map of all the different locations of our troops. I worked on the map for three days and two nights; I did not sleep. I then went from Montigny with my Captain Joachim von Tilly to Rouen on a Sunday morning to deliver the map to General Rommel, but he told us, "Sorry, I don't have to look at it. It is too late; we can't do anything any more." Sure enough, soon thereafter the Allied forces drove the German Army back to Germany, and we took shelter in little villages so we wouldn't be hit by airplanes.

One day we failed to get orders because U.S. paratroopers captured our general. Our unit experienced a great surprise attack because no one knew or could warn us. At noon three U.S. tanks appeared on top of a hill looking at us. It took only minutes to get into our trucks and run. My captain, Hans Joachim von Tilly, his driver, Hans Gaedt, and I in the backseat of our Ford V8 convertible, were able to escape. But soon our car broke down.

Our leader, von Tilly, jumped into another car of our unit and said to us, "If there is no time to fix the car before the enemy arrives, just leave it and run." The two of us pushed the car into the woods and started to fix the problem, but it got dark and our flashlight needed a battery. So, we both sat in the car and slept. I woke up around five in the morning, said my prayers, and walked carefully toward the village, where I met a German farmer. I asked him, "Are the Americans here?" He said, "No, we are all surprised. I think these Americans do their war from 8 AM to 5 PM." So we fixed our car and soon joined the rest of our company.

As those three tanks had surprised us, I had no time to secure my briefcase with all my important belongings, especially my precious photos of my family. When I met up with our company, my friend Joachim Berber from Berlin surprised me. He said, "Walter, in the last minute I saw your briefcase and took it." What a great joy this was for me that someone would be so thoughtful to think of someone else. We stayed in contact for many years after the war.

Shortly thereafter, we went to the Rhineland, and at Cologne we drove over a partially destroyed bridge over the Rhine River that completely collapsed soon after we drove over it. All the other signal-corps vehicles had to be left behind at the Rhine River, and our soldiers swam across the river. Shortly after this, we were completely surrounded by the enemies and I saw thousands of our soldiers walking with their white flag into prison.

It was still possible to send mail, even while surrounded by enemy troops, so I sent a letter to my father on the Yugoslavian front and to my brother Hans, who was on the Russian front, and notified them of the new address of our family in Tremsbuettel near Hamburg. I got the address when my stepmother wrote me a letter while we were surrounded in the Ruhrgebiet area. Others and I began to retreat so that we might avoid becoming prisoners of war. Many of my group gave up as the American prisoner of war camps were rumored to be decent. There were twelve of us soldiers retreating together. While enroute to hide in the woods, we saw many trucks burning. The Germans were destroying their trucks so they would not fall into the hands of the enemy.

We stopped and everyone stood there looking because we could see a few loaves of bread in one of the burning trucks. I told everyone to please step aside, and I jumped through the fire, got one loaf, and then jumped back out again, which earned me great applause from the soldiers. Later, this loaf was our iron ration and saved us.

In another instance, we were hiding in a ditch in a village at night, when a British jeep stopped right in front of us. We heard them going into a house but wondered if someone had stayed with the vehicle, as it was customary in the German Army.

I was lying flat on my stomach all the way on the left of my friends; in all, there were twelve men. Then I heard someone coming toward me through the woods with a gun. I prayed, no, I cried, "Oh, Lord, the war will be over any day. Please save my life." It turned out to be another German soldier who had checked the Jeep already and confirmed that no one was in it.

We hid in the woods for three days and three nights, waiting for things to quiet down. During most of those three days we were bombarded by artillery fire. Then, after the third day, U.S. soldiers walked through the woods calling, "German comrades, come out!" But we did not go.

After three days, on April 15, 1945, we twelve soldiers, together with our company leader, started to go north. We began our journey in the Ruhrland between the cities of Altena and Iserlohn. We only walked at night, following the North Star. During the day we slept. This went on for one week. The war was still going on.

At one time I heard the sounds of English-speaking soldiers. So I went all by myself to the edge of the woods and saw the U.S. soldiers on roller skates with baseball gloves, throwing the ball to each other. Then I saw their army trucks. I was amazed! They were new and big, and there were so many. It made me smile because we Germans had destroyed our junky old worn out trucks so the U.S. soldiers would not get them.

One night we walked up a steep hill in the woods, and I lost my bread (the iron ration). It was very dark, and we had no help of light from the moon. But I was a praying man, so again I cried to the Lord. Then I notified the other eleven soldiers of my dilemma. We all walked down the hill again and found the bread in the dark.

After one week of marching nights, we went to German farmers, and they gave us civilian clothes. The farmer's wife asked me, "How far are you planning to walk?" I told her, "To Hamburg." She was shocked. She said, "That is impossible! It will take you weeks. You will never make it because the war is still going on."

I said, "I know it seems to be impossible, but with God's help, I will make it." She smiled and then gave me some old clothes. We left our army uniforms, revolver, and compass in the woods. Now we were able to walk during the day, and at night we could sleep in the woods. Unfortunately, in our civilian clothes it was too cold to sleep outside, so most times we stopped at farms. At most we got food before we retired and in the morning had breakfast. But there was a time when we did not eat for three days.

In the meantime, our group split, as some lived in different directions. As we arrived on May 1, 1945, in Hannover, we saw the Russian soldiers celebrating their biggest holiday. They would rob people on the street and get whatever they wanted from the stores for free. At every window, the Germans displayed the Russian red flag to celebrate the Russian holiday, having just taken down the Swastika of Hitler's flag to demonstrate their allegiance to the communists. Just the day before, we, the men in the army, were the heroes of the Fatherland, but today we felt like criminals in hiding.

In the end it was only Hans Gaedt and I still marching north. It was interesting to learn on this escape that it was mostly the German refugees that would help us. They felt for us, and at times insisted we sleep in their beds while they slept on the floor.

One day as the two of us came out of the woods into a village at noon, we saw two ladies talking with each other on the street. One of them called us over and asked, "Are you soldiers in civilian clothing trying to get home?" We confirmed her observation and she told us to come with her. We then met her husband, who was a shoemaker, and she fed us and then, for the first time on our escape, we were provided with food to take along on the road. It was touching, so I asked her, "Please tell us why you are so kind and helpful?" She said, "I have a son on the Eastern Front in Russia. I hope he is on his way home just like you by now, and I pray he will find help as you found it today with us."

Twice we were stopped by the U.S. Military Police and let go. A little later a young man helped us with his little boat to cross the River Elbe at night, a great accomplishment.

I marched for over six weeks to Hamburg, Germany, to my new home in Tremsbuettel, from Iserlohn/Altena. My family had landed there after leaving the city of Schneidemuehl, the place where I grew up. They left just minutes before the Russians invaded the city. Hamburg was hundreds of miles from Schneidemuehl. While walking north for those six weeks, I prayed constantly. I anxiously waited to get to my new home to do what I was told in Normandy, to study the Book of Mormon.

When Hans Gaedt and I arrived in Tremsbuettel, it rained for the first time in our long journey. We stood in the doorframe of a farmhouse for shelter. When the rain stopped, we went to the address of my family. But we found out that

WALTER KINDT FILE

German soldiers pose outside their administration headquarters.

they had moved to another address.

The war had just ended two weeks before we arrived. Everyone warned us, former German soldiers, that there were hundreds of British soldiers in that little village. We had an invitation from an army buddy, Hans Behnke, who was a banker, to stay with him. I had worked with him in the office in the army. So now we walked again all the way to Hagenow because it was too dangerous with so many British soldiers where my family lived and Hans Behnke found us a job with a butcher. It was important after the war to find employment as soon as possible.

We worked there only for room and board. I picked up the cows from the farmers and assisted in butchering them. One day they asked me to kill a lamb, but I just couldn't do it. It was easier with the cows, as it was not easy to bring them from the farm to the butcher. One day I walked with a cow over the city square in Hagenow, and I could tell something was going on. I heard that tomorrow the American soldiers would leave and the Russian soldiers would occupy this area, according to the Potsdam and Jalta Peace Agreements. Hagenow is about thirty kilometers south of Schwerin and ultimately became part of East Germany.

With my cow, I went to a parked truck full of

RUMORS OF HITLER AMONG CHURCH MEMBERS

With his ascension as Chancellor of Germany, Hitler began to institute a variety of organizations and programs to help achieve his many goals. For the German Latter-day Saints, these programs bore a disturbing similarity to the programs and organizations of the Church, many of which were ironically banned during Nazi rule.

Like the Church, Hitler organized the people according to age and gender with the purpose of education, albeit for very different purposes. For children to the age of thirteen or fourteen, Hitler introduced the Jungfolk (Young People). When old enough, young boys were inducted into the Hitler Jugend (Hitler Youth), and girls became members of the Bund Deutscher Maedschen (League of German Girls). By the age of seventeen or eighteen, all young adults were expected to participate in Arbeitsdienst (Labor Service) for twelve to eighteen months. Men were given public works projects such as building roads, bridges, and in the late 1930s, defensive installations and military barracks. Women were assigned to work on farms and in orchards in rural towns and villages. All adults were expected to be members of the Nazi Party, and local party officials organized groups for women to meet together to discuss topics such as womanhood, child rearing, cooking, and cleaning.

F. THUESON FILE

Adolf Hitler salutes a passing military parade.

Among the many programs instituted by Hitler's Nazi Party, one stands out in comparison to the Church. In 1933, the Nazi Party instituted *Eintopfsonntag* (One Pot Sunday) to be held on the first Sunday of every month between October and March. On this Sunday, each German family was to prepare only one simple meal in a single pot. The money saved through this act was to be donated to the poor, through the local party. While this program was instituted as part of a broader winter assistance program, it was soon adopted as a propaganda tool to demonstrate the unity of the German people and lack of social segregation under Nazi rule. Many propaganda photos showed Hitler and other high profile Nazi leaders participating in "one pot meals."

Source: Saints at War, various files, World War II in Europe an Encyclopedia (Volume 1: 688-689)

potatoes. The driver said he was going to Luebeck (about sixty kilometers away) and would be leaving in one hour. The butcher didn't want me to leave him, but when I sat on that truck on top of the potatoes, his daughter and others were on it also. She asked if her father gave me anything, which he didn't, because her dad was busy hiding his smoked meats so the Russians wouldn't find them.

In Luebeck, I visited Brother Mohr's home (the branch president), and from there I went to the expressway to walk back to Tremsbuettel. I started at eleven o'clock in the morning and arrived there at seven in the evening. There was only one car driving on the expressway all the hours that I walked. The driver stopped and invited me to go with him, but it was seven o'clock and I had to get off the expressway to walk to Tremsbuettel. The other side of the expressway was packed with U.S. military trucks, tanks, oil, ammunition, and other war material. I was glad to get home, and I was then finally able to start studying the Book of Mormon.

I noticed in the weeks to come as I studied the Book of Mormon how it literally changed me because I was more helpful and kinder to others. Think of it. My family lost everything they once owned. Yet, in my prayerful pursuit, studying the Book of Mormon, I found a great joy in my heart. I never felt sad for being poor in material things, because I felt that having lost the senseless war finally gave me the time to read the Book of Mormon. Every time I started to read the Book of Mormon, I prayed for the Holy Ghost to be upon me. Every time my prayers were answered.

It was 1945 and I was twenty-one years old. The war was over, and I had lost much because of the war. My first task was to apply for a job as a land surveyor for the surveying department of the city of Wandsbeck, a suburb of Hamburg. While I was home, I was able to go to church again. I will never forget when I attended my first sacrament service after being deprived of it for so long (about four years without church, except for some Sundays while on furlough). This gathering was held at a member's home, situated in a beautiful garden. We didn't have enough chairs, so half of the congregation stood outside in the garden, where we received the sacrament. Brother Rudolf Kaufmann was married as part of this service, located at the Lehmkappel. Brother Kaufmann was half Jewish and was finally able to get married.

I will never forget that day. There I stood. I had lost my mother to cancer when I was only fifteen. Now I was twenty-one and I had lost my home, all my belongings, my beautiful bank account, my friends, my job, and my hometown. I had even lost the war.

It was ironic how Hitler had tried so hard to be the head of a new "Millennium," and how he had deceived many people with his new man-made religion. Millions lost their lives trusting him. His kingdom lasted only twelve years. It helped me realize, more than ever, not to ever "trust in the arm of flesh."

So at this sacrament meeting at the cottage, my first church gathering in four long years, I felt the spirit of the Lord as I had never ever felt it before. I was facing a seemingly impossible situation, starting over with my life. Yet, I rejoiced in God. I prayed and promised my Heavenly Father that I would do whatever was necessary to have this power of the Holy Ghost, this wonderful peace I felt at this moment on this day, all the days of my life. I also prayed for the Lord's help to give me the strength to help others feel likewise.

WALTER F. FASSMANN

Walter F. Fassmann was born January 31, 1922, to Walther and Anna Fassmannn in Zwickau, Germany, birthplace of the great German composer Robert Schumann. Walther and Anna were lifelong members of the Church, their families having been baptized by the missionaries in the early part of the century. Walther was a veteran of the First World War and served in the German Navy. Returning home from the service in the spring of 1919, he walked into the chapel for sacrament meeting still dressed in his naval uniform. He was spotted by Anna, who had never met him before, who decided right then that he was the man she would marry. They were married a year later.

Walter and his older sister Erika were born in the midst of the terrible post-war depression that had ruined Germany's economy and left millions starving. Though earning enough to feed their growing family required hard work and long hours, the Fassmannn home was happy, and the children grew up strong. Walter's childhood consisted of much play and taking care of his two younger siblings. Though not an important part of his daily life, the political changes that began to occur during the 1930s were not unnoticed by young Walter.

One could say that the war really started on January 30, 1933, on the day Hitler came to power in Germany. I can still see before my eyes columns of SA and SS men marching through the streets in torchlight parades. Then I heard rumors about arrests. Certain schoolteachers all of a sudden did not show up for classes. Synagogues were destroyed and Jewish cemeteries desecrated. Apartments that had been occupied by Jews were vacated. Many of the things that were happening I could not yet clearly understand. In 1936 I was transferred from the Jungvolk organization to the Hitler Youth organization. National socialism was taught in school, in the Hitler Youth organization, and at work. The youth and many of the adults were convinced that Hitler was the man of the hour. Everyone was experiencing the prosperity of the German nation.

Unemployment disappeared, and with it, poverty. Most of the people now could afford new luxuries. Industry and business were booming. But the sufferings of those who were persecuted were unknown, and by now it was too late to do anything about it. Many had voted for Hitler to give him the opportunity to show what he could do. They were under the impression that they

WALTER KINDT FILE

Young members of Hitler Youth set off for an outing.

could vote him out of office again whenever they wanted to. But, in that respect, the masses were mistaken. Hitler's first official acts established his dictatorship, and every opposition was beaten down mercilessly.

I was too young at the time to properly evaluate the happenings and circumstances of the time. I only knew that we were much better off than we had ever been. We could afford an automobile, we went on trips, and we no longer had to be so careful about spending our money. Every summer I could go to camp with the Hitler Youth, and then I even became a group leader. I shared in the pride of the German people when Hitler declared the Treaty of Versailles invalid, when the German Army marched into the demilitarized zone, when conscription was instituted again, and when we occupied Austria, the Sudetenland, Czechoslovakia, Eugen-Malmedie, the Memel region, etc.

Then things all of a sudden became serious. On the morning of September 1, 1939, all of the apprentices at the plant of Jacob Brothers were assembled in a hall to listen to a speech by Hitler on the radio. At that time we heard that since the early morning hours of that day German troops had returned fire and crossed the Polish border. That was on a Friday. On the previous Sunday we had already received food ration cards, and blackout operations had been organized long before. Everything had been carefully prepared for the attack.

On Sunday, September 3, extra editions of the newspapers announced that England and France had declared war on Germany, and the war was in full swing. Three weeks later, Poland lay beaten to the ground. In his victor's ecstasy, Hitler declared, "With man and horse and wagon, the Lord has smitten them!" (In German this expression rhymes: *"Mit Mann und Ross und Wagen hat sie der Herr geschlagen."*)

As I grew older, my enthusiasm for national socialism waned. As had occurred previously, it happened that the meetings of Hitler Youth and our MIA (Mutual Improvement Association) conflicted. I went straight to my unit leader in the Hitler Youth and told him that I was not coming and that I was going to my church. He said, "That is too bad, because with us you could become someone." When I entered college, I left the Hitler Youth movement and used the excuse that I needed more time for my studies, and besides,

I needed to join the National Socialist Students' Union. That was the time when I started to listen secretly to foreign radio broadcasts. The love of freedom and the democratic thinking exposed to me by the American missionaries had influenced me a great deal.

After the conclusion of the Polish campaign, it appeared for a long time as if there was peace. Only the blackouts and food rationing reminded us of war. In the spring of 1940 Denmark and Norway were occupied, and in the summer of 1940 France was brought to her knees within six weeks. Then the bombing of cities on both sides began, even though Goring had loudly boasted that no enemy planes would ever fly over German territory, and if that happened, his name would be "*Meier*." (This is about the same as when we say, "If such and such happens, I'll be a monkey's uncle.")

We frequently had air raid alarms. Every time we had such an alarm, two or three men had to go to the meetinghouse of our branch to fight a fire, in case one should break out during an air raid. Each week two young people were designated for the job. Two or three times a week I started out on my trek to the meetinghouse in the middle of the night! Even young girls did the same, and all on foot. To top it off, the whole town was blacked out. A blackout meant that absolutely no light could be visible from the outside. The windows of the houses, trains, and streetcars had to be completely covered with black material so that absolutely no ray of light was visible on the outside. The headlights on cars were covered in such a way that the light could only penetrate through a very narrow slit. During an air raid alarm, all traffic had to stop. If you stepped out of the house, it would be pitch black until your eyes got somewhat adjusted. This was especially bad at the new moon when there was no moonlight. At other times, the moon gave us a little light that could not be blacked out. Up until that time, I had not even realized that the moon gave off light.

Then came January 31, 1941, my nineteenth birthday. On that day, I received my orders to report for the Labor Brigade. A week later, I was on my way to Koniggratz (Hradec Kralove) in Czechoslovakia.

The Labor Brigade had existed long before Hitler came to power. Then it was called the Volunteer Labor Brigade (*Freiwilliger Arbeitsdienst*). Young men under the age of twenty-five could join. They lived in camps and received free room and board, clothing, and twenty-five *pfennige* (less than a dime) daily. In return, they had to work on public work projects, such as building roads, flood protection, emergency housing, etc. Even before Hitler came to power, the Volunteer Labor Brigades were dominated by the National-Socialists German Workers' Party (NSDAP), Hitler's political party. In 1935, Hitler changed the Volunteer Labor Brigade into the Compulsory Labor Brigade. From then on, every young German, men and women between the ages of eighteen and twenty-five, had to serve in the Reich's Labor Brigade (*Reichsarbeitsdienst*).

Now it was my turn. In the town of Koniggratz (Hradec Kralove) in Czechoslovakia we were unloaded and taken into a huge gymnasium. There were 180 beds and 180 lockers in the large hall. This was to be our lodging for the next six months. First we received our uniforms; then our personal clothing was packed in suitcases and sent home. Then a bed and a locker were assigned to each of us, and we were instructed how to keep everything in order. Many of the instructions did not make sense to me, and I did not intend to follow them. After I had finished things my way, I sat down and read a book.

Shortly before the time appointed for inspection, I noticed that others were still busily engaged in getting their beds and lockers in order. Strangely, at the time of inspection I was not only *not* found to be lacking, but I was found to be a little better than others.

These 180 men were a division, and we were subdivided into four platoons. Each platoon had three squads (fifteen persons each). I belonged to Platoon 4, Squad 11. First, we had several weeks of military drill, and then we were assigned to our work projects, building splinter protection ditches and machine gun ranges at an air base. The drill and garrison duty did not bother me much. Even during punishment drills, I didn't lose my sense of humor; but the morning run, right after getting up, did me in. How happy I used to be when it was raining, because then the morning run was canceled. Otherwise, I was a pretty good member of the Labor Brigade.

Once, during drill when the command was, "Division about turn," I made a three-quarter turn instead of a half turn. My platoon commander was so happy to be able to find fault with me. The three-quarter turn had happened because the back edge of my heel had been standing on a

THE RISE OF THE NAZIS

In the aftermath following the Versailles Treaty of World War I, small political parties and groups of dissidents abounded all over Germany. One such group, the German Workers Party, formed in Bavaria and, like others, sought for more representation for the lower-middle class in the new government. In 1919, the German military ordered Adolf Hitler to attend the meetings of this party and spy on their activities. Hitler was soon convinced of their ideas, joined their ranks, and left the army. He attended a local university to learn public speaking and soon became a leading spokesman for the party.

KENNETH BATEMAN FILE

A Nazi war rally near Berlin.

In less than a year, Hitler had risen to become a top leader in the party, and called for it to be renamed the National Socialist German Workers' Party or Nazi Party. The party adopted a set of doctrines, "Twenty-five Points," which closely mirrored Hitler's personal views, and began to gain in strength and popularity. Seeking to emulate the fascist movements in Italy, Hitler began to reorganize the leadership and structure of the party and established a paramilitary arm, *Sturmabteilung* or SA, to help enforce the party's policies.

With the political situation in Bavaria beginning to crumble, Hitler felt that the time was right to stage a military coup and overthrow the government. The attempt failed, and Hitler and other party leaders were imprisoned. Though he only served a minimum sentence, Hitler emerged from prison in 1924 with a greater resolve and more refined vision for the Nazi Party and the German people. He began to reunite the party and spread its influence throughout the entire country. Though the elections of the late twenties were disappointments for the party, Hitler redoubled efforts, and in the 1930 election, the Nazis gained a large number of parliament seats. By 1933, the Nazis had gained enough influence that they were able to persuade President Hindenburg to appoint Hitler the chancellor of Germany. Soon Hitler passed legislation that barred the creation of new political parties and the banishment of opposition parties, and Germany became a one-party state under the control of a *Fuehrer*, with a puppet government at his total control.

Source: *World War II in Europe, an Encyclopedia* (Volume 1: 706–8); *The Simon and Schuster Encyclopedia of World War II* (427–28).

pointed rock and that had propelled my turn farther than I had anticipated.

After four weeks, we were finally permitted to leave the camp alone. It was a Saturday afternoon. I was still busy cleaning up when the order came, "Ready for inspection!" Quickly I put on my coat over the work clothes I was wearing, put on my cap, and ran outside to line up in front of the building. There I stood, unwashed, unshaven, my hair not combed, the arm band only half sewed on, dirty boots, my old dirty suit underneath the coat, and without gloves.

When inspection was over, less than half of the men were allowed to leave camp. Unbelievably, I was among them, but unfortunately we were not allowed to go back into the building, and I had to go to town filthy and dirty as I was. In town, things were available that we had not been able to buy in Germany for quite some time. The language was no problem since most people knew some German.

During the first few weeks it was quite cold on the job. We always worked outdoors. The worst part was cleaning our tools—shovel, ax, and spade—at the end of the workday. With our bare hands, we needed to clean them with snow, causing our hands to become ice-cold. Every time I had to do that, I felt like weeping.

The happiest moment came when we sat in the bus again that took us homeward. Then things were not so bad anymore. Naturally, we had to keep the barracks spick-and-span, peel potatoes, keep our clothes washed and mended, etc. The collar protector (the one I used for the work clothes) got the worst of it. First I could see it becoming dirtier and dirtier, until there was no room for more dirt on it. Then the dirt started rubbing off on my neck and the protector became whiter and whiter. This cycle kept repeating itself until I finally worked up enough guts to wash it.

With the arrival of summer, the work became more fun. As soon as the weather permitted, we took off our shirts and let ourselves be tanned by the sun. By carefully and slowly exposing myself to the sun, I managed to acquire a nice tan without ever getting burned. After my skin had become used to it, I could expose it to the sun all day, even on the hottest days, without putting on any cream. We were all in peak physical condition and could shovel, hoe, and dig all day without getting tired. To see this group of young men in gym trunks was a treat! The muscular, brown bodies were glistening in the sun. It really could be said of us that we were "hard as Krupp steel, tough as leather, and nimble as a greyhound." (This was Hitler's favorite saying when he talked about the German youth: *"Hart wie Kruppstahl, zah' wie Leder, und flink wie ein Windhund!"*) After the strength of the sun rays diminished in August, our suntans began to fade. Never again did I manage to get such a marvelous suntan.

After we were sworn in, it became easier to get permission to leave until we were finally permitted to spend all our free time outside the living quarters. Koniggratz was not a large city, twenty thousand inhabitants at the most, yet the city created a "metropolitan" impression. There was an old town and a new town. The old town was laid out like any German town since this region had at one time been part of Germany. In the new town everything was very modern—government buildings, modern high-rise apartment buildings, a railroad depot, parks, boulevards, etc. This kind of architecture I had seen in Germany only in large cities. There was also a residential section with modern elegant villas whose strange, unsymmetrical architecture caused us to chuckle and make fun of it.

We enjoyed taking walks through Koniggratz and the surrounding countryside. If we did not feel like walking, we only had to step into the building next to the gymnasium. There was a movie theater and also a restaurant. A few steps farther was an indoor swimming pool, and across the street we could have fun in rowboats on the Elbe River. Often we preferred just to stay in camp. Then we segregated in small groups and sang, talked, played cards, or everyone, but me, got drunk.

The food in camp was very good and plentiful, especially the cocoa, which we drank by the liter. Often we were in such a hurry to empty the jug in order to have it filled up with cocoa again that we burned our mouths and throats. The cook became famous for his saying, "The top brass get the sausage and butter, and the men get a good soup." (In German this sentence rhymes, after a fashion.) He said it in his south German dialect.

The camp orchestra was known all over town, and when our whole group marched through town singing, everybody enjoyed listening to us.

On a peaceful Sunday morning in July, we were awakened by a loud voice coming over the loudspeaker. It took me awhile before I knew what was going on. Then I recognized Goebbel's voice; slowly I began to grasp what he was saying. He tried to explain to the German people and the world how necessary it was for Germany to attack Russia at dawn on this day. Germany had previously made a friendship and nonaggression pact with Russia. Nobody seemed too surprised about the announcement. Political bombshells like that were common since January 30, 1933.

Then came the day of our dismissal. We had written home for our civilian clothes, and they were sent. The uniforms were turned in, and we were free men again. But the freedom was not to last long. On August 22, 1941, I arrived at home. Three or four days later, I received my orders for military service. The place I was to report to was a school building in Chemnitz on August 31, 1941.

The orders read that I was called to an SS division. My first thought was of the SS (Hitler's elite storm troops in black uniforms). After some inquiry I learned that SS stood for "*Schiffsstamm*" division. Then I was somewhat relieved, because it meant that I was called to serve in the German Navy. That I liked pretty well. Several hundred men were assembling in a large hall in Chemnitz. There was hardly one among them who didn't know someone from his service in the Labor Brigade, and groups began to form in the hall. Each time a new man entered the hall one group or another let out a yell of joy about seeing an old comrade from the Labor Brigade again.

Then we were loaded into a special train and moved to an unknown destination. Finally, we were let out in Stralsund and led into large barracks. This was the headquarters of the First SS Division. Rooms were assigned to us, and then they let us have a few days of leisure time. All day there was nothing to do but bum around, and yet we were not allowed to leave the barracks. The examinations and issuing of uniforms proceeded very slowly. We even had to pass a written exam.

Two weeks later, those who had been assigned to the Navy Coast Artillery were on the move again. First we went by train across the island of Rugen to Sassnitz. There we were put on a railroad ferry and taken to Tralleborg on the southernmost tip of Sweden. By train we went on through southern Sweden to Oslo, the capital of Norway. The trip through Sweden was interesting. We passed clean cities, idyllic villages, and a beautiful, ever-changing countryside. Now and again we saw groups of young men threatening us with their fists, but that didn't bother us too much. In the evening we were fascinated by the brightly illuminated cities. In Sweden they did not have nightly blackouts of the cities, as we had in Germany. To see a lighted city again after two years was a feast for our eyes.

In Oslo, we made a stop and were allowed to leave the train. In the cafe of the railroad station we (a few of my old buddies and I) ordered cake. It tasted terrible! They were using ammonia as a rising agent. We gulped it down anyway. Then we took a short walk into town. Later, the train proceeded to Kristiansand, which is situated on the southern tip of Norway. There we were loaded on buses and trucks that brought us to Flekkefjord.

I was fortunate to be assigned to a bus. But, at any rate, the trip was extremely frightening. We traveled on a treacherous road, up and down steep, rocky mountains. The hairpin curves were so narrow that oncoming traffic could not be seen, and passing was impossible. In spite of all that, the convoy was moving so fast that it was hair-raising. One open truck, carrying about twenty men, collided with a passenger car. Everyone on the truck was thrown out, hitting their heads against the rocks. Fortunately, the soldiers were all wearing their steel helmets, which prevented serious injuries or even deaths. Only one man sustained a serious knee injury. We didn't see him again until four weeks later. How relieved we all were when we boarded a train again in Flekkefjord! The countryside on this treacherous trip was truly beautiful. We went from one valley to the next, each one luscious green, clean, and well maintained.

From Flekkefjord, the train took us to Stavanger, and from there we went by boat to Haugesund. Military trucks took us to a nearby coastal battery. All in all, a few more than fifty new recruits had been assigned to this location. The training crew welcomed us with the customary remarks, intended to frighten us. But all of us had recently finished our duty with the Labor Brigade and were well acquainted with the tricks training crews used to intimidate newcomers. When the training started, they soon found out that we were not greenhorns. The only thing new to us was the gripping of rifles instead of spades. We survived the eight weeks of recruit training pretty well and were not tormented unnecessarily.

We all lived in barracks close to the ordnance emplacement and hardly had any contact with the regular battery personnel. On November 13, 1941, we took our oath. For this occasion, a large group of naval officers and a band came to our camp. A naval officer with the rank of major, by the name of Rohvetter, administered the oath.

During our training period we got to Haugesund only twice. We didn't miss very much, because it was only a very small town with nothing to do there. But any chance to go "on land" was naturally welcome to us.

Life on a rocky cliff, with nothing to see but the same old faces, can become monotonous. But I was fascinated to be so close to the sea. For hours I listened to the roaring and thundering of the waves. When the wind was blowing hard, the water was thrown so hard against the high, steep rocks that it sprayed high above them and sounded like thunder. We often climbed some of the rocks so we could sit by the sea.

Not far from the place where we often played, a huge rock protruded from the water about 100 to 150 meters from shore. We were often told how dangerous it was to swim out to that rock because the surf was so strong that one could not swim back to shore. I simply could not believe that. One sunny November day, I put on my swimming trunks, got into the frigid water, and swam out to the rock and back. The surf did not bother me nearly as much as the ice-cold water. I was so stiff that I could hardly pull myself out of the water. While I was still in the water, I could not even bring my fingers together. Alas, nobody was impressed by my heroic deed.

At the end of November, after our training was finished, the fifty men were distributed to different assignments. With a few others, I was assigned to the island of Kvitso. To get there, we first went by boat to Stavanger and then with another boat to Kvitso. From Stavanger, it took about two to three hours. Kvitso is a small island located at the entrance to the Fjord of Stavanger. A few hundred fishermen and their families lived on Kvitso in two small villages. The island is well known for its lobster fisheries.

On this island were situated four 21-cm cannons from the last century. They were supposed to protect the Fjord of Stavanger. Now I was one of those who were expected to take care of these pieces of ordnance. We all had the feeling that we had been exiled to this island, because we could not leave it under any circumstances. We explored the island in all directions. One Sunday afternoon, a buddy and I rowed clear around it. During the six months we were there, I only got to Stavanger once.

The work was not strenuous, and we had

PRESERVATION OF THE BRANCHES

CHURCH ARCHIVES

Citizens survey damaged buildings in Freiburg.

Many miracles occurred throughout the war to ensure that the members of the branches of the Church were preserved and allowed to continue in their meetings:

"Prior to the air raids on Hamburg, leaders of the Hamburg District called upon the local Saints to conduct clothing drives. Brother Berndt felt inspired to instruct the branches to bring all this clothing to the Altona Branch hall. . . . During these raids all the branch halls were destroyed with the exception of the Altona Branch where the clothing was stored, and the brethren were now in a position to help the Saints, most of whom had lost all their belongings, and return to them the clothing they had contributed."

"It was customary that during the meeting a member of the branch presidency would listen to the radio for information concerning any possible air raids. On a Sunday during sacrament meeting of the Altona Branch the branch president Herbert Baarz was listening to the radio and everything seemed to be in order. Brother Baarz felt inspired to tell the members to leave the meeting immediately and go to the shelter, a ten minute walk. The meeting was closed and members left. They had no sooner arrived at the shelter when Altona was attacked by American bombers, leveling the area close to the meeting hall."

"During the Nazi time we expected our branch to be closed, and the spreading of the gospel to be forbidden, as it was done to most sects, and a sect we were considered to be. During this time Friedrich was called to serve as branch president. The Gestapo started taking leaders of the various religious 'sects' in for interrogation, usually resulting in their being forbidden to continue any kind of meetings. Friedrich knew the Gestapo would be coming for him so he gathered his scriptures and church books together and noted every reference he could find showing that the church believed in honoring, obeying and sustaining the laws of the land and would not be a subversive influence. Sure enough, the Gestapo came for him. He took his books and scriptures and went with them. I do not know how long he was gone but it was worrisome. He succeeded in convincing the Gestapo that he and his branch of church members would not be a subversive group and they allowed him to continue to hold regular church meetings."

Source: *Regional Studies in Latter-day Saints Church History: Europe* (Brigham Young University, 2003).

plenty of free time. I had to learn to service the ordnance properly. The emplacement and living quarters had to be kept clean. Occasionally we had a training session, and sometimes we had a chance to see a movie for entertainment. Once in a great while they even sent a variety show to our island. That was a great pleasure for us.

All of us had to "stand guard" a lot. Naturally, I had to do my share of it. That meant standing guard for two hours and being free to rest four hours. That routine was repeated for twenty-four hours.

What really frightened me was to stand guard at the ammunition bunker during the night. The bunker was some distance from the emplacement, and I was out there all alone. During the night the wind would whistle through the rocks and the waves could be heard thundering against them. During the day it was beautiful out there, especially when the sky was clear and the ocean calm. The sea murmured softly, the blue sky reflected in the water, and the tiny waves glittered in the sun. Ships would slowly glide by. That's where I learned to love the sea.

Things were not always so peaceful. At one time, a sad feeling inspired me to write the following poem:

Ganz einsamfremd und unbekannt
Steh' ich infinst'rer Winter's Nacht
Im Norden tiefin Feindesland
Und haltefiir Gross Deutschland Wacht.

Es fehlen deutsche Wiesen, Felder
Nur Felsen stehen rings umher
Und statt der dunklen Nadelwalder
Erblickt mein Auge unendliches Meer.
Darauf ein Schifflein schwimmt 'gen Suden
Es fahrt der fernen Heimat zu
Ich ruf: Mein Deutschland sollst du grussen
Wo's fur mich Frieden gibt und Ruh'.
Der Ruf verhallt in Meeresbrausen
Und ich erinn 're mich meiner Pflicht
Doch einmal nimmt das Schiffda draussen
Auch mich an Bord—mehr will ich nicht.

This is a rough translation:

Unknown, strange, and lonely
I stand in the dark winter night.
Way in the North, in the land of our enemy.
Standing here to guard Great Germany.
Oh, how I miss German meadows and fields,
Only rocks stand all around me,
And instead of dark evergreen forests
My eyes only see the endless sea.
There a ship is floating southward,
Toward my beloved homeland it moves.
I call out, "To Germany take all my love,
Where my soul could find peace and rest."
The rushing waves swallow the sound.
I am reminded of my duty.
Someday, a ship out there
Will take me along—who could wish for more!

We could often observe the northern lights. On occasion, they were unbelievably beautiful. The roots of the bundles of rays shimmered in the lilac-bluish colors that turned to white the farther they reached out into the firmament. In waves, the light grew more and more intense. Very interestingly, in summer, the nights remained as bright as the days. Around midnight there was a short period of twilight before the sun rose again out of the sea. On the other hand, during the winter months we only had a few hours of daylight.

In spring, we noticed the many, many seagulls that had their nests in the rocks. Their constant shrieking sometimes made it hard to sleep. As a reward for us, we would gather their speckled eggs.

In the village they had a few milk cows. What sad looking creatures they were! Only bones held together by skin. They were kept alive by some food that looked like paper. The sheep didn't fare much better. Summer and winter they had to scrounge for their food. As soon as the weather permitted us to peel our potatoes outdoors, the sheep literally snatched the peelings from our potato peelers. We gave them many a good morsel.

As already mentioned, we did not have to

endure too many hardships on that island but, nevertheless, almost every soldier dreamed about leaving it. This dream was fulfilled for me and another fellow in June 1942.

That spring, there had been a notice on the bulletin board that the navy was looking for men who could be trained as artillery mechanics. Two of us volunteered. We were both metal workers and had studied a few semesters at a school of engineering. I had completely forgotten about that application when one day Fritz Weinhold and I received the order to report to Wesel on the lower Rhine River to be trained as mechanics. Naturally we were delighted. We could go back to Germany and civilization!

On a beautiful day in June 1942, we said good-bye to Kvitso. With the marching order in our pockets, we started our journey. Again we traveled for a while through Sweden. But this time we also went through Denmark and crossed the Big and Little Belt on a railroad ferry. What impressed me as tragic was that on the Swedish side the shore was brightly illuminated and on the Danish side it was pitch dark. For a long time I stared at brightly lit Sweden while we traveled deeper and deeper into the darkness. That's when I fervently wished for peace.

The soldiers who were going home on furlough from Norway were loaded like pack mules. They almost broke down while they were changing trains. Besides their customary luggage, some had a barrel of herring on their backs and another barrel in each hand. Some of the barrels were leaking, which created a terrible stench.

Full of hope, the two of us—Fritz Weinhold from Chemnitz and I—reached Wesel on the lower Rhine River. At the depot we asked where the barracks were, and they sent us into town. From there we were directed to other barracks close to the railroad station. That same evening we went out on the town. That was my first real evening out since being in the Navy.

A few days later, all candidates for the course of instruction were assembled, approximately two hundred men. We all received blue Navy uniforms, were divided into groups, and assigned to our quarters. Then the course began. The classrooms were in the barracks in town. Four times daily we had to walk the distance between the two barracks, a half hour each way. School was easy for me. I hardly had to pay attention, and then only when the various pieces of ordnance were discussed that I had not yet seen. At the end of the course, I knew as much as I had known at the beginning.

Every day we had permission to go into town. The various duties, from drill to peeling potatoes, were easy. We also had enough to eat. War was raging far away in Russia and Africa, high up in the air, and on the oceans. Already at that time I had my doubts that we could win this war.

—•—

By the end of October, the course was finished and we were assigned to various detachments. To my surprise, I was sent to a FLAK battery (anti-aircraft site) in Kiel. Since I was traveling alone, I first took a little side trip to Berlin. My sister Erika was serving in the Berlin LDS mission office, and I had not seen her for many years. By coincidence my brother-in-law, Alfred Neumann, was visiting the mission office at the same time, and we had a good time together in Berlin. We spent the night in the subway traveling back and forth. At that time, I also met Irmgard Gottschalk, who made a great impression on me.

Then I proceeded to Kiel where I had been assigned as a FLAK battery mechanic. The people in the military office noticed that I had taken more time than necessary to get there. The next thing I did in Kiel was to request a furlough, which was promptly granted. On November 11, 1942, I was on my way home. Unfortunately, the two weeks passed much too fast. During the few weeks I spent in Kiel, we had very few air raid alarms. I cannot remember that anti-aircraft guns were shooting even once.

After finding out the address of an LDS branch in Kiel, I started out one Sunday to go to church. I had to walk a long time before I reached the place, only to find a sign on the door that read "Closed for remodeling." That was the only time I had a chance to go to church as a soldier.

A few days later, I was ordered to Swinemunde. Again I made a long trip out of a short hop by taking a side trip to Hamburg, where Aunt Frida was living, and also to Berlin to the mission office. In Hamburg, I saw for the first time what bombs could do. Whole sections of the city were actually leveled to the ground.

In Swinemunde, for one reason or another, my superiors did not like me. It came to a head one day when I passed the sergeant and the commanding officer, while riding a bike, without saluting them. The bad thing was that they had saluted, expecting me to return the salute at the same time. However, I had not even recognized them. A few days later, I was on my way to Russia.

In Swinemunde, it had been boring. Mostly, I had to stand guard. I never got close to one of the large guns where the officer candidates were being trained. Before I was shipped to Russia, I spent a few days in the military hospital. There I could follow on the radio the news about the tragedy of Stalingrad. My orders were to go to Ust-Luga, on the Gulf of Finland. I went through Berlin again. This time it was really hard for me to say goodbye. When the train that was to take me to Russia rolled into the Berlin station, I felt like turning around and running. Finally, I took courage and got on the train.

It took days before I reached my destination. By then it was the end of February 1943. I had a hard time finding someone to direct me to the unit to which I was assigned. During the trip, the soldiers had made fun of me about the clothes hangers that I had fastened to my backpack. "You won't need those in Russia," they had said. Later I understood why. Our shelter was an earth bunker. But it was quite comfortable and homelike there, especially in the evening when we were toasting our slices of bread on the iron stove. The winter did not last much longer, and spring brought wooden barracks, beds, lockers, tables, chairs, china dishes, etc. Soon our emplacement was furnished very nicely. We were located directly at the mouth of the Luga River where it flowed into the Gulf of Finland, about 120 kilometers west of Leningrad (now St. Petersburg). During the summer months, we went swimming several times a day. The water was very warm. I also went sailing twice.

The emplacement consisted of four 10.5 cm Russian cannons. As an artillery mechanic I had a pretty good position. A few times I even was sent to neighboring emplacements to repair weapons. Fortunately, everything turned out well each time.

Like every place else in the navy, I stood my ground as far as the Word of Wisdom was concerned. This often meant alienating some of my fellow soldiers, and even my superiors. On one occasion I was ready to give in just a little bit. A high-ranking navy officer paid our unit a visit. Later in the afternoon he wanted to socialize with the garrison for a little while. On these occasions I was often asked to play the accordion. Since I was sitting right close to the officer, he turned toward me, indicating to clink glasses with me. One of our officers handed me a glass. "I wonder what is in it?" I was thinking as I put the glass to my lips. In order to not embarrass the VIP or my company officers I was ready to drink a swallow. It was only water. This proved to me that they respected my beliefs after all.

A few kilometers from our base, a raised wooden platform had been built in the midst of some planted fields. The Russian young people from the surrounding villages met there to have some fun and dance. The platform could hold twenty or more couples. Even the German soldiers liked to go there to dance with the Russian girls.

One Saturday evening I went with some of my buddies to the platform. It did not take long

RUTH BIRTH FILE

A German soldier receives full military honors at burial.

before they asked me to play some German music they could dance to on the accordion a Russian teenager was playing. The boy turned the accordion over to me and I began playing. The Germans enjoyed dancing to my music and encouraged me to keep playing. Then a young pretty Russian girl came over to me and whispered in my ear, in perfect German, "If you don't return the accordion right now the boys here will kill you." I stopped mid-song and immediately gave the instrument back to the Russian musician. Thus ended my first and only visit to this place.

—•—

Since we were quite far north, the nights during summer never were completely dark. The northern lights were visible but not as beautiful as in Norway. Almost daily we could witness a fata morgana. To the north of us, in the Gulf of Finland, were two islands that belonged to Russia and were occupied by Russians. Using a telescope we could see these islands, with the buildings on them, reflected upside-down in the water. Again and again I was drawn to the telescope to observe this strange phenomenon.

The mosquitoes bothered us a lot, so during the night, while standing guard, we had to wrap ourselves up like it was wintertime. But, even though we had a mosquito net over our heads and all our bare skin was covered, the mosquitoes still found some openings to get to our blood.

I slept with two other mechanics in a room. At night we did not go to bed unless we had closed the door and windows tight and had conducted a mosquito hunt. Otherwise, I considered this assignment as if it had been a vacation spa. Yet, I was delighted when I was told that at the end of July I would get a three-week furlough, and after my return I should go again to Wesel to participate in a mechanic petty officer's training course. This was good news to me. So, I started my journey home.

I began to enjoy traveling. Overcrowded trains and vagabonding around didn't bother me at all. In Berlin, I barely had enough time for a short visit in the mission office, about which I'll report elsewhere. I hardly have any recollection of the time I spent at home. Liane Richter, whom I had been dating before leaving Zwickau, had jilted me some months before, giving me an indescribable feeling of freedom. I enjoyed my furlough immensely.

The trip back went well with the exception of the fact that somehow I had been infected with scabies. Shortly after my arrival in Ust-Luga, I was sent to the field hospital, where I had to stay a few days. After my release from the hospital, I had to get ready for my trip to Wesel. During the last night before my departure, shooting started at the neighboring emplacement. A few Russian boats had tried to land. I thought it was high time for me to scram. A few months later, I learned that not long after I had left the whole front was overrun by the Russians.

Well, I was on my way to Wesel again. I had them write into my orders that I had permission to stay a few days in Berlin. The trains were overcrowded again. Once, during the trip an SS sergeant was sitting opposite me. From time to time, he put his hand to the back of his neck and pulled out a worm. Finally he was fed up and demanded that the suitcase above him in the luggage rack be opened. And what did we see? In the suitcase was an untanned sheepskin, crawling with thousands of small worms.

When I arrived in the mission office, Erika disclosed the sad news that my brother, Heinz, had been killed in Ssokolowo, Russia. That reminded me of a dream I had during the trip. Alone in a train compartment, I had fallen asleep in the middle of the day. I can no longer recall the details, but I was aware that Heinz had lost his life. I could trace back the day and hour of that dream and found that it coincided with the day and hour of his death. My mother had a similar experience; at that same hour she heard him call, "Mother!" I immediately inquired at the commandant's office in Berlin whether I could get permission to go home for a few days. My request was denied, and I stayed in Berlin for five days.

At the beginning of September 1943, I reached old familiar Wesel. This time I knew exactly where to go. How happy I was when I saw Fritz Weinhold and many other acquaintances again. This time our group was only a third as large as it had been the previous time. School was fun, duty was not bad, and every night we could go into town. Only the air raid alarms had increased significantly. There was hardly a night when we did not have to run down to the cellar at least once or twice. In the morning I often could no longer remember how I had gotten down or back up again. But since Wesel was never really bombed, it did not bother me too much.

At one time, all the apprentice groups participated in a singing competition. Our leader practiced two snappy sailor songs with us. (He knew what the judges would like best.) While the other groups were presenting their songs during the competition, I lost all hope that we had a chance to win. They were singing "schmaltzy" songs in perfect harmony and very artistically. I could not believe my ears when it was announced that we were the winners. Now I can say that I once won a singing competition, even though I only played the accordion.

During the first part of December 1943, my request for a weekend pass to go to Zwickau was granted. Because of the long trip, I did not have much time to spend at home, and the many delays of trains caused by the bombing made things very difficult.

To this day I have vivid memories of hearing over the radio at home for hours and hours that a very important announcement of serious consequences was forthcoming. Finally we were informed that the Japanese Air Force had bombed Pearl Harbor and that the American fleet had suffered great losses. They also said that, with this development, the war had entered a new phase and that from then on Japan and Germany would combine their forces. Only recently did it come to my attention that this could not have been Pearl Harbor, and what it was all about I could not find out. The whole thing could have just been propaganda.

In March 1944, our training course was finished. The next step toward becoming a *mechanic maat* (machinist's mate) in the navy was an eight-week training program for infantry petty officers in Eckernforde. Our group was sent there, where things were a little livelier. We had to drill a lot and crawl around in the terrain. That did not bother me. I was always happy when it was my turn to stand guard in the harbor. The harbor was teeming with fishing boats. I enjoyed watching what was going on. During the night I was fascinated by the phosphorescent, flashing, and splashing waves. I could look at the water for hours. If there was an air raid alarm, the whole countryside would be "fogged in" by huge smoke generators. We could hear the allied airplanes coming and going, devastating German cities.

In May 1944, this phase of our training was over and all of us, with few exceptions, could sew the gold stripes of a petty officer onto our shoulder straps. Our group was sent to the transit camp Neustrelitz. That meant a marching order to the south. Could it be Africa? Fritz Weinhold was with me in the group. It took longer than a week before fifteen mechanic petty officers received their orders to go to Athens, Greece. We had only one common traveling order for the whole group. It stated that we had to travel to Vienna and that we could not ride on express trains. That pleased us all very much. So, we started our journey. Our first stop was Berlin.

In Berlin we joined a troop transport headed for Munich. But on the way we decided that would be too fast for us. Some of us hailed from Leipzig and the surrounding countryside, and we wanted to make a stop there, so we made the following plan: As soon as the train would stop in Halle, we would get off and hide behind pillars until the train left.

The train pulled into the station in Halle. Before it even came to a stop we heard over the loudspeaker that on a specific track a train to Leipzig was ready for departure. Immediately we spread the word among our group that we all were going to try to catch that train. Quickly we ran down the stairs, through the tunnel, and up the other stairs just as the train started pulling out. While it was slowly moving and picking up speed, we all jumped on. Only then did we notice that an officer of the troop transport had been running after us, shouting for us to stop. He had stopped and was standing on the platform looking at us with his eyes wide open. Everyone had made it! We had lucked out!

In the Central Station in Leipzig we had another conference. At least half of us were from Saxony and wanted to make a short visit home. Because we had only one order and ticket for the whole group, that was not so simple. So, we decided that each would travel wherever he wanted to go, at his own risk, and two days later, we would meet again on a certain train to continue our travel. I took the risk to go to Zwickau. The trip took three to four hours, and during all that time I was constantly afraid that a ticket inspector would come through the compartment. Fortunately, no inspector showed up.

When the train reached the Central Station in Zwickau, I got off. However, I could not go through the exit gate because, first, I had no ticket; second, I had no military order; and, third, the exit gates were all guarded by the military. So I waited in the station for a train that would go to Zwickau-Polbitz. There the exit gates were not guarded and, besides, I could have bought a ticket for that short stretch in Polbitz. But I had to wait for hours before a train would go to Polbitz.

Suddenly, I noticed an open gate on the side of the station and it led directly out on the street. Quickly I got up enough courage, jumped across a few tracks, sneaked through the gate out onto the street, into a streetcar, and I was gone. No one had seen me. At home, everyone was naturally quite surprised to see me show up so unexpectedly. I spent one and a half wonderful days at home and with Inge.

When I had to leave again, I bought a ticket to Reichenbach, and for the previously mentioned reasons, boarded the tram in Zwickau-Polbitz. Everything went smoothly. When I arrived in Reichenbach, the previously designated train was standing there, and my buddies were waving to me. I was the last one to rejoin the group; all had gone well. My buddies had been worried about me because they had expected me to join them in Werdau. Peacefully, we continued on to Vienna. We traveled during the day and spent the nights in various lodgings. In Nuremberg we stopped over for a little longer time, since this was the hometown of one man in our group. In Passau we visited the famous cathedral. We also made a stopover in Salzburg, Austria.

I don't remember how many days later we finally arrived in Vienna. There, we had to wait a few days in a transit camp, which was fine with us. We used the time well to see the sights of Vienna, which made a great impression on me. I even rode around on the giant ferris wheel in the "Prater." In one of the huge churches, I attended an organ and violin concert. The high apartment buildings, with their ornamental facades, looked to me like castles. Finally, the transport going to Greece was assembled. It took quite some time before we reached Athens.

There, I was again put in a transit camp, and a few days later I was assigned to a unit. This was a completely new experience for me. It was a FLAK unit, stationed directly in the harbor of Piraus. Our unit was servicing the large weapons on transport ships that were bringing replacements to the islands in the Mediterranean. All transport ships were small Greek vessels that were equipped and manned by us. It was my task to supervise the installing and mounting of the ordnance. Fortunately, I never had to go out to sea. Sometimes ship and crew returned safely, sometimes only the crew returned, and sometimes members of the crew were missing. For me, the bombs that the British dropped on the harbor were sufficient.

Now and then I had to lead a street patrol during the night. We had to see to it that nobody was out walking the streets and that the rules of blackout were strictly obeyed. Once we passed a house in which one single light bulb was lighted and the window was not properly blacked out. I ordered one of the men to knock on the door. When no one answered, I gave the order to shoot out the light bulb. To my great relief the man hit the bulb with the first shot. Very satisfied, we continued our patrol.

Since we were in a malaria-prone region, we had to take Atebrin daily. This is a medication that protects against malaria. However, it was not that simple with "Papadatschie Fever." This disease is spread by a fly of the same name, and everyone could count on coming down with the disease within three months. It hit me exactly at that time. Besides having a high fever, one is also very sick to the stomach and has to vomit. It usually lasted about five days.

In Athens I did not have close contact with my buddies in the group. I did not participate in the drinking bouts with the petty officers and commissioned officers. My friend Fritz Weinhold was in the same division but belonged to a different FLAK unit.

Greece made a very deep impression on me. Here I felt like I really was in a strange country. I could never see enough of the tropical environment that man and nature had created there. It was hard for me to understand that a khaki uniform, when washed, could dry within an hour. I could not comprehend how the juicy fruit being sold in the marketplaces could have grown and ripened in that hot and dry climate. Again and again I was astonished that marble palaces and beggars' hovels could stand side by side. I enjoyed wandering through Athens and Piraus. Of course, I was especially interested in the ancient ruins. The Acropolis stood on a hill in the center of town. The outdoor movie theaters, some of which were on flat roofs of buildings, were new to me. The shoe-shine boys who wanted to earn a few coins from the soldiers were a bother to us. It was fun to swim in the Mediterranean, but the water was warmer than necessary.

But my stay in Greece was not to last very long. In September 1944, German troops began their retreat from Greece. At the beginning of October the large passenger ship *Zeus* made her last trip from Athens to Thessaloniki. I was on it. The trip took about fifteen hours. Fifteen long hours exposed to enemy mines, submarines, destroyers, and planes. Fortunately all went well. During the night we could observe a sea battle raging in the distance.

In Thessaloniki we were distributed to various lodgings and waited to see what would happen next. There I came down again with Papadatschie Fever. I felt miserable, while the others could enjoy the good food. A few days later it was our turn to go to a transit camp where all men from the army, air force, and navy were assigned to marching columns to start their long trek home, on foot!

The same evening I heard that fifteen specialists from the navy were to be ordered as escorts for an evacuation train for the wounded, bound for Berlin. I learned that my friend Fritz Weinhold and I were among them. Very late in the evening I finally found a little space on the floor where I could lie down. It was then that my whole career in the navy passed before my eyes and it became clear to me that my Heavenly Father had always protected and guided me so that I never had been directly involved in the battles of the war. During my service in the Labor Brigade I had been far away from the danger zone. In Norway I was completely untouched by the war. I had been transported through neutral Sweden instead of through the Skagerrak, where many transport ships were sunk. Even though Wesel was close to the Ruhr region, the town was never attacked from the air. And, as I had been told, Kiel never had as few air attacks as during the time I spent there.

In Swinemunde the war was not noticeable. In Russia things became risky only after I left. The people who were in the mechanic petty officers' training course following mine were ordered into battle against American troops in the west. Except for hearing the humming of the American air squadrons passing over us, I had not noticed anything of the war while in Eckernforde. Just a few days earlier my ship transport had landed without being attacked by the enemy, even though many ships had been sunk before on the same route. And now I had been selected to get back to Germany by such comfortable means!

While I was pouring out my heart in a prayer of gratitude and thanksgiving, I suddenly saw gruesome, grotesque faces approaching me. They looked as if they were made of thick strands of wool. After coming directly in front of me they vanished into thin air. But more and more multitudes of them appeared from nowhere, rushing toward me. I was wide awake. Opening or closing my eyes did not change anything in the gruesome apparition. These ugly, terrifying faces were grinning and looking at me as if to say that from now on the wind would blow from a different direction.

The next morning fifteen very confident specialists of the German Navy started toward the designated place where they were supposed to board the evacuation train that very same day. Anxious not to miss the train, we camped long days and nights next to the railroad tracks. Finally the train pulled in, but to our consternation we were told that this was the "end of the line." The railroad tracks ahead had been destroyed by the enemy. There we sat dumbfounded, with our marching orders in our pockets. After a short deliberation, we decided to find a way to Berlin on our own.

Soon we discovered a munitions supply train going in the approximate direction we wanted to go. I don't remember how much time we spent on that train sitting on boxes of ammunition. It must have been a week or longer. Often we were disconnected from one train and joined to

While I was pouring out my heart in a prayer of gratitude and thanksgiving, I suddenly saw gruesome, grotesque faces approaching me. They looked as if they were made of thick strands of wool. After coming directly in front of me they vanished into thin air. But more and more multitudes of them appeared from nowhere, rushing toward me. I was wide awake. Opening or closing my eyes did not change anything in the gruesome apparition. These ugly, terrifying faces were grinning and looking at me as if to say that from now on the wind would blow from a different direction.

another one. Then we stood for hours in one spot before moving on for a few miles. Fortunately, the Partisans (Marshal Tito's communist Yugoslavian resistance fighters) did not attack us. During the night we helped guard the locomotives. Once, while again standing still for a long time, we heard that not far away there was a completely evacuated village. Immediately, I joined others to investigate. Sure enough, we found a village utterly deserted. Neither man nor mouse was there. The huts were completely furnished, with sausage and meat in the cupboards, cheese and dried fruit in the pantry, etc. Furniture and dishes were all intact. The inhabitants had fled with the Partisans into the mountains, from where they made their treacherous attacks on the retreating columns. Everyone who found something to eat took it along because our provisions were very meager. While looking for something edible, Fritz Weinhold and I came to a field of corn. As much as we looked, we could not find any cobs of corn. We even pulled some stalks out of the ground, thinking that the corn might possibly be in the ground, as is the case with carrots. We had given up our search when we met a soldier who showed us how the cobs are hidden in the leaves.

After many long days and nights, we finally reached the town of Kraljevo, Yugoslavia. We were told that the Russians were only three miles from the town, and then we heard the thunder of cannons. The train would definitely not move farther. We found shelter in the storeroom of the airport at the edge of town. Bombs and explosives were stored there very close to each other. They were to be detonated before the troops left the place so that everything would be destroyed. We hardly had settled down when a few grenades hit nearby. Never since have I gotten under a table as fast as I did then. The others also quickly found cover wherever they could. Fortunately, none of the explosives were hit. In spite of this scare we spent the rest of that night on top of that powder keg.

The next morning we marched into town. We hardly had arrived there when we were greeted by an infantry officer. He was not too impressed by our marching orders; he gave us an order to look for quarters and then to report to him. He wanted us to go to the front, and mentioned that a whole submarine crew was fighting there, and that some of the brave sailors had already died a hero's death. We replied, "Yes, sir!" and left, very dejected.

After walking around for a while, we saw an infantry transport detachment with their trucks camped at the outskirts of town. We asked them if they could use a few more men, and we were hired on the spot. (That's how we escaped being sent to the front.) That was a real break. They fed us, and we did not need to do too much. Some of us had to assist, occasionally, in transporting supplies to the front, now and then a plane flew low over the town firing machine guns.

Exactly one week after our arrival in Kraljevo, on a Sunday, a large convoy of air force trucks pulled into town. Soon we learned that they were to be loaded on a train with the destination GERMANY! That was exactly where we wanted to go! Secretly, we packed our belongings and sneaked to the loading dock. Sure enough, there they were, with most of the vehicles anchored securely to flatbed railroad cars. Without being seen by anyone, we found a truck that was covered with tarpaulin already fastened to a railroad car. After getting into it, we waited impatiently for the train to pull out. Finally it started rolling. We had not been detected! We all could see ourselves arriving in Berlin very soon.

For about fifteen hours we had rolled along very slowly, when the train stopped. Peeking out, we saw military police taking other "blind passengers" off the train. My impulse was to stay on and hide from the police, but our leader and others thought it prudent to leave the train. Not until two months later, after I had reached home, did I realize how wise this decision (which I at the time considered to be stupid) had been. The troops that had continued on that train, traveling through Albania, were literally chased to death like wild animals. Only very few survived. I heard a report about their horrible fate at the hands of our enemy over the radio. It still makes me shudder when I think what would have happened to me if I had not left that train with the others.

We found ourselves in the railroad station of Mitrovica, Yugoslavia, and were led to a place where thousands of soldiers were camped outdoors. Two or three days later I marched at the head of a column of approximately 250 men with a machine gun on my back. By now it was November, and those of us who had come from Greece had no warm clothing. I had stopped shaving, and the bristles of my beard grew longer and longer. We marched about twenty-five miles each day. During the nights we slept on the frozen ground. The countryside through which we marched was beautiful. I still remember seeing the veiled women as we marched through Novi Pazar, a picturesque small town with an oriental touch.

Our column had marched approximately one hundred miles when we reached the Mileseva monastery, close to Prijepolje, located high in the mountains. It was now being used as a military hospital and army officers' headquarters. There we were detained and ordered to relieve an air force marching column that was covering the retreat route. We were supposed to do that for three days and then be relieved by another marching column coming through later. But those three days were to stretch out into six long, hard weeks.

We climbed up into the mountains and took over the emplacements of our predecessors. We moved into their scanty shelters made of branches and foliage. Fritz Weinhold and I found a small lean-to, barely large enough for two men to stretch out in. Since we believed that our stay would only last three days, we did not bother to improve anything in our miserable shelter. But when more than a week later the promised relief had not arrived, we gathered more branches and straw to make our shelter more livable and weatherproof. No matter what we improvised, we always were wet to our skin when it rained or snowed. Every morning we were all crumpled when we crawled out of our hole. Food was always scarce, but we somehow kept alive with the provisions that the peasants gave us voluntarily, or sometimes not so voluntarily.

One morning, we found a chicken—plucked, cleaned, drawn, and ready to roast—hanging on our shelter. Since we assumed that it belonged to someone else, we left it alone. When it was still there the next day and nobody had claimed ownership after we had inquired around, we decided to take care of the poor chicken before it spoiled. In the afternoon the chicken was put in a pot together with a few stolen potatoes. We hung the pot over a little fire that we had started laboriously with a few wet twigs. Just as our fire started burning, we heard wild shooting from the neighboring strongpoint just above us. A few minutes later a soldier came running and told us that their strongpoint had been overrun and that he probably was the only survivor.

Immediately our whole camp was put on alert and a squad was sent up into the mountain to see what was going on. My friend Fritz Weinhold and I were in that squad. We were indeed sad when we had to leave our chicken in the pot with the fire still going, but we had to march off. When we reached the place of attack (I was at the head of the group with a machine gun in hand) we found out that everything was okay. The Partisans had merely stolen a machine gun and retreated. There weren't even any wounded. When we returned to our camp, we ran quickly to our shelter to see what had become of our feast. To our pleasant surprise, we found that the potatoes were cooked into a delicious mash, and the chicken was tender and tasty, ready to eat. If that "attack" had not interfered, we probably would have wolfed down the potatoes half-raw with the chicken only half-done and tough, because our empty stomachs would not have allowed us to wait until everything was well done.

—•—

On another occasion, I was standing guard

all alone at an advanced position during the night. Suddenly, a grenade exploded nearby. Quickly, I pointed my machine gun in the direction of the detonation and fired. The lock of the gun only clicked, but no shot was fired. Then I drew the cock again and fired a few salvos through the calm of the night, and the whole camp was put on alert. For the rest of that night the guards were reinforced.

The next morning a patrol was sent out to investigate the reason for the detonation. We found that one of the land mines we had installed had apparently been detonated by an animal during the night. Suddenly someone yelled, "Cover!" I threw myself to the ground and BANG!—another mine exploded. One of us had accidentally detonated it. The only casualty was one of the men who got a splinter in his buttock. I had to help transport him on a stretcher to the monastery. That was quite a climb up and down the hills.

Occasionally, I went down to the monastery. Sometimes when I could see that I would not be able to reach our strongpoint during daylight, I simply found a little corner in one of the buildings of the monastery and spent the night there. On one such occasion, I came dangerously close to patients suffering from typhus. Once I also experienced an air-raid alarm there. In no time, the place was deserted because of a few low-flying planes, and I could see no reason to take cover. Since it was mealtime, I could help myself to a meal from the field kitchen without being seen by anyone, because the crew, officers, and cooks had all scrambled to safety.

After about four weeks, we were ordered to go to another higher mountain stronghold. There we first cut down a few trees to reinforce the position with logs. A few shelters were standing there. In the meantime December had arrived, and it became colder and colder, and more and more snow fell. My shoes were in shreds. While standing guard, I could only avoid freezing my toes by moving them constantly.

To my great relief we were ordered to abandon that particular strongpoint. I was only too glad to obey that order, because I felt it was too risky up there anyway. The next few days we spent in the vicinity of the monastery doing nothing. At that time I found out the reason for the unbearable prickling and itching all over my body. Often I would undress completely, even in the severest cold, to shake what I thought to be straw out of my underwear and clothing. As soon as I was dressed again, the itching and prickling continued. Finally I found out that my clothes were full of lice! A doctor gave me a written order to go to the field hospital to be deloused, which helped.

Finally, in the middle of December, we continued our march. Somehow Fritz had procured a pair of boots for me. Unfortunately, only one of them fit, so I went on my way wearing one boot and one old, worn-out shoe. I was also able to get rid of my machine gun and got a rifle instead, which was not as heavy. Again we marched all day long and camped at night.

A few days later we reached a village close to Visegrad, Yugoslavia. There we made a stop, and those of us who had foot trouble were separated from the others. At my request I became one of the group who had foot problems. We were transported by train the few kilometers to Visegrad, where we were left to our own devices. Here I have to add that previously I had found out that the leader of our marching column could issue written orders stating that the bearer had foot problems and should be given all possible help in moving forward. I had requested and received one of those orders.

The first thing after arriving in Visegrad was to start looking for food and a way to move on. But there was no prospect for either. Toward evening I came to the railroad station. As luck would have it, they were just unloading a railroad car full of bread. I offered my help and it was accepted. As a reward I received a few bread crusts and a dish of soup. Then I started walking all by myself along the road. At the outskirts of town I saw a number of field kitchens dispensing food. After a long wait in line I received my share and continued walking.

MAX BOETTCHER FILE

German POWS at work in Italy.

In the meantime darkness had descended. At first the road had been quite crowded. Every now and then I was stopped by military police. After seeing my written order saying that I had foot problems they let me pass. The later it got, the fewer people were on the road. I walked long stretches without meeting a living soul. Occasionally I overtook a marching column that had to go slower because they were moving along with pack mules. The road I was taking was a mountain pass. It became colder the higher I got. At the top of the pass I met a guard and chatted with him for a while. Then I continued my way downhill. I fully expected to run into Partisans at any moment.

I really must have been a sight! Just imagine: My disheveled beard was crusted with ice. Over my head I had pulled a lady's stocking to keep my ears warm. On the top of my head I wore a filthy field service cap. For a shawl worn over my gray leather jacket, I had another lady's stocking. (Where these stockings had come from, I can no longer recall.) For gloves I had two socks. On one foot I wore a boot and on the other a shoe. All my possessions, consisting of a few toilet articles and a few pieces of underwear, were in a haversack. I carried my rifle upside down, like a stick over my shoulder. The haversack and a cooking pot were dangling from it.

In such a get-up I walked along the road all by myself until dawn. Then I chanced upon a truck that the driver could not get moving. He had built a fire under the motor to warm it up, and after a while the motor did start. The driver gladly took me along. So, I traveled the whole day "luxuriously" in the back of a truck, covered with a tarpaulin. After dark we were stopped by military police. I had to get out, and the truck continued in a different direction. With a few other soldiers I had to wait in a guard bunker for a vehicle that was to bring us to Sarajevo, Yugoslavia.

The next few days, until Christmas Eve, I spent in overcrowded barracks in Sarajevo. We were literally lying on top of each other on the floor. The sanitary conditions were indescribable. In order to get to the latrine, we had to wade through human excrement. Thousands of soldiers had to endure these horrible conditions in that complex. On Christmas Eve I was transferred with 175 other men to another camp. The marching column to which I belonged had not yet arrived in Sarajevo. Since I did not belong to any unit at this time, I was assigned to this group to become part of an emergency squad. Before we started our march we each received some sweets as a Christmas bonus. Then we marched off to the train depot. It was bitter cold and it had started to snow.

Our destination was about eighteen miles away, and we had to travel in open boxcars. It was very cold. Around midnight we were packed into the village schoolhouse. Again we were so crowded that we had to almost lie on top of each other. After I found a little spot and everything had quieted down, my thoughts wandered back in time to my home, and I remembered the many wonderful times when we celebrated Christmas. But I thought, "Even if things don't look too rosy now, I still can find reasons to be grateful." At least now I had a roof over my head and was not cold. Finally, I dropped off to sleep.

When I woke up it was Christmas morning. That was when in years past we always received our wonderful Christmas surprises. Even on this morning I was not without a surprise; it was in my pants. As quickly as I could, I carefully crawled over the other soldiers and went outside. Behind the schoolhouse I found a little brook that was almost frozen over. There I undressed, cleaned myself, and threw the old long johns away. I still had another pair in reserve.

Our food on this Christmas day was plentiful. We could eat as much stew as we wanted. In the afternoon we all had to line up. The first question asked was, "Who in this group belongs to the navy?" I stepped forward with a few others. "All navy personnel go back to where you came from!" was the next order. The same afternoon we were transported back. What became of the others who were not navy, I never found out.

After our arrival back in the barracks in Sarajevo, I was notified that my marching column had arrived. At least I finally belonged to a unit again. It was December 27, a day I will never forget, as it happened to be my sister Erika's birthday. On that very same day our group was assembled to be transported back to Germany and I was among them! The only bad part about the whole thing was that the railroad car into which I was loaded had only wooded slats as side walls. As well as we could, we stuffed the openings with tent canvas and anything else available to be somewhat protected from the draft. Most of the time I managed to sit near the fire we had started in the middle of that cattle car. The side of my body close to the fire was roasting, and the other side was ice cold.

During one of the many stops, I met a soldier who was beside himself with grief because his rifle had been stolen. I gave him mine, and from that day to the end of the war I had no weapon. When I slept again close to the fire one night, I woke up in the morning with another "surprise" in my pants. At the next stop I got off the train and said farewell to my last pair of underpants. By now I was sick and tired of the horribly cramped conditions in the packed railroad cars. On December 31, 1944, I vowed that I would not spend New Year's Eve in that railroad car.

When the train stopped in a small town in Croatia (we never traveled during the night because the Partisans preferred to attack trains during the darkness, or they would blow up the track) I went with two others (as I recall, Fritz Weinhold was one of them) to the local commandant's office and asked for lodging for the night. Since there was none available, they invited us to stay right there in the office. We gladly accepted their kind offer. I was sick and really felt rotten. A few sips of cognac and a few glasses of hot tea with rum revived me. I never considered this drink to be against the Word of Wisdom. In the condition I was in, the alcohol did me a lot of good.

At the hour of midnight all the officers were called to assemble in one office. Among them were many high military officers. We three unkempt and filthy soldiers certainly were not fit for their company. But they all, without exception, were very friendly and cordial toward us. They were very glad to see how much better off they were compared to us common soldiers. At the stroke of midnight, a speech by Adolf Hitler was broadcast over the radio. I believe it was his last one. "Vienna will always be Vienna!" he shouted out into the world. (Five months later, the "Thousand-Year Reich" ended, about nine hundred and eighty-seven years ahead of schedule.)

After the speech we were given permission to spend the rest of the night in one of the offices, where we bedded down on the floor. How heavenly that was! For once we could stretch out our legs and turn around without bumping into someone. In order to be able to wash up well we had intended to get up bright and early the next morning. But, being so tired, we overslept. When we woke up it was daylight. Quickly we packed our bundles, thanked the people for their hospitality, and raced toward the railroad station. The train was just pulling out but we managed to get on.

In Zagreb, Croatia, we changed trains. (Little did I realize at that time that I would spend more than two years there as a prisoner of war.) Since we had a layover there, I shaved off my beard. Everybody, civilians and soldiers, had been gawking at me, and I had enough of that. Then we traveled a few more hours to Cilli, in northern Croatia, where we were deloused, had a bath, got a haircut, had a medical examination, and got a completely new set of clothing. I felt like a human being again! It was great. I even looked so different that my old comrades did not recognize me. Everyone had thought I was an old man. After the cleansing I looked much younger, like a young man who would turn twenty-three in three weeks.

I was assigned to a new unit, a navy FLAK unit in Trieste, Italy. My faithful comrade, Fritz Weinhold, was assigned to the same unit. But first we all got a furlough. During the second week in January, I arrived home. They were overjoyed to see me alive, since they had not heard from me in months. Thus, the retreat from Greece ended happily. I was allowed to stay at home for two weeks. Then I traveled to Trieste, in northern Italy. I was assigned to a FLAK battery and Fritz Weinhold went to the neighboring one. My life there as a naval mechanic petty officer was quite comfortable and quiet. While the others had to scurry around during air raid alarms, I could stay in bed. From time to time I got up and went from one cannon to the other to see that everything was in working order. If I found that everything was okay, I went to bed. Enemy planes flew over day and night. There was a lot of shooting but no planes were hit. The port of Trieste was being bombed heavily. Upon Monte Bello we could hear the whistling of the bombs. Our neighboring FLAK battery was completely wiped out one day. Luckily, the life of my friend Fritz Weinhold was spared. Shortly thereafter our battery was almost annihilated. One of the bombers dropped three heavy bombs next to our encampment. The bombs blasted three deep craters into the soft ground. Otherwise, there was no damage. One man who was in the washroom at the time of the attack was slightly wounded. I was just walking from one cannon to the other when the bombs hit. The concussion literally threw me into the hole where a cannon was placed. Had the bombs been released just a fraction of a second earlier, there would have been nothing left of us.

The war was going very badly for Germany. In the east and the west, fighting was already raging on German soil. We were probably the soldiers who were the farthest away from Germany, with the possible exception of those who were in Norway. In those days I often discussed the war situation with Fritz Weinhold. He still was holding out great hope for the "secret weapons" Hitler was bragging about. I very gladly let him lead me into believing him.

One day some soldiers came back from town where Partisans had disarmed them. We also learned that the Yugoslav Partisans were coming closer to our camp. Soon we were aiming our guns at land barricades, and toward the end of April the Partisans were only a few hundred yards away from our position. They established themselves in the schoolhouse just opposite from us. At that time I accomplished my one and only heroic act. Our auxiliary light generator was out of order, and our only other one was stored in a shed at the far end of our battery, very close to the enemy position. Since I was the mechanic petty officer, they assigned me a few men to go and get that object out of there. We reached the shed without incident, got the thing out of the shed, but when we started on our way back with it, the shooting started. Instantly all my men took cover in holes. I stood by the generator and had a hard time getting my men to abandon their cover. Finally I succeeded and we were able to bring the generator to our command post.

—•—

In the morning of May 1, 1945, the Partisans started overrunning our position. All our guns were manned, and a fierce battle ensued. Machine gunfire was cracking all around us, but another petty officer and I sat in our room (as maintenance mechanics, we were not part of a squad) eating our fill of the available food and preparing our haversacks and briefcases for the escape. The shooting around the building increased in ferocity. Finally I went downstairs to see how things looked and what could be done. There I met the first of our soldiers who had left their positions, which had been overrun by the Partisans, and the commanding officer ordered us to retreat. I had my haversack with me. But when I ran back to retrieve my briefcase that I had left by the door, it was nowhere to be found. I frantically looked for it for quite a while, but when I noticed that most of my comrades had left, and I was almost the last one still around, I ran off without it.

We raced down a wide path toward the city of Trieste as fast as our legs could carry us. Occasionally I turned around to see if the Partisans were pursuing us. My greatest worry at the time was that the Partisans might be chasing us or shooting at us with our own cannons, which I thought were still in working order. As I learned later, my worry was unfounded, because all the big guns that our people had to abandon had been rendered useless, at least temporarily. Most of the men in our FLAK unit were gathered in a naval supply camp at the foot of Monte Bello. When they started to reorganize the troops into new defense positions, I simply disappeared. I was told later that the commanding officer of our battery had told his men that they were free to run and to fend for themselves, and afterwards he shot himself.

While I and two others were wandering through the town like lost sheep, a woman who spoke German invited us into her house, saying that we could stay there until things quieted down. Very gladly we accepted her invitation. After getting rid of our weapons (as I mentioned before, I had none left, except one hand grenade), we got settled down in the basement of a five or six-story apartment building. That was around noontime. For four hours we heard the incessant rattle of rifles and machine guns. Quite often we could hear grenades hitting close by. Then suddenly, all was quiet, and the three of us fell sound asleep. We were rudely awakened by loud yelling voices, "Out! Get out!" That is how I fell into the hands of Yugoslav Tito Partisans. One of the Partisans immediately took everything away from me that looked interesting to him. When he found my watch, he really started searching me thoroughly, because I had initially told him that I had no watch on me.

Later we were all herded together at the base of Monte Bello. During the middle of the night we were finally brought back to the very same place where we had been when the attack had started. From there, we were taken into the schoolhouse right next to our former FLAK battery. We spent the rest of the night in a room packed like sardines. How are things going to be, and what will become of us, were the questions on everyone's mind.

During the next two or three days more prisoners of war joined us. Most of their clothing had been taken away, and instead they had been given the lice-infested rags that the Partisans had been wearing. Once I saw a group of men looking like Partisans coming up the hill. Ah, I thought, there is going to be a change of guard! But I soon found out that it was another group of German prisoners of war in Partisans' rags.

Another rather amusing episode happened there. An older Austrian soldier, who must have been in his forties, approached me. Pointing out a certain Partisan, he demanded that I kill that man or do something else terrible to him. His reasoning was that I was still young and did not have a wife and children at home to consider; therefore it would not be so bad if I got killed. His gripe was that this particular Partisan had just taken his gold watch, which was an heirloom from his grandfather. For a moment I was speechless. I thought of the scripture where it says that none has greater love than he who is willing to lay down his life for his friend. But this case did not involve a friend—but a gold watch! I tried to explain to him that he already had the opportunity in life to have a wife and children, while I was still looking forward to that experience and that he should take revenge on the Partisan himself, since he had already lived the greater part of his life. But he could or would not understand this line of reasoning, and therefore the loss of his gold watch remained unrevenged.

After about a week we were brought to a nearby collecting center. Thousands of German prisoners of war were gathered in the place that formerly had been a German supply camp. To my great surprise, I ran across my brother-in-law, Rudi Miller, Erika's husband. I was so surprised that all I could utter was, "Oh, my goodness, are you here too?" (In truth, I said something much more colorful, but it isn't worth repeating.) Each of us had a friend, and from then on the four of us stuck together. It was not too cold, and being outside day and night did not bother us.

A few days later, the whole camp had to march on in the direction of Rijeka. The supply camp was being completely vacated, and everybody scrounged together all the foodstuffs they could lay their hands on. The four of us found very little to take along. The long daily marches were very tiring, and those who had hoarded food could not carry it any longer, so they simply dropped what was too heavy for them. We picked up what we thought useful, and soon we had so much that we could hardly carry it.

When we were about halfway to Rijeka, we stopped for a few days. While there, a Partisan took my comfortable shoes. He gave me his, which were not too bad, but were too narrow. I had no other choice but to cut the shoes in the places where they were too tight. After more prisoners had joined us, the march continued. It became more and more difficult. All day long we had to march without getting anything to drink.

At the outskirts of Rijeka we walked by a beautiful country home. There a young girl filled our pots and cans with water. We all crowded around her to get our share. I, too, was lucky enough to get some water. (By that time I had learned by experience how much energy can be created by just one sip of water.) The Partisans aimed their rifles ready to shoot her if she did not stop giving us water. The prisoners were desperate enough not to care whether or not they got shot. But the girl showed no sign of fear, and continued to pour water. I had to move on to make room for others.

Beyond Rijeka, the march ended in a wide canyon with a creek running through it. The few days we spent there was hell for the thousands of prisoners. Worn-out, sick, hungry, and ragged, we were a mass of humanity destined to die.

One day we were told to line up along the road and then move back toward the entrance of the canyon. The hours we spent on the road were used by roving groups of Tito's soldiers to take away the Italian money we still had on us. Every prisoner was being searched and had to give up all he had. Three prisoners lay dead by the side, shot right where they had been ransacked. These men had broken the comb or the watch that the Partisans had wanted rather than let them be taken from them, and that had cost them their lives. In the canyon we settled down again. Every day we waited on what was to happen next.

We had to form ranks again and march on, but only a short distance down the other side of the highway into a hidden bay on the Mediterranean. I presume this was done so that nobody could see our misery. Fortunately, there was a sweet-water well close to the seashore. On Whitsunday in the middle of May 1945 we boiled four pots of water and used our last herbs to make tea. That was our nourishment for almost three days. On Whitmonday the four of us volunteered for a work detail, hoping that the reward would be some food. A few hundred men were led back to the canyon where we had been and we had to pick up the rocks that our soldiers had set up for their camps and cooking. Every time I bent over everything went black before my eyes. When it was dark, we actually did get some food. The next morning we had to close ranks again and march on. Over dusty roads we were led into the interior of Yugoslavia. Like a huge monster, the mass of prisoners writhed slowly through the streets of the towns and villages. The sight was heartrending. Hungry, thirsty, and sick, we dragged ourselves along.

In flocks, the German prisoners ran to the houses along the way to fetch a bite to eat. If one got something, the others fell all over him and in the end the precious food was trampled into the ground and nobody got anything. I saw a woman come out of a house with an apron full of bread. A pack of prisoners rushed toward her like wolves. She was so frightened she dropped the apron and fled back into her house. Dozens of men were struggling on the ground for that bread.

Orchards were plundered of fruit that had hardly developed from blossoms. Many a death was caused by this. I never took part in any such struggle for food. Hungry and thirsty, but steadfast, I patiently marched mile after mile. Occasionally, every prisoner got a handful of flour. We mixed it with water and baked it on hot rocks before we ate it.

Later we were allowed to march during the night. Our column stretched for miles. At that time we were able to get water from the wells in the villages. That way at least the problem of thirst was solved. Once we saw hundreds of women walking along the road with baskets on their heads. We assumed that they were carrying their harvest to market. They ended up at the same place where we had our next rest stop. What they had carried on their heads was food, meant for us! Divided among so many prisoners, each one of us merely got a bite.

In a small town where we stopped I tried to care for a buddy who had been shot in the abdomen when he had been caught trying to beg at a house. He was being dragged behind us in a horse-drawn cart over the bumpy road without getting medical attention. Still, he uttered, "The pain and sorrow I endured during those few hours I would not wish on my worst enemy." Then a Partisan chased us away from him with a whip. What became of him? How much chance of survival did he have? On and on we marched, covering twenty or thirty miles every day. My friend and I often locked arms to hold each other up. Looking back, I have since marveled many times how I often marched hour after hour and was still capable of admiring the beautiful countryside as the morning began to dawn. "Walk and not be weary, run and not faint!" These experiences have become to me a testimony for the Word of Wisdom.

In Petrinja, we stopped in a large camp with barracks. It was June 1, 1945. Was the time of the death marches over for us? We all were assigned barracks and our heads were shorn clean. Very much surprised, we looked at each other. One day later we had to go on, but it was only a part of our group. I don't remember how long it took before we reached Kostajnica. By that time there were only a few hundred of us. We were housed in a few barracks there. What misery! All of us were sick and weak. The mass deaths had begun! We got some food every day, but it was slop that pigs would not have eaten. We devoured it anyway. Every day groups were sent out to haul rocks. I also participated once or twice.

At one time I volunteered as a roofer, hoping to get some decent food from the people in the village. Rudi also came with me. We helped to thatch a roof. But the man was not too satisfied with our work, and the reward we had expected was not so great. One day I mentioned to Rudi that I would rather march again because we had it better then than now. The next day the request came for two hundred men to move on. Rudi and I were among them. That was a tiresome march to Karlovac. Just as a chicanery, the guards very rarely led us to drinking water. The thirst became so unbearable that we were forced to drink putrid water.

A group of six men, Rudi and I included, decided to flee. At a convenient moment we disappeared behind some bushes where we first wanted to rest for a while. The others kept going another two or three hundred meters farther; then they also stopped to rest. Now we didn't know what to do. Should we continue our attempt to escape with the other prisoners and guards so near to us?

The weather was pleasant, but we had poor prospects for finding anything to eat. We had courage, but no good plan of action. It was a difficult situation for us. I decided then that we would wait until morning before doing anything else. If the column was still there, we would return to them. If they were gone, we would continue on our own as best we could. The others agreed with my decision.

The next morning our group was still close by, and we rejoined it like good boys. I don't know if my decision to return to the column was inspired or just my good luck, but it undoubtedly saved our lives because I later discovered that escaped prisoners were shot when they were found by the Partisans. I am sure that had we continued on our own we would have been captured and killed.

It should be mentioned that before our "escape," I had pretended that I could not walk anymore and that the others were helping me. This had only been a trick to enable us to stay behind the rest of the group. Maybe that was also the reason why they made an earlier rest stop.

The tormenting continued. Suddenly, a few Partisans attacked one of the prisoners. I could never find out for certain why they did it. They hit him, threw him to the ground, and stomped on him. A few shots were fired. When it was all over, the German soldier was dead, and the Partisan who had tortured us the most had been hit by a ricochet in the chest and did not survive.

—•—

I cannot recall how many days it took before we arrived in Karlovac. For me that had been the worst march, as thirst was the greatest torture. I was to the point where I would have drunk poison just to get some liquid into my throat. It was not that there was no water available; there was plenty of it. They withheld it from us on purpose just to torture us. At any rate, the hunger marches ended for me in Karlovac. Tito's Partisans had taken the lives of thousands of German soldiers, including that of my good friend, Fritz Weinhold. I was told that those who had fallen down by the road because they could no longer walk were shot. Thousands were so weakened by the marches that they died later. The very young ones and the very old ones were the worst off. Those who were about my age could take more hardships.

In Karlovac we were divided up into work gangs. I participated in the building of warehouses and bridges. We mostly slept outdoors, but we got food regularly, most often a mush made of corn. This corn had at least been ground and was seasoned. In Kostajnica, the corn had only been crushed.

For some time I was camped by the river Kupa. That gave me a chance to bathe and wet my ragged clothes. Another time, our group, which consisted of about fifty prisoners, slept right next to the platform of a train station. While people were boarding the train, we sat on a pile of sand, stark naked, hunting lice in our ragged clothing.

During that time I found a new comrade. Once I was walking with him along the road when he begged a whole loaf of white bread from a Yugoslav. I asked him to give me just a tiny piece so that I could taste for once how white bread tasted. His answer was, "Before I would give you a piece I would rather throw the whole thing into the river." On another occasion someone gave him a handful of berries for both of us. I purposely refrained from asking him for my share, and he did not give me any. What a contrast between him and other soldiers who had offered me some bread during the hunger march, even though I had not asked for it and was a stranger to them.

When festering sores started developing on my hands, I no longer had to go to work. My daily chore was to keep the flies away from the wounds since there wasn't anything available to bandage them with. When those sores started breaking out on my genitals, I was sent to a prisoner hospital camp nearby. Some ointment and bandages helped to heal the infection. It was now August 1945. The conditions in the hospital camp were devastating. There was absolutely no help available even for those who where seriously ill. Many of them were merely skeletons with puffed up abdomens. The moaning and groaning humanity lay in barracks that were very crowded. I was sheltered with a few others in what was a kind of cave. Vermin of all kinds did not let me sleep. Lice, fleas, and bedbugs were torturing me continuously. Two nights and days I lay awake, scratching. Finally on the third night pure exhaustion brought me some sleep. That cycle continued for several weeks.

One evening I heard someone in the barracks yelling, "Help! Someone help me get up!" It seemed that nobody paid any attention to him. Then, someone snarled at him, "Shut up!" "Be quiet!" etc. I went in and helped him sit up. During the ensuing short conversation, I learned that he came from a neighborhood of Plauen, which is close to my hometown, Zwickau. Suddenly he heaved a few sighs and fell backward as I was holding him in my arms, and then all was quiet. I felt his pulse, but he was dead! I thought to myself, now the others could be satisfied and no longer needed to yell at him. In the morning I saw the orderlies carrying him out. He was a somewhat older man.

I cannot recall how long I stayed there. What had become of my three comrades, I didn't know. In Karlovac we had still been together, and then each one of us had been assigned to a different work detail. I really was kind of glad about it because those three had been fighting among themselves in the worst way. It was disgusting to me, but I personally had gotten along well with every one of them.

Suddenly the order came that all those belonging to a certain work detail had to report back to the work detachment. As soon as all were assembled in Karlovac, we were loaded onto a freight train and transported to another place. In Petrinja we were told that all those who had been in the field hospital near Karlovac could get off the train there. Those who were not sick should continue on the train. Anyone acting contrary to this order would be severely punished. Even though I felt pretty good and the sores had healed, I got off. Not until much later did I realize how fortunate that was for me. It was unknown where the others were brought.

In the field hospital in Petrinja I found the same misery as in Karlovac. We had to sleep on the bare floor in the barracks without any pad or blanket. The condition of most men was deplorable. Men were dying every day. The doctors, who were also prisoners, walked among the sick, unable to help, as the scant supply of medicines was completely inadequate.

A few days later I became seriously ill. Like so many others, I had dysentery. I lost my appetite and had a strong aversion against all food; to even look at food made me gag. My body became weaker and weaker. Every hour I had to run to the restroom, just to expel a thimbleful of blood. There was no paper to wipe with. Every morning I went out in search of twenty-four large leaves to serve that purpose for one day. No one can imagine what an effort it was to pick those twenty-four leaves every morning. At first the doctor thought that I used the leaves for smoking.

Now and then the doctor gave me some opium medication that brought relief for a few hours. The others in the room cared for me as well as they could. They made me get up every morning and refresh myself at the well at the same time I picked the leaves. They never divided the remainder of my food among themselves until I simply refused to eat another bite. Only because they urged and encouraged me did I manage to swallow five or six spoons full of food. I was so weak that I could not understand how others could have the energy to climb out the window or to sweep the corridor with a few birch branches.

I cannot recall anymore how many days this condition lasted. I assume somewhere between ten and twenty days. Then one day my appetite suddenly returned. The doctor looked at me and immediately knew that I was better. Then things started looking up again for me. Sick people came and were released as being healed and well. The doctor let me stay, even though I felt quite well.

In the meantime the food rations were to become larger. It is unbelievable how much food we could devour. Someone must have added some fat to the barley mash (that was our main nourishment) one day, as the whole camp was sick. Our bodies could not yet digest the fat. We also got a lot of cornbread. Cornbread with a thick mush of barley spread on it was our usual fare.

At Christmastime we got pancakes made with white flour. For a while we received one pound of white bread per day. Every day a group of prisoners had to walk into the village to get the loaves from the baker. This assured us that we were not completely forgotten, because the white flour and the barley were furnished by the UNRRA (United Nations Relief and Rehabilitation Administration).

Another problem we had was fuel. Even our guards had none. Occasionally a group of prisoners went with a Partisan to steal some wood from the forest. Every prisoner came back carrying a log on his shoulder. The wood they brought back, however, was only for the Partisans. We prisoners dismantled a nearby empty barracks. One night the barracks collapsed because all the wood that held it up had finally disappeared. A few men from our room, me included, even stole the entrance gate to the prisoners' compound.

The worst epidemic of deaths was over with. How they used to hurriedly dispose of the bodies during that time of mass deaths, I don't know. But now whenever a man died he was carried up to the cemetery on a bier. While they carried him past the gate many of the prisoners formed a lane and sang "Ich hatt' einen Kameraden."

I had one faithful comrade 'ere we heard the trumpet's call,
And we pledged our hearts forever in battle joined together,
To beat the foe or fall.
A musket shot came screaming to seal his fate or mine
Right at my feet he stumbled, and friendship's shrine it crumbled
Around that friend of mine.
His hand is blindly seeking the clasp I cannot give
For duty calls me onward, farewell my dying comrade,
Our love shall ever live.

Slowly the procession made its way through the village and uphill toward the cemetery. Many of the villagers made the sign of the cross or took off their hats. Others took off their hats, but acted as if they just wanted to scratch their heads because they were afraid of our guards. When the procession arrived at the cemetery, they found a hole that had already been dug. The blanket was taken off the bier and the naked body was simply tossed into the hole. I attended several such "funerals."

Months went by. Somehow the prisoners got hold of musical instruments—even a piano found its way into camp. Various groups were formed. There were musicians, actors, singers, and artists of all kinds. We had high quality programs. I especially liked a man who sang folk songs, accompanying himself on the guitar. He sang the song about a deceitful gypsy in a masterful way. There was also another excellent tenor among us, and we never tired of listening to him. A religious group was also formed in which prisoners exchanged thoughts about their religious convictions.

—•—

Spring 1946 had come, and the doctor had not yet released me. Every morning while making his rounds he asked me how I was. I simply answered that I was fine. And he walked on. Many others came and were discharged again. If anyone tried to fake illness, he was immediately dismissed. Then word came that in April a transport of sick soldiers was to leave for Germany. A group of us were sent by the doctor to Zagreb from where the transport was supposed to leave. I was among them. In Zagreb we were again examined by Yugoslav doctors. They accused me of faking illness. Only very few from our camp were sick enough to be sent home to Germany.

So, back to Petrinja we went. What was actually wrong with me? I didn't know myself. I felt very well. Why had the doctor kept me for such a long time in the field hospital? I really don't know. Could it be that Heavenly Father had something to do with it? I think that I would not have survived in that first work camp where we had to lift such heavy loads. Promptly upon my return, the doctor again assigned me to a room in the field hospital in Petrinja.

Again a few weeks passed. Then news came that the field hospital was to be disbanded. A Yugoslav doctor examined us all and sent me along with a few others to the work camp located in the same complex of barracks. The others were transferred to the prison hospital in Zagreb. Thus my stay in the field hospital ended approximately nine months after I had entered it because of festering sores.

Summer 1946 had come. During the days we worked in our assigned details. We had to do all kinds of jobs. At the moment just a few come to mind: building houses, stacking bales of hay, unloading grain, etc. None of these chores were too hard for me.

The grain we were unloading came in sacks. Many of the prisoners stole some of those sacks to use as a pad or cover for the night or to make clothing. One day I worked up enough courage to steal one of those sacks. I was promptly caught by a Partisan. He took me into a hut where I fully expected to be beaten up. But nothing of the kind happened; they simply let me go again. Later, I was able to get a sack by exchanging it for some cigarettes that were rationed out to all prisoners. Now I had a pad to lie on. For quite a while all in our camp were getting twenty cigarettes a day. I gave mine away and only occasionally did I trade some in for things I could not get any other way.

I still owned a thin, threadbare blanket. In cold weather I rolled up like a ball, with the blanket over me. My warm breath collecting under the blanket gave me some comfort. During the night we often lay against one another which gave us enough extra warmth so that we could at least sleep.

At that time I took a great interest in classical literature. (Those kinds of books were the only ones left on the shelves in the camp library.) Soon I was crazy about literature. I even took a book along when we went out to work so that I could read during the lunch break. It became easy for me to prove a point by quoting literature, the same way it is often done with the Bible.

At the beginning of December 1946, the small groups of prisoners still in the camp in Petrinja were transported to Zagreb. Not one of them was as badly dressed as I. With my short, patched pants, the ragged jacket, and boards for shoes on my feet, I really looked wretched. Fortunately, the weather had not yet turned cold. In Zagreb we were all put in the barracks of a transit camp and held there for a few days.

Shortly before Christmas I and a few others who also had metal working experience were assigned to a work unit and transferred to camp 101, located at the outskirts of Zagreb. There were about twenty prisoners in our group. Every morning we were led by a guard to the center of town (the walk took about thirty minutes) to an automobile repair shop which was run by the Partisans. Together with a few Partisans we worked on their cars and trucks. By now the Partisans had become the Yugoslav Army. As far as we were concerned, they were still Partisans.

Christmas Eve 1946 was approaching. The barracks was so overcrowded that some of us, including myself, had to sleep on the floor. I lay next to Otto Hold, an Austrian who was a few years younger than I and was on the same work crew with me. The two of us were lying close by the entrance door, and we were hungry. As far as we could see, all of the others had somehow been able to get hold of some goodies that could be considered a dainty morsel. One fellow took pity on us and gave us each a cookie. We reminisced together of past Christmastimes at home until we fell asleep.

I don't know anymore how Horst Grigo, Georg Weinhold, and I managed it, but all three of us occupied top bunk beds right next to each other in the barracks. Horst Grigo was something like a squad leader for the "Auto-Radiona" (the repair shop) squad. Horst tried to get Georg in with us at first, but did not succeed until much later.

—•—

It is very probable that at least two or three months had passed since that Christmas Eve before I started bunking next to Horst and Georg. During that time I came down with a very severe cold. The medical orderly let me spend two weeks in the sickroom. When I recovered from this illness, I had completely lost my sense of smell and my balance. I could not walk straight and would weave back and forth as if I were drunk. The camp leader admitted to me later that when he saw me lying in the sickroom he thought that I would never make it.

In this camp we received food regularly, but it never was enough. I seemed to be hungry all the time. Once, after I had received my food and sat down at the table, another man came by and accidentally bumped the table so that my dish almost fell over. I became outraged and yelled at him, "If my dish had fallen over now, I would have hit you in the trap so that you could not see straight!" He only looked at me and answered, "I never would have thought you capable of using language like that!" This probably was the only time I lost my temper. Things like that were not expected of me.

When Easter came I was occupying the top bunk next to Horst and Georg. In the meantime a few prisoners had formed a band with a few musical instruments. They made good music together and were the main attraction when we had programs in the evenings. Easter 1947 was a very beautiful day. We saw the citizens come out and take a walk through the forest. Our band was giving an outdoor concert. Many people stopped to watch and listen. Most of the men in camp behind the fence were wishing that they could go for a stroll too.

Suddenly a girl about thirteen years old climbed up the slope, put her hand through the fence, and gave me a colored Easter egg. I was confused, and she ran away very quickly. It was quite risky for her to come so close to the fence. I cannot remember into how many pieces we divided the egg. Nobody got much. But a gift under these circumstances was something special, not only for me, but also for the giver. The effect of this gift was profound. From that moment on, I was no longer hungry all the time.

After our working hours, Horst, Georg, and I often volunteered to participate in some work details. We never got anything for it, except maybe some food. But it gave us an opportunity to see other things and places. We had to do all kinds of work. Once they needed someone to shovel coal in a hospital. Otto Hold, my Austrian comrade, and I had to shovel coal into a shed. The others were led away to another job. The two of us worked in our usual slow tempo. Now and then the guard came by, and it appeared that he wanted us to work faster. The idea did not appeal to us.

A few hours later, we were led into the dining room of the hospital to get something to eat. There we met the others and found out how much harder they had worked of their own free will to get all of their coal into a cellar. Apparently the guard had tried to make that clear to us. Another time we went to a shoe factory. That gave us a chance to exchange our worn-out shoes with shoes that were just lying around. I have to mention here that soon after our arrival in the Auto-Radiona we had discovered a supply of used, but still usable, clothes of all kinds belonging to the Partisans. That gave me a chance to finally acquire some decent clothing. What I was able to get a hold of there in the line of clothing and underwear was sufficient to last me to the end of our captivity.

The winners of a special prize were men who were chosen to shovel coal in a boarding school for girls. (Of course, when volunteering, one never knew beforehand what he was getting into.) Aside from the fact that some girls were flirting with us, we were the first ones to receive money for our work. Later, we were also given money for our work in the "Auto-Radiona." It wasn't much, but we could afford to occasionally buy a special treat or a toilet article. It simply came about by itself that Horst, Georg, and I lived the United Order. All income, money, and articles were pooled. In this way, the three of us, as a unit, could afford many more things than a single person could.

I didn't know anything about the work in the Auto-Radiona. Soon Otto Hold and I volunteered for the job to carry the meals for all from the camp to the shop. We enjoyed walking through town, seeing pretty girls and new things from time to time. At first a guard always went with us, but later they let us go alone. A guard also led the group to work in the morning and back to camp at night. Occasionally, purposely, a man got "lost" on the way and later returned to the Auto-Radiona. I did that once too, in order to get myself some eyeglasses for reading. Later the guards did not even go with us anymore.

That's the way things went until shortly before Christmas 1947. Suddenly, we were removed from the Auto-Radiona and brought to another camp. Our United Order had to be discontinued. After a short time we were together again. But then we did not only work in the Auto-Radiona in the middle of town, we lived there too. We got food from the Partisans who had a kitchen right next door. (Later on we were allowed to cook our own food.) That made us, for all practical purposes, free people. After work, we were at liberty to go wherever we wanted.

At that time the prisoners were given the option to become free men if they would pledge to stay in Yugoslavia for five years as laborers. Not too many accepted that offer. As it turned out later, they really had been cheated because soon after that all prisoners could move around town any way they wanted. Those who had pledged—after paying for rent, food, and clothing—had less money left to spend than we received as pocket money. As prisoners we did not have any expenses. The German prisoners also were never lacking initiative to find some additional income. Soon we had a better living standard than the Partisans. We made ample use of the opportunity to move around freely. In the streets, cafes, and stores many German soldiers could be seen. All were well dressed. I also had good clothing by now.

We no longer sent our letters through the prisoner of war mail but directly, privately. At the beginning the mail service had been very poor. My people at home received the first word about my whereabouts six months after I had been taken prisoner. Anyone can imagine the anxiety and worries of our families. We received our first mail from home nine months after being taken prisoner. Then we could send one letter a month through the official channels, until we found out about the other way. All the necessities of life were now taken care of. We also had sufficient recreation. But we were still prisoners of war! And each one of us had only one wish: to go home to our families! But even after three years, there was no thought of it yet.

—•—

In the middle of the year 1948, our whole group was transferred to another Auto-Radiona. Our living conditions became somewhat better, too. Here the trucks of the Yugoslav Army were being repaired in a production line. Naturally they were all American Army vehicles. Together with the Partisans each one of us had to perform a certain task. Mine was to install the front fenders and the grate protecting the radiator. Because of the primitive tools and the bad conditions the parts were in, the job wasn't always easy. Every day they wrote down how much of the expected output we had achieved. Whenever I thought that everything had gone well for me, they only registered me with 80 or 90 percent of the expected output. But on other days when I didn't feel like working at all and nothing seemed to go right, my output was judged to be 100 percent. How they decided what to put down, I don't know. Our watchword was: as long as the vehicle makes it out of the gate on its own power, we are satisfied!

Very unexpectedly and to our great surprise, it was announced in September 1948 that a plan had been drawn up about the time when the various camps would be released. We in Zagreb were to be the next-to-last transport, in January 1949. I knew in which camp my brother-in-law, Rudi Muller, was and that his camp was to be one of the first ones in October. Soon we found out that those transports going to West Germany always made a stop right close to the Auto-Radiona. I also knew with which transport Rudi was supposed to come. Sure enough, when the time came, after some inquiry, I found him in one of the freight cars. We could talk to each other for a while.

The time dragged on very slowly. Everyone was trying to buy a few things to take home with them, like honey, cigarettes, leather goods, etc. Christmas 1948 I still spent in the Auto-Radiona. Finally, the first part of January, our turn had come! Camp 101, to which our group belonged, was transported to Belgrade. There we were held in a camp for a few days until a train was put together to take us home. Horst Grigo left a day or two earlier to go to West Germany. Georg Weinhold and I traveled together, packed in freight cars, via Hungary and Czechoslovakia to East Germany.

How we rejoiced when the train finally entered our homeland in Bad Schandau! In Dresden some family members were waiting for their fathers, sons, and brothers, whom they had missed for such a long time. However, nobody was allowed to leave the transport. Everyone first had to go through a transit camp in Lobau, Saxony. The process of release took a few days. While I was in that camp I dreamed one night that all my possessions that I had brought from Yugoslavia had been stolen. How relieved I was when I found out that it had only been a dream! I had not brought much, but it was all I owned, and I had obtained it through hard work and sweat.

Finally, after a few days, my name appeared on the bulletin board announcing that I was free to go home. As we were getting into the train, a big argument developed between the returning prisoners and the workers on their way to work. The train was already overcrowded when we came along, and we wanted to board it too. Each side claimed to have more right to be on the train than the other. Many a harsh word was spoken. I quietly pushed my way onto the train and arrived in time in Zwickau.

Thus, the most difficult period of my life had come to an end. I had been away from home almost exactly eight years. Seven months in the *Reichsarbeitsdienst* (labor brigade), three years and eight months in the German Navy, and three years and nine months as a prisoner of war in Yugoslavia. Many people would consider time spent under these conditions as time wasted. I do not share this feeling. I value this span of my life because during this time I had experiences I could have had no other way. These experiences have enriched my life, strengthened my character, and strengthened my testimony of The Church of Jesus Christ of Latter-day Saints, and brought me closer to God. I have never had feelings of hate toward the so-called enemy, even when I was mistreated by them, and I never needed to point a gun toward another human being.

MIRACLES AT THE MISSION HOMES

During the war, neither German mission was forced to close, and missionary work continued on a limited scale, mainly in support of the local branches and districts. Berlin was bombed on the night of November 22, 1943, and all of the homes around the East German Mission home were destroyed. The windows of the mission home were broken out, and its roof and ceiling received some minor damage. At about noon the next day, Brother Paul Langheinrich, second counselor in the mission presidency, felt a strong impression to evacuate all of the sisters working in the office to his home. He instructed them to pack their belongings and all of the mission records and leave at once. Several hours later, President Klopfer, the mission president, who was home on leave from the army, decided to visit the mission home. Finding the doors locked and having no key, he set out in search of his first counselor. Moments later the bombing began again, and the mission home suffered a direct hit from a five-hundred-pound bomb, completely destroying it. However, because the promptings of the Spirit had been heeded, no one was injured.

The West German Mission home in Frankfurt was spared destruction from bombing that destroyed 70 percent of the city. Though it had suffered some damage from bombs exploding nearby, it was miraculously saved from complete destruction in 1944, when a four-thousand-pound "Blockbuster" bomb landed in its courtyard but did not explode, only cracking a few of the walls from its impact. The sister missionaries working in the office had heard the bombs approaching block by block and hurried to the basement, where they knelt in prayer and asked for their lives to be spared. The explosion of the bomb would have completely destroyed the entire city block and would have killed the entire mission staff.

ARTUR SCHWIERMAN FILE

The destruction of Essen.

Source: Frederick W. Babbel, *On Wings of Faith* (Bookcraft: Salt Lake City, 1972), *Saints at War* various files

Though the war was over, the fight for freedom had just begun. After a few months, Walter was able to reenroll at the university to complete his engineering degree. In 1950, Walter and Inge were married, and though required to share an apartment with Walter's parents, they were happy. Though some things were in short supply, life was comfortable, and Walter found great happiness serving in the Church as accompanist and organist for the Zwickau Branch, as well as helping distribute Church Welfare shipments to the members of the branch. However, soon the propaganda and lies from the communist government began to wear on Walter and Inge. Walter's sister Erika had already escaped to the West to join her husband Rudi, and soon thoughts of leaving began to form in their minds as well.

One incident changed everything, however. My father had received permission to visit my sister Erika in Langen, close to Frankfurt/Main, for two weeks. At that time, Papa was the first counselor to the mission president, Walter Stover, and district president of the Zwickau District, simultaneously. On his return trip from Langen, he took a side trip to the mission office in West Berlin. When he did not return to Zwickau at the appointed time, we were very worried, so I telephoned the mission home in West Berlin. I talked to President Stover and explained the situation. His only reply was, "If your father did not arrive at home, he must have been arrested." I immediately went to police headquarters. There I could not get any information either, but I had the distinct feeling that they were keeping something from me.

For a whole week I went to the police every day without being able to get any news about Papa. The whole district arranged a day of fasting and prayer for him. Then he suddenly showed up. What had happened? President Stover had given Papa twenty-five thousand East Marks to deposit in the East German bank account of the Church, over which my father was in charge. Shortly after the train had reached East German territory, the police checked the papers and belongings of each passenger.

A police woman asked Papa to open his briefcase. Right away she spotted the monthly Church statistical reports of the Zwickau District. She did not know what to think of those papers and escorted Papa to the police compartment of the train. The first thing they asked him was to empty his pockets. That is how the money was found. Nobody was allowed to have that much cash, so Papa was immediately arrested and taken to Leipzig for investigation. Papa told them all about the money and whose it was. The district president of Leipzig was hauled in and interrogated. Since his statement corroborated Papa's and no contradictions were found, Papa was allowed to go home again, but only after paying for room and board for the time he had been detained. There was to be a hearing in court later. But the twenty-five thousand Marks were gone, and the mission never saw that money again!

My father had enjoyed the two weeks with Erika and Rudi. He told us of so many wonderful things about life in the West, and after the experience he just had been through with the authorities in the East, he gave me some urgent advice, "Walter, scram to the West!" That was my signal! If I had only listened to Inge, we would have gone long before. From that moment on, we started our preparations for the flight. By that time we finally had finished furnishing our little two-room apartment the way we liked it. Our last acquisition had been two nightstand lamps. A week later we bartered them away again.

We told Inge's sister Marianne and her husband, Alfred, about our plans. They immediately decided to join us. Then Alfred showed us some letters from a missionary living in Canada whom he had met while he had been a prisoner of war in England. In all his letters he offered his help if Alfred could get out of East Germany. We wanted to keep up that contact, but we could not risk mailing these letters in East Germany. That meant trips to West Berlin to write letters, mail them from there, and then come back later to pick up the answers from Canada.

Mama's friend Lilly Ackermann, who served as an intermediary for us, let us stay in her apartment in West Berlin anytime we needed to. She also had food for us every time we came. I traveled to Berlin quite frequently, taking along in suitcases things we wanted to get to the West. Fortunately, my suitcases were never searched. The things I brought to Berlin I sent from there by mail to Langen, where I already had rented a room from Heino and Irmgard Muller. In West Berlin I tried everything possible to find a way to get out, but I simply could not get the necessary permit for residency in West Berlin. So, we had to find another way to escape to West Germany.

For people who knew how to go about it, it was not too difficult at that time to slip across the border illegally. Even my mother, all alone, as well as Helga, had crossed over and back. But if someone was caught and they found out that this person had "burned his bridges" behind him, he was in real trouble. However, we had no other choice. Liesbeth Mannek from Plauen came to our rescue. She was a sister of Linda Schotz, who in turn was my mother's good friend. She was willing to help us get across the border whenever we were ready for it.

Finally, all preparations were made so that we could set a definite date. We did not dare sell any of our belongings; that was too risky. At one time, when I had offered a book for sale in my school of engineering, the immediate reply was, "Are you planning to desert?" That was my first and last attempt to sell anything, with the exception of my toy train with all accessories, which I sold to an old school chum for three hundred Mark. But all the dishes and linen that could be removed without creating suspicion, we took to my parents' apartment in a little handcart.

Nobody knew about our plans except my parents, my sister Helga, Inge's mother, and Inge's sister Johanne Oeser. Alfred didn't even tell his mother. Inge's sister Lotte and her husband, Klaus Sauberlich, did not know a thing. We planned it all with the Neumanns in secret sessions behind closed doors and drawn curtains. All this was going on while I was finishing my schooling as a mechanical engineer. In order not to create suspicion I even applied for a job as an engineer after receiving my diploma.

Finally, the time had come. In the middle of August 1951, just two weeks after receiving my diploma, we started out on our journey toward freedom. There were six of us: Inge and myself, Alfred and Marianne Neumann (Inge's sister), their sons, Rainer, age seven, and Holger, two and a half years old, in his baby buggy. We planned to meet at the *Hauptbahnhof* (the main railroad station). The Neumanns were to take the streetcar to the main station, and we were to go by train from the little station in Polbitz to the main station.

Before we left my parents' home, we knelt together and Papa said a fervent prayer. He asked Heavenly Father to send his angels ahead of us to prepare our way to freedom. Inge's mother went with us to the little station. The train arrived, we boarded it, and in less than a minute we were on our way. Below the tracks on the street stood Inge's mother. We waved to each other, conscious of the fact that in all probability we would never see each other again. Inge could not hold back the tears. I tried to console her by telling her there was hope that someday we would be together again. Somehow, I was convinced at that moment that it would happen, and it did.

As prearranged, we traveled with the Neumanns on the same train to Plauen. However, Liesbeth, who was going to guide us through the forest to the border, was in Berlin at the time where a gymnastic festival of the Socialist World was being held. We could not return to Zwickau. The Neumanns had "burned all their bridges behind them." In our case, it would not have been too conspicuous to return. The two sisters living with Liesbeth allowed us to stay with them. For two or three days we waited impatiently for Liesbeth's return. Finally, she arrived! The next morning we would start right away.

It was a cold, clear, sunny August morning.

We left very early by train toward the border. We got off at a small station and had barely walked about ten minutes toward a village, when two border guards on bicycles stopped us. They wanted to see our passports and inquired where we were headed. Liesbeth gave them the name of a farmer in the village and asserted that we were just going there for a picnic. I was trembling all over from fear and cold. The two men looked us over very strangely, returned our passports, and said that they would check with the farmer to see whether we were telling the truth. What prompted them to let us go could only have been the consequences of our prayer.

As soon as the guards were out of sight, we "got lost" in the forest. Liesbeth knew the countryside very well. Avoiding highways and roads, we walked through forests and over fields and meadows. Approximately an hour later Liesbeth pointed out the direction and said that the border was not too far away. She wanted to return, so we continued on our way by ourselves. Later we met one or two farmers who gave us more advice about the right direction. Then we could hear vehicles moving back and forth. We concluded that there must be a road ahead of us. Alfred volunteered to try to find out where it would be safe to cross the road. We hid behind a hedge deep in the forest and waited patiently. When Alfred had not returned two hours later, we had to assume that he had been caught. After talking it over, we decided to try to get across the border without him. If worst came to worst, we could turn back anytime.

At first, we walked to the left along the hedge and found a path leading across the road. Since it appeared to me to be the right direction, I intended to follow the path to get across the border in a short time. Marianne was of a different opinion. She insisted that it was the wrong trail and steadfastly refused to follow it. Against my personal conviction, I turned around and we crossed the road again, returning to the spot where we had originally waited for Alfred's return. (As we learned later, angels had guided us!) But there was no trace of Alfred! So, we went along the hedge again, but this time to the right and crossed the road again. When we were in the middle of the road, two border guards came down the hill on their bicycles. We hid behind some trees, and the guards sped past. This crossing of the road was not more than a hundred meters away from the first one.

For about a half hour we struggled with the baby buggy through the forest, when we met a gamekeeper with his rifle strung over his shoulder. He asked us for our passports and wanted to know what we were doing there. There was no other choice; I had to admit that we were trying to get across the border to the West. He looked at us, returned our passports, and after pointing out the direction as I had asked him, he disappeared.

On we walked through the forest. We also had to cross fields, but we no longer were too cautious while crossing them. We just kept on walking. Then we came to fields in which there were some small groups of trees we saw a row of white rocks about three hundred meters ahead of us. Could that, by any chance, be the border? In the distance I saw a farmer working in a field. The others hid behind a group of trees while I asked the farmer about the borderline. I told him that I was coming from the West, and wanted to know if I was standing in the East and if the white rocks were the border. Yes, the white rocks were the border. I ran back to the others, and as quickly as we could do it with the baby buggy, we hurried toward the white rocks. In the distance, we heard the farmer calling to us that we were going the wrong direction. The white rocks were behind us! An indescribable feeling of joy and freedom overcame us. We had made it! But where was Alfred?

A church tower showed us the way into the village of Muenchenreuth. We asked a boy where the bus station was so that we could catch a bus to Hof. He quickly disappeared without saying a word. A few minutes later the boy returned with a West German border guard. At that time we did not yet know that West German border guards were to be feared more than their East German counterparts. Like criminals, we were locked in a cell. It was about 2:00 PM. We were told right away that we would be taken back to the East as soon as a guard was free to take us.

Now, we were really in trouble and at a loss of what to do! The first thing we did was to kneel down and send a prayer to our Heavenly Father asking Him not to forsake us. At that point in time we did not yet know that all this was part of His plan to get us safely across the border. Approximately an hour later we were interrogated by an American officer. He rejected my request to let us go in a very stern and unfriendly way. Again, we were locked up.

At 6:00 PM a guard appeared ready to escort us back to the border. Very sad and discouraged we trotted back toward the place from which we so wanted to flee. While we were walking, I asked the guard how the roads and borders were running in order to be better informed. I also begged him not to return us via the road, but to let us slip back through the forest so that we would not be caught by a guard on the other side. He was kind enough to agree to that.

At the border he stopped and watched us disappear in the forest. As soon as he was out of sight, we stopped. The women and children were crying. There was not much counsel to be expected from them at this time. So, I very resolutely turned the baby carriage around, and marched back toward the West. Only this time, instead of walking toward the village, I stayed close to the border, and then turned toward the right, hoping to somehow be able to reach Hof.

We walked through forests and fields. But soon it had become dark, and we didn't know where we really were. Now and then we met a kind soul who showed us the right direction, only to get lost again. Suddenly we saw a light in the distance. To get to it we had to cross meadows and swampland. In places we had to carry the buggy because it got stuck in the mud. In order not to attract the attention of border guards, we only whispered. At first the children cried because they were hungry. But all we could give them were sweets. Then they cried because they had an upset stomach from the sweets.

Finally, we reached the light. It was a railroad signalman's house. A dog started barking fiercely and a woman came out. She advised us to follow the tracks to the next road, to turn right, and follow the road into the nearest larger village where we could find lodging in an inn. Along the tracks it was not too bad, but on the road there were lights coming toward us constantly. Were they guards on bicycles, motorcycles, or in cars? We didn't know. It was pitch-dark and we were terribly afraid.

Finally, toward midnight, we stumbled into the village named Feilitsch. The baby buggy rumbled on the street. At the railroad station many people came to the windows and looked out, wondering who was wandering around with a baby buggy in the middle of the night. About two hundred meters farther on was the inn. At last, we made it! All the time Holger had been carried or pushed in the buggy. But seven-year-old Rainer really had accomplished something! Faithfully and patiently he trotted along all the way!

Fortunately, people were still up at the inn. We told them our story and that we could not get any West money until the next morning, when we could ask for it by telegraph from Langen. For Marianne and her children they had a room, and they allowed Inge and me to sleep in their living room on the sofa. At least we had a roof over our heads. We were so excited that we did not sleep very much and we woke up very early the next morning.

Thinking that Inge would be less conspicuous, I sent her to the post office to telegraph for money. She was able to do it without any trouble. But before she did that, she had taken all of our shoes down into the courtyard and cleaned off, as well as she could, all the mud that was on them from the previous night's trek.

I sat at the window, wrapped in a blanket, observing what was going on outside on the street.

First, I noticed that there were border guards walking in and out of the restaurant, which was part of the inn. Some of them kept walking up and down the street. While Inge was downstairs cleaning the shoes, one soldier was standing across the street from the inn watching everyone who was going in and out of the railroad depot. Never before in my whole life had I felt such fear as I did while sitting at that window! I was literally trembling with fear and cold. Inge told me later that I had looked like an old man while sitting at that window.

During my lifetime I had been in many dangerous and life-threatening situations without feeling so afraid. But here it did not concern just my life, but freedom, and not only mine, but Inge's, her sister's, and also the children's.

During my lifetime I had been in many dangerous and life-threatening situations without feeling so afraid. But here it did not concern just my life, but freedom, and not only mine, but Inge's, her sister's, and also the children's. On top of it all, there was the constant worry about Alfred's whereabouts.

The innkeepers told us that there was a train to Hof at 9:00 AM, one at noon, and another one in the afternoon. After the 9:00 AM train had left the guard disappeared. What would happen to us if the guard returned to watch the train at noon? Was it possible that all trains departing from here were being watched? That really worried me greatly.

Inge had finished cleaning the shoes and was out of sight of the soldier in the street. At 10:00 AM I sent her to the post office again to inquire about the money. It had not yet arrived. Half an hour later the wire transfer was completed, but the post office would not give the money to Inge because it had been sent in my name. I had to venture with her through the village to the post office. Every time we met a soldier my heart started pounding. Feilitsch must have been a garrison, because so many soldiers were walking around. We made it back to the hotel with the money, paid our bill, and thanked the innkeepers for their kindness.

By now it was 11:00 AM. The train was standing in the little station, but there was no guard in sight yet. This was our chance! I sent Marianne ahead with the two children because I thought we would be less conspicuous that way. A little later Inge and I followed her without any incident. Quickly, we bought our tickets and boarded the train. We had to wait an hour before the train departed at noon. To us, this seemed like an eternity, since we were constantly worried about soldiers coming to check the passengers. Finally, the train left! Less than a half hour later it pulled into Hof. At each little station in between, we trembled with fear that border guards would come in to search the train. In Hof, we immediately inquired about trains to take us farther.

Marianne's train to Bavaria left at 3:00 PM. Ours did not leave until 9:00 PM. Marianne had some East Mark that she could exchange here. With that money, she bought the tickets and something to eat for the children. Inge and I stood beside their train until it pulled out of the station to take them to Bavaria, where Alfred's sister-in-law, Gisela Neumann, was living. The Neumanns wanted to stay with her until they got a chance to emigrate.

As soon as the train was out of sight, I first heaved a sigh of relief. In this undertaking the two children had not only been a great responsibility for me but also a great burden. Since Alfred's disappearance I had felt responsible for the Neumanns. Would Marianne find him at Gisela's? Alone with Inge, I felt much safer. Without three extra people, and most of all, without a baby buggy, we were more flexible. The very first thing we did was to go to a butcher shop and a bakery. With our rolls, butter, and sausage we sat down on a bench in a park and enjoyed a picnic.

After eating we went to the post office to

send a telegram to my parents with a prearranged coded message that our escape had been successful. Full of joy, we were skipping down the wide steps of the post office when suddenly Inge gave me a shove and began leading me sideways across the stairway. She had recognized the border guard who had escorted us back to the East coming up the stairs towards us. All I noticed was the green uniform. He passed us. Did he really not recognize us? It was possible, since the two children and Marianne were not with us. In order to get out of the streets, we went into the closest movie house. At least it was dark there!

The movie theater was showing an American film about a man and a woman escaping across the desert. I cannot remember the movie's title, but the story was so gripping that for a short while I forgot all about our own danger. When Inge reminded me around 7:30 PM that it was time to go to the railroad station. For a moment I did not even realize where I was. With heavy hearts we started walking toward the railroad station. Since our train was already standing on the track, we immediately bought our tickets and boarded the train.

Standing by the window, we observed what was going on in the station, hoping fervently that no green-uniformed border guard would show up to check the passengers. We were still within the twelve-mile border zone which was constantly being checked for refugees.

If one of these border guards had entered the train, we would have somehow tried to make ourselves invisible. About an hour later, which to us seemed like a very long time, the train started moving out. As the distance between us and the border grew, our hearts became lighter. Nonetheless, we still talked to each other only in whispers, as we had always done during our flight. It took us a few days to get over that habit. We stayed awake until we reached Frankfurt/Main at 4:00 AM. There we had to transfer to go to Langen. Finally, about 5:00 AM, we stood in front of the house where Erika and Rudi Muller lived.

It was Sunday. Since they were renting from people, we did not dare to wake them up that early, so we sat down in a nearby meadow and devoured our remaining rolls, butter, and sausage. We finally dared to savor the feeling that we are now safe! Our fear had vanished and gratitude filled our hearts. We were free! But what had become of Alfred? Three hours later we finally dared to knock on the door and ask for Erika. Our joy to see each other was great. I had not seen my sister since 1943. Their landlord allowed us to stay with Erika and Rudi in their tiny two-room apartment in the attic for a short time.

We did have a rented room of our own, but it was still empty. It took us a few days to find a few pieces of furniture. Papa had a bank account in Langen, and we could borrow from that account to buy the barest necessities. In the past whenever he had a chance to get some East Mark across the border he had done so, even though he had to pay four to six East Mark for one West Mark.

While we were staying with the Mailers, Inge made herself useful by helping Erika with the household chores. I was running from one government office to another in order to get the necessary permits for residency in Langen. I also looked around to find a job. Soon I found one in Egelsbach, a neighboring village, at Fleissner and Son as a toolmaker. We also were granted a West German passport, but only a temporary one, since we told them that we intended to emigrate.

As we were carrying a load of our meager belongings to our room, Birkenstrasse 22, we saw Marianne, her two children, and Alfred walking toward us. Where on earth had they come from? In that small village in Bavaria it had been impossible for them to find lodging or work, so they had decided to come to Langen, where there was more industry and therefore a better chance to find a job. There was no other choice but to let the Neumanns move into our little room.

About a week later a family right close to our place let the Neumanns move into a small room

TRUE TO THE FAITH—JOHN L. FLADE

One of the consistent patterns of German Latter-day Saints during the wartime period was that they were stalwarts in the Church both before and after the conflict. A fine example of this is found in the life of John L. Flade.

John was born in Kemnitz, Saxony, in Germany in 1926. His parents were converts to the Church. At one time, his father was branch president in the Kemnitz Branch, a branch which John described as possibly being the largest in the Church at the time with over 600 members. Brother Flade grew up strong in the Church. He eventually joined the German Army in 1943 and was a Forward Observer.

John was distressed at having to fight the Allied forces as he knew there were LDS members on the other side, including his own cousins. He worried about shooting a brother and so reflected that whenever he had the chance he would shoot, but would purposely aim poorly. He wondered if perhaps he was the reason the Germans lost the war.

John was eventually taken as a prison of War by the Americans and was transported to the United States. After the war John moved along with his wife, Alice, to the United States. There they established their family in Utah. Later, Brother Flade returned to his beloved homeland, where he served as a mission president.

Editor's note: *John Flade's story is one of many featured in the 2001 BYU documentary work,* Saints at War, *directed by talented director and writer Matt Whitaker.*

in their attic that had just been finished. There were about a dozen houses in that neighborhood that were called the Mormon settlement. All the refugees from the East worked together in building these houses with money borrowed from the government. I also did my share of helping with that project.

It seemed like a miracle to us that Alfred appeared so suddenly. We were overjoyed to see him. But what had happened to him in all that time? The story he had to tell sounded to all of us like a novel! I let him speak for himself. This is his story:

When I left you at that hedge in the forest, I stalked very carefully up to the road. Upon reaching the slope I stuck my head through the bushes only to find out that I had landed directly next to two border guards. I barely managed to duck back into the bushes without being noticed by them. I did not dare move for fear that they would hear me. I waited and waited in vain, hoping that they would move on. I could, from time to time, clearly hear the wailing of my children in the distance. Finally, two other guards came on their bicycles to relieve them. [Those were the two guards who almost had caught us while we were crossing the road.]

That gave me a chance to get away from my hiding place. But when I finally got back to the hedge, nobody was there. So, I backtracked on the path on which we had come, while calling out your names loudly. But all was in vain. Finally I decided to cross the border by myself, thinking that I could return anytime if something should have gone wrong with you. So, I crossed the road and found a path leading in the direction toward the West Zone. [That was the path that Marianne had so steadfastly refused to travel.]

After following this path, which led through a forest, I suddenly found myself among a group of border guards who were conducting some sort of field exercise. Without being noticed by them, I managed to hide in the brush. [We probably would have come upon the same group of soldiers had we followed that path, but with two wailing children we could not have hidden from them.]

When the soldiers had left I continued on the path. After climbing over a crossbeam I knew that I was in the West Zone. A church tower was my guide toward a nearby village. Approximately half a mile beyond the border I asked a farmer working in the field if he had seen someone looking like you. While talking to him I saw a group of people coming up the road. It was you, with the border guard taking you back to the East. There was nothing left for me to do but hide behind a large haystack. You walked right by me and I saw you disappear into the forest. A while later, the guard came back alone. He stopped by the haystack to chat with the farmer for a while. Then I saw you come out of the forest and disappear in another direction.

Since the guard was still standing there it was impossible for me to follow you. When he finally went on his way, all my running and calling for you did not get me anywhere. It seemed like you had vanished. I found the road leading to Hof and followed it, not on the road but parallel to it, through gardens, fields, and over fences. After it got dark, I felt a little safer and walked on the highway. There, the going was much easier. I had not traveled on that road more than five minutes when a border guard stopped me and recognized me as a refugee. (If Alfred had found us, we certainly would have walked with him on that road, and would have been caught by a border guard for the second time.)

I was locked up and interrogated. The American officer soon found out that I belonged to your party, and he mentioned that you had been taken back to the east a while ago. Whereupon, I told him that I had seen you returning to the west. At any rate, I was told that I too would be brought back to the border. After spending the night in a cell a soldier brought me back to East Germany. I did the same thing you had done. As soon as the guard was out of sight, I turned back again. This time I was luckier and reached Hof without any incident. After inquiring, I decided to travel by bus to my sister-in-law in Bavaria. The bus was cheaper and departed two hours earlier. [Had he chosen the train, he would have met us and his family there.]

After arriving there, I was very discouraged because Marianne and the children were not there, and I cried bitter tears. I assumed that you were far ahead of me since I had to spend that night in a cell. [Alfred did not know that we had not reached Hof that evening, but had stayed overnight in Feilitsch.] How happy I was, about midnight, when Marianne finally showed up. From the railroad station, she had to walk for hours through the forest in the middle of the night to the village where my sister-in-law lived. When she finally arrived there, the baby buggy collapsed.

That was Alfred's story. My father's prayer before our departure had been answered. Angels had led the way and brought us safely to freedom!

Both Alfred and Walter were able to quickly find work and begin applying for visas to the Americas. As the months passed, they were privileged to welcome into their small home many of the families from their home branch in Zwickau who had also chosen to escape the East. In April 1952, the family was granted a visa to immigrate to Canada and from there to the United States.

Ruth Birth

Ruth Birth was born March 12, 1920, in Schneidemuehl, West Prussia, the second of eleven children. Though not born into the Church, her parents readily accepted the gospel when Ruth was a little girl, eagerly inviting the missionaries in to teach the family. The Birth family was a great addition to the Schneidemuehl Branch, and Ruth's father, Friedrich, was soon called as branch president, where he would serve for many years. Friedrich, who had served as a soldier during the First World War, was a successful glassmaker by trade, and his wife, Emma, ran a small market to help support the family.

Learning the gospel together, the Birth children became very active in the branch, serving in the Primary organization and attending the many youth activities in the area. Ruth was musically talented and often provided accompaniment with her accordion at activities and meetings. Though she hated going to school, she received training as a secretary and, because of the war, was easily able to find work in the war offices of Schneidemuehl. As the war began, family life continued remarkably unchanged. Soon, however, her brothers Gerhard and Nephi were drafted and sent to the front. Both were killed in battle, which was a tragic blow to the family. Ruth's father, while too old to serve in the military, was called to serve in the Civil Defense forces of the city.

Ruth met Kurt Bratz, a young member of the Church, and the two began dating. As the war started and Kurt was drafted, their relationship continued through letters and postcards. Kurt wrote regularly, often writing postcards and letters from the battlefield. On leave, the two became engaged and began planning and waiting for another leave to be married. As the war for Germany worsened, the prospects of Kurt receiving leave dwindled. Early in 1944 Kurt was wounded and hospitalized not far from Schneidemuehl and in a city where Ruth's aunt and uncle lived. While Ruth was confident that Kurt would recover, it wasn't long until a telegram arrived for Ruth from her relatives with only three words: "Kurt is dead." The news was devastating. She did as much as she could to keep busy, but it was difficult to get over the grief of her loss. As 1945 began, Ruth decided to begin keeping a personal journal to help her with the loss.

Sunday, January 14, 1945—Today, a year ago, my Kurt died. Is it possible that it has been a full year? I can hardly believe it. How wonderful it was to be together, and what a marriage here on earth we had imagined for ourselves. The question of whether or not I will ever be ready to marry another man, I just don't know.

RUTH BIRTH FILE

Kurt Bratz's grave.

This afternoon, once again, we had a few lovely hours. Edith conducted Sunday School and substituted in the adult class. She thinks I should take the assignment in February.

I played the piano for an hour and read a little, but it was noticeable that something was missing.

Monday, January 15, 1945—A quiet day has passed. I think again and again about the last year. I received the telegram that Kurt was dead. I couldn't grasp it. Every part of me fought against what I was hearing. But Heavenly Father knew what was best. I was so egotistical and only thought about my own happiness.

It wasn't long before the events of the war began to come closer to the city of Schneidemuehl.

Thursday, January 18, 1945—Today, I wanted, above everything else, to visit Sigrid in the hospital, but nothing came of it. I, instead, had to man a display, with which I wasn't finished until 6:30.

Everyone is restless and excited. In the east our troops are fighting against 150 divisions who are pressing quickly forward. They are already to Litzmannstadt. The train station is full of refugees. Here the people are also thinking of fleeing. Papa thinks that he might never return from the Civil Defense. On the bridges, next to the tank barriers there are guards. Will we also have to leave here?

Sunday, February 4, 1945—Now I want to finally write in my journal again. I will try to remember all that's happened in the past few days. The Russians came closer and closer and the thoughts of the people edged closer and closer to the need to flee. On Saturday the 20th, I bought train tickets to Kreuz for Ulla and me. There was supposed to be a special meeting for Relief Society presidencies. Ulla was worried about leaving her little one. I, however, thought that something would certainly happen if we didn't go. The train was scheduled to leave at 6:10, and we needed to get up at 4:30 to make it. I asked Ulla to knock on my window at this time to wake me up because I was afraid of oversleeping. During the night someone knocking woke me. At first I thought it was Ulla, but I soon realized that it wasn't my window but the window above and that it was only 2:30. I couldn't hear what the matter was, but then I heard my mother very upset and begin to moan and cry.

We quickly jumped out of bed and heard the terrible news from the Party ordering us to quickly prepare to leave. Now I imagined that mothers with children should be the first to leave, but mother would hear none of it, and insisted that we had to stay and immediately began to cry again. We quickly got dressed. Naturally we put one shirt over another and one dress over another. We looked awful, even though it didn't matter, and packed up our small suitcases and bags, as we realized when the entire of Schneidemuehl had to leave so quickly there would be no way to carry a large suitcase. Morning came, and my trip to Kreuz was naturally out of the question. Midday came and we still heard nothing from the Party. At 10:00 PM I went to work. Everyone just stood around excited. We should have completed our assignments to fill out our shipping orders. They were, however, laughed at and forgotten.

At 12:00 AM we had an air raid warning. There were no airplanes coming from the west, so there must have been Soviet planes there. I pulled on my coat and left without any good-bye. It was beautiful winter weather. The horrible cold from this morning was somewhat lessened by the sun. Only the frost hung finger thick on all of the branches, and the fences looked like white walls. It was an amazing sight. The snow crunched with every step. As I was halfway home, the all clear signal sounded. At home there was a great lunch waiting. After I ate, and turned myself around a few times, I went with Christel back into the city to the office.

When we finally returned home it was already dark. A crashed airplane was burning in the fields next to Goennersweg. Mr. Schmidt was there for a short while and pled with us to come to him in Dresden if we had to flee. Papa also came home for a short time from the Civil Defense and complained that the people, through the Party, were becoming unruly. He calmed us considerably as he told us that it wasn't as bad as we were hearing. There had only been two trains that had left with women and children. We slept pretty soundly this night.

Early Monday, I went singing to the office. The winter world was so beautiful that it was almost too much for me. I thought back with affection on my beloved young Kurtl. The soldiers have built and are continuing to build defensive positions on our street and in our fields. The dirt was frozen so deep it required explosives to break up. The explosions were very powerful, but we are familiar with this kind of thing.

Everything was crazy at the office. In my office was a huge box, like in every other. We were supposed to get everything ready to pack. In the yard, the work papers and records were already burning. By midday we had packed all of our things in the boxes. We had even torn out the telephone. The registration office also packed. At noon I brought my case home with me. Suddenly in the afternoon came the watchword that there was no danger expected for Schneidemuehl and everything had to be unpacked. Himmler was there and made sure that no one was able or allowed to leave. Mr. Lohse ranted that the telephone had been torn out. So after close, I returned home with my case. The Teske furniture factory burned brightly. It was Arson.

I was very happy again on Tuesday morning. In the office was the same lousy mood. Mr. Timm reconnected our telephone. The business should be able to continue. Nothing went right for me. The prisoners of war escaped again in the night. Also my card index had been picked up in the morning so I couldn't straighten anything out. Everyone stood in little groups all over and held "camp meetings." In the afternoon we all had to sit in the conference room and endure a business lecture. In the evening I had to go out again for fire watch. Mr. Ludtke came and pled with Mother to come with him in the luggage car of the next train. Mother still wouldn't hear any of it. She did, however, eventually realize that it would be better if she also left when the children did. Mr. Kirbis also came and advised that we should leave.

So on Wednesday, Mother left with Eva, Gretel, Werner, Gitti, and Peter in the luggage car of a freight train for Dresden. Papa took her with him in the morning to the train station. Luckily he had a little free time at that moment. As I came home that evening, the house felt pretty empty. This evening, a train with relocated people left. The artillery explosions were already sounding very close.

Now every morning we are awoken by the loud shooting. The noise began this morning at 4:30 AM. On Thursday, Ulla left with her mother and children on a transport that was supposed to go to Greifenhagen. I went home today for lunch. Mr. Kirbis was there and advised us that we should be out of the city in at least three days so Schneidemuehl could be properly encircled and defended. I retrieved one of Kurtl's suits from the basement and altered the legs. These I put on and went again to the office. In the evening Mr. Kieger went to a Party meeting. There it was once again pointed out, that Schneidemuehl was in no danger, and that mothers and children could leave of their own free will, but that for workers to leave would be considered desertion. So for us that meant we had to stay, but I felt that Edith, Imi, and Christel should leave with Mrs. Kieger. We couldn't sleep very well during the night.

Early Friday I went once more safely into the office. The boss gave us all a little speech, that we couldn't leave, that our eventual departure as an entire group would be taken care of, and that Schneidemuehl was in absolutely no danger. We went back to work feeling much calmer. I burned all of my files. Then I called Edith once more and told her that she should, before anything else, get all of our bags and suitcases packed onto the sleds so that we could leave at a moments notice. I then went back to my office and worked further on my carton. At noon I suddenly received a call from the commander of the defensive positions. I threw on my shoes that I had taken off because my feet were too warm, without even tying them, and ran across the floor to get to the phone quickly. I didn't even make it to the phone. Suddenly I heard two explosions. My first thoughts were—bombs. I immediately turned around. Everyone ran to the basement. The soldiers from above us almost beat us to the cellar. The booming, explosions, and noise were incredible. The Russians were shooting at us with Stalin's Organ. After the attack was over, we made sure that the office could still function. I ran home. You could see evidence of the attack from the bomb craters in the street the whole way home. On Eichbergerstrasse, the corner house was burning brightly. At home, everyone was there with everything packed on the sleds. They all wanted to get out of the city. Wilford came on his bicycle. We saw to it that he returned home and quickly gathered his things to come with us. At the time of the attack, Marie was with her children at the train station. The train left immediately after the attack was over. I went into the entryhall and called my boss. He wasn't willing to give me the pass that he had promised to give us when we left. So I left without one. In the afternoon at 4:30 PM, we began to move with our sleds out of the city in the direction of Lebehnke.

On the way we lost Christel, Mrs. Kieger, and her twin daughters. They had to stay behind, as something wasn't right with their sled. We couldn't wait, as the streets were absolutely packed with sleds, children, and dog-pulled wagons. As we left the city we all had to hide, as Russian tanks were approaching. We left our sleds standing and ran off the road. When we heard no shooting we returned to our sleds and continued further. There were explosions in front, next to, and behind us. The only thought I could muster was: only forward, that way we don't have to endure the constant shooting and explosions any more. When a military or Red Cross vehicle came, the entire line of people came to a stand still. The mothers with their smaller kiddy wagons couldn't move very well in the snow. Here and there a wheel would come off of a wagon. It was eleven kilometers to the train station in Lebehnke. We went only another two until we came into a village because we were so thirsty and so tired. We received some coffee and a pile of straw as a bed.

A half meter of snow fell during the night and a snowstorm was blowing. How would we ever get to the train station? It was almost impossible. We sent Wilford to the train station. He was to determine if another train was going to leave. As he came to the train station, a transport train with 250 officers and refugees was just about to depart. He hurried back, but was sure that the train had already left without us. I had the feeling, however, that we had to be on that train and we should go, so we grabbed our sleds and left. It was a terrible hurry. A soldier, who was also staying with the farmer, helped us. As we approached the train station we saw the train still standing. It appeared that it could leave at any minute. At the train station they could now see us coming. The train's anti-aircraft team ran out to us and helped us, as we could hardly make it any farther. Everyone, sleds, suitcases, and all were thrown into the train, which immediately began to move, right at that moment the first shot, probably from Soviet tanks, fell into the village. The officers repacked our sleds that had come unpacked when they were thrown in. We were on our way, and for that we were very grateful to our Heavenly Father.

By Jastrow the train was packed. Two kiddy wagons were with us in our train car. It was very cold. The train stopped all over the place, sometimes for hours. The train was supposed to stay in Katzebuhr until the next morning. I went with a Lt. Lehmann to find straw and coffee. We were also able to get something to eat. The mothers with small children were supposed to be brought into the village. So we also took advantage of the invitation of a very nice family and lay down for a little while. I was given a little tiny room upstairs. The feather bed was just right. The Lieutenant slept in the kitchen on the floor. I fell asleep right away. We awoke after only a half an hour. The train was about to leave. We thanked our guests and left for the train station. We hadn't quite made it to the train station when we saw the train already rolling away. We went to the station conductor, who gave us the advice that we had better start following the train. So off we went on the railroad embankment. It was extremely difficult as the snow came up very high. Sometimes we sank up to our knees. The icy snowstorm blew so hard, that I soon had to begin to rub my face as it started to freeze. We talked back and forth, however, and were able to laugh about things. At one point we saw on the railroad embankment the outline of a tank. Luckily as we came closer it turned out to be just a clump of bushes. The going was extremely tough, but how happy were we when we finally spotted the train from far off. By Lottin we had finally reached it. We clambered into the luggage car and warmed ourselves up a bit. Then I had to lay down for a while to rest. It was too cold, however, so I pulled myself once more in front of the oven, and so passed the night.

On Sunday morning, our train arrived in Neustettin. All of the officers were required to get off the train. Our car filled up. There were also refugees from Neustettin. Just before departure the officers came back. We were glad, as they had taken care of everyone before. Finally in the afternoon our journey continued slowly on. How often the train stopped, or for long, I can't remember anymore. I stood the entire day next to the small oven, cooked coffee, warmed milk and bottles for the small children, and even roasted some liver in the evening that the train conductor had in his bag and all of this without a table or any other cooking utensils. It went okay, however. In the night we all slept half standing, half sitting.

No one was allowed to use the toilet, as we had converted it into our refrigerator. Wilford sat on it and would make us something when we were really hungry. He also made things for the officers as they had not received any food for several days. We had become friends with all the officers in the meantime. We had included all of the officers into our big family; their names were Rudi, Hermann, and Jupp. At one stop, I passed a child out of the car to Rudi. The platform was slippery and he slipped and fell with the child. The little one was just fine, but Rudi bruised his ribs pretty badly. Right after, Hermann smashed his finger. It must have hurt like crazy as he went unconscious. Rudi rubbed snow on his face, but it took awhile before he came to. Again, in Falkenburg, we had many delays. There was a hospital train on the tracks there, so Rudi went to the doctor. Besides his bruised ribs, he was also coming down with malaria. The first attack came quickly. As evening approached we arrived in Dramburg. I went with Lieutenant Lohscheidt, I mean Hermann, into the city to find food. First, we needed to find food for the officers, but weren't successful. We then went to the NSV who were shocked to hear over a thousand refugees in the train. They quickly cooked soup, made sandwiches, and organized everything necessary. They gave us a pot of coffee and a sandwich. We went back to the train to let them know that the food would soon be delivered, but the train was no longer there. That was the last thing we had expected. So again, we began to follow it. It was about five kilometers to Janikow. Nighttime, a snow storm, and deep snow on the train tracks made for extremely strenuous travel. We were very glad to find the train in Janikow.

For the longest time we stood just before Stargard. It had to have been twenty hours. In Wangerin, a tiny village just before Stargard, I went with Lt. Weber, whose first name is Jupp, to shop for food. We needed bread the most. We went from one baker to the next, but bread was sold out everywhere. Finally we came to a shop where we had to wait a little while, but we did receive bread, still hot, just out of the oven. We then were able to buy tea, sugar, grits, and other items. All packed up we returned toward the train station. On the way we stopped at a house, as I wanted to wash. Nicely enough, the people there allowed me to do so. As I was half finished we heard our train whistle. We received a quick sandwich and began to chase after the train. Soon a sled came up and took us to Rufnow. This time we arrived there just before the train did. Jupp took me with him into the army food kitchen and gave me a plate of soup. Then we went to meet our train and unpack the food we had bought. We then went with Hermann and Ingrid once more to the NSV to eat some cake. In Stargard, the officers were finally able to get food. The train left quickly to travel further. From here on we were fed through the officers.

In Angermuende we were forced once more to endure delays. However, we were able to receive lots of fresh, hot milk from a dairy there. We also met up with two other refugee trains from Schneidemuehl. We were very worried about Rudi. He was very weak from the many attacks and high fever of the malaria. He wanted to go the hospital in Dresden.

On Thursday evening we arrived in Berlin-Pomkow. Here we received sandwiches. The officers had to leave the train except for Rudi, who was to stay with us. The farewell was very difficult for them. Jupp had an especially hard time. I was also almost inconsolable. I could hardly stay standing. To top it all off the air raid sirens began. We had to stay in the train. Of course we were terrified, which only got worse, as we saw the trees catching on fire and heard the bombs exploding. Rudi was very loving. He grabbed us little scared rabbits, Imi and me, by the hand and kept us calm. When he could tell that I was okay, he made sure that there was a place made for me to lie down in the straw at the back of the car. I immediately fell asleep. Above me the wagons rocked, and all around me were packed children's feet. I couldn't even stretch out my own feet. But I slept, and so soundly that I didn't even notice when we drove out of Berlin.

In the morning, around 6:00 AM, I was awoken. Rudi was having another attack and needed my place. Our train drove further. We came to Sachsen. We were very happy, because we all wanted to make it to Dresden. We continued with our train until Riesa. The transport was to continue on toward Thueringen. Our trip into Dresden continued without too many difficulties. In Dresden we were received by many helping hands. Hitler Youth took us from the train station into the city. We rode the street car to Plauen and were then brought by a nice man with his father and his son up to Doelzschen. It was still a difficult thing, as Christel had sent a telegram from Berlin, so little Eva and Werner had already gone to the train station to pick her up. We were finally able to sleep in a bed that night. It was wonderful.

Feeling that she and her family were finally safe, Ruth searched for work in Dresden and began working in the Labor Office, arranging work papers for the many foreign workers who were in the city. As the air

RUTH BIRTH FILE

The Friedrich Birth family outside their Schneidemuehl home.

raid sirens woke her out of bed on the thirteenth of February, Ruth watched as the city of Dresden exploded in fire. The family wanted to leave, but the attacks continued and all felt it wasn't safe. Finally on the sixteenth of February, it seemed like they could get out.

At 5:00 AM, I woke Wilford and Christel and we began to pack our things. Mrs. Guenzel had already packed her wagon. For Mrs. Kroehnert we had a small wagon and a large suitcase as she wanted to come with us. At 8:30 AM we were finally able to leave, with five small hand wagons and one child's wagon. It was a terrible cruelty. Up and down the mountains. At times I thought I wouldn't make it. We had already traveled a fair distance when Mrs. Kroehnert decided she couldn't go any further. The children just wouldn't make it. We gave her the large suitcase and the small wagon that I had pulled for so long. I was very sad to see them go as I had come to really love the Kroehnert family. Would they make it safely back home? We continued further. I helped Mrs. Guenzel pull her wagon. The streets became better as we went further. The two Peters took turns sitting on top of the wagon. Two times we had air raid warnings, and one of those times a full alarm. We had to get to a shelter. But nothing ended up happening. Mother could hardly go any further. At 4:30 PM we arrived in Heidenau. There we could continue on by train. It was a good thing, as we were all so dog tired. In all of the places we had pulled our things through, the bombs had created complete havoc. Sometimes we even had to carry our heavy wagons, in order to make it around the bomb craters. First we rode the train to Pirna, where we waited an hour. Then, very late, we were able to ride farther to Bodenbach.

Around 6:00 AM we began again. This time Mrs. Guenzel was going a different direction, so we parted. We were able to ride in a D. train, or D. wagon with first and second class. That was wonderful, as we could even sleep. We always had to switch cars, so the unpacking and repacking of all of our wagons and luggage was difficult with each transfer. The wagons had to be lifted into the luggage cars each time. In Komotau the train was already packed full, and we still had to get in. With great effort we made it. In Weipert we had to change trains, thankfully for the last time.

This transfer was also very difficult, but we made it. Now we were finally in Annaberg. We had to stay at the train station as we didn't know where to go from there, and had no address. We finally thought to call Geyersdorf, where we immediately connected with Gretel. She was shocked to hear our voices, but said that someone would be there to pick us up. After an hour the ladies from Geyersdorf came with three small hand wagons to pick us up. We still had two wagons ourselves. So we moved into Geyersdorf in the dark. We were greeted warmly from the brothers and sisters of the village. We only wanted something to eat and then to be able to sleep as long as we could.

In Geyersdorf, the members welcomed the Birth family and provided them with everything they needed. Ruth quickly found work in the nearby city of Annaberg, and the family quickly settled into a normal routine. From the local members of the Church came a great strength, and Ruth found great joy meeting with the Saints, even in the face of adversity.

Saturday, February 24, 1945—In the afternoon we walked to Wiesenbad and then took the train from there to Scharfenstein. The train was so full that we could only get on by forcing our way on. From Scharfenstein we had an hour's walk to Drehbach. Because the train had been over an hour late we arrived at the house meeting very late. We were only there a few minutes when Brother Schaarschmidt, who was speaking at that moment, was called outside. Outside was a police officer who was there on assignment from the secret police. We had to end the meeting. The devil just will not allow for a congregation in Drehbach. He is obviously quite mistaken, as the word of God will continue to be preached there. The journey back to Scharfenstein was beautiful. The moon shone through the high pines that stood in its way. We sang the whole way and had to run the last few steps, so we could make our train.

Sunday, March 4, 1945—Today was fast Sunday, a wonderful day. Mother now comes with us, regardless of weather, the whole long way to the meeting. What a joy. In Schneidemuehl we prayed and fasted so many times for this and now our fasting and prayers are answered. How wonderful our gospel is. When I think of how great the blessings are that our Heavenly Father gives us every day, I know that we don't deserve so much love and goodness. In testimony meeting almost all of the testimonies were from members who have either been bombed out or have fled their homes. I couldn't have stood up as my tears were flowing so hard.

Sunday, March 25, 1945—We went to conference. What wonderful words for us, especially those of us who have had to leave our homes. We slept very well at the Fassmann's, but did have to get up rather early so we wouldn't be late to the meeting. I will never forget the pie we received for breakfast, as it was especially good. The first person I saw that I recognized at the meeting was Sister Schmidt from Kreuz. We were so happy to see each other. Then I ran into almost all of the members from Tilsit. Even Brother Schulzke was there. It was almost like I was in Tilsit. I could have cried the whole day for joy. Brother Schmidt was especially happy. The theme of the conference was "obedience, the first path to progress." Our wonderful gospel was once again presented in conversation, poems, and talks. I felt especially how worthwhile the gospel is for us. Everything was full of a wonderful spirit. We actually wanted to return on Sunday but there were no more trains to Annaberg. So we went to the Gangiens. We were able to experience a few more wonderful hours there.

Even with the strength of the gospel, the realities of the war looming near were not lost on Ruth and her family.

Thursday, April 5, 1945—The people are becoming angry about their situations; they aren't receiving enough to eat anymore, the danger of air attacks is present everyday. Today we had three air raid warnings and three full alarms. Some claim they can even hear the shooting from the front.

It could be possible, the Americans are moving quickly, and if it continues, they could be here in a week. There is fighting already in Thueringen. Only a few still believe that Germany can win. I haven't given up hope yet, I am German after all. This evening we had a house meeting again. It was very nice.

Sunday, April 8, 1945—This was once again a very eventful day. I didn't get up until 10:00 AM, as we weren't able to get to bed till midnight last night because of an alarm. As we went to meeting, we had the third full alarm of the day. We went ahead anyway and by the time the all clear came we were almost to Annaberg. I went as if in a dream, as Edith had shared something with me right beforehand; papa might have been killed in Koenigsblick. I can't and won't believe it and only hope that it isn't true, because how can Mother handle it. No, it can't be true, that we'll only see our Papa first after we die. How is Mother supposed to endure this difficult trial? But the hope is still there that it is just a mistake.

We had a wonderful meeting. We were told that we had no need to fear. Every Wednesday at 7:10 PM, every member in Germany will join in prayer. Now that will be a great power. In the evening we also had a wonderful house meeting. Thirty people were there, including five elders. Erika also spoke. She said we must be a light to all people, especially in these times. I really want to try to bring a little joy into the lives of those whom I meet. Afterward we sang, which is always such a wonderful thing.

Monday, April 16, 1945—It is not nice; the whole day we had to sit in the office and couldn't do a thing. As a result there is a terrible tension in the air. We can't do anything except wait for what's to come. There were no warnings the whole day. But there were strafing attacks again. The planes now come over a whole lot. We have to always be ready to jump. This morning in Weipert they had an invasion alarm. It was called off by noon. The Americans are already coming from the direction of Bayreuth-Egerhoch. There is fighting in the areas around Leipzig and Chemnitz. Sometimes the sound of shooting is so loud and close, that you think it was only twenty kilometers away. This evening I sat in front of our door and played the accordion. We promised that when anything came we would go down to the cellar.

NATIONAL ARCHIVES

Women searching for food in bombed out Leipzig.

Tuesday, April 17, 1945—I wasn't able to sleep well in the night. The military vehicles are still driving past through our neighborhood. In between you can hear the foot soldiers, some of whom look like they might be staying in our area. Our bus is still going. The bombers are making it really bad. They were there the whole day. Because of them I couldn't even go to lunch. I went to Bastian's, and wasn't a second back in the office when a full alarm sounded. The planes were already over us. In the office basement I just didn't feel right, and as about four hundred airplanes were flying over I ran with Ms. Unger all the way up the horrible mountain to the Bastian's. I shouldn't do that again, as I was half dead by the time we got there. In total, there were about six hundred planes over us along the way. They were flying very low. In Geyersdorf, two vehicles were destroyed by fighter planes. Shot and burned out.

As news of armies in the neighboring villages and cities grew, there was great fear. Yet, with this news also came news of a different sort. As the American army grew closer, word started to spread among the Saints that contact had been made with LDS soldiers. From them, the German Saints learned that President Heber J. Grant was still alive and leading the Church, and that there was great concern over the welfare of the German Saints. It was a great relief to finally be free of the isolation from other members of the Church. On May 7, the unconditional surrender of Germany was announced. For Ruth it was a great shock but also a tremendous relief.

May 8, 1945—I could hardly sleep the whole night. The line of refugees hasn't let up. The entire military from the area of Dresden-Freiberg is coming too. I didn't go to bed till midnight last night. Downstairs at the Schaarschmidt's they are busy providing quarters for as many as they can. All of the soldiers want to go to "Ami" (the Americas). They buy whatever they can and then leave again. In the morning I fried liver for some of them. There is no peace for anyone. In the afternoon came the news; the Russians are in Wiesenbad, which is only a few kilometers away. They are coming to Annaberg. In the evening a few of them arrived on motorcycles but drove further. All of our soldiers are gone. A few have come back, with white bands on their arms, as we are supposed to be at peace, even with the Russians. I sure imagined peace to be different.

May 9, 1945—Now we are under Russian control. A lot of Russian military moved past our street this morning. Some of them go into the houses and take what they want. It is terrible. Everything is rifled through. They are especially interested in watches and rings. At midday we heard that the Americans were going to come here. That would be nice. It doesn't look like it will actually happen, though.

A few times I was completely alone as the Russians with raised weapons came in. I wasn't scared and continued my work. They stayed standing in the doorway and then left without even touching a thing.

May 19, 1945—This morning I awoke to the sound of horse hooves and loud talking and yelling. A quick look out the window told me that once more Russian troops were moving through. I wasn't able to go over to our room till 5:30 PM. I had a lot to do the whole day, because tomorrow is Pentecost. Yesterday the girls came back from Chemnitz. It must be terrible there. Ninety-three percent of the city is just rubble. There is hardly anything to eat and you can't drink the water without boiling it, as it is contaminated, probably from the many bodies lying in the waterway. Potato peels are dried, ground, and used as flour. We eat green cabbage, nettles, and common sorrel, but it tastes very good. Today we cooked our Pentecost cake with flour, sugar, and water. I have never baked a cake like this. It should taste very good, however. We're just glad that we still have a cake.

May 20, 1945—First day of Pentecost and with it horrible, cold, rainy weather. Also this morning I had a terrible headache. At 9:00 AM we had Sunday School and I had to teach. It went well, which made me very happy. The topic was "striving above." Afterwards we went to Sister "Marie" Schaarschmidt, and brought her some flowers and sang the song, "Oh, how wonderful was my latest dream" then today is also Mother's Day. You hardly notice any of these special days this year. As we were returning from Sister Schaarschmidt's we began to run as we saw Soviet infantry troops coming up the mountain. I dove through the window—with German uniforms and caps some Russians look very German, there were even some handsome young men with them. It was already 11:30, high time to get to Church. We went out and as we got up onto the country road, all of the Soviets were gone and we were able to make it to Buchholz without trouble. On our way back we had to sneak in the back as in front of the house some Russians were fiddling with a car. They were drunk and Mr. Klaus was being forced to help them. They were at our door three times, but Mother shut it in their faces. You could hear very loudly through the entire house "open up!" Mother thought we wouldn't be able to eat our lunch, but I said that if we blessed our food, no one would bother us and no one would be taken from us. And that's what happened, too. Afterward we had to watch as two Russian women plundered through the Kaufmann's house, and there was nothing we could do to stop it. Edith had all of her stuff taken from the house, because she sleeps there. Everything was gone. Her best clothes were there. The Russians in front of our house weren't finished with the car, as it was time to get to the Schaarschmidt's for our house meeting. We went as quickly as we could across the street but they grabbed Christel and she had to clean their car. I was so furious, but I couldn't do anything.

As conditions worsened, it quickly became evident that no refugees would be able to remain in the Annaberg area. If they did, they would not receive ration cards, and would be unable to eat.

On Friday, the sixth of July, Luci Meyer stopped by and told us that in Buchholz an announcement had been made that all refugees had to go and would no longer receive food cards. Now it was our turn also to leave. Where should we go? On Saturday, Luci and I traveled to Zwickau. We figured we could round up all of the members who had been quartered here or were refugees and travel to Meklenburg. We also wanted to find a good priesthood holder and were thinking about Brother Schulzke. In Zwickau, our plan failed, as there and in the surrounding area, all the refugees were still allowed to stay, including the Schulzke's. On Saturday evening we traveled to Steinpleiss where we were taken care of by a lovely sister and allowed to sleep. Brother Schulzke had suggested that we all come to Zwickau, until they also might have to leave, so we were excited and tried to find a place to stay in Zwickau and Werdau. On Monday we were given a few places where we could stay and a few pounds of salt, so we returned to Buchholz, or Geyersdorf, with the news.

Later, we met a sister who shared with us a wonderful message. Brother Lehnig and Brother Krause were there. The refugees were all to travel and camp at Cottbus and in the evening there would be a special meeting at Bastian's. That was such wonderful news. We couldn't get home fast enough for lunch to tell Mother and the others. In the evening, the meeting was exactly what we were hoping for. We knew both Brother Lehnig and Brother Krause. They spoke with fire and with such an excitement that we were carried along. What a wonderful chance for us to hear the word of God preached with such power. Afterward I went to speak to both brethren about our upcoming trip. In the evening Brother Ranglacke and Brother Langheinrich, from the mission leadership, came. On Saturday, the four brethren, as well as Brother Schramm and Brother Wagner, came to visit us in Geyersdorf. We had another special meeting. Mother received a testimony again, as after the meeting Christel arrived from Doebeln, and brought us bread, so much that we were able to give some to the brethren.

Our trip was set to begin early Tuesday. Monday was a tough day, as we hadn't packed anything yet. I also had to go to Buchholz to get instructions from Brother Langheinrich, as I had been chosen as travel leader with responsibility for thirty-one people traveling to Cottbus. Edith was also able to come. She had also been called by Brother Langheinrich to work on genealogy in this area. Eva had to stay here. Sister Bendler, who I would rather call Ingrid, a new missionary, also came along. On Monday evening we moved to Buchholz with our luggage, two handcarts full, where we stayed with other members in the Froebel school. On the way we were surprised by a downpour that soaked us to the skin. Our first travel day arrived, extremely cool from the great amount of rain falling. We had to plan for four days of travel.

The brethren had come personally to the train station to see us off, early, as our train left at 5:12 AM. I took over my responsibility, 31 people, including two babies in carriages and three handcarts full of luggage, not including all of the luggage that the members were carrying

CHURCH REFUGEE CENTERS

With more than 85 percent of Church members left homeless, and thousands more refugees and scattered across the country at war's end, Church leaders authorized the formation of refugee centers for Church members to gather. Not only did these locations provide needed relief and support, but they also allowed leaders to take note of who was still unaccounted for.

In some locations, like the East German cities of Chemnitz and Cottbus, these centers were simply a concentration of Saints in an area where local government restrictions on refugees were not strict, and it was possible to gather enough ration cards to support everyone. In other locations, such as Wolfsgruen and Langen, members where able to obtain property and structures to house the growing numbers of refugees needing help. In Wolfsgruen, for example, Church leaders located a mansion in which approximately one hundred Latter-day Saints could be cared for at any given time. Although great challenges still confronted those who lived there, the facility served as a safe shelter, a place for convalescence, and a Church center. Everything from constant shortages of food and other supplies to harassment from local authorities were a part of the experience of the Saints at Wolfsgruen and the other centers. Nonetheless, many Saints regained hope and started new lives.

Source: *Regional Studies in Latter-day Saints Church History: Europe* (Brigham Young University, 2003).

CHURCH ARCHIVES

The Wolfsgruen Chateau provided a safe haven for displaced members of the Church.

CHURCH ARCHIVES

Saints gather at a Church refugee center in Langen, central Germany.

themselves. I already had to deal with the fact that I was a little queasy. But just for a moment. The train arrived already full. With a lot of effort and urgency we were able to get everyone on. Brother Langheinrich made sure we knew that Chemnitz was our first station. We had a few hours wait there. I sent Edith and Werner to the Kinder's to get some warm coffee. No one else was allowed to leave the station as I had all of their tickets in my bag. Around noon, Edith returned with the sisters from the Relief Society who had brought us hot coffee and tea. Our journey continued at about two in the afternoon. Everyone was pushing and shoving to get onto the train. Once more with a lot of effort we were able to get all of the members on, especially the sisters with carriages and our carts with the luggage underneath. The other carts and a few cases we were able to get up onto the roof. Ingrid scrambled into the last car with Werner's help. We secured everything very tight with rope, and after I had made sure that everyone had made it aboard, we sat down on the buffer. It was very cold. On the way, the conductor gave me a little place to sit in one of the cars. And so we went till Riesa. We had to stay overnight there. This time in a former hotel. For our place to stay, we received a dirty room. We were very happy to get it though, as we were completely alone and could actually say a prayer.

The group continued on, and with great help from the Lord they were able to make it to the Church refugee camp in Cottbus. For Ruth, the stay was short, as she was called to return to Annaberg with her sister Edith to work as a missionary collecting as many genealogical records as possible. After a few months, Ruth was called to serve as a full-time missionary in the mission home in Berlin. The mission home was located in free zone of Berlin, so when her service was completed after two years, she chose to remain in West Germany. She continued to volunteer in the West German mission home, and then traveled to England to work as a nanny before immigrating to the United States. Once in Salt Lake City, Ruth was able to arrange for sponsors for the rest of her family, who by this time had left East Germany, to allow them to also come to America.

Edith Birth Rohloff

Edith Birth Rohloff was born February 18, 1923, in Schneidemuehl, West Prussia, the third child of Friedrich and Emma Birth. Her parents were baptized only three months after she was born. Edith loved the gospel, and especially the branch in Schneidemuehl. While she always dreamed of being a teacher or nurse, she was responsible for helping her mother run the family market. While she was never able to teach by profession, she found great joy teaching Primary and the youth of the branch.

While we younger folks didn't realize what was coming up, the older generation did. Hitler had taken back one piece after another of former German land, taken away after the First World War and given to other nations. It was a matter of time when other more powerful nations would not go along with what he was doing. My hometown was a border town on the Polish border. Many German soldiers were stationed there. When Germany attacked Poland on September 1, 1939, we really feared to see war action in our town, but surprisingly not much happened. Of course no one knew the outcome of the war. For five and a half years Germany would battle the world and at the end be in rubble and ashes. We lost our homeland, our home, two of my brothers, Gerhard and Nephi, and my fiancé, Helmut. All three were killed in action in Russia. My younger sister Eva died after the war of typhoid fever. Every family in Germany was affected by this terrible war.

My brother Gerhard was the first in our family who had to leave home. He was drafted into the German Army. After a short drill in Germany his unit was transferred to Russia and was engaged in action. Gerhard was wounded on the battlefield and transported to a military hospital in the city of Koenigsberg. Here he met Helga Meiszus, who later became his wife. Helga, from the city of Tilsit, was attending district conference in Koenigsberg. The youth attending the conference visited the wounded LDS soldiers. On Gerhard's next furlough on the eleventh of February 1942, he married Helga in Tilsit. After only four days he had to return to the battlefield in Russia. He was killed in the war on the first of April 1942. We all were shocked and saddened.

RUTH BIRTH FILE

Gerhard Birth and Helga Meyer, 1942.

We all had sweet memories. It was not so long ago, he had taught me how to drive a car and now he would not return. It was hard on my parents. Father lost his son who helped him in the beginning with his business which was now flourishing nicely. How devastating this news must have been for his wife, Helga. We all wished the terrible war would come to an end.

Our district conference in Schneidemuehl was always a spiritual feast. We expected many visitors from our district and from the mission home. Brother Paul Langheinrich, the counselor of President Herbert Klopfer, and a lady missionary, were our guests. During the conference my dad said to me, "Edith, Brother Langheinrich wants to talk to you." The way he said this brought fear into my heart. When I met Brother Langheinrich, he told me that our mission president wanted me to serve a two-year mission in the mission office of the East-German mission in Berlin. My heart stood still. Why me? Everyone in our branch was very excited about my call, and I was nervous.

In September 1941, I started my mission for The Church of Jesus Christ of Latter-day Saints. The war had started in 1939, and the mission president, President Rees, and all American missionaries had been called home to America. Elder Herbert Klopfer, who was living in Berlin, was called to be the acting mission president in the East-German mission. He was a very fine man and very capable to be the president. He was married and had two small children, Herbert and Ruediger. He took two local brethren as counselors, Brothers Richard Ranglack and Paul Langheinrich. Both were still working.

The mission had twelve districts, from East Prussia in the east to Thuringia in the west, and from Mecklenburg and Pomerania in the north to Silesia and Saxony in the south. At that time all young men were drafted to serve in the war. We did not have any missionaries in the field or in the mission home. Only lady missionaries could be called to serve. There were four of us lady missionaries at the time, Ilse Reimer, Erika Fassmann, Irmgard Gottschalk, and I. Later Ilse Reimer was honorably released, and Gretel Dzirson took her place.

It was my first time being away from home. After a short time, I got used to my new life and enjoyed it very much. I became independent and loved what I was doing. Our work was mostly in the mission home. I was in charge of the Primary in the mission. While at home I had started teaching Primary when I was only thirteen years old, and now I was directing the activities in all the Primaries in the mission. At home I had learned to teach. I learned now how to lead, to instruct, and to help. It was surprising how fast I was able to learn because of my calling. There was no connection with Church headquarters in Salt Lake City and not much sympathy from the German government. After all, we were a church with headquarters in America, Germany's enemy.

The greatest need was for lesson material for all the organizations. In my diary I wrote about the many manuals we had to type and print, the manuals for the Sunday School, Primary, genealogy, Gospel Doctrine class, the monthly *Sonntagsgruss* (Sunday greeting), etc. We had a little printing press in one room of the office, which was always in use. All these printings had to be packed and taken to the post office in a little hand wagon. At one time I remember a heavy rainstorm surprised us and we had to take home all the packages and repack them. We were very busy but we enjoyed every minute of it.

The mission home was in the most beautiful place in Berlin, near the *Tiergarten* (zoological garden). We visited the garden as often as it was possible. What was not so nice, even dangerous, were the Allied air raids over Berlin that increased as the years went by. At that time these air raids came by night. We were barely asleep when the sirens woke us up again. Sometimes we were just too tired and we stayed in bed, but when we heard the bombs falling, we would jump up and run to the nearby cellar. Sometimes we would sit for hours in the cellar, which was always cold and smelly. Sometimes we would run to the bunker which was located under the *Siegesaeule* (victory pillar) but cellars and bunkers saved the lives of many people.

There were highlights for us missionaries when we visited with the brethren at the district conferences, which were still held. Some branches had to be closed because the meeting rooms were taken away or no priesthood was there anymore. Others now held meetings in homes. But many still functioned well, even though many brethren were in the armed forces and many had been killed. But all the members looked forward to the district conferences. These conferences strengthened our testimony and kept us together and gave us support to stand up for the teachings of Jesus Christ. We had to teach and speak in these meetings. It was always uplifting and felt so good being party of it. Even later people remembered me from those years.

In the fall of 1942, I visited the district conferences in Zwickau (Saxony), Koenigsberg (East Prussia), and Danzig (West Prussia). I also attended the district conference in Chemnitz in the state of Saxony. At the conference meetings, I had to speak, as usual. After the meeting in Chemnitz I met a young man, Helmut Kinder, who was on furlough from the army. He complimented me on my talks and told me how impressed he was with my thoughts. Chemnitz was his hometown. We talked and after he had to go back to his unit, but to my surprise I received a letter from him. We kept in touch by writing to each other. He was four years older than I, and he was a tall, handsome man.

RUTH BIRTH FILE

The Birth sisters outside their Schneidemuehl home.

My father with his large glass company was always in demand when large towns were bombarded. All the broken windows had to be repaired as fast as possible. My eighteen-year-old brother, Nephi, had to go to Hamburg with a group of craftsmen. Hamburg had another terrible air raid and needed help. On his way home he visited me in Berlin. This was the last time I saw my brother Nephi alive. It was August 1943, and a month later he was drafted into the army and was sent to Russia. In the spring of 1944, he was reported missing in action. He never came home. It is very hard to hear that one of your loved ones has been killed in action, but it is even harder to read that he is missing in action.

RUTH BIRTH FILE

A Church conference held in Dresden in 1946.

Because of the circumstances in the prison of war camps in Russia, you never knew how they died. Nephi was such a special, fine young man. How did he die? Was he shot? Was he taken prisoner? Did he die of starvation as so many did in the Russian prisoner of war camps? Just missing in action—that was hard to take.

The last district conference I visited was in Berlin. Here I had to give my last talk as a missionary. My father and four of my sisters, Ruth, Irmgard, Eva, and Gretel, were in attendance. My wonderful mission call came to an end. I was released on the third of November 1943. For more than two years I had the great opportunity to serve, learn, and appreciate the teachings of Jesus Christ as a missionary. I made many friends, met wonderful people, received a greater testimony, and learned to love the Lord so very much. Many wonderful people found a place in my heart. How grateful I am that I accepted that calling.

I appreciated the work and guidance of my mission president Herbert Klopjer and his wife very much. His counselors, Brother Langheinrich and Brother Ranglack, and their wives were an inspiration to me. They did so much for us young girls. I loved each one of my companions and appreciated the great friendship we had with each other. In the time I served my mission, our mission president, Herbert Klopfer, was stationed in Berlin with his army unit. He was a stalwart, good-hearted man, but as the war went on, he too was sent to Russia with his unit. He was taken as a prisoner of war and died in the camp. A comrade saw him die and reported it to the Klopfer family after he returned home.

In the night of November 22, 1943, I had been home for just two weeks, when the part of Berlin where the mission home was standing was hit by a terrible air raid. All the houses around the mission home were destroyed. The windows of the mission home were broken, and the ceiling and the roof were damaged. The sisters cleaned up the mission home the next morning and roughly repaired the ceiling and roof. In the midday Brother Langheinrich came. The spirit had whispered to him to bring all the sisters out of the mission home immediately. He placed the lady missionaries in his home. The following night the mission home was completely destroyed. Our brethren were really inspired; they took all belongings, especially the genealogical records, out of the building during the day between the attacks.

On my first weekend home we had a visitor. Walter Rohloff was on his way from the Russian front to his garrison city, Schwerin, to attend the army officer academy in Thorn. He visited us, of course, without having permission and a furlough permit. He had to pass by Schneidemuehl again on his way to the academy and stopped by our home again, once again without a permit. He just couldn't pass Schneidemuehl without seeing us. We were always happy to see him. He was always such a nice happy man, full of pep.

Four months after my mission, Helmut Kinder, the young man I met on my mission, got furlough from the army and visited me and my family in Schneidemuehl. We took the time to get to know each other better. We found that we had a lot in common. We loved to read, loved music, and loved the gospel. We enjoyed every minute we had to together. It was a wonderful time for me. He had to give a talk, and we even sang a duet together in church. My family liked him very much, too. We fell in love and got engaged on the eighth of March 1944. Before he returned to his unit he gave my sister, Irmgard, enough money to always buy me fresh flowers. He was very attentive and mindful. His unit was stationed in France, and we hoped it would stay there, and that he wouldn't be transferred to Russia. We wanted to get married as soon as possible. We met once more in Dresden, where he had come as a secret courier. We spent the day hiking in the beautiful mountains surrounding the city. It was a lovely winter day.

Later the news reached me; Helmut had been transferred to Latvia, Russia. I had misgivings about this. My brother Gerhard had lost his life in Russia. In July of 1944, we had received the news that Nephi, who was also on the Russian front, was missing in action and in all probability also had been killed. Now Helmut was also in Russia. The radios and newspapers didn't bring much comfort. Allied troops had landed in France and were marching toward Germany's border. German troops had left Africa and were now fighting on Italy's soil. Italy, the much praised friend of Germany, had turned against Germany and was fighting for the Allies. Wherever you looked, the German Army was in retreat. In Russia, the army retreated and had heavy casualties, but what we experienced most at home were the air raids.

I had written in a letter to Helmut that my beautiful wedding dress was ready and we were preparing for our wedding. I placed the letter on a crystal bowl in my bedroom to mail the next day. The next morning (September 9, 1944) a noise woke me up; it sounded like someone had thrown a rock through my window. I jumped up and saw that my crystal bowl was broken. The crystal fragments had formed a heart and a cross. When my father saw the fragments, he said, "I am sorry, my child, but I have to tell you, your fiancé was killed this morning. He did this to let you know he was dying." I didn't want to believe it, but from that time on my letters were returned. I later learned that on the ninth of September 1944, Helmut and another soldier were laying telephone lined between army units in Latvia. They didn't return from this assignment, and no one knew what happened to them. It was hard to understand how fast a dream can end. It ended for me.

—•—

The condition for Germany was hopeless. The Allied troops had reached Germany's western border. The Russians were standing before Warsaw. The air raids increased and it was hard to travel from one place to the next. Now boys fourteen and fifteen years old were drafted into the army. My father was drafted into the *Volkssturm*, an old man's guard. He was fifty-one years old. This Volkssturm was organized all over

Germany. Old and handicapped men, who up to now had not been drafted, were called up. It was the last effort by the Nazis to sacrifice the very young and the old so they could live a little longer. This Volkssturm was poorly trained and poorly armed.

Of course the question arises, "Why did the people go along with these orders?" There are many reasons why they did. First of all, only a few protested and took action. These few were killed and were labeled as traitors. Second, there was the fear to be imprisoned. Hardly anyone would say a word against the government because no one knew who was an informer. Most everyone knew about someone who had spoken and was taken away and never returned home. Then there was the Joseph Goebbels propaganda. I think most people recognized him as a liar, but then many felt there must have been something right about what he said. He couldn't lie that much. He talked about a *Wunderwaffe* (miracle weapon) which would change the outcome of the war. In regards to that, he didn't lie; Germany was working on the atomic bomb. Only the Allied bombardment of the plant and the fast progress of the Allied troops prevented Germany from having the bomb first.

By order of the government on August 11, 1944, the defense of Schneidemuehl was prepared. People were ordered to dig trenches around the city. My sister Christel helped dig these trenches. We were all worried what the next days would bring. The large stream of people coming from the East who had left their homes and fled before the Russian Army made us think that we might also have to join them and perhaps experience the horror stories they talked about, being mistreated, raped, or killed. We prayed a lot to the Lord for guidance.

Christmas 1944 was the last Christmas in our old homestead. A dear friend of our family, Walter Rohloff, snuck in, as he had done many times before. His unit was on Germany's western border, and he had made it through all the battles. He had received a furlough for his bravery. The Lord had protected him during all of the war action. On Christmas Day his unit was part of the German Army that started the last major German attack against the Allied forces. He was glad to be with us and not with his unit. An uncertainty lay over all of us. No one knew what would come tomorrow.

Our cousin Sigrid Kindt was in a hospital with nerve paralysis. She was released even though she was so sick. My mother took her into our home. Because she couldn't walk, her fourteen-year-old brother, Wilford, put her on a sled and brought her over to our house. After a few days, we didn't see any improvement, and my father felt she needed a priesthood blessing. In the blessing he promised her complete recovery. After the blessing she was well and when her stepmother, with her little children, left town to escape the Russian Army, she was able to carry their heavy suitcase.

With Father drafted, we lost our leader. My mother was very worried. We had two businesses which we had to keep open by order of the government. Mothers, with smaller children, were permitted to leave town. We begged our mother to go, but she didn't want to leave. She was too afraid that she would never see her older children alive again. We prayed about it, and like a miracle, the next day our neighbor came over and told us that he would drive a train to Berlin the next day and that he could take our mother and the children along. That was an answer to our prayer. We tried to convince our mother that we would be okay. We were sure that we would be protected and guided. Mother took the train with Eva, Gretel, Werner, Brigitte, and Peter to Berlin and from there continued to Dresden. We took an offer from Mrs. Guenzel, a friend of our family, that in case the Russian Army threatened us, we could move our home to Doelschen-Dresden.

We girls who stayed in Schneidemuehl kept our businesses open. Irmgard took care of the glass and art store, and Christel and I ran the grocery store. Ruth had to return to work in a government office.

We thought we would be safe for a while. We were never so wrong. Only two days after Mother left, the Russian Army started bombarding our city. We knew Schneidemuehl had been declared a *Festung* (fortress). We didn't know what to do, so we prayed. We felt that only God could give us the right feeling. We didn't want to be part of the Festung Schneidemuehl.

Many of our neighbors packed what they could carry and went their way westward to escape the Russian Army. We saw them moving and asked ourselves if we would soon be part of the thousands of fleeing and homeless.

While under bombardment we packed two children sleds with food and warm clothing. Children sleds were the safest transportation to pack. They could travel through deep snow and could be left in case of danger. I took my father's scriptures he loved so much and my own scriptures and diary along. Then I thought of our ration cards and thought they might help us later, so I took them along as well. Everything else we left behind.

My cousin Wilford Kindt came to us and asked if we would take him with us. His stepmother with the small children and his older sister Sigrid could leave by train, but the military police wouldn't let him go. He was fifteen years old, and they felt he should be a soldier. We were happy to take him with us. We locked our house and left. It was the twenty-sixth of January 1945, and a foot of snow was on the ground and it was very cold. We had grown up here and it was a terrible feeling to leave everything behind. We loved this place, where we used to sing, play music and games, and had our harmonious family life. We loved our neighbors, our friends, and we loved our LDS branch. But I think we loved our lives more than anything else and we left with the hope, one day to return. That day never came. Our decision to leave must have been inspired by God.

Big craters covered the streets, but when we went on our way through the city the shelling stopped. We were a part of the many people who were trying to escape before the Russian Army could reach us. Our neighbor Mrs. Rieger was with us. She had a large down comforter on her sled. It had started to slip and Christel gave her a hand tying it down when the call came that there were tanks ahead. Everyone went for cover and in the confusion we lost Christel and Mrs. Rieger. Christel saw us from a distance, but because of the large crowds of people could not reach us. She was all by herself with nothing, not even money. The only thing she had in the pocket of her winter coat was a sandwich. We felt terrible and waited and looked everywhere but couldn't find her. We worried much about her, but we hoped we would see her in Lebehnke, the next village, where we wanted to stop. We didn't meet her there, but we had as consolation, the knowledge that she knew the address of Mrs. Guenzel in Dresden where we had planned to meet our mother and brothers and sisters.

Through the deep snow we walked along the highway northward, close to the River Kueddow toward the next village. It was minus twenty degrees Fahrenheit. We were dressed warm, but our shoes were not made for walking in the snow. Pulling the sled was hard on us, but we didn't feel it much. All we could think about was getting away from the Russian Army. We stopped in Lebehnke, but the farmer who we were supposed to meet was packing, too. Unknown to us, the Russian Army had just conquered the town of Schoenfeld only eight miles east of us on the other side of the river. Every able body was fleeing the Russian Army. Men from the German Army had made their quarters in the farmer's home. He made room for us and allowed us to stay the night in the living room. Early the next morning, the farmer left with only what he could place on one wagon. There were still horses in the stables and cows waiting to be milked and chickens running around the farm. After the farmer had left, the soldiers made themselves comfortable and started to kill the chickens. They tried to talk us into staying with them, but we were not interested in becoming their maids.

We could hear the thundering of guns coming close. What would our fate be?

We could hear the thundering of guns coming close. What would our fate be? We remembered there was a railroad station about one and a half miles away. We thought there might be a train there to take us away. My cousin Wilford had a bike and we sent him to the station. There was a train at the railroad station. He was told to get on the train, because it was supposed to leave any minute. Wilford told them he had to notify his cousins who were waiting for him in the village. The man asked him if it was more important for him to save his own life or his cousins'. But bless Wilford, he took the risk and hurried back as fast as he could and told us about the train. The train was filled with army officers and refugees, but by now it was probably gone. I said, "The train is an answer to our prayers, and if God will, we will reach that train." We hurried as fast as we could. The soldiers had given us big boots to wear. They were warmer, but it was harder to walk. From a distance we could hear the whistle of the train giving the signal to leave. Now, so short before our goal, we weren't sure if we would make it. We could hardly go any faster, but then soldiers from a nearby anti-aircraft unit saw our effort and came to help us. With their help we made it to the train. Barely inside, the train started to move. Out of breath and exhausted but deeply moved, our thanks went up to our Heavenly Father.

Under normal circumstances, the train ride from Schneidemuehl to Berlin would take two and a half to three hours. It took us eight long days and nights. The conditions in the freight car were very poor. There was no food, no heat, no water, and no toilets. The food we had brought from home we shared with other people. We three sisters were young and strong and helped wherever we could. When the train stopped at a railroad station, we would take the half frozen babies out to get them warm again. Babies and small children and old people had the hardest time, and many died. We were asked many times by our fellow refugees if we were working for the Red Cross. Of course we were not, but it felt good to help and comfort people in need. Everybody was tired, hungry, and cold, and the train was so very slow and the people so afraid that the Russian Army would catch up with us that some people just left the train. I never considered leaving the train; I thought it was still the safest way to escape. My sister Ruth left twice to look for straw and food, and when she returned each time the train had already left. The train was so slow that she could catch up again.

We made many detours over Neustettin, Angermuende, Polzin, Stargard in Pommern. In Neustettin many high ranking officers came into our train and they were really a blessing for us. They had to be in Berlin as fast as possible, and that gave our train priority over the others. Because of that we passed some trains that had been standing at the railroad stations for days.

One night I was up late writing in my diary. Everybody around me was asleep. I was sitting on our hard sled and my back was hurting. The train had been standing for more than twenty hours, and we didn't know why. We had no radio and didn't know how far the Russian Army was from us. What would be our fate? The fear of falling into the hands of the Russians never left us. But when I prayed, a calm feeling came over me. Still sitting with my thoughts, I heard other train refugees singing. Death had taken their little baby and they found solace in the hymn, "So nimm denn meine Haende" ("Lord Take My Hands and Lead Me).

Lord take my hands and lead me upon life's way
Direct, protect, and feed me from day to day.
Without your grace and favor I go astray;
So take my hand, O Savior, and lead the way.

Lord, when the tempest rages, I need not fear;
For you, the Rock of Ages, are always near.
Close by your side abiding, I fear no foe,
For when your hand is guiding, in peace I go.

Lord, when the shadows lengthen and night has come,
I know that you will strengthen my steps toward home,
And nothing can impede me, O blessed friend!
So, take my hands and lead me unto the end.

(Words by Julie Hausmann, Tune by Friedrich Silcher)

A melancholy feeling came over me. Tears were rolling down my cheeks. I remembered this hymn from when we would sing it at home or in church. But now we were sitting here in the dark and the future was bleak. Yet, somehow this hymn lifted me up and made me feel good. The horror pictures that other refugees had impressed upon my mind about the Russians

"I THE LORD AM BOUND"

Throughout the course of the war, it seemed that almost no German city or town was spared the utter devastation brought by constant allied bombing raids and advancing enemy troops. Civilian casualties mounted, and almost everyone had lost homes. As Church officials attempted to ascertain Church members' conditions and the condition of the branches throughout Germany, it became readily apparent that the Church as a whole had been spared by miraculous means. Though close to 85 percent of the members had lost their homes, and almost all meetinghouses had been destroyed, the number of members killed during raids was surprisingly small and scattered. There were countless stories of miraculous preservation and timely promptings that warned Church members and their leaders of impending danger and allowed them to flee to safety. This protection was attributed to the members' faithfulness and obedience to the commandments.

Unfortunately, the protection seen generally among the members of the Church was not felt by all. Frederick W. Babbel, who accompanied Elder Ezra Taft Benson on his tour of Europe after the war, reported the following:

We learned that our branch in Pforzheim was virtually wiped out. During the war years considerable dissension had arisen among the members, and this mounted until it was found necessary to discontinue meetings altogether. Since their city was a costume jewelry center rather than a prime military target, the people of Pforzheim felt reasonably secure. Each time military planes flew overhead, however, on their way to military targets to the south and east, the people would seek the added protection of their air-raid shelters.

After one particular bombing group had passed them by and the "all-clear" had been sounded, the people returned to their normal duties. Then without warning the bombs began to fall. Apparently the British attacking force had encountered heavy German fighter opposition and had been unable to deliver their bombs on target. Lightening their planes in an effort to reach the safety of their own shores, they unloaded their entire bomb-load on this unsuspecting city. The city was left 95 percent demolished. As far as was known, only one family of Church members had escaped the onslaught.

We were assured that where unity prevailed, most of our people suffered far fewer casualties.

Source: Frederick W. Babbel, *On Wings of Faith* (Bookcraft: Salt Lake City, 1972)

faded and a positive outlook returned, knowing the Lord was with us. Standing at the railroad station and knowing the Russian Army was coming nearer with every hour had aggravated our fear, but now I felt good in the knowledge that with the Lord's help we would safely reach our destination. When the train was rolling, this fear, of course, was minimized.

After eight long days we arrived in Berlin and right into an air raid. Our train was left outside the railroad station until the raid was over. From Berlin to Dresden, the train traveled normally, just like in peacetime. Here it was warmer and there was no snow. We didn't know what to do with our sleds. We took the sleds with us to the streetcar and to the end station, but there we had a problem—we didn't know how to get to Mrs. Guenzel's home. A man saw our dilemma and asked us where we had to go. We told him we needed to go to Doelschen. He said, "That's on top of the mountain. Stay here. I will get my car and bring you up." This friendly man did get us up there and we met our mother and younger brothers and sisters. Here Mrs. Guenzel had everything well arranged for our family. At neighboring homes we were given bedrooms to stay for the night, but during the day we were able to stay in her home. This nice woman let us use her kitchen to prepare meals for our family of eleven. It must have been quite a change for Mrs. Guenzel to have so many people in her house, but she was very generous. A telegram had arrived from Christel saying she was in Berlin and would arrive in the evening. Except for my father, all living family members would be together again in a safe place.

Doelschen was a small village in the mountains overlooking Dresden and was about fifteen minutes away from the city by streetcar. Dresden was a beautiful town, maybe the most beautiful in Germany. It had irreplaceable buildings and treasures from the Baroque period. Not only was the town beautiful, but the surrounding mountains and the winding river through the city were beautiful too. We were planning to stay here until the war ended and then return to our home in Schneidemuehl.

It turned out much different than we had planned. In the night of the thirteenth of February 1945, the air-raid alarms woke us up. I slept in a neighbor's house, but it was close enough to the others that I hurried over to my loved ones, who had never really experienced a heavy air attack. I remembered the air attacks from Berlin and tried to calm my loved ones down, but this attack was much worse than the attacks I experienced in Berlin and I was frightened, too. The airplanes released the bombs mostly over Doelschen and it sounded terrible. Some windows in our house were broken and the roof damaged, but we were so lucky, Doelschen was not the target. After the air attack we went out of the house and looked over to Dresden. The entire city was a burning torch. The Allies had dropped explosives and incendiary bombs over the city. These bombs set the buildings and even the streets on fire. People who tried to save themselves from the fire were sucked into it. They became living torches. Some of the men from the village went to the city to help extinguish the fire, and to help save the people that were buried in the rubble.

Only about thirty minutes later, the attack was repeated. It was just like the first attack, except much worse. Not one of the men who went to help in the city returned home. Because Dresden was full of refugees from the east, no one really knows how many people were killed. The estimates are as high as 300,000.

After the two terrible air raids, my mother, us children, and Mrs. Guenzel were so scared we didn't want to stay another night. But where could we go and find a peaceful place? We didn't know anyone here. We hadn't made contact with the LDS ward in Dresden yet. Then I remembered, on my mission I was with Gretel Dzirson and she lived in Geyersdorf in the nearby Ore Mountains. We packed our few belongings and took the fifteen-mile walk to the nearest working railroad station in Pirna. No busses or streetcars were going, so we had to walk. It was a walk through the ruins and the damaged streets, all a horrible picture. It was very hard on my mother, now already over fifty years old and not in good physical condition for a march, but she was determined to leave and we helped as much as we could. Shortly before Pirna we boarded a train, exhausted, but on our way. We had to change trains a few times and after two days we arrived at our destination.

From Annaberg I called Gretel and explained our problem. We were very tired, but these wonderful LDS people had food and beds for everyone in our family of eleven. The next day I spoke with the mayor of the village and explained our situation. With the help of this friendly mayor, we found places to stay. It was heartwarming to see how these people were willing to help. Of course we had to split up because of the size of our family. We got rooms with different families, but we had a roof over our head, furniture, and a bed to sleep on.

In Geyersdorf we didn't have any air raids, but we had to watch for low flying planes. They shot at everything that moved. When we walked to church to the town of Buchholz-Annaberg on Sundays, we had to watch out and take shelter when the airplanes attacked. On some Sundays we had to stay in Geyersdorf and have our meetings in the home of the Schaarschmidt family. It was too dangerous to walk to church.

From the first day we liked the Ore Mountain region. We loved to walk through the mountains, the fields of flowers and the green meadows. These six months in this region was a special experience for all of us. We loved the people and the large LDS branch. It felt so good to be with members and to be able to attend church and have these spiritual meetings. My mother liked her stay as well. Yes, she missed everything she had lost—her home, her business—but for the first time she had the time to read the Book of Mormon from the beginning to the end. She gained a great testimony of the truthfulness of the gospel.

Yes, she missed everything she had lost—her home, her business—but for the first time she had the time to read the Book of Mormon from the beginning to the end. She gained a great testimony of the truthfulness of the gospel.

I looked right away for work and found a job as a saleslady in a meat store. Everyone could buy products with their ration cards. When the Russians moved in, it didn't change for us Germans, as we still used our cards; but the Russians took whatever they could get. They came into the store with their guns and threatened to kill us if they did not get what they asked for.

One day about five Russian and Czech soldiers came into the store and demanded all of the sausage I had, which I gave them. They wanted more and I told them honestly that I did not have anymore. They pointed their guns at me and told me they would check the house and would kill me if they found anything. My heart was pounding but I stood by what I had said. They believed me and left without checking. While I was talking with the soldiers, my boss stood behind the door and listened to what was going on. He had worked all night long to make more sausages, so there were plenty in the house. Had the soldiers looked, they would have found them, and I surely would have been killed.

Up to that time we had not heard from my father. We knew our hometown had been declared a fortress and that there had been much fighting there. Of course we hoped our father was still alive and maybe just a prisoner of war. One day our cousin Wilford Kindt got a letter from a friend. He reported that he had heard Mr. Birth had been killed in action and was buried in Koenigsblick, a forest by Schneidemuehl. We girls wanted to protect Mother from this sad news. She had already lost her two sons Gerhard and

Nephi, and now her husband. We all tried not to show our sadness and sorrow when she was around.

Somehow my mother must have felt that there was something we weren't sharing. She knew I kept a diary, so the next day while I was at work she looked for my diary. She found it and found what we were hiding. She had Peter, my little six-year-old brother, with her. She took him with her into her room and cried and prayed for a long time. After a time, a particularly strong feeling came over her that my father was not dead but needed our prayers. She called us together and we decided to fast every Friday for him. From that day on for thirteen weeks we fasted and prayed every Friday.

Our LDS branch members didn't understand why my mother would make her children fast every Friday, when she had already heard that her husband was dead. But she was not moved by these comments. Her faith and her feelings were so strong, she knew our father needed help and we needed to support him. This power of faith no one could take away from her.

The war finally ended after six years. Germany surrendered on the May 8, 1945. We were glad it was over, but sad about the condition of Germany. It had been divided between the victorious nations, Russia, Great Britain, the United States, and France. The area we used to live in became part of Poland, and all Germans still living in that area had to leave. There was no hope we would be able to return to our home. Our family was divided and we were living in different homes. People were nice to us, but it was not a condition we could live in for very long. We needed ration cards to buy food and there were no cards for us in Geyersdorf. So far, Brother Walter Fassmann, who was living in Zwickau, had registered us as living there, so we could get ration cards, but we knew he couldn't do that forever.

One day, we had visitors from the Cottbus branch of the Church. The brethren, Fritz Lehnig and Walter Krause, invited us to move to Cottbus. Brother Paul Langheinrich from the mission presidency was with them. In Cottbus, the brethren had converted a part of their meeting house into a refugee camp. Many LDS members from the former East German provinces were coming and had found a place to stay. The brethren invited us to move there as well. It was hard for us to leave Geyersdorf, where we had lived for six months and loved it, but we felt it was an answer to our prayers.

We were thirty-one women and children, including two babies and one young man who had lost his leg in the war. Lucy Meyer and Ingrid Bendler were in charge to bring us to Cottbus, and my sister Ruth and I helped. It was a large undertaking because no regular trains were going. In Annaberg we entered a train going to Riesa. It was raining hard and the train windows were mostly broken out and the roof was leaking. I saw the damage the air raids and the war had done. Whole blocks of homes were burned and destroyed. It was terrible what this war had done to our beautiful homeland. It took us all day to reach Riese, only about eighty miles away.

We stayed there all night at the railroad station. It was the safest place to be as thousands of people were still on the road looking for a place to settle. The next day we waited for a train to arrive. At midnight, a passenger train came, overcrowded like every train we saw. People were sitting everywhere, even on top of the train, but we managed to get everybody in. We had to help my mother in through a window. That train brought us only to Pristewitz. Again we had to get out. We organized some potatoes and beans, and cooked a soup on an open fire, and then we waited.

Finally, we got a message that the next train would be going to Cottbus. At 10:00 AM the train arrived, but it was not a passenger train. It was a freight train. Fear gripped us, as we saw that the train was full of Russian soldiers. We chose to take this train anyway, as the thought of another night on the street was just as scary. I don't know about the others, but I never prayed so long and constantly in my life. We all lay down on the straw, the Russians on one side of the car, and we on the other. My mother couldn't sleep and kept watching everything. What she saw amazed her. Everybody lay down except the Russian officer. He was up and if a soldier so much as raised his head, he would command him to lie down. He was our guardian angel, and nothing happened that night.

We finally landed in Cottbus, hungry, dirty, but safe. We had felt the hand of the Lord so much on this trip. The camp my mother and my younger brothers and sisters joined now was really a blessing at that time.

The stay at the refugee camp was a blessing for the family. To help alleviate the strain for food, many of the girls sought work in the surrounding cities and villages. Edith and two of her sisters, Ruth and Eva, were called on genealogical missions by the mission presidency. They returned to Annaberg and began collecting as many records as they could. One day in Zwickau, the girls heard great news.

At the railroad station we met Brother Schulz from Berlin. He told us he had seen Father in Berlin. He said our father was very skinny and looked old. He had lost his right arm and looked different, but it was like a dream come true. Our father, who we thought was dead, was alive! He was on his way home. In the beginning of August 1945, our father had been released from a Russian prisoner of war camp. He didn't know if his family was still alive or where they might be. He went to the LDS mission home in Berlin and, of course they knew where we were. On the ninth of August, he arrived in Cottbus. My mother and the children were so excited to see him come home. My mother's feelings had not betrayed her! She knew all the time that her husband was alive! It was a great reunion. He had lost his right arm and was thin and old looking, but was full of enthusiasm and plans to start over again.

RUTH BIRTH FILE

A meeting of the Schneidemuehl branch Primary organization.

He had been with the German Army in Schneidemuehl to the bitter end. The day after we had left, he visited our home and found it ransacked. He was tempted to burn the house down, but didn't. On the thirtieth of January, the Russians completely encircled Schneidemuehl. My father fought with his unit in defense of our hometown. When the German Army tried to break through the Russian lines, they left the *Volkssturm* soldiers and my father behind. Father became a prisoner of war. He got an infection in his right arm while in the POW camp and was treated with medication without success. For thirteen weeks he lay in bed with a high fever and lost eighty pounds. The doctor thought he would die any day. They felt the last thing they could do for him would be to amputate his right arm. After the amputation, the fever broke and his condition improved. Our fasting and prayers were answered.

Walter K. Rohloff

Walter Rohloff was born June 4, 1922, in Neubrandenburg, Germany. He was the oldest child of Bruno and Irene Rohloff. The branch in Neubrandenburg was large, and Walter enjoyed the association of the members. His father was a very faithful member of the Church and taught Walter the importance of standing up for his beliefs. As Hitler's influence increased across Germany, many employers required their workers to join the Nazi Party. Of course, being a member of the Church disqualified one from being able join the party and to work. Not willing to denounce his beliefs, Walter's father was forced to find new work. For young Walter, who was in school, the example his father set would remain an important legacy for the rest of his life.

In the spring of 1937, I started my training as a machinist (*Maschinenschlosser*) in a factory close to my home. The factory was built after 1934 on a property the size of a city block. The house we were living in bordered on the factory's edge. To get to the entrance I had to walk a little ways. The *Mechanische Werkstaetten*, as the company was called, fabricated mainly parts for airplanes. The company had an excellent training program, which was part of the technical trade college in town. It was hard to get a place there. Boys from all over Germany received training there. One had to go through special tests to be admitted. Of the twenty-six boys in my class, only a few were from my hometown. The training contract called for four years of training but was later reduced, during the war, to three and a half years.

I was class president for all the three and a half years. Even after I became student body president, I kept my job as class president. I communicated well with the boys, and I was not afraid to represent them when it was needed. Of course they teased me—not because I was a Mormon, but to persuade me to smoke cigarettes and drink alcohol. But in the end, they left me alone. Later, some funny situations came up. I was dismissed from the Hitler Youth (for disrespect I showed toward the Hitler Youth flag) but was still kept as student body president. On holidays we had joint school activities and I was in charge. Among other things, I had to give orders for the flag ceremonies. All students were members of the Hitler Youth and were standing like soldiers in uniform. I, being in civilian clothing, gave the orders. The director confronted me and asked me why I was not wearing a uniform like everybody else. I told him I was not a member of the Hitler Youth anymore. Though he wore the party badge on his jacket, I don't think he was a Nazi by heart. Like so many people, he was a member of the Nazi Party only to keep his job. He never asked for my release, and I was student body president till I graduated.

October 12, 1940, my father's brother Kurt got married, and our family was invited. Father and Mother couldn't go, but my sister Elfriede and I did. It was in Ferdinandshof, Pomerania, on the Vetter family farm. I was very much impressed with the amount of food which was served there. I had never participated in a meal like that. There were many young people of my sister's and my age, but I and the girl assigned to sit with me had to sit with the adults. Having heard about the drinking going on at those parties, I went to my uncle and told him I wouldn't drink alcohol, and I asked him to respect that. He said he would. It is the custom in Germany to toast for the health of the newlyweds. Knowing this, I turned my glass upside down so as not to be filled. Before the meal, everybody stood up, raised their glass, and drank to the well-being of the couple. I raised my empty glass too and wished them well. After everybody sat down, my uncle got up, lifted his glass, which had been refilled, and toasted toward me. I had no choice. I stood up and raised my empty glass. Everyone told me (and I didn't know anyone except my uncle at the table) that I had to fill my glass and had to drink. I didn't give in. To make things right, I had my glass filled with milk, and I did drink to the health of the couple. The laughter of the ones present didn't bother me.

I had courage there, but later in the year, when I graduated from college, I almost gave in. After graduation we had a nice party for all who graduated, and we even had a band playing. My friend Hermann Cziborra played in the band. Of course these parties were more or less drinking parties and I had tried in the past to stay away from school parties of any kind. This one I could not miss. We had already visited a brewery and witnessed the process of how beer was made. At the end of the visit we had been given a case of beer. Now we had it for the party. All evening long I was teased and invited to drink. "Just one sip," I was told. "It won't do you any harm." After I heard it often enough, slowly I started to believe it. When someone toasted toward me, I raised my filled glass and brought it toward my lips. At this moment, I looked over to the band and saw the waiter offer my fried Hermann Cziborra a glass of beer. He shook his head and didn't take the drink. Without drinking, I put my glass of beer down and was ashamed of myself. Here I was ready to drink, and over there was my friend, whom I had taught not to drink and he had declined! It was a good lesson for me. Slowly I learned in the adult world to stand up for what I felt what was right. In all the situations I later came to, I had no problems doing what was right.

—•—

Our branch grew, and we needed more and better rooms. We moved from the Wollenweberstrasse to the Eisenbahnstrasse, which was close to the railroad station. The rooms were nice and almost made just for us. We had a large assembly room for sacrament services and some small classrooms. The growth did not last long. With Hitler in power, living conditions improved. People again had work. Before 1932, one third of the work force was out of work, but now there was not enough manpower to fill the jobs. Hitler built new roads (the Autobahn), new factories, new aircraft and airports. A new army was built and an *Arbeitsdienst* was founded. Young men before joining the armed forces had to labor for six months with shovels and spades on government projects. They were drilled like the army but had no guns. People didn't think much about the preparation for war, until I think in 1938 before the war. Butter was rationed. More and more people thought about buying their own home. Even my father was thinking of doing it because the financing was affordable.

Most people probably even agreed with Hitler when old territory Germany had lost after World War I was taken back by the German armed forces. The better living conditions in Germany, the Nazi youth program, and the Nazi indoctrination resulted in the loss of more and more members in the Church, especially the youth who became an active part in Hitler's party. When war broke out in 1939, many of our young men were in the armed services. Only Egon Toebe, the son of our branch president, and I were left at home. From the girls my age, only the Bauers' girls, Frieda and Anni, were active.

In 1941, we lost our meeting hall and we kept only the classrooms. While some of our branch members were in the armed services, many had left the Church. The ones still attending church didn't live in harmony with the teachings. After Brother Toebe was released as branch president, my father was asked to preside over the branch. I was asked in November 1941, to be the president of the Sunday School. Only for a short time I could do this. Then I was drafted (in February 1942) to the army. We lost the classrooms later too, but when I came home on furlough, we called the members together for a service in our home.

After graduating from trade college, I kept working for the same company. I had to work in production. More and more men were taken out of the work force and placed into the armed services. Women took the place of the men, and I supervised and prepared the work for about twelve to fourteen women. Many of these women were from out of town, some from Austria. Our department was small, only about thirty people. We had two groups, and all were older than I. In the other group was a man who had a family with five children. When he opened his mouth, filthy jokes and songs came out. At first I thought it would not bother and influence me, but I was surprised when I caught myself humming the same songs he was singing. I didn't want that. I had warned him many times to quit these stories and songs. He just told me to mind my own business. He didn't belong to my group, so I went to my boss and told him that I did not want to work in the same room with that man anymore. He tried to talk me out of it. The man was a good worker. But I had made up my mind and would have left the department if no change was made. He was transferred to another department.

WALTER ROHLOFF FILE

Walter Rohloff

As the war went on and more nations were pulled into the war against Germany, people got worried. I remember in contrast, how people smiled when we were sitting in our eating hall at our company on the first day of September 1939. We were expecting a *Sondermeldung* (a special announcement) by the *Fuehrer* Hitler. Many were smiling even after hearing that Hitler had declared war with Poland. (Hitler said in this Sondermeldung that war was declared in retaliation for Polish troops storming the radio station in Gleiwitz, Silesia, which was a big lie.) Now in 1941, German troops stormed into Russia and one victory was reported after another. But many, especially the older ones who had lived through the First World War, were worried, and Father said, "How will that end?"

I worked long hours. After my regular 8.5-hour day, I worked in research, developing new materials. I had to work many Sundays. Many times I didn't go home but slept on the workbench. I made good money but couldn't buy anything with it. On one payday, my pay was less than I expected. After inquiring, I was told that because I was young and should be in the armed services, my money had been taken out and given to finance the war. I didn't like that a bit and went over to our union leader. He was, of course, a Nazi and favored this arrangement. I was straightforward and told him how I felt about them stealing my hard-earned money. If there was money needed, I would make the decision about how much I wanted to donate, and besides, would he guarantee me that I would not be in the armed services tomorrow? After our talk, I was afraid I would be put in jail. What I had said was not in line with the Nazi Party thinking. But I got my money and didn't have the problem anymore.

Yes, the army wanted me too. First came Hitler's SS. The first time when I was asked to appear for a medical examination for the Waffen SS, they smiled at us. They wanted us (we were a large group), but I didn't want to go. I knew they liked men like me. Just as the *Soldatenkoenig* in Prussia wanted tall men for his army, Hitler wanted tall men for his SS. I am over six feet tall and had a healthy body, just what they wanted. I was prepared for them. I fabricated a lie and told them I wanted to join the air force. At that time, Hermann Goering, the *Reichsmarschall* of the air force, was still favoured by Hitler, and the SS couldn't touch their recruits, so they couldn't draft me into the Waffen SS. When I received notice the second time to appear for a medical examination for the Waffen SS, I stood by my lie. This time, they pushed much harder, but when I didn't give in, they let me go.

When I was asked the third time, at the end of 1941, to appear for an examination, I knew my old trick wouldn't work anymore. Before the examination, we (about fifty young men) were kept in a room that held just that many. One of the SS men gave a stimulating talk about the excellence of the Waffen SS and why we, as good Germans, should join the SS. After the talk, they moved the tables so that just one man at a time could pass through. Alongside the opening were SS men, and they asked everyone to sign up. I was sitting in the rear, but I could see that almost everyone did sign up (some after a long discussion). I looked for a way to get out. In the rear was a double door which led to the outside. I checked the door and found it was in poor shape. I went a few steps back and then threw myself, as hard as I could, against the door. The door broke open, and I and many others left as fast as we could. (In 1941, joining the Waffen SS was what they called voluntary. Later, men were drafted just the same way as to the other armed forces.)

I knew sooner or later I would be drafted into the army. My friends were all serving in the armed forces already. It was no fun going any place without them. In cafes or restaurants I needed ration cards to buy a piece of cake. I couldn't afford it. The card was not enough to satisfy my needs. Dancing was forbidden. More and more men much older than I were being drafted. The war had spread out over many more nations. After Germany and Russia had divided Poland, Hitler sent the armed forces, early in 1940, into Denmark and Norway. Then in May 1940, action started on Germany's western borders. After an armistice treaty was signed, Hitler sent German troops to Africa to help Italy, who had entered the war on Germany's side. My father remembered World War I and said, "Italy won't do us any good. It will be our downfall." Italy had started to attack Albania and got strong resistance and asked Germany, in early 1941, for help. German troops went not only through Yugoslavia, they also conquered Romania, Bulgaria, and Greece. That agitated Russia, who had taken part of Romania. It now shared a large border with the German Army. In June 1941, Germany attacked Russia and the German armies went far into Russia. They became stuck in the snow. An unexpected early winter stopped the German attack.

I was not yet in the armed forces for a simple reason; my company had declared me *unabkoemlich* (essential). The army had tried to draft me too, but I had orders from my company to give the *Stellungsbefehl* (order for compulsory draft) to them. They took care of it. In February 1942, I again received a *Stellungsbefehl*. At this time I asked the company to let me go. They didn't understand why I wanted to go while everyone else tried to stay. My father couldn't understand me either and wanted me to come over to his company. I didn't want to. I liked my company and my work. I wanted to go because none of my friends were home anymore. All had been drafted and had joined the armed forces. Some had already died in war action, and when I met their parents, they asked me why I was still home. I was embarrassed and hated it. They probably thought I was a draft dodger. I was not afraid of going into the war, even though I did not really understand what it meant. It was only because I worked hard and the company appreciated my work and wanted to keep me.

The war was now more than two years old, and no end was in sight. After many victorious battles in Russia, the winter of 1941–42 brought a change. The German armies were surprised by the earlier than usual winter and by the bitter cold. They were not prepared for the cold, and many soldiers froze to death or had frozen body parts. All over Germany, people were asked to donate blankets and coats to keep the troops warm. Of course it came too late for many. While food had been rationed since the beginning of the war and butter even before the war, the rations became smaller and smaller. Money was plentiful, but it was almost useless. For all that you wanted to buy, you needed ration cards. There was a black market, but drastic penalties kept it small. Air raids were not yet a problem. The general of the air force, Hermann Goering, had declared at the beginning of the war, "No enemy air force would penetrate German air space or his name would be Meyer." Since the allies bombed Hamburg, everyone called Hermann Goering, Hermann Meyer. Listening to enemy radio stations was forbidden, but people did it anyway. All reading material had been censored since Hitler came to power. You heard only what was approved by the Nazi Party.

On a beautiful morning, February 18, 1942, I reported with others for duty at the railroad station in my hometown of Neubrandenburg. From here we would be transported by rail to Schwerin, where the Infantry Regiment 89 was stationed. Because the train was not expected to leave until the afternoon, the commanding officer gave us furlough on our word of honor to be back in time. I liked that and visited with my girlfriend. My feelings were different once we arrived in Schwerin and the gate to our barracks had closed behind us. I felt as if I were in prison.

Before I left home, my father talked to me about things I would have to face in the army and the need for me to stay firm in the gospel. He gave me a pocket-sized New Testament with the words that "I should make good use of it." While I said "thank you" to him, in my mind I thought, "I will leave this New Testament in my clothing when I mail it back home." That's the way I thought, and that's what I did. After we were issued uniforms, I packed my clothing in a carton and left the New Testament in my jacket. I don't know why the mailing was delayed, but for many days the boxes with our clothing laid on top of our lockers.

Every morning we had our uniform inspection and got instructions. One morning our drill instructor stood before us and I heard him say, "Rohloff?" "Yes, sir," I said, and ran in front of the company. "I read in your *Soldbuch* (passport) the entry under religion. I can't understand that. What does it mean?" Well, if I were reading it myself, I wouldn't have understood it either. The day I had to give all this information, I told the man, "I am a member of The Church of Jesus Christ of Latter-day Saints." He said, "There is not enough space" and wrote, "Jes.Chr." Now, while the officer was asking me, I felt very uncomfortable in front of so many men and turned red in my face and said, "It stands for 'Church of Jesus Christ of Latter-day Saints.' " "What is that?" he asked. I asked myself, yes, what is it? I was completely unprepared for this question. In all my years of attending church and going along with what had been said, I had done very little thinking on my own. I hesitated, and before I answered, he had me return to my place.

All morning through the drill, I couldn't get rid of the thought, "What is that?" At noon when we got back to our barracks, I went into our room. I shared it with about eleven others. I took the carton containing my clothing, opened it and took the New Testament out. I was eager to find a satisfying answer to the question. From that time on I studied the scriptures intensely to find an answer to the question, for myself, and for others when they asked me. The next day, the boxes containing our clothing were gone.

While the drill was hard and strenuous, it was not hard for me. Having been actively engaged in sports and keeping the Word of Wisdom, I was well prepared.

While the drill was hard and strenuous, it was not hard for me. Having been actively engaged in sports and keeping the Word of Wisdom, I was well prepared. Soon the platoon leader called on me to continue the drill with the platoon while he talked with the noncommissioned officers. He must have given a good report to the company leader, a captain, who called me into his office and asked me if I wanted to become an officer. I was surprised and asked him to give me a week to consider it. I wrote my parents and explained what had happened and asked for advice. My father felt it was not good enough information to write an answer. We needed to discuss the details. By train he came over on Sunday. We spent the day together. He told me it was all right for me to become a German army officer. "Mormon and Moroni were officers in the Nephite army, even though they disliked the doings of the Nephites," he said. "This will mean much work for you. Accept the offer, but keep the Lord's commandments. Stand up for what we believe in."

The next day I gave my affirmative answer. I learned that besides me, three others had been chosen to become officers. We four were now partly removed from the rest of the company and had extra instructions and drills. One of the instructions we got was horseback riding. My companions were the sons of well-to-do families, and their fathers were reserve officers in the German Army. Not so with me. My father hated serving in the army and made it only to the rank of private, in spite of the many years he served. Also, my fellow officer aspirants had had instructions on horseback riding before and looked forward to this hour of training. I had never sat on a horse and wasn't excited over that. In the first lesson, the instructor told us we needed to get acquainted with our horses. We had to get under the horse and then stand on top of the saddle. While standing on the saddle, he wanted us to jump over the horse's head. That was easier said than done. Jensen, one of us four, tried to step on the head of the horse to make it over, but the horse moved his head out of the way and Jensen fell to the ground, hurting himself. We others did all right. At the end of our first hour of instruction, the instructor put up a hurdle. We were instructed to jump our horse over the hurdle and while doing so, to lift up our cap from our head and call the name of the horse. Jensen tried it first, but the horse just went around the hurdle. Siems's horse did just the same, even though he tried hard to get the horse over the hurdle. Now the instructor got mad. Harmann was next. The horse, seeing the whip in the instructor's hand, went over the hurdle. Harmann clung onto the horse for dear life.

For me, sitting in the saddle with no stirrups was already an accomplishment. I knew I would have problems. I decided I would do as instructed, but I didn't know how to get the horse moving, as before my horse had just followed the other horses. Now it needed to move when I wanted it to. I tried everything I knew, but it wouldn't move. Then the horse saw the whip in the hand of the instructor. It started running toward the hurdle and jumped over. During the jump, I lifted my cap and called the name of the horse. With a high arch, I fell from the horse. The horse jumped for joy. But I had not only the pain, but also the loud laughter of all present. It surely didn't make me look forward to the next hour of instructions.

We four *Reserve Offizier Anwaerter* (reserve officer candidates) had a great time together. The drill was hard, but we helped one another. Many of our instructors were noncommissioned officers and tried to make our lives miserable. We took it with humor and tried to tease them back as much as possible.

We also had weekend furloughs. They were easy to get when your home was within a hundred kilometer radius of the garrison. It was more difficult to get if your home was further away. I applied for weekend furlough and, to my surprise, I got it even though my hometown was more than a hundred kilometers away. I had a great time at home. I had to be back by 9 AM on Monday. Somehow, when I looked up, the arrival time of my train had changed. I thought it would arrive before 9 o'clock. I arrived thirty minutes later. I tried to explain, but no one believed me. It hurt me that my officer would think I was lying. Well, I got three days in prison on water and bread.

In prison I had plenty of time to think things over. I decided that if no one believed my story, why not do as they thought I had done, only I would make sure I was never caught. No, I didn't think to give up weekend furlough. I just devised a plan to have furlough more often and without problems. From now on I would take weekend furlough with permission or without. Whenever I felt the time and conditions were right, I would take weekend furlough. Back at my unit I talked to Harmann. His home was in Guestrow. It was on the way to my hometown, and it was within the hundred-kilometer circle. I asked him if he had any objections to having my father bring my bike over to his place. I would apply for furlough to his hometown and from there I could go by bike to my home and back. He had no objection, and it worked out very well.

Jensen, one of the four of us, was from our garrison city of Schwerin. His mother wanted to give us a treat and invited us and four beautiful girls to a party with us. Toward the end, Grandma Jensen came, and we were introduced to her. The first to be introduced was Siems. After she asked him about his well-being, she asked, "What profession is your father, Herr Siems?" "Professor at the university in Rostock. Right now captain in the army," was his answer. "Very welcome, Herr Siems." Next was Harmann. "You are Herr Harmann?" she said to Harmann. Then after the same questions she had asked before, she asked, "What is your father doing?" "He is head of the department for construction and development in the state of Mecklenburg. Right now, he is serving in the army as a captain." She was delighted. Next was her grandson. He, of course, didn't have to tell her what his father did to make a living. His father had been directing the post office in town. Right now, he was serving as a major in the army. Now it was my turn. I didn't have the credentials the others had. "O Herr Rohloff," she said, and after the same introduction as the others, she asked, "What is your father doing?" "My father is an office worker," I said. She looked at me for a second as one does who is wondering, "How does this fellow come in here?" Then she turned around and left. She didn't shake hands as she had done with the others, nor did she welcome me. Our hostess was upset with Grandma's behavior and tried to explain it to me. I told her not to worry; it didn't bother me. It surely didn't. I had met these people before. They accepted only their class of people. All others were dirt.

—•—

We had the same drills as the other soldiers, along with some additional duties. Before the other soldiers started, we had to go to the stables and brush the horses. How well we cleaned the horses was always checked. Most were reasonable when they checked our work over.

Our training was with the 7-mm guns. We officer-aspirants had opportunities to practice directing and working with a crew. Then came the day we could practice shooting with real ammunition. We could compete with the officers and noncommissioned officers in this drill. Targets were assigned to us and we brought, one after another, our gun into position to destroy the target. I had my turn close to the end of the practice day. Up to that time only one crew had destroyed their target. Many officers were standing around and watched us closely and critically. I brought my crew into position, and I could see the target through my field glasses. I gave the orders and the first shot was too far, but I could see I had the right direction. The next shot was too short, but with the third I could see the debris flying through the air. We had a direct hit. I turned toward the general standing nearby and reported, "Target destroyed." "Thank you," said the general. "Very well done." My crew and I were delighted.

My training received a setback, when on the twenty-seventh of June 1942 I was admitted to the military hospital. I had a fever and a sore throat that later was diagnosed as diphtheria. I was taken to the quarantine station of the hospital into the room I would be placed in. I was asked some questions by a male nurse about myself and about my sickness. When the nurse asked me about my religion and I answered, "Church of Jesus Christ of Latter-day Saints," one of the soldiers in bed spoke up and said, "Are you LDS because you believe in it or because of your parents?" Though I was dizzy and felt miserable, I could think clearly. I said, "Because of my parents."

The days went on, and I got my medication and every day I felt a little better. We eight men in this room had much time on our hands and we talked a lot. There was really not much for us to do. Because we were in quarantine, we had to stay in our room or in a small surrounding area. One day when we talked about religion, I tried to explain my belief. The fellow who asked me the question when I was admitted, spoke up and said to me, "You don't believe it yourself." "How can you say that?" I asked. "The day when you were admitted," he continued, "I asked you about your belief and you told me you were a member of that church because of your parents." This hit me like a blow to my head. I had completely forgotten this incident, but I remembered now. It took me a while to gather my strength. Then I said, "I am sorry and beg your pardon. I didn't have the courage at that time. I am a member of the LDS church because I know it is true."

I wrote home for more Church literature, and my father acted right away. I realized, to defend and strengthen my belief, I had to know more about what the Church taught. I used my time wisely and studied the scriptures and Church literature. On the fourteenth of August 1942, I was released from the hospital and returned to my unit.

When I returned, my three companions had graduated and were already transferred, but our drill instructor was still there. He was ready to start training for another group of officer aspirants, and he wanted me to join that group. Before the training started, I got two week's furlough for recovery.

Being home, I wanted to prepare myself for the strenuous drill ahead of me. Running around the block, I found out I dragged my legs, and when I drank anything, the fluid came back through my nose. When I returned to my unit it got worse. My instructor, knowing me well from the past course, took me aside and asked me what was wrong. I told him I didn't know. Everything looked healthy, but I had poor control over my legs. He sent me over to the doctor. The doctor checked me over and sent me back with a sealed report. My instructor read the report and told me, "The doctor says you are faking." He took me by the arm, and we both went over to see the doctor. By now I was dragging my feet badly, and he had to help me along. There was nothing nice in what he told the doctor. He told him that if he didn't know what was wrong with me, to get me another doctor who could help me. He knew I was sick and needed help. The result was I had to go to the hospital for further examination.

To go was easier said than done. Going by bus to the hospital was all right, but getting into the hospital was another story. I had to go up about ten steps to the entrance, but my legs didn't want to do it. I had to crawl. I felt terribly helpless. A doctor examined me, and I saw he did things completely differently from the first doctor. He told me I had nerve paralysis, and he kept me right there. I wrote home and told my family about my problems. On Sunday my father visited with me. As he saw me, he cried. I had never seen him do that before. In his memory he had me as a sportsman, and now I hardly could move. "Buby," he said, "the war is over for you. You will never walk."

On Sunday my father visited with me. As he saw me, he cried. I had never seen him do that before. In his memory he had me as a sportsman, and now I hardly could move. "Buby," he said, "the war is over for you. You will never walk."

No one in the hospital had illnesses which I was familiar with. Most of the men had epilepsy and looked healthy, except when they had a seizure. Others had similar problems as mine. Many lay in bed all day long. I tried to move around as much as possible. In the morning the nurse came around to give us our shots. On my chart, I could see the medication my shots contained: strychnine, prostrychnine, and insulin. I didn't know what that was and had no way of looking it up. Rumor had it that the doctors were trying new medication out on us. My condition got worse. On one of my "walks" in the hallway, I slipped and fell. Unfortunately, my head landed in a pail full of water. With only the help of a nurse passing by, was I able to get out of that situation. The pails were standing in the hallways to fight incendiary bombs in the event of an air attack.

I couldn't see much improvement in my condition. I thought and prayed about it and came to the conclusion to exercise daily. I chose the backyard for that purpose, as I wanted no one to see me. In the morning, I dragged myself down the stairs to the backyard and started to "walk" around a small piece of lawn. After that, I tried to do some body exercises, like knee bends. It was very hard on me, but soon I could see some improvement in my condition, which encouraged me to do more exercise. My activity didn't stay unnoticed for long from the other patients. They would stare out the windows and mock me. I had already seen enough improvement in my condition; it didn't discourage me from going on. When the doctor saw my improvement was much better than anyone else's, he made every patient do the same but left me alone. I could go on with my way of doing exercise. This didn't make me popular with the patients, for they didn't like to exercise. Soon after, I was dismissed from the hospital. It had taken almost four months from October 2, 1942, to the January 23, 1943, to restore my health. I was KV (fit for active service) again.

My unit gave me a fourteen-day convalescence furlough. My parents were delighted when they saw me and how well I had recovered. We all were very grateful to the Lord, who had answered our prayers and had restored my health.

Our little branch of the Church was almost nonexistent. After discussing this with my parents, I visited the remaining members, and we had Sunday meetings at our home. I understand that they continued meeting on Sundays in our home until the Russian Army invaded Neubrandenburg in 1945.

—•—

After returning to my unit, I found none of my former comrades there. All had moved on, including many of the staff. No officer training course was planned, but my superior insisted that I continue my training. I was transferred to a training course in the town of Gnesen in the state of Posen, close to my father's hometown of Hohensalza. The course was already in progress, but I had no difficulty catching up. I reached the goals of this course and was made a *Gefreiter* (private first class) on June 1, 1943.

Here in Gnesen, I received for the second time *Bau* (prison). We came back from an exercise and had to prepare for a roll call. When taking the roll

RUTH BIRTH FILE

Members of the Schneidemuehl Branch celebrate New Year's Eve, 1944.

call, the officer looked through the barrel of my rifle and said he could see some dirt. I could not, but he could and that got me three days in prison. I had a single cell and had to live again on water and dry bread. That was far too little for me. The only exercise we got was a half-hour walk in the prison yard, between the walls. There were many men walking, and I don't know what they had done. I was in this prison with another aspirant from the school. He took it very seriously. We couldn't walk and talk together. Everyone had to walk alone. I was hungry, and the thought hit me that he might still have his bread. I walked faster than the others and passed him by but could only say one sentence without the guard seeing it. Passing him the first time, I asked, "How are you?" "Terrible," he said. The next time, when I passed him, "Did you eat?" "No," he said. Next, "Do you have bread?" "Yes." And then, "Where do you have the bread?" "On the window sill." When we were ordered back into our cells, I was one of the first to enter. I hurried over to his cell, found the bread, and went into my cell. No one saw what I did. It was not enough, but helped. After being released from prison, I continued my training.

Shortly after I arrived in Gnesen, I wrote home for the address of the nearest branch of the LDS Church. Father wrote me all the information to be able to find the branch in Schneidemuehl. Brother Philipp Bauer from my home branch was now living in Schneidemuehl. I used his address and name to get furlough to the city. I got weekend furlough to Schneidemuehl and visited the branch there. It was the first time I had visited a branch of the Church outside my home branch. I had visited the church before in Demmin, but that was when we had district conference.

Standing in front of an apartment building

with the address my father had given me, I couldn't see where in this building church meetings could be held. After looking at other places close by, I entered the building and walked up the stairs, but all the doors were apartments. As I came down the stairs, I saw two young men crossing the ground floor hallway. I asked them for the LDS Church. "Come on with us," they told me. "We have district conference tonight and tomorrow." We walked to the backyard, and there was what I was looking for, the rooms for holding church meetings. The branch had very nice rooms, and I was very favorably impressed with the membership in attendance. Of course the many young sisters in attendance caught my attention too. I noticed a young sister—Ruth Birth, I learned later—sitting on the harmonium. It was a good, spiritual meeting with many young members participating. After the meeting, I made the acquaintance of some of the youth and went home with Brother Philipp Bauer.

After the Sunday morning meeting, there was a meal given for all in attendance by Brother and Sister Birth. It was a good meal, and after we young people were filled, we went into the nearby park and talked together. It was a fun time. I told many made-up stories and in one, I called myself *Vati* (dad). That name Vati stuck to me. From that time on, my name by the youth of the branch was Vati.

After the meeting, I was invited by Brother and Sister Birth to visit their home on Goennerweg 74. I consulted with Brother Bauer, my host, and gladly accepted. Here I met the Birth family and many of the young people I had seen before. When I left Schneidemuehl by train, I felt enriched and had a great desire to return. During the following week, I wrote home about my visit and the experience I had visiting the branch in Schneidemuehl. My father wrote back that he was delighted. I also wrote Brother and Sister Birth and told them how much I was impressed with their hospitality and with the branch in Schneidemuehl. They wrote back too and invited me to come anytime and stay with them. That was just what I needed.

Carefully I planned my next visit. I knew I couldn't get another weekend furlough so soon and would have to wait. But I didn't want to wait. I would go without a permit. On Saturday shortly after our drill was over, in the early afternoon, I went to the railroad station and bought a ticket to Schneidemuehl. In those days, the platforms at the railroad stations were sealed off, and you could get there only through a control station. Beside the railroad employee who checked the tickets, stood a man from the military police (MP) who checked the furlough permits of the soldiers. I had a ticket to travel with the railroad, but no furlough permit. I couldn't get through the control station, but I had made up my mind beforehand. I decided to climb over the high fence which surrounded the station and reach the platform that way. It worked out well. In the railroad car I met some of my fellow aspirants, and I asked them to help me watch out for the military police, which would be checking for permits on the train. When one of them told me the MP was in the next compartment, I checked the restroom to see if it had a door on the other side. It had none. As the train stopped, I wanted to change compartments to avoid the MP men. To my great surprise, there was already an MP man standing at the door, with his hands on the door handle. I turned around and went through the back door and reached the next compartment. At the next station the MP and I traded places again, except they didn't know it. Safely and without any problems, I reach the railroad station in Schneidemuehl. I even had a seat on the overcrowded train.

I got down on the platform and didn't know what to do next. I didn't know the station well enough to know how to leave without running into an MP man. Between the platform where my train arrived and the main platform were railroad tracks. In the dark I could see MP men walking up and down on that main platform. Everyone else had left already, but I was still standing there with my small suitcase. I could see the MP men standing together and talking and looking over

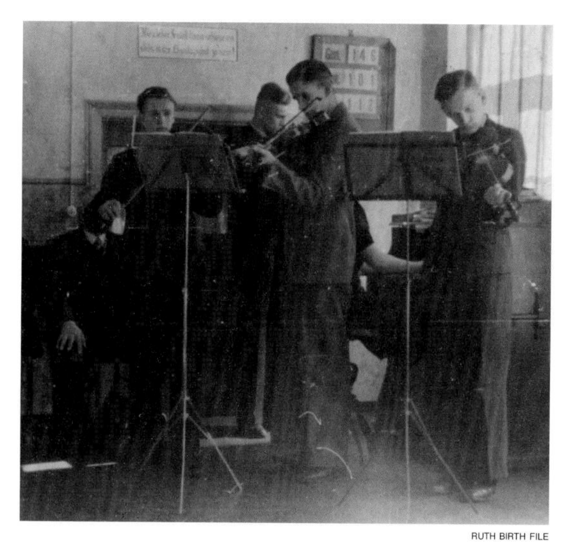

RUTH BIRTH FILE

Five youth perform a musical number during sacrament meeting in the Schneidemuehl Branch.

to me. Then I saw the MP men cross the tracks and come toward me. Now I had no choice. I ran away in the opposite direction, crossing many, many tracks, toward a wooden fence. I threw my suitcase over the fence and grabbed the top of the fence and tried to swing myself over. With great noise the fence broke down, and I walked over the fallen fence. Once on the street, I outran and lost the MP men.

I had lost my orientation. This was only my second visit to Schneidemuehl. After a little thinking, I found the right direction and the street *Am Goennerweg*. When I arrived at the Births' home, it was dark. I didn't want to wake up the family and looked for a place to stay the night. Nearby were garden plots. In one of them I saw a small *Laube* (shed). I climbed the fence and found the Laube open. On a board, I made a bed and slept well into the morning. Then I went over to see the Birth family. Father Birth greeted me. "Where do you come from?" "From Gnesen." "There is no train from there at this time." "No. I slept in a Laube. Everyone over here was asleep when I came by. I didn't want to wake anybody up." "We will change that." Mother Birth said, "You knock on my bedroom window and I will let you in." "By the way," Brother Birth said (and having been a soldier himself for many years during World War I, he knew army life), "how did you get furlough so fast again? Do you have a permit?" "No," I said. "I took furlough without permission." A big smile appeared on his face as he said, "I like that." Many times after this first time without a permit, I visited the Birth family in Schneidemuehl, and I never got caught. It was always close, and one wrong move would have been devastating for me. Why did I do it? I felt loved and wanted in the family, and I took every opportunity to visit them. The discussions I had in the family and with Father Birth encouraged me to study the scriptures. In my spare time in the training course, I studied the Bible. Every time I went to the Birth family and the Scheidemuehl Branch, I felt strengthened and encouraged to stand up for God and Jesus Christ against the atheistic Nazi ideology and do what was right. These experiences in Schneidemuehl and my father's letters had a deep influence on me and gave me direction for my life.

After finishing the course in Gnesen, about ten of us from the twelfth infantry division had to return to our garrison in Schwerin. Here we received all that we needed to go to the front in Russia. Before leaving for Russia, we applied for furlough, which was granted. I had furlough to my hometown, but after a few days I asked my parents if they had any objection to my going to Schneidemuehl and visiting with the Birth family. Because I had furlough only to Neubrandenburg and couldn't legally travel to Schneidemuehl, I put on civilian clothing and traveled by train, without difficulty, to Schneidemuehl. I had, as usual, a great time there. Upon returning to my unit, I took the same men I was in charge of before and we went by train to the Russian front.

It was the fifth of August 1943 when we started on our way to the German East Front. Our division was stationed east of the town of Mogilew. On the way, we got a little insight into what had been happening. All the forest had been cut away on both sides of the railroad tracks for about a hundred yards. By doing this, one could oversee the tracks and the sides better. Russian partisans had blown some of the trains off the tracks. We could see railroad cars and locomotives lying off to the side. To avoid this, our locomotive pushed a few cars in front of it as it went along. I could see that fighting had gone on here, but I still had no fear and no real understanding of what war meant. After I had been in the battles and was wounded the first time, I learned and recognized the danger and protected myself. Our ride went smoothly, and after marching some miles, we arrived safe and in good spirits at our division headquarters.

Here we were split up, and I had to join the third infantry company in the eighty-ninth regiment. In the evening, protected by the darkness, we moved into our emplacement. My new home was a hole in the ground, covered with big logs and plenty of dirt on the top. The bunker, as we called that place, was connected to the *Hauptkampf Linie* (front line or trench). A squad of about six to eight men occupied a bunker. I was placed in a squad and introduced myself to everyone. One of the men was standing guard; the others were sitting in the bunker playing cards. When my turn came, I had to stand guard by a machine gun. From that place I could see, as much as darkness permitted, the no-man's-land. About forty yards in front of me, we had a barbed wire entanglement. I couldn't see the enemy line, but I could see the flash from their rifles. Sometimes the Russians would shoot with the *Stalinorgel*, a rocket gun which could fire many rockets at once. When a rocket hit the ground, the detonation looked like a big mushroom of fire. It was pretty to see, and while watching that, I got careless. I felt the touch of a hand on my back. My corporal had come up behind me. He reminded me of the danger and that I should protect myself. He told me the Stalinorgel is not very accurate, makes lots of noise, and seldom hits its target. While we were not bombarded with it, it could still stray over to hit us.

The next morning I went along the trench and visited the place were the rockets had hit our line. There were the first dead I saw, and I told myself to be more careful in the future. It made a deep impression on me. I was lucky to be stationed at a relatively calm front, where only a little fighting was going on. After being at the front only a short time, I got my own squad. I don't think the men in my squad liked the idea of having me as their leader. I had the same rank, *Gefreiter* (private first class), as some of them. Their main concern was that I was a greenhorn with no frontline experience. First I had to prove that I was able to lead. We were assigned a section to protect and had to build our own bunker. While the enemy could see our trenches, they couldn't see where we had our bunker. To dig the hole was not hard, but getting the hole covered was. We went to the nearby forest and cut the trees we needed. Then we carried the logs on our shoulders to our hole. I noticed that the men let me carry the heavy end. I didn't mind. I wasn't afraid of hard work, and I knew what I wanted. With every log we carried, the men came nearer to me, and it didn't take long until everyone did his fair share of the work. This helped us to make a good squad, and I could feel more trust toward me by the men. While I was on the front, I experienced no heavy fighting, only a few touch ups on both sides.

I had to attend another training camp. This time the course was attended only by men of our division. It was another selection, and the ones who passed would go to the academy. The training was from October 9, 1943, to the thirtieth. Before the training started, on the first of October 1943, I was made an *Unteroffizier*, an NCO or noncommissioned officer. For me the course was easy. I worked hard and did what I could to become an officer. The only problem I had was that after fourteen days, I turned sick with a kind of yellow fever. It kept me in bed for a time. Then I was able to participate again, but I had not fully recuperated when the course ended. Some of the men attending the course didn't pass the tests and were sent back to the front. To the six best in the course, the officer showed the grades on their report cards. Even missing so much time in training, I was one of the six, and I was very satisfied with my grades. There were about ten of us that were not sent back to the front but went on to the academy. I was put in charge to bring the men back to Germany.

—•—

One tragic thing happened while we were still in training. When I became ill, I was transferred to the nursing station. My replacement in the course used my bunker and bed. He didn't pass but didn't want to go back to the front. He was afraid of the war action, and he told us he would rather kill himself then return to the front. We didn't take him seriously and didn't pay much attention. He first told the officer he was sick. The doctor examined him and didn't find anything wrong with him. When we returned on our last day from an activity, we found him dead in his bunker. He had placed a gun against his head. The whole place looked awful.

—•—

We had to walk a distance to reach the railroad station. After we boarded the train and traveled toward Germany, I had a great idea. I went ahead and talked it over with my fellow aspirants. Our train had to pass through Schneidemuehl and Neubrandenburg, and what could be better than to stop there and take a day or two off. "How would it be if we all took two or three days off at the town of our choice and then meet at a certain place in Schwerin?" I asked the men. Of course, I had to do plenty of explaining and convincing till we all agreed. We would take three days off and meet after the three days, in the evening at a café in Schwerin. I would be the first to leave the group. I wanted to stop in Schneidemuehl. That was the first city any one of us was interested in stopping at. I trusted my fellow officer aspirants would do as we had agreed, and I left the train in Schneidemuehl. I spent two days with the Birth family and then went on to Neubrandenburg and stayed with my parents for a day. It was great to be together with the ones I loved. Then I went on to my garrison city of Schwerin. Shortly before midnight I arrived at the café where we planned to meet. Everyone was there, sitting around a table. With a great hello I was received. When I asked my comrades how it was at home, everyone was quiet. They told me no one had stopped and visited at home. They were afraid they would get caught and lose their rank. When they arrived in Schwerin, they reported at the office and told the officer that one man was missing (me). They received orders to wait until the missing man arrived and then report. Now I was a little concerned. I told them to have their uniform spic-and-span and to look sharp. We would report tomorrow morning.

In the morning in front of the office, I had every man stand in line for inspection. I made sure everyone looked good. I went into the office reporting to the officer, "The officer aspirants of the twelfth infantry division returning from the front are ready to attend the academy in Thorn." Not realizing that I was the missing man, he asked me, "Did the missing man arrive?" "Yes, sir," I answered. He came out into the hallway and looked us over. He liked what he saw. He asked me what we wanted to do next. I said, "We would love to have two weeks of furlough." He thought for a minute, and then he said, "I have nothing against it. Go over and report to the battalion commander and if he agrees, it is fine with me."

After he released us, the men hugged me and were all excited that we might get furlough. We went over to the commander's office, where I did just the same as I had done before. I went inside and reported to the commander, and he came out. He was impressed with us young fellows and asked us many questions. How were our troops doing? How was the morale, and so on. Then he asked me too what we wanted to do next. I said the same thing to him as I had done before. "That's fine with me," he said. "Come by this afternoon and I will sign the permits." *After noon,* I thought, *my train will leave shortly after noon, and I would have to wait till the evening.* "Sir," I said, "how about me running over and doing it now?" "Go ahead when you can," he said with a smile. I guess he knew the slow progress it would make in the company office, but I wanted to give it a try. I had to convince the office they could do it with my help.

"Yes," the men in the office said. "It can't be done." I had some convincing to do and offered my help. When I had been in the hospital, I had had much time on my hands and helped at the office. I knew what to do and how to do it. They explained to me their procedure and, with their help, I went to work. I had our company leader sign and went over to the commander and had him sign. He was not a little surprised when he saw me. He signed and wished us well. I gave every one their permit, and we all hurried to the railroad station. You should have seen the eyes of my mother when she opened the door and saw me. "What did you do now?" she asked. "Nothing is wrong," I said. "I even have a permit this time." She couldn't believe it. I had just left last night and here I was back again.

—•—

After my return to Schwerin, we had to leave for the academy in Thorn. We left in early December 1943 and had a few days before the deadline for our arrival. The group wanted to stay in Thorn, but I was not interested in staying longer than necessary in the barracks. Especially not when I could spend my time in Schneidemuehl with the Birth family. I stopped again in Schneidemuehl while my comrades went on to Thorn. Edith had returned from filling a twenty-four-month mission in Berlin, serving in our East German Mission's headquarters. While I loved everyone in the Birth family, for Edith I had a special liking. We would go out together. At times we would study the scriptures and exchanged our thoughts. She helped her mother in their grocery store.

In the evening of the last day of admission, I arrived at Podgorz, a suburb of Thorn. Because there were so many latecomers, the master sergeant had to help out, and he took all needed information from me. He asked me all kinds of general and personal questions. Then came the always interesting one: "Your religion?" "Church of Jesus Christ of Latter-day Saints." "Let us write, *EV* (for Lutheran church)." "I am not a Lutheran" I said. "Well, then, let's write *Kath* (for Catholic church)," he countered. Now I got a little upset. "I am not a Catholic. I am LDS and listen, you write what I tell you, will you?" He looked at me, astonished. I guess nobody had ever told him that.

The rooms in this building were large. About ten to twelve men occupied one. I liked the group in my room; we made a good team. On the third day I was asked to come into the office of our commander, a major, decorated with many medals, including the *Ritterkreuz.* He met me standing in his secretary's office. After I saluted, he asked me about the welfare of my father and mother. I knew he didn't have me come up to ask me those questions. I thought I knew what he was after, and I was right. Then came the question I had expected: "I don't understand. What is that religion you belong to?" "It is The Church of Jesus Christ of Latter-day Saints," I told him. "I never heard of that church," he told me. "Oh," I said. "Herr Major, you know this church. You have heard of the Mormons, haven't you?" "You are a Mormon?" he said and took two steps back. "Yes, sir, I am a Mormon."

We talked about the Church and the doctrines of the Church. I asked him if he would like to know more about the Church and read some Church literature. He said he wanted to, so I hurried down to my room and brought back three books, The Book of Mormon, *The Program of the Church* by John A. Widtsoe, and another one, the title I have forgotten. When I presented him with the books, he told me he would read them and would discuss my case with the other *Herren* (gentlemen), the commander of the academy, and the section heads. He also told me he could not guarantee that I would remain at the academy, and he would tell me what the outcome was. I saluted and left.

About fourteen days later, I was called back to see the major again. This time he was sitting at his desk. He told me he had read the books and discussed my case with the Herren. They all agreed I could remain at the academy. Then he explained to me the advantages I would have if I would leave the Mormons and become a Nazi. When he saw my negative stand toward his proposal, he told me my religion was changing its doctrines. I asked him what doctrine had changed. He told me, "*Vielweiberei*" (polygamy). I always like a discussion. When he said this, I bent over, planted my hands on his desk, and looked him straight in his eyes and said, "Vielweiberei, Herr Major, is what you see around here, men being married, taking out and having sex with other women. Mormons who had more than one woman were married to them and honored that marriage covenant." "Rohloff!" he said, and that reminded me he was a Major and I an Unteroffizier. I stood at attention. "Here are your books. You can remain, but we will have a special eye on you." I was released and could go. I must say, he was always fair to me. In classes which he taught, he handled me the same as the rest of the other students. When I had to teach a class on the duties of a German soldier, his judgment was fair. He even told me my presentation was very good, which was seldom heard. His final remarks on my report card were understandable; I had no loyalty to the Nazi Party and didn't consider changing.

The charts from the course previous to ours were still hanging on the walls for the first week. To my surprise, I saw the name of the son of my branch president on the chart. I wondered how it was that I was the first Mormon at the academy. Later I learned he had turned his back toward the Church. He apparently couldn't stand the heat.

During all this and what later happened, I was always in touch with my parents and got much encouragement from them. My father would write me, "Stand up for what you believe, but do your best. Be tops in your exercises. Let them show their colors, so they have to admit you did your job, and it was your religion that is held against you." The only thing we differed on was me taking furlough without a permit. He didn't want me to do it, but I loved it and did it whenever I had an opportunity. I needed the relationship and encouragement of the Birth family and of the youth in that branch. When I returned from there, I had strength to go on.

The drill was hard, but I didn't mind. I knew that anything I learned here could save my life later if I were in war action. I was healthy, kept the Word of Wisdom, and sports had made my body strong and flexible. We not only had physical training, but we also had to learn how to instruct and how to lead. We would sit until late in the night to prepare for that. When I felt I was prepared well enough for the next day, I would get out my Church literature to prepare not for war, but for a mission for the Church.

During one of the preparation hours, I was sitting at the head of our table with the entrance door at my back. I had finished my preparations for the next day and had spread out my Church literature on the table. Through the door came the master sergeant, checking on us. Stopping at my place first, he looked over my shoulder for a while and then he asked, "What is that book?" "The Bible," I said. "Let me see the other men first and then I will talk to you." That was fine with me. He went and talked and checked on the others one after another, and then came back to me. I knew he didn't believe in a living God, and my chances to convert him were slim. After he asked me about my beliefs, I explained to him the teachings of the Church. He listened for about half an hour and asked many questions. When he wanted to leave, he turned to me and said, "I can't prevent you from doing this, but you and I have nothing in common anymore." We did not have anything in common before.

WALTER KINDT FILE

Young German soldiers celebrate Christmas, 1942.

The next day we had to give a presentation. You guessed right—it was me who had to instruct the class. Not only was the major, who usually instructed this class present, our master sergeant was there too. I presented the material, and after my presentation everyone in class had to evaluate my presentation. It was always done after anyone's presentation. To my delight, the major's critique was, "Very good, Rohloff."

—•—

I felt that I made good progress in the training to become an officer in the German Army. Most of our instructors helped me to be successful. We all were grateful to be at the academy and not somewhere on the front. Things didn't look good for Germany. There was very little progress made anywhere. In Russia, the army fought a losing battle at Stalingrad, and in Africa the army retreated. Goebbels propaganda said, "The army was straightening out the front lines so as to have better positions." Rumors had it that our allies were no help. At the first confrontation with the enemy, they left their positions and ran. At home there was a bleak outlook too. The air raids had increased. For the people, the workload was much longer and harder and was mostly carried out by women and older men. Most of the able-bodied men were in the armed forces. My mother had to go to work too. She worked in an assembly line in the same factory where my father was employed. She didn't like it but couldn't make a change.

We here in the academy worked hard to complete our training, knowing that everyone who was successful would be an officer, a lieutenant. It was announced that a few of us, the best, would be promoted two or three weeks before the others. My group and I counted on my early promotion, and we were very disappointed when it didn't take place. I started to think something must have gone wrong. Except for the master sergeant, no one had treated me any differently than the others, and that included the major, our commander. I kept hoping I would be promoted before we returned to our units, but I had already the feeling it wouldn't happen.

At the academy, the final days came and my feelings hadn't betrayed me; I didn't become an officer. I was not told why, but apparently others knew more about it than I did. On the last day a sergeant came and asked for me. He introduced himself as being a Lutheran minister and said he wanted to get acquainted with me. He was older than I, and I am sure he had a family. To me, he didn't look like a Lutheran minister. He looked more like an army officer. He had a well-built, athletic body, like a man who does many sports. Shaking hands with me he said, "I wanted to get acquainted with you. I understand you didn't become an officer because you are an active Mormon. I don't think well of the Mormons, but I respect you for standing up for what you believe in." He left as fast as he came. Apparently he was an active Lutheran and shared with me the same destiny. It was not as easy to take as I thought it would be. Now I had to salute the ones who, only a few days ago, I had helped in their preparations. Especially hard to take was that the ones I had helped the most through this course were the first to turn their back on me.

—•—

I returned with the others to Schwerin in the middle of March 1944. Again I received two weeks' furlough and spent it between Neubrandenburg and Schneidemuehl. It did me much good to be with my family and the Birth family. I still carried some disappointment, and being with them encouraged me to go on and to stand up for what I believed. After returning to my garrison in Schwerin, two others and I got orders to leave for the East Front in Russia. This time I was lucky; the parents of one of my comrades lived in Schneidemuehl. We stopped there, and I went to see the Birth family. While at the Birth home, I received a call from my comrade. He had our reports there and had opened the envelope over steam. He told me of his report card, and it was no good. Then he read all the entries on my report card, and I had all "good" and "very good" marks, but under remarks was written, "Religious fanatic, belonging to the Mormon sect. Politically not trustworthy." Now I knew why I didn't become an officer, and now I felt good. It gave me a great lift. I had accomplished what my father and I wanted. They had shown their true color.

We extended our unauthorized stay for three days and then we went on to reach our unit, the twelfth infantry division and the eighty-ninth regiment. We found our regiment east of the town of Mogilew. My two comrades were invited into the commander's shelter first. I stood outside the door of the bunker and could hear what was going on inside. Inside it sounded like a thunderstorm. The commander told the two they were a disgrace to his regiment and they hadn't represented the unit well. For quite some time he raised his voice, and when he released the men, they looked like something had hit them. That didn't make me feel good either. When he ordered me in, I expected the same treatment. After he opened my report and read it through, he looked at me and said, "There is nothing we can do. You have your belief and we have ours." Then he continued to my surprise, "Do you have a wish?" It caught me unprepared, but I asked to be returned to my old company, the third. He told me he couldn't do that, but he would send me to his old battalion and to the seventh company.

The next day I got my own squad and shelter. Our front line ran along the foot of some small hills, and we had our shelter connected with the main trench. The shelter of the platoon leader was behind the hill. There was no trench from the battle line to his shelter, and no visual contact between him and us. On the other hand, he could move around without being seen by the enemy, while we had to put our heads down during the day. We had great respect for the Russian sharpshooters. When I was on patrol at night, I found we had only a few men to guard a large section and there were long distances between the guards. Not much was going on in this section of the German front, and we hoped it would stay that way. Men were needed in many other places, so we were glad we were here.

In one of my first days at the front, I was ordered to see the company commander, a captain. To my surprise, when I entered his shelter, he had one of the poorest. He had water on the floor and had to place boards over the water. That made the ceiling very low. He invited me to sit across from him on a piece of wood. He had read my report card from the academy and felt that a man with my talent should change his beliefs and become an officer. He explained to me his point of view, the Nazi theory. This theory he felt anyone could understand and was superior to any other theory. On the other hand, there was I, with my impossible belief in a God no one had ever seen. He could comprehend someone believing and praying to the sun, but to an unseen God, that was incomprehensible. I told him I appreciated him taking time out to talk to me about my beliefs. Then I explained to him what I believed and why. He had a little temper, and every time I contradicted him, he would raise himself from the wood he was sitting on and hit the ceiling. The face he made after hitting the ceiling was so funny; I had a hard time not laughing. I couldn't convert him to change his philosophy, and he couldn't convince me to change either. We parted after a long discussion, and I never heard from him again.

—•—

North of us, the front had collapsed and we were taken out of our position to reinforce our troops. That sounds so easy, but it was hard work. We had to carry our own equipment and had to help the horses to pull the wagons. None of us were permitted to sit on a wagon. We had to walk all the way. The unpaved roads were in terrible condition. Some were, of course, better than others. Now in the spring, all the roads were soft and slippery, and the holes full of water. The only good thing was, there were no airplanes around.

In the night, we moved into our new positions. This place was higher, and there was no water in the trenches, but the trenches were full of the dead. Dead soldiers were lying all over the field, and some were even hanging in the barbwire entanglement. We started to clean up and buried as many dead as possible. Where we found identification, we sent it back to our supply unit. Many trenches we covered with dirt because they were full of dead, and we had no way to take the dead out. All this had to be done at night. Sharpshooters didn't let us lift our heads above the dirt wall in front of our trenches. There was nothing we could do about the dead hanging in the entanglement or those who were lying in no-man's-land. We didn't want to risk our lives. Later when it was warmer, the dead who were lying around started to stink, and that was really unpleasant.

When there was no action, the daily life in the trenches was boring. Only one guard was, for about two hours, on duty at a time. All the rest were in the shelter and played cards, read, or slept. Playing cards was for money, and because you couldn't buy anything there, it was spent freely. Drinking alcohol was a big problem. Fortunately, the Russians never knew that; at times, I was the only one in the trench sober and awake.

In early June 1944, I was ordered to appear before the battalion commander. Arriving at his shelter and notifying the clerk of my arrival, he came outside. He made me stand at attention while he read from a letter: "The cadet Unteroffizier Walter Rohloff is, as of this day, dismissed as a cadet and from further officer training. The reason, 'In politics not trustworthy, since he is a religious fanatic and belongs to the Mormon sect by order # B I B from 2.6.44 Ziffer 7.' He told me he was sorry and dismissed me. Maybe I should have felt bad about it, but I didn't. I felt very good. Now for the first time, I heard officially why I did not become an officer. On my way back to my unit, I passed a small piece of forest. I went in, and on my knees thanked the Lord that I could do this little thing for Him. He was always with me, and I was really happy I could do something in return.

Another try was made by my new company leader, a captain, to have me become an officer. He called me to his shelter and told me I could become the leader of a company (120 men), but the men in this unit were convicts. That would be the last thing for me to do. He didn't realize how little I cared to become an officer, but he thought he could help me with this offer. I never had seen a *Strafkompanie* (a unit of convicts), but I assumed many would be political prisoners. I asked—no, I begged—him not to recommend me. Apparently he didn't. I never heard a thing about that again. In our unit every one loved his country, but I didn't know of anyone who was a Nazi.

One early afternoon I was lying and dreaming on my bed. In my dream I saw that we were attacked and I was wounded and taken back, all the way to Germany. Then I thought, "If you got wounded, what books would you take with you?" I opened my eyes and thought, "What nonsense!" But I went outside and looked over at the enemy and didn't see anything suspicious. It was as calm as usual. Back inside our shelter, I looked over my books. I had made a hole in the dirt wall where I kept my books. I took the New Testament, the Doctrine and Covenants, and the Articles of Faith out and put them in my pockets.

On the next day, June 21, 1944, mine was the last tour before dawn to check the guards in the main battle line and to make contact with the neighboring division. When daylight came, I went over the hill to the shelter of our platoon leader. His shelter was on the other side of the hill and quite a distance from our main battle line. It was quiet, and I hadn't seen anything important to report. My platoon leader was talking to another platoon leader on the phone when I heard the words, "*Ivan im Graben* (The Russians are in the trenches)."

Without saying a word, I hurried out of his shelter and went to join my men. It was the place I should be. I had to cross over the hill, but the Russians were laying artillery and mortar fire on top of the hill. They sealed our line off from the rear so no help could come from the rear. I had no choice; I had to cross the fire. By listening to the flying grenades, I knew when to run and when to lie down. My men were already in the trench, and I informed them what had happened and placed them in position. When everything was almost over, I expected to see some Russians in the entanglement. After a salvo missed us, I put my head up to see what was going on. A late grenade hit the ground a few yards in front of me, and some fragments hit my face. It didn't penetrate my skull, and I never lost consciousness.

After things calmed down, I went to the company leader's shelter for first aid. The doctor told me the wounds were not life-threatening, but an infection could be. He sent me back to the nearest hospital in Mogilew. I was not sure what I wanted to do. My company leader told me I could stay or go, it was my decision. After the doctor made me aware I would be responsible for what happened, I disregarded my platoon leader's pleading for me to stay and went. I had to take another wounded man along, on a wagon pulled by a horse, a heavily wounded man. We reached our *Tross* (baggage unit) in daylight without any problems, and from there we were transported to the hospital. The hospital was packed with wounded men, and they tried to move out as many men as possible. Because my wounds did not need attention right away, I was placed in an *Erholungsheim* (convalescent home) nearby.

A chess tournament was planned on my first Sunday in the convalescent home. I like to play chess, and I was thinking of participating in the tournament. In the past, I had always tried to have a spiritual hour on Sundays when I studied the scriptures. When it was possible to attend a church of any denomination, I attended church, preferring the Lutheran faith. In all the years I never met a Mormon, nor was I stationed near an LDS church, except when I was in officer-training in Gnesen and Thorn, and that was not really near a church either. I was debating with myself between my love of chess and my commitment to keep the Sabbath holy and find a church to attend. The town of Mogilew was new to me. Because this was deep in enemy country, we were told not to go alone. I checked around, but no one was interested in going to church. I went anyhow. Mogilew is a large town, and because I didn't know where to find a church, I walked along the streets looking for a sign on a building. Usually church meetings were held close to a military installation. I had walked for a long time when I saw a sign that said, "*Evangelische Lutherishe Soldaten Gemeinde*" (Lutheran army branch). I walked in and noticed a few soldiers in the room, and a minister getting ready for the service. I have forgotten details of the service, but the theme I remember, "And we know that all that happens to us is working for our good, if we love God" (Romans 8:28). This really was true for me. This scripture didn't leave my mind for the next several weeks.

After returning from the service, I was not interested in playing chess anymore. I studied my scriptures and read other books. Only a few days had passed since I was wounded, but my wounds didn't bother me much. I went to bed early. During the night, a toothache woke me up. Looking around for help, I found the place in uproar. After asking a member of the home staff, I learned the Russians had broken through our main defense line and were moving in our direction. Later I learned the Russians had broken through our defense line at the place where I was wounded. This was typical in planning the attacks. The Russians were able, on the day I was wounded, to penetrate our defense with an assault party. It showed we had a weak spot, and a major attack followed. This time, no fortification of our line was made, and the Russians were able to break through. We were quite a distance behind the front. I thought it would take some time till they would reach this place. I didn't recognize the seriousness of the situation. After getting a sedative, I went to bed and slept well.

Getting up the next morning and looking around, the house looked like a beehive. Things were packed, and material and men were moved to the railroad station. The staff was able to take almost all the personnel and patients on the train, except for a few who were able to move on their own. Eleven men didn't make it, and I was one of the eleven. Most of the men were very disappointed, but in my mind was the scripture from yesterday: "When we love God, all things will be to our best." We were advised to return to the hospital.

We did return to the hospital, but there we were greeted by the same conditions as in the convalescent home: confusion. It took us a while to find someone in charge. He was very helpful but had room on his train for only five of us. I was one of the six who were still left behind. This was not encouraging, but the thought from Sunday made me feel it was for my good. He instructed us to walk to the city commander. The commander's office was on the main highway through Mogilew and in a beautiful villa. His message to us was very short and clear. At 6:00 PM, Mogilew would be declared a fortress. No one would be permitted to leave and no one permitted to enter. The city, he said, would be defended up to the last man. We could do whatever we wanted—leave before 6 PM or stay here and fight. Well, I was really not interested in dying in this town, nor in becoming a prisoner of war.

Walking from the house toward the street, I heard someone from a big, bypassing truck shout my name. Talking to them, I found out they were part of my unit and had to go back for material. They took me along and we went westward. They told me what had happened, and that little of my unit was left.

—•—

It was only June 1944, but the end of the war for Germany was in sight. The Allied forces had broken through the German defending lines in France and Italy. Here, the Russians had now broken through too. There were many people who disliked Hitler and the Nazi Party, and they tried to work against him. On our way, we saw trains loaded with tanks and heavy equipment standing on the railroad tracks. These tanks and artillery were needed on the front, but someone kept them sitting here. Later, army officers tried to kill Hitler (in July 1944), but it didn't work out. Many lives would have been spared and much sorrow would have been prevented had these men succeeded. It was not only the German Army who retreated westward nearer to Germany—many Russian civilians, too. Rightfully, these people feared their own people more than the Germans, and later happenings showed they were right. I saw this large body of Russian civilians fleeing before their own army, some with horse and *panje* wagon, but most walking and carrying their belongings. I thought of my family at home and hoped they would never have to leave home, and this would never happen to them.

The next morning I went over to the main highway crossing. One man from the military police (MP) was stopping and placing men who needed transportation in the vehicles. I joined the group but was kept waiting till he had given transportation to every other soldier, even though my turn should have been much earlier. A van came by and had to take me. This was not an ordinary van; it was a mail transporting and sorting station. It was very comfortable inside and (what was very important for my well-being) they had plenty of food. I helped with sorting the mail. It was just too bad that this vehicle didn't go all the way to the city of Minsk. I was planning to be admitted into the hospital and have my wound treated there. I had to transfer trucks a few times, till I reached the outskirts of Minsk. The truck I was riding in carried not only me, but many other soldiers. Before we could enter the city, the truck was stopped by the military police. All the men had to get off the truck, and the MP kept everyone there, except the truck and me. I had the little tag which I got when I was wounded and arrived at the first aid station. Later after I arrived in the hospital, it was taken away from me. It had all the information about me and my physical condition. I was the only one who had this tag, and that was the reason the MP let me go on. How I still had the tag, I don't know. Before we arrived at the hospital, the driver stopped the truck, leaned out the window, and asked me, "Should I take you to the hospital or to the railroad station?" This unexpected question made me think a minute and then I said, "To the railroad station."

In one of the many barracks at the railroad station, I found an empty upper bed, and I fell asleep. Later it seemed I heard a faraway voice shouting, "Everyone who wants to go to Germany get over to the railroad station and on the waiting train." That woke me up, and seeing the commotion, I knew it was real and not a dream. I had nothing to carry but myself. I was quickly at the railroad station and in the train. I found a window seat but chose, because I was so tired, to climb into the suitcase net above the seats and fell asleep instantly.

I didn't hear how the railroad car filled, nor if anyone complained about my filling the suitcase net. Neither was I aware how everyone was checked by the MPs, which surely had happened. Apparently no one could get me awake, or they saw my tag and left me alone, I don't know. When I woke up, the train was moving and we were near the town of Vilnius in Lithuania. That was a long distance form Minsk.

My wounds by now had healed, but the fragments were still inside. I met a comrade who had been on the staff of the convalescent home in Mogilew. What he told me was not good news. He was one of the few men who had escaped when the train, carrying the men from the convalescent home away from Mogilew, was attacked by the Russian Army. The Russian tanks were faster and stopped the train, and the men who tried to escape over an open field were mowed down by the guns of the tanks. How good it was that they hadn't taken me along. The word of the Lord was fulfilled: "All that happens to us will work for our good, if we love God."

The Russian tanks were faster and stopped the train, and the men who tried to escape over an open field were mowed down by the guns of the tanks. How good it was that they hadn't taken me along. The word of the Lord was fulfilled: "All that happens to us will work for our good, if we love God."

I was kept in Warsaw only for a short time. Then a hospital train was put together, and we were transported into Germany. On July 7, 1944, we arrived in the town of Kirchhain, in the *Nieder Lausitz*. Upon our arrival we were examined, and because my wounds were healed and no danger of infection existed, I was placed in a gymnasium. This big hall was full of patients and beds. Here I had the opportunity to write to my parents. They wrote back and also visited me. The high command had notified them I was missing and possibly killed in action. How happy they were when they heard from me. Not only were they grateful I was still alive, I was too. The Lord had really guided me through this difficult time. I had not thought of my dream far away in Russia, but now I remembered and marveled how it came about.

I was informed by my parents where to find the nearest branch of the Church. I applied for weekend furlough to the city of Cottbus, but my application was rejected. There was not much to do in the city of Kirchhain. This city was known for the many tanneries which were located here and made the city smell, not especially good. The surroundings of the city, I never explored. What I wanted was to visit the branch in Cottbus. I made plans to go there without a furlough permit. I found out there were no MPs at the local railroad station. Leaving the gymnasium was a problem because the doors were locked and the windows were very high.

I decided to try it anyhow. Early on a Sunday morning while everyone was still deep asleep, I moved a table under the window, another smaller table above it, and a chair on the top. Now I could reach and climb through the window. Without any difficulty, I reached the railroad station, bought a ticket to Cottbus, and was on my way. Having never been in Cottbus, I inquired of the passengers how the station was built, and after admitting I had no permit for furlough, I asked them how I could leave the station without having a problem. One lady spoke up and told me there was no MP on platform 4, only an inspector from the railroad.

After arriving in Cottbus, I went right to platform 4. Many people left the station through this gate. Because only one person could pass by the booth, we had to stand in line. When it was my turn to give the inspector my ticket, he told me I couldn't leave the station through this gate; I had to leave through the main gate. I told him I couldn't leave the station through the main gate because there was an MP standing there and I had no furlough permit. When he heard that, he insisted in no uncertain terms, that I go through the main gate. I smiled at him, placed my ticket on the counter, and I was gone.

The meetinghouse of the Church was close to the railroad station in the *Lausitzerstrasse*. I was early and took the opportunity to talk with the members who arrived early. Brother Fritz Lehnig, the district president, was present, and I talked to him. He asked me among other things, if I was married. When I told him no, he invited me to take a close look at the girls of his branch. I didn't need this invitation—I did it anyhow. After the morning meeting, I met his daughter, Jenny, and other sisters of the branch. The meetings were uplifting, and I felt right at home among the members of the Church.

Between Sunday School and sacrament meeting, I was invited to dinner by Brother Guido Schroeder. As we walked along the streets and I was saluted or had to salute someone from the armed services, they raised their hand in the Hitler salute while I used the army salute. That was strange to me, and I felt uneasy and I asked Brother Schroeder to use other streets where there was very little traffic. What I didn't know was that on the day before, July 20, a Colonel von Stauffenberg had planted a bomb in Hitler's headquarters, but Hitler was not killed. All connected with this attempted assassination were looked for and later killed. To show their solidarity with Hitler, the army had ordered everyone to use the Hitler salute. There were not many friendly feelings between the army and Hitler's SS anyhow, and this change annoyed many more.

After sacrament meeting, I went with Gerda Eckert to her home, and she brought me to the railroad station. I didn't know any other way to enter the station (I of course couldn't use the watched over gates), so I had to jump the fence. The fence was about six feet high, but that was not the main problem. All along the fence were *Lanzer* (soldiers) standing and kissing their girls good-bye. I said good-bye to Gerda and went over to the fence. I excused myself by one of the soldiers who had his girl in his arm, and I explained to him what I had to do. He was irritated but gave room, and I jumped the fence. Without any problem, I was back in the gymnasium and in bed.

In the morning, one of the male nurses came by and told me I had been reported missing yesterday and would have to appear before the captain. I polished my uniform and everything that goes with it, to make a good impression. At the appointed hour I reported to the captain. He was an elderly gentleman, a reserve officer, nice and friendly. He made me stay at attention and read a report to me. It was reported I was looked for and missed at nine o'clock in the morning, also at noon and at three o'clock in the afternoon. He asked me then what I had to say about the report. I told him the report was correct. I was not in the building at that time. He looked surprised. Apparently he had not expected me to admit that I wasn't in the building. Now came the question I couldn't answer: "Where have you been?" "I can't tell you. If I tell you, you'll have to punish me," I said. "But," I continued, "I didn't do anything wrong." I knew there was a punishment for leaving the hospital, but the punishment for leaving the town was even greater. I don't know how he felt and what went through his mind. He took my *Soldbuch* (passbook) and looked through it. After reading it for a little while, he asked me, "Under religion, what does it mean? I don't understand what is written." Usually the entrance in that spot was "EV" for Lutheran church, or "Kath" for the Catholic Church, but mine was "Jes.Chr." apparently for Jesus Christ. I told him it stands for "Church of Jesus Christ of Latter-day Saints" and that we are better known as Mormons. He asked me if I believed in the teachings of that church, and I said yes. He said, "I wonder what your minister would be saying about your past actions." Well, I couldn't tell him I had just seen my minister. I told him I had not broken the laws, only rules, and I didn't think my minister objected. Then he asked me questions about the teachings of the Church, which I gladly answered. After a friendly discussion, he dismissed me with the words he wouldn't punish me, but should I be caught again, he would have to do it. I promised he wouldn't have to do it. The next time I got a permit for weekend furlough.

After being in the hospital for almost three weeks, the doctor looked at my wounds and decided to take out the fragments I had in my forehead. It was done by local anesthesia. I could hear the doctor working on my bones, but didn't feel anything. Only a few days after the operation, on the eighth of August, I was dismissed from the hospital.

What I heard in Schwerin was not good. Our twelfth infantry division had been completely destroyed in Russia. A new twelfth division would be formed near the town of Dirschau, in West Prussia. None of the men I talked to felt good about it. My father at home had told me already, he felt Hitler wouldn't give in until Germany had been completely destroyed. He couldn't stand Hitler anyhow. My uncle Willy Tank was with the police and stationed somewhere in Czechoslovakia as a guard in a concentration camp. He had told my father some things that were going on there, which my mother later told me. My father had asked my uncle why he did not quit the police, but that would probably have been difficult without persecution. It almost came to a break between the two of them.

Most men in our garrison in Schwerin felt we should give up, and the few who didn't feel that way believed Goebbel's propaganda. There was always talk about a *Wunderwaffe* (miracle weapon). You could occasionally see the new airplanes (the jets), in the air, but only a few knew that we didn't have enough gas to fuel them. Then they had heard about the rockets, V1 and V2, being shot over to England. The air raids over Germany were far more devastating than the few V1s or V2s. We felt we had superior weapons, a new machine pistol, a machine gun, the 8.8-mm anti-aircraft gun, and so on. But these new weapons were more an apple of discord between the SS, who got all this stuff and the army, who just knew about it. It was depressing. At home people worked hard during the day in the factories. At night, they got very little rest. Many times they had to hurry to the shelters to protect themselves from the air raids. Food and clothing was rationed and very little was available. It was frightening when you took a look at a map and saw the many nations who were fighting Germany.

In 1943, the German Army started to retreat under the pressure of the Allied forces, and under the shortage of men and material. Up to that time, the German Army had marched deep into Russia, in Africa, to the border of Egypt, and kept Allied forces out of France. Now the forward advance of the German armies had ended. In Russia, Italy, and France, the resistance of the German Army gave. By this time, in the fall of 1944, the Russian Army was moving toward the Polish border. The Allied forces had a stronghold in France and were close to the German border. In Italy, Allied forces had landed and moved slowly northward. The SS had a new division called *Hitlerjugend* (Hitler Youth), mainly from boys seventeen and eighteen years old. My father was drafted, being fifty-three years old, into the *Volkssturm* (Folks guard). At home everyone had to work, and many people from the occupied territories had to work in Germany too.

With others, I was transferred from Schwerin to Dirschau in West Prussia, not far from Danzig. Here my division was restored, and all the units got their old (traditional) names. I didn't know any of the men. I saw all new faces. The old guard was either dead or captured in Russia. The equipment we received was pitiful. The once proud German Army now had old machine guns and the old, but reliable 98k rifle. To carry our equipment, we received panje wagons which the Russian Army had used before us, with the little horses that came from the same place. We looked more like a circus than an army. I would laugh, but it was very serious. As soon as they could get enough men together, we were loaded on a train. We crossed Germany and moved toward the German west border. We received no training, no practice, and no preparation whatsoever. It took us a few days before we arrived at night, near the city of Aachen. Unloading went fast and without any incidents. We marched a few hours that night, till we stopped and received the order to protect ourselves (*Einigeln*) on all sides. This order made me suspicious. I went over to our company leader and asked him why. He told me there were no German soldiers around here, and our assignment was to show resistance. My feeling was not really great. I realized we were being used as cannon fodder. I wondered who of us would see the next evening.

By sunrise we had moved into a forest below the village of Schevenhuette. Between us and the village was an open field, and close to the village were some enemy tanks. There was no preparation for our attack. We had no tanks, no artillery, nor mortar guns under which protection we could have moved forward. Of course we had to cross the open field during our attack, and the smart Allied troops let us come close before they started to shoot. Our rifles were no match for the tanks. We had to turn and try to get back into the forest. There we gathered whoever was left, regrouped, and went over to the next small village. At noon we attacked that village. This time they smothered our attack right when it started. As we now gathered, we saw that we had lost two-thirds of our men. But that was not all. With the few men we had left, we attacked a third village in the evening. When we returned from that skirmish, only eleven men were left of about forty before. Somewhere we went to sleep. Then I remembered it was my mother's birthday, September 17, 1944. What a day. I was tired but otherwise unharmed.

Conditions didn't improve, and even with additions of new men, no new or heavy equipment or weapons were added. The men were soon driven back from their positions. As they regrouped and reformed into defensive positions, Walter quickly recognized the danger of their situation.

I was not much pleased with this new defense line. On the hill there was no place to hide. There were no trees and no shrubs, only grass, and to my big disliking, a trigonometric marker. This marker was entered on every map, and the artillery could easily hit it. An even greater disappointment was the ground water level. It was here, on top of the hill, very high, close under the turf. We did what we could to build some kind of protection for us. I found a crater a grenade had left and used that as a foxhole. It was really a few feet in front of our defense line, but I had a good view over the field in front of me. During the night, our battalion commander came and wanted to make a counterattack and get the lost position back. We talked it over and decided to infiltrate near a sharp bend in the front line. It was a clear and beautiful night, and the moon was bright. We could see well, but so could the enemy. We walked one behind another. I was right behind the commander. We came to a clearing and he wanted to cross, but I wanted to walk along in the dark under the protection of the trees. He didn't listen when I explained my concern. He walked right on, crossing the clearing, while I kept standing in the dark for a while and let the men pass me by. It was too bad that I was right. He had just passed a little beyond the middle of the clearing, when all hell broke loose. From many sides I saw rifle fire coming, and while we saw only the flash of their rifles in the dark, we made an excellent target in the clearing, in the moonlight. It looked like they had been waiting for us. The man before me got hit in the leg. I gave him first aid and told him to keep calm and raise his hands. He would be treated well. I crawled back to our former position, gathered the returning men, and built up our defense. I didn't see the commander again but heard he made it all right, and got decorated for this fiasco with the *Ritterkreuz* (Knight's Cross). Maybe I should mention here that I was decorated on October 17, 1944, with the Iron Cross Second Class. I told the presenting officer I would have preferred furlough to getting the medal.

We were still sleepy in our holes when the morning broke. Looking around, I couldn't see much of interest below us. Behind us, the little village seemed to be still and asleep. Then I thought

I heard tank movement. It didn't take long until I saw tanks coming up from the valley toward us. What now? We had nothing with which to defend ourselves against the tanks. The little shallow holes we had were no protection against tanks. There was no help in sight. This was the end. I prayed. I always said my prayers, but this time it was different. It was a cry for help. I didn't want to be run over by tanks. Helpless, I watched as the tanks came closer and closer. When the tanks were about fifty yards from me, I thought I heard a noise behind me. I looked over at the village. There I saw a Volkswagen-schwimmwagen pulling a 7-mm light infantry gun behind it, come over the field. In almost no time, I had the gun ready and fired. At this short distance the first shot was a hit, and the tank started burning. Then they hit the next one. The rest of the tanks moved back, and soon the tanks were out of sight. That gun crew must have been old-timers. They knew their business so well. Thanks went up to my Heavenly Father.

When we would lose many men and were overtired, we would be taken out of the main fighting line and could get a little rest. While we were in reserve, the men we had lost would be replaced with new men. Most of these men were completely unprepared, and many were unfit. The time we spent with these men was very short and they got little training from us either.

Again, plans called for our division to be taken out and restored to full strength in men and equipment. My company leader told me to go and make quarters for our company. He gave me all the information I needed to make quarters. Walking along the highway, I had to pass through a forest, where I saw many gasoline barrels stored and many SS men walking around. There was not much love lost between the SS and the army. As I walked on, two SS men came along the road. I could see they were officers, but instead of saluting, I just kept my hands in my pockets and looked the other way. When they had passed me, one of them turned around and stopped me and asked why I had not saluted an SS officer? I asked him, "How am I to know who is an officer in the SS?" The markings of their ranks were much different from ours. Our not-so-friendly argument ended when he reached for his pistol. I had mine in my hand already and warned him not to move. In no time, I was surrounded by SS men and had to go with them to their commander, the same officer I had passed on the highway. He gave me a long lecture, and then instructed two men to turn me over to the military police.

As we reached the highway, I saw a company of soldiers coming toward us. I compared that unit with the SS unit I had just left. The SS had all modern, new weapons and equipment, not to mention the nice, comfortable trailer the commander had. This unit we met looked worn out, and had only horses with panje (Russian flatbed) wagons and old guns. What I saw confirmed only what I had heard and seen before—the SS was favored in every way, and the army was used as cannon fodder. As we passed them, I heard someone calling my name. When I turned toward the caller, I recognized my company leader, a lieutenant. He asked me what had happened, and after I told him I had not saluted some SS officers, he told me to go and take my place with my platoon. To the two SS men, who had the order to turn me over to the military police, he said he would give them as many men as they wanted from their own SS unit, who didn't salute him. I don't know what would have happened to me if my unit hadn't crossed my way. I had seen soldiers left hanging on the trees on my way.

While we were in this section, we had no major attacks, just the usual exchanges, skirmishes, and casualties. After we were there for a few weeks, I was asked by the commanding officer to go to the regimental headquarters and meet men from other companies to make quarters. When I arrived, the men had already left, and I was told that I could follow the others or return to my unit. They would take care of my assignment. I was going to go back to my unit, when my inner voice clearly said, "*Tue wie Dir gesagt wurde* (Do as you have been told)." Usually this voice warned me when there was danger ahead, but when I looked toward the front, I couldn't see any danger. The front was calm, but still I did what my inner voice told me. After I had made quarters for the company as I was asked to do, I went to bed. We expected our units the next day.

When I slept, it was always a deep sleep, and it was hard to wake me up. But this night I woke up from the noise outside and the vibrations of the house. When I went outside and looked over to the front, it was lighted as far as I could see. Countless airplanes were crossing over the front and dropping bombs, and the artillery from both sides was in action. It was a major attack. I later learned that another unit had moved into our position, and my unit had barely left the trenches when this attack came. It couldn't have been at a worse time. An exchange of units always brought some confusion. The attack was a complete surprise. Now I knew why my inner voice had warned me, and I was very happy I had followed the inner prompting. For over a week I waited for orders to return. I reported daily to my superior, but was told to stay where I was.

I was well rested when the call came to return to my unit. When I reached the battle zone, I was concerned how to make it through the artillery fire, because they were shooting at any movement. I walked along the road and used the trees along the road as cover. As I came close to the artillery fire, I saw a medic walking along in the open field, waving a Red Cross flag. Where he went, the artillery fire stopped until he had passed. Under the trees, I walked along with him and made it safely to my regiment's headquarters. In the dark I went on to my unit. My unit was now called a battalion, even though it was smaller than a company. All the men who used to belong to the battalion were grouped together in this unit. The rest were wounded or dead. When I arrived, my former company leader, now the battalion commander, asked me to be his adjutant. Our assignment was to prevent the enemy from crossing an elevated railroad track. On the crossing was a signal house, which we used as our headquarters. All our men were lying around the crossing in a half circle. We had only rifles, not even a machine gun. I got acquainted with the defensive line and made adjustments as needed.

During the night, we talked together (the commander, my friend, the school teacher, I, and others). They wanted me to give the men alcohol, and I objected. I told them, with a clear head, they would be much better off for the upcoming attack than if they were drunk. My argument was not accepted, and even my friend from Berlin told me off. My commander had been pretty neutral in this argument, but then he told me to give alcohol to the men, which I did. It happened as I thought it would. When I patrolled the men in their emplacement in the morning, I found many didn't have a foxhole and were just carelessly lying on top of the ground. One of them was my schoolteacher. He was drunk. As I confronted him, he reminded me that he was higher in rank than I, and he knew what he was doing. I loved that man, but I couldn't talk him into digging the hole. He was always careful when he was sober. I felt sorry for him but had to give my attention to other things. It was the last time I saw him.

In the night my other friend, the opera singer, had visited me in this little signal house. He looked pale, but all the men were nervous and irritable. He told me he was sick. I couldn't see anything wrong with him but had a medic look at him. The medic reported to me he couldn't find anything wrong with him either. I had to send him back into his foxhole. He had told me that he would die tomorrow. I tried in vain to change his attitude and was very concerned about him.

In the morning, the enemy artillery bombarded our position. That was expected, but then we ran out of luck. Our own artillery started to hit us, and that was deadly. Now we couldn't hear what would hit us, and we started to lose many men. The wounded we brought into this little house for protection against the fragments. Our medic was very busy giving aid to these men. We had no way of bringing the wounded back to a hospital. Our little house was already filled up when I saw two men bring in, in a canvas, another man. When I looked at the man in the canvas, it was my friend, the opera singer. In pain he looked at me as if he wanted to say, "Didn't I tell you?" It turned my heart over, but there was no way I could help him except to send him back to a hospital. I asked the men if they would take him back where he could get more help. They did, but I learned later that they were shot at by a tank. He was killed instantly.

While all this was going on, we were also under constant fire. We had to lay flat and get up all the time, to protect ourselves. So far, no shells had hit the little building. Then I saw tanks breaking through, and the little building blew up. I saw only one other man nearby. To get away from the tanks, we had to cross a little forest pass. A tank nearby shot everyone who crossed. The man closest to me tried to run over the pass, and he was hit right away. I crossed after him and ran crisscross through the low woods in front of the tank. The machine gun fire followed me, and I could see how the twigs got hit. But I made it unharmed, out of his way. When I was out of the machine gun fire, I came into the artillery salvos. I came through those untouched too. By now I was so nervous I feared I would have a nervous breakdown.

When I reached our baggage unit, I looked so terrible the men didn't even recognize me. The result of these last three weeks of fighting was that of over two hundred men we began with in the battalion, only eleven were left. For most of us, requests were prepared to decorate us with the Iron Cross First Class and the *Sturmabzeichen* (Award for taking part in three skirmisches). For some like me, who were in more than fifteen skirmishes, the *Nahkampfspange*. When I was told about this, I told them I would prefer furlough much more. My commander felt I needed a rest and gave me *Tapferkeitsurlaub* (furlough for bravery). On the twelfth of December I was on my way home, and didn't have to return till the third of January 1945.

As usual, I didn't stay only in Neubrandenburg, but also went to Schnidemuehl. Both places were, up to that time, untouched from the war. I don't think anyone believed the war could be won. Most people had given up and looked forward to the day when the war would be over. Only the party members kept hoping a turn would come. My father now belonged to the Volkssturm, an old folks' organization. They carried rifles and were supposed to enter the war. Youngsters in their early teens were put in the *Luftabwehr* to fight the air attacks. Young ladies served at the railroad stations to help with refreshments and food when trains, loaded with wounded soldiers or refugees, would come through. Everything was organized in detail and it still worked. The tracks of the railroad were destroyed many times, but after a short repair, it would be functional again. Factories were damaged, but they too were soon in operation again. Some factories were built underground and in caves. My factory where I used to work was still in operation, but I didn't know if they still made parts for airplanes. We didn't use many airplanes anymore. They were standing around ready for action, but no gasoline was available.

But there were dark clouds on the horizon. I enjoyed my stay with my family and the Births. When I was with the Birth family, I would get up early and study the scriptures with Edith before she went to work in her mother's grocery store. I was very surprised when I heard the news on the radio that the German Army had started an attack on the German West Front. I was sure my unit was involved in the action, because it was in the vicinity where we were stationed. The Rundstaedt offensive was a surprise to me and to the Allies too. I didn't believe it would be successful. I thought of the men and equipment and weapons we had. I assumed the other units, with the exception of the SS, were similarly outfitted. There was no way we could change the war. I was very glad I was home. To me it was Hitler's last attempt to change the outcome of the war, and when he would lose this battle, he would end the war. How wrong I was.

—•—

When the day of my departure, the third of January 1945, came, my father and my mother accompanied me to the railroad station in Neubrandenburg. We all felt that terrible things were ahead of us. The German defense had further deteriorated. The Russians were marching through Poland and would soon reach German soil. The attack in the west had been stopped by the Allied armies, and they had started counterattacks. Father said to us, "Apparently Hitler wants to sacrifice us all. Should we come through this all alive," he continued, "let us contact the LDS mission headquarters to find out where we are. We don't know what will happen here, and you don't know what will happen to you." He told me, "Stay close to the Lord," and he quoted from the scriptures: "For everyone who loves the Lord, everything will be to his good." I had the strange feeling that we all would see hard times, but we would come through alive.

My father told me, "Stay close to the Lord," and he quoted from the scriptures: "For everyone who loves the Lord, everything will be to his good." I had the strange feeling that we all would see hard times, but we would come through alive.

On the eleventh of January I arrived at my unit, eight days later than I had permission. Only once on the long way was I questioned why I was late. It was in Dusseldorf in an air raid shelter. It was in the evening when the man from the MPs asked me why I was late. I asked him if he could read. By that time my permit was full of official stamps I had collected at the different railroad stations. Wherever there was an open spot, there was a stamp. I couldn't see what he did because he stood at my back, but I could hear him turning my permit over and over. He gave me my permit back, shaking his head, but didn't say a word. Maybe the little word in the upper right corner of my permit, *Tapferkeitsurlaub* (furlough for bravery), might have helped me. All these men tried to stay in their safe place and to keep away from the front. Stepping on the toes of someone who might have a little clout could be dangerous and bring them to the front.

My unit existed only in name. It had changed completely. All the men were unknown to me, and their attitude was below zero. On the day I arrived, we had to leave the quarters my unit had occupied. The SS moved into the rooms, and we were given the hallways. I saw the hate our officers had toward these SS officers, but they did as they were told, even though our officers were higher in rank. What was especially disgusting to me was the way the SS treated the civilian population here in Belgium. They took the last food away from these people. When I tried to intervene, one of them pointed his gun at me and said, "Just say one word and I'll blow your head off." I knew he would and I kept my mouth shut. For the behavior of the SS, I had to pay later anyway. When I became POW in Belgium, the people saw not much difference between the SS and the army. We were all Germans, and they hated us and treated us like *Boche* (pigs).

On the morning of the eighth of March 1945, I walked toward the Rhine River to find a way to cross the river and get to the other side. As I walked through the streets, people asked me to give up fighting and go home. Of course I had given up fighting, but going home was a difficult thing. The housewife where I had been in quarters gave me some sandwiches, and on my way to the river I ate. Not much was going on at the riverside. A motorboat was there with the motor running, ready to leave. I went over and talked to the driver, and he told me the general wanted to get to the other side and would use the boat. He agreed to take me along. We talked and waited, but then about noon, we got news that the general wouldn't go. He wanted to stay and become a POW. Just the thought of becoming a POW made me uneasy. I decided to cross the river on my own. I had no idea where the enemy was. I could hear shooting, but I didn't think they were close enough to give me a problem. That I had never used a paddle boat didn't bother me. I felt I could handle it. I didn't even think of the danger involved.

Walking along, I saw a paddle boat lying there with the paddles inside, ready to go. I took my belt off and put it with my gun into the boat. When I sat in the boat, I felt comfortable. I pushed away from the riverside. I could steer the boat with my feet. I had paddled the boat only about fifteen yards out when a bullet passed me. Now I realized the danger I was in. The river was wide and deep, and the current strong. Should a bullet hit me or hit the boat beneath the water line, it would mean death for me. In this strong current, the cold water, and the winter clothing I wore, I would not survive.

I thought I couldn't turn around. It would be too slow, and I would be even a better target than I was now. I made myself as small as I could in the boat and said a short prayer, "Lord help me," and paddled for my life. The noise from the passing bullets was terrible in my ears, but no bullet hit me or the boat. I almost reached the other side when the cord to my rudder broke, and the boat went against the current. "It is all over," I thought. Then I felt the boat hit something on the bottom. In that second, I remembered learning in school that the rivers had underwater dams. Those dams went from the riverside toward the center of the river, but only for a few yards. The purpose of the dam was to reduce the flow and to keep up the underground water table. I saw I was about ten yards away from the shore, so I got out of the boat. I grasped my belt and my gun and turned toward the riverside. As I turned, a bullet hit me.

Luckily for me I fell forward on my knees, and my knees came to rest on the dam and not to the side. Had I fallen into the deep part of the river, it would have meant sure death. I got up and went along the dam. The "dam" was only about two inches under the water. After reaching the shore, I crawled up the bank and through the bushes. Now I was out of breath and felt weak. But German soldiers helped me along. I started to feel pain, and when we opened my clothing, we saw blood coming out of my abdomen. It was a clean shot, entering from the back of my body and going out in the front. "You need help right away," said one of the men, and they gave me two first-aid packs which I held on both ends of the wound. I knew very well I needed to be on the operating table or it would be the end of my earth life. But I was calm and confident. Two of the men helped me to the nearby highway.

We just waited a few minutes, and then a Volkswagen came by and was stopped by my helpers. They requested the man to bring me as fast as possible to a hospital. He declined as he had to deliver a written order to the commander of a Rhine bridge and was in a hurry. The soldiers talked to him until he agreed to take me to the nearest first-aid station. He took me and went to find a first-aid station. His fast driving hurt me terribly, but I didn't say anything. I was just glad to get help.

When he found a station, he left me on the lawn, I think without notifying anyone, and went on. It was a beautiful day. There were many wounded soldiers lying on the lawn. I laid there for a time before a medic came around and asked if I wanted something to drink. I told him I didn't think I could drink water because I had a shot through my abdomen. "How long have you been laying here?" he asked me. I didn't know, but it seemed to me it had been a long time. He went away in a hurry, but it still took a while till he returned with a doctor who examined me and dressed my wounds. When he was through, I was placed on an ambulance and we went further into the mountains.

In the evening after dark, we reached a convent by Siegburg, where we stopped. There were four men in the ambulance, and I had the upper place by a window. I could see and hear what was going on outside. Under a darkened light, the driver and a

R. JONES FILE

Captured German troops are trucked to makeshift POW camps.

doctor stood and talked. The driver wanted to leave us at the convent. The doctor told him no. Then he explained that this convent was already under artillery fire, and bombs were being dropped nearby. Also there was no electricity. After an argument, I was the only one taken out. The driver felt I wouldn't make it to the next hospital, and the doctor agreed with him. After placing me on an operating able, a nun came and prepared me for an operation. She asked me what my religion was. I told her, "Church of Jesus Christ of Latter-day Saints." She didn't know this church, but she had heard about the Mormons. I guess they wanted to bury me right, but I didn't want to be buried; I wanted to live. In spite of all the pain, I felt good on the operating table and thanked the Lord for His help.

When I woke up, I was lying in a large room filled with wounded soldiers. It was daylight, and I was in much pain. A medic came to see me and talked to me. He asked me about my parents and if I had a girlfriend and many more things, and while doing this, he stroked with his hand softly over my head. It felt very good. He couldn't do it for long. An air attack came, and he (and everybody else) went for shelter in the basement. I was lying all by myself in the big room. Some of the bombs fell close by. The windows broke, and the room was filled with dust. The building shook, but I had no fear. I had too much pain to think or feel anything else. When it was over, the medic came and gave me morphine.

While I was asleep, I was moved to the basement. Seven others, all heavily wounded, were lying with me in a room. A Catholic priest was giving the one across from me the last rites. Then later, he did the same to the one next to him. Both were carried out dead the next day. The man next to me was wounded like I was, with a shot through his abdomen.

I felt better now. The pain was bearable with medication. One day, it must have been noon (only by the activities could I tell if it was daytime, since we had no windows in the room) the nurse came with a nice, cooked meal. I had not eaten a good meal for so long. It was just what I wanted, and it smelled so good too. The fellow next to me took it and ate right away, but I was more careful. "Did the doctor give permission for me to eat this?" I asked the nurse. She didn't know. "Would you please go and ask?" She went, leaving the meal on the night table. What a temptation it was to eat. My neighbor couldn't resist the wait and ate. When she came back, after what seemed to me a long time, she took my meal, and I got my glass of milk again. The next morning when I woke up, the fellow next to me was dead.

Though his wound had been serious, it was turned out to be a blessing. While in the hospital, the American army moved in and Walter was made a POW. Though there was little food, conditions were much better than those who had been captured by the Russians.

Many men worked for the English Army, and I got to know quite a few. With one, Klaus Wiggess, I became pretty close. He belonged to the Lutheran church, and we had long gospel discussions. Later, two others joined us, and one day we put up a tent where we lived and had lengthy discussions. We started our discussions after the ministers of the Lutheran faith, who had held daily meetings, were sent home. Catholic priests had taken over, but we didn't like the way the meetings were held, no gospel discussions, only the mass. We decided to hold meetings ourselves. I had offered to help to teach these interfaith meetings. After they heard I was a Mormon, it was not accepted.

We four men of different faiths studied the book of Hebrews in the New Testament together. We sang German church hymns and folk songs. During the day we went to work. The three of them cleaned up the town of Paderborn, and I worked in the kitchen. One of the men brought me a Bible he had found in the rubble of the city. I was delighted. I made good use of it and studied whenever time permitted. Most of my knowledge of the gospel I learned in those days. I used my time wisely. I had the book the Doctrine and Covenants, also with me, besides the little New Testament. Germany was divided into four zones: American, English, French, and Russian. Men were discharged into all of the zones, except the Russian. The state of Mecklenburg where I came from lay in the Russian zone, and rumors had it we would be discharged soon. My friends, with whom I shared the tent, were from the English and American zones and were soon discharged. I moved back into the barracks with others from my home state. In August, we heard it would be our turn next. We were loaded into railroad cars, the animal type, without windows and some without roofs. We thought we would be transported close to home but soon found we went in the wrong direction. Now we realized our POW time was not over, but just beginning. I thought of the offer one of my friends had made to me, to go and change my home address and be discharged to his hometown. That was possible then, and done by some. Now there was no way out. I thought of escaping, but the doors were well locked. Through Germany we went, and through Holland, to Belgium.

I was not aware of the great hate people had toward us Germans. Many times after we left Germany, the train passed under bridges. People stood on top of the bridges and threw rocks at the POWs in the open cars. The car I was in was covered, and we were protected. We had a little hole in one upper corner of the car which permitted us to take glimpses outside. When we stopped in Belgium at railroad stations, people would stand and move their hands across their throat and call, "*Sall boche*" (German pig). There were not just a few. No, everyone on the packed station platform would do it. I was shocked to see the hate those people felt against us. It was sobering as we realized, this was the nation we would stay and work in.

Though the thought of not being released for such a long time was quite depressing, the treatment received by their British captors was decent and the men were grateful for their situation. Walter continued his study of the gospel, praying for his family's safety as he knew they were under Russian control.

Then I received my first mail from home. It was shocking. The Russians had taken my father and put him in a concentration camp. The good news was that everyone was still alive. Mother wrote me later, that when I come home, the mission president wanted to send me on a mission. I would gladly go. It was always my desire.

I had many gospel discussions with my fellow POWs. My bed neighbor had apparently watched me very closely when I went to bed. I had the upper bunk. He lay next to me and had seen me kneel in my bed and pray. He told me he used to do it too, when he was on the front and in danger, but didn't do it anymore. I asked him why he didn't pray anymore. He said there was no need for prayer, he was safe now. I asked him if he was not a little ashamed of himself to call on the Lord when in need, but to forget him in better times.

In the beginning, Walter worked in a coal mine. Due to his height of over six feet, this was a tedious job, and he found himself hitting his head on the rock ceiling more often than not. After a time, he found a way to transfer to a farm detail and was assigned to work with a local farmer.

The farmer was delighted when he found out how well I could repair his equipment, but he also found out how stubborn I was when things were against my principles. On Sundays I declined to do any work except feed the pigs. On one Sunday morning in the harvest time, he came from church (he was a devout Catholic) and told me the priest had told the congregation today they could bring in the harvest. I told him it didn't make any difference to me what the priest said. What the Lord had said was important to me, and the Lord said, "Keep the Sabbath day holy." That was what I intended to do. I always found a quiet place where I would study the scriptures, and so held my devotions. The farmer took everybody else who worked for him to the field to harvest the crop. In the early afternoon a storm came up, and it rained hard. Everybody came back wet to the skin. I watched them return. As I stood in the door frame, the farmer passed by me. I could not help but say, "Well, farmer, who is right, the priest or the Lord? Remember the Sabbath day and keep it holy."

The farmer was convinced that Walter would try and run away. Though he tried to convince him that he wouldn't their conversations often centered on how he could get away with it. Finally, Walter began to make plans for escape. With the help of some in the village, he was able to obtain some money, civilian clothes, and a map. As Walter began his escape, the problems of nerve paralysis he had experienced before returned, and he was captured and taken back to the POW camp.

Soon, Walter was able to get himself on another farm detail, and once more found work for a sympathetic farmer, who was very kind to him. The farm was small, and Walter enjoyed the work he was able to do.

Like at the other places, I worked hard every day except for Sundays. I fed the horses and cows, and that was the end of my Sunday work. One Sunday, the family had to leave and had no one to milk the cows (it was done by hand). I volunteered, and that was a mistake. From that time on, I had to milk the cows every Sunday. I did not object to milking cows on Sunday; I knew it needed to be done. I just didn't want to do it. I wanted to have Sunday for myself.

It was now November 1947 (two and a half years after the war in Germany ended in May 1945). The farmer took me aside and asked me if I wanted to stay in Belgium and not to go back to Germany. He painted everything in beautiful pictures to get me to stay. He had already talked to the government in Brussels, and they had told him it was all right for me to stay. He offered me good money and a place to stay. I had heard of other POWs who did not go back to Germany, but it was not for me. I missed my affiliation with the Church and felt I was needed there. I wanted to support my mother while she was alone and my father was in a concentration camp. Mother always felt that Father was still alive, even though she hadn't heard from him or from the government as to how, where, or what he was doing. Respecting my decision, the farmer talked to my camp commander. He agreed to let me stay on the farm until the day before my departure. On that day, I was hurried through the formalities, and on the next day, we were on our way to Germany.

Though things were still very difficult in Germany, Walter was glad to be home. His family was overjoyed to have him back, and the opportunity to be active and serve in the Church again was a real blessing. The branch in Neubrandenburg was quite small and much help was needed. It didn't take long, however, before Walter was called to serve a full-time mission.

Artur Schwiermann

Artur Schwiermann was born July 22, 1927, to Luise and Friedrich Schwiermann in Essen, Germany. He was the second child of the family, his older brother Fritz having been born in 1920. Essen was part of the huge industrial complex of the Ruhr Valley, and because of the depression that had crippled Germany's economy, the city was hit particularly hard. Artur's father was very politically active and an outspoken critic of the Nazi Party and Adolf Hitler. When Hitler came to power, Friedrich was arrested and sent to a concentration camp. Due to the fact that he was a decorated war hero, a disabled veteran of the First World War, and that his wife wrote a scathing letter to the Nazi Party, he was released after seven months of incarceration.

Of course, the experience only served to increase his dislike of the party, and influenced what Artur and his siblings learned at home about politics and the world. Artur's mother had joined The Church of Jesus Christ of Latter-day Saints and was an active member in the local branch. On Tuesday afternoons, she would gather up Artur and his brother and sister, as well as all of their friends, and take them to Primary. When he turned eight, Artur wanted more than anything to be baptized, but his father refused to give his permission until he felt Artur was old enough to understand the religion. By the time Artur was ten years old, his father finally relented and Artur was baptized on June 5, 1937.

In that same year, 1937, I was required to join the German Young Folk organization, which was the lower division of the Hitler Youth. We had to recite the following oath: "I swear to devote all my energy and my strength to the savior of our country, Adolf Hitler. I am willing and ready to give my life for him, so help me God." The training sessions were held on Wednesdays from 4 until 7 PM and on Saturdays from 3 until 7 PM. We were required to wear uniforms. They were available at lower prices than regular street clothing. At first, I found the training to be hard but after a while became accustomed to it and began to enjoy the activities. The marching, singing, sports, shooting, and handicrafts, all in a competitive environment,

RUTH BIRTH FILE

Official party decorations adorn this Schneidemuehl house.

brought out the best in all of us. We received badges for achievements in sports and shooting. Aside from the physical activities, we were taught to read maps, use a compass, and learned survival techniques. We also went on outings, slept in castles, and generally speaking, had a good time. We were taught German history as seen through the eyes of Hitler's party; I believe there was certainly a coordinated effort between the Hitler Youth and the public schools to teach us. We were told that the German nation was treated badly after World War I and that the territories and colonies had been wrongfully taken away from us. Hitler felt that now was the time to restore Germany's rightful boundaries. We saw movies of the new German Army, Navy, and Air Force. We were encouraged to be proud of our heritage and to look at the past and present achievements of German scientists, composers, and other artists.

Attending Church services on a regular basis had a balancing effect on my thinking and attitude. Hitler and his men captured the enthusiasm of most German people. On national holidays, practically every household displayed a flag, although the window of the Schwiermann apartment was an exception. When Hitler and Duce of Italy visited the Krupp Works, we as members of the Hitler Youth formed the first line along the route of the motorcade. Behind us stood thousands of people waving their flags and cheering the heads of state passing in open convertibles.

The time seemed to be passing in giant steps. By now Austria had become part of the German Reich. Hitler's meeting with the English and French prime ministers in Munich gave the people hope for peace and signaled the beginning of the end of Czechoslovakia. What would happen next?

On November 10, 1938, my teacher and vice principal entered the classroom to inform us that according to the latest radio news, members of the SA and SS (two political party organizations under Hitler) were on the rampage and destroying homes, businesses, and synagogues owned by Jews. Our class was dismissed, and we were told to go and witness the injustice done to the Jewish people. What we saw was hard for us to understand; the destruction that took place seemed nothing to be proud of. The synagogue, the finest and most majestic edifice located in the center of our town, was engulfed in flames. Firefighters stood idly by; they only protected the adjacent buildings.

During the following weeks, the Nazi Party, with its propaganda machine, tried to whitewash the action of the SA and SS, hoping that in due time the German people would forget the incidents or not care about them. It was mandatory for Jewish men and women to wear the Star of David with the inscription "Jude" (Jews) on their clothing, so that they could be identified as being Jewish. These people must have been horrified.

At age eleven, my concerns centered around going to school, doing expected chores around the house, playing soccer, riding bicycles, roaming around the fields, swiping apples and pears from neighbors' yards, and at times, building fires for a potato roast. During the winter months we enjoyed the snow and zooming down the icy, slippery roads. Then the day arrived when Hitler went on the air to inform the nation of the persecution and suffering of people of German descent living in Poland. To stop the tyranny and the shedding of blood of men, women, and children, he ordered the armed forces to invade Poland to put an end to these atrocities. The process took only eighteen days. The people of Germany felt that the German Army was invincible; the citizens were not surprised when they were informed of the invasion of Norway and Denmark. This was done to neutralize the effects of the British navy blockade. With every victory, more and more young men wanted to join the armed forces to become a part of history. We noticed a momentary stalemate prior to the German invasion of France, Holland, Belgium, and Luxembourg, but in a matter of months these nations also surrendered and Great Britain became the target of concentrated bombardment. The Royal Air Force retaliated by bombing our cities. But, the German government told us that it was only a matter of time before the British would also give up, which, of course, never happened, thanks to the help of the American Air Force.

Our spirits were very high after so many victories. The government justified the invasions by telling us that the wrong done to Germany after

ARTUR SCHWIERMAN FILE

Artur and Fritz Schwiermann.

World War I in Versailles had been corrected and the shame of the past erased and supplanted with pride and joy. There was a feeling of indignation among the Germans which turned into laughter when our ally, Mussolini of Italy, said that victory was guaranteed only after the Italian forces had entered the war. Looking back at past accomplishments, the German people felt confident and sure that the war would be won.

As time went by, the war was still progressing with no end in sight. We were constantly being reassured by our government that victory would be on our side. The food was rationed and other restrictions were placed on the people, e.g. listening to foreign broadcasts was outlawed and punished with incarceration. Since my hometown was located in Germany's largest industrial area, it was constantly bombed by the enemy. The government did not want the children to have to live through this horrible experience, so it started evacuating school children to rural areas in other parts of the country. I was evacuated to Bavaria. A Catholic monastery, located on a hill, was my new home. Our activities were well organized and covered by strict rules: early rising, body care, breakfast, in-house school sessions with lots of homework, physical exercise and preparation for the Hitler Youth achievement, and marksmanship badge. We completed all tasks enthusiastically, not realizing that with every accomplishment we reached another milestone in military training.

One day during the early morning hours, we were surprised to hear that the German forces had entered the USSR. They were hoping to conquer Russia quickly. Almost hourly, the High Command reported that the German troops were advancing and capturing one city after another. They also took huge numbers of prisoners, among them the son of Stalin. Moscow was not far away, and upon receiving this news the whole nation was jubilant, but then the unexpected happened. An early and especially cold winter struck the German armies. Napoleon had been defeated and could not fight the Russian winter; neither could the German Wehrmacht. On the home front, the civilian population was encouraged to knit and donate gloves, wool, socks, sweaters, warm underwear, and other items that would be useful and keep the soldiers warm. The government also encountered shortages of precious metals and again called upon the German civilians to donate brass, copper, and other metals of strategic value. The population was reminded of the sacrifices made during the reign and struggles of Friedrich the Great when the people exchanged their gold wedding rings for iron bands.

In the meantime, the enemy air attacks intensified, but most of the anti-air guns had been withdrawn from the cities and were now used on the front lines to combat tanks and infantry assaults. These were useful and destructive weapons and greatly missed on the home front. Our cities became very vulnerable to the ever increasing air assaults by the enemy. During one of the first raids, the building housing our LDS branch was hit and burned. Since we were unable to return to the gymnasium to hold our meetings, they were held in private homes. Our faith was constantly tested, but we continued the services during the air raids and disregarded the exploding bombs.

More and more planes penetrated German air space and dropped their devastating bombs on the already badly scarred cities. They also dropped leaflets on German soil, which read, "Germany, a fortress, cannot be besieged from the outside, but must be burned from within." People lost their homes, belongings, and often their lives in a matter of seconds, but the NSDAP kept reassuring us that our cities would be rebuilt in a fashion never known before once victory was achieved. I lived through raids conducted by approximately one thousand planes. Essen alone was subjected to an excess of 275 air raids, and 75 percent of the city was destroyed by the end of the war. Due to a shortage of manpower, we youngsters would help fight the fires to save as many homes as possible. Those nights of destruction were gruesome in one respect, but interesting in another. We witnessed fireworks we never saw before—the bursting of 8.8- and 10.5-mm grenades, 2-cm tracers, searchlights, planes exploding in midair, and the burning of different sections of our city.

The war continued without any sign of ending soon. When the conflict started, I never thought that someday I would also be a participant. My dad, who was a foot soldier during World War I, had experienced the tough army life with its daily discomforts such as rain, snow, heat, and cold, in addition to the danger. He counseled me to volunteer for the air force and become a pilot, hoping that by the completion of my training the war would be over. I followed his advice and signed up to join the air force. Prior to my acceptance, however, I had to serve in the *Fliegerjugend* (Youth Flying Corps). Our training was done on weekends, and we learned how to handle and fly gliders. All of us looked forward to Saturdays with great excitement.

During peace time, in order to join Hitler's party, the NSDAP, a person had to be at least eighteen years of age. At the onset of the war, however, to give more people the opportunity to become a member, the age limit was lowered to sixteen. This enabled me to join the party. Some forty-five years later, I cannot recollect the reason for joining. I wonder if it was the pressure to protect my father and make him look less anti-Nazi, or if I was a product of years of indoctrination. I really don't know.

WALTER KINDT FILE

German office staff at work.

I was proud when the draft board, after physical and mental examinations, classified me as "A1." This meant that I could be drafted by any branch of the armed forces. Only a few young men could brag about such fitness. One day I received two letters. The first contained a draft notice for six weeks of flight training. The second letter was a greeting from Hitler and an induction order for the Conservation Corps, which every young man had to join prior to military service. The induction order had priority over the flight training; needless to say, I was very disappointed. On a cool, rainy morning, my father escorted me to the station to board a train to Steinfeld located on the Drau River in Austria. During the last moments of our time together, and speaking from experience, Father admonished me to behave myself since it would make my life much easier. Reluctantly, I stepped on the train and, like many other recruits, was ready to report for duty. After we reached our destination, we lined up for roll call and marched to our camp. New events started happening in rapid order. We received instructions pertaining to the new lifestyle and were assigned our quarters. Uniforms and boots were thrown at us, and we had to exchange them until all twenty-six cadets found the correct size. Our training started immediately. We were taught how to handle and use firearms and spent many hours learning to identify enemy and German planes. We were also assigned kitchen duty. The most hated tasks were peeling potatoes and cleaning vegetables for the daily meals. When we were asked to accompany the disliked chores with songs, we became so incensed that we sang a song mocking the system.

One day while leaving the mess hall, an officer shouted, "Enemy plane!" Everyone took cover and deliberately broke his dinner plate. This act of defiance prompted the leadership to retaliate. At four o'clock the next morning, we were ordered to be combat ready in ten minutes. We spent all day in the mountains practicing tiresome and exhausting war games. On the way back to the camp, we had to march and sing. We sang the same tune over and over again. We went out again the following day but this time marched to the low lands where war games were conducted in the swamps. By the end of the day, we could barely move. On our march home, we were ordered to sing again, and just as we had done on the previous day, we repeated the same song. The officer, bewildered by our persisting defiance, congratulated us on our unity and acknowledged the strength therein. He admonished us to use the same determination during combat.

Having been trained to handle and operate guns and other supporting equipment, it was time to participate in the real action. We operated out of an installation located in Villach, a Yugoslav-Italian-Austrian border town consisting of twelve anti-aircraft guns. During the following months, we were involved in many air battles.

One day the announcement of an impending inspection caused a great commotion. We immediately started to clean and polish our equipment. It turned out that the visiting officers were not interested in inspecting the equipment but were looking for three young men from our unit who were 172 cm tall with blue eyes and blond hair, had no birthmarks, displayed good manners, were educated, and politically reliable. Since I met all of the requirements, I was one of the three chosen by the officers. We were told that we would be privileged to look in the eyes of high government officials but should not be intimidated by their status. Three men had been selected from each unit. We all received special training without being informed of the assignment. At the end of the training sessions, we were told that from approximately 125 young men, only 90 were needed and the elimination process began. After receiving additional mental and physical evaluations, 92 men completed the process successfully, and two had to be eliminated. Since I had previously signed up for the air force, and to avoid inter-service rivalry, I requested to be dismissed. It was not until months later, when I recognized one of the 90 young men who happened to be on the same train as myself, that I found out that the group had been assigned to protect Hitler's estate, the Eagle's Nest, located in the German Alps.

When I returned to my unit, the commander chose me for his assistant. I was in charge of the kitchen, mess hall, supply room, and the uniform and weapons depot. I also looked after his personal needs. Due to my job, I enjoyed many special privileges. In addition to the thirty German marks base pay, I earned forty marks for the extra work. Since we were under the age of eighteen, we received candy in lieu of cigarettes. We all thought that this practice was a mockery, and it was the general consensus that if you were old enough to die, you were certainly old enough to smoke. None of us smoked or had the intention of doing so, but since cigarettes sold for a much higher price on the black market, we felt cheated. The higher echelon realized the unfairness of this practice and changed it. I sold my cigarettes and added another forty marks to my savings account. I was offered a promotion but did not accept it since I would not only lose my position as the commander's assistant, but also the money and prestige. A new officer assumed his duty in our unit. He was unaware of my position. He and I locked horns on his first day. He reprimanded me for my slow movements and for keeping my hands in my pockets since it was a rule to walk swiftly without putting one's hands into pockets. I told him, in a sarcastic manner, that my boots would not permit me to walk at a faster pace. This blew his mind, and a fellow officer had to calm him down. When the commander left for two weeks to attend a seminar, I became free game, and this new officer saw his chance to retaliate. I had to stand guard practically every night. This was basically an honor duty, but he used it as a punishment. During one of those rainy and foggy nights, the officer walked over to the generator shack with the intention of stealing the key and pulling the alarm. The generator could not be started without the key and would render the guns and radar useless, and of course, get me busted. When he reached a real wet spot and thought he was undetected, I requested the password; he did not comply. Instead of repeating my request two more times, I shouted, "For the last time, stop!" and emptied my submachine gun of all thirty-two rounds. He tried to hide and threw himself to the ground. I commanded him to spread his arms and legs and left him in this uncomfortable position until the watch commander arrived requesting an explanation for the shooting. I pretended not to know the mud-covered officer and turned him over to the commander.

I received the news that my father was hospitalized again and became very depressed. The following day, a telegram informed me that my dad was expected to live no more than a few days. Leave was only granted when a death in the immediate family occurred. In my case the commander made an exception. He handed me an important looking envelope and asked me to act as his courier and deliver it to his friend who happened to be on the draft board in Essen. The envelope contained a letter with the provision that in the event of my father's death, my leave was to be extended by three days. I boarded the military train to Salzburg and continued my journey to Munich, where I encountered a problem. The only connection to Essen was an express train, but its use required special clearance from the military station commander. He put his seal on my travel orders but had second thoughts and refused to sign them. Since I was fighting time, and the next train did not leave until hours later and stopped at every small station, I thought that my world had come to an end. A captain standing nearby must have read my mind and asked me if I had a problem. I explained to him that I had to get to Essen as fast as possible. He took my documents and signed them. As I boarded the express, I noticed that all compartments were occupied with the exception of one, which was reserved for disabled soldiers. Up to this point, I had been standing on the trains and could not bear the thought of having to stand up all the way to Essen. In desperation, I took the reserved sign, quietly moved it to the next compartment, and made myself comfortable. I was finally able to relax. Shortly after I sat down, I heard a commotion next door. The military police was asking everybody to move out so that the disabled soldiers could be seated.

Upon my arrival home, my mother and I went straight to the hospital to see Dad. He was slipping in and out of a coma but at one point was awake long enough to recognize me and inquire about my well-being. He was always worried that I did not have enough to eat. After I reassured him that everything was fine, he fell back into the coma. Since I had been deprived of much needed sleep, I went home to rest. My mother remained in the hospital, and when she came home the next day, June 12, 1944, she told me that Dad had died. Even though my father did not show much affection to his children, he was always concerned about their welfare and was an excellent provider for his family. I was so sorry that he was gone forever. We notified my brother and made arrangements for Dad's funeral. Fritz came home, but I had to leave before my father was buried.

When I returned to my unit, I heard rumors regarding the withdrawal of anti-aircraft guns from our city. They were badly needed on the battlefield in Hungary. Since enemy planes were flying at such high altitudes that they outdistanced the deadliest of the guns and radar was no longer useful, our crew was transferred to Graz in Austria. I became an orderly to a general. This was a boring and dissatisfying job. My trouble started immediately after I failed to salute the head of the Nazi Party in Austria. When I was questioned regarding my failure to do so, I replied, "Since when do I have to salute every street car conductor in town?" I was reprimanded for my so-called "bad behavior" and had to face the possibility of being court-martialed. Since I was bored with my job and feared the punishment, I requested a transfer under the assertion that men fit to bear arms should be given the opportunity to do so. My request was granted. A short time later, I went home for a few days before I had to report to the Hermann Goering Garrison in Berlin Reinickendorf to become a soldier in the escort battalion of Reichsmarschall Hermann Goering.

I received short but rigid training sessions in tank, anti-tank, and general assaults. Since I was experienced in fighting enemy aircraft and partisans, it was hard for me to follow the orders of the instructor, who had never been in combat. My rebellious attitude was reported to my superiors, and of course, did not help me. My spirit had to be broken and the officers found different ways to achieve total submission. When other soldiers were given a day off to go into the city or attend church services, the free-spirited ones spent their time crawling in dirt on their belly, running with a gas mask covering their face and holding a rifle above their head. One time I had to line up the troops and report to Sergeant Schroeder. I commanded attention and while facing the sergeant, I reported, "Twelve members of the Airborne Tank Corps of the young nation ready but unwilling to report for the Emperor Wilhelm's memorial hour." For this act of defiance, I was ordered to put on a gas mask again, but this time the officer pierced my filter with a pencil. The carbon dust penetrated my nose and throat and made breathing almost impossible. When the so-called "attack" ended and I removed my mask, my face was black. The icing was put on the cake when I had to crawl on my stomach through pastures. I tried to go around some fresh cow dung but was forced to go back and take the shortest way. I was covered from the torso to the toes with cow dung. One can only imagine how I looked and smelled. In a fit of anger, I told Sergeant Schroeder that the first bullet shot from my weapon would fly in his direction. He smiled and assured me that I would change my mind. After a short stay at Karin Hall, Goering's residence, all of us were shipped out to the Eastern Front to fight the Russian's invading Germany.

—•—

We had been told all along that our retreat, to consolidate the troops and shorten the battle lines, was well organized. The rumor also persisted that Germany had developed a secret weapon which was more effective than the V2. This new weapon would help Germany to achieve its victory. Our unit was ordered to stop the enemy when they broke through our lines. We were very successful, which led us to believe that the war would be won. Quite often the enemy outnumbered us 10 to 1, and our tanks were useless due to the shortage of fuel. For this reason, fighting had become very difficult and casualties were on the increase. We moved from place to place to help, when required to do so we stopped and drove the Russians back until the infantry took over. One night, the noise of mortars warned us of an incoming armored assault. To forestall such an operation, Sergeant Schroeder asked me to accompany him and penetrate the Russian line. He also added that I now had the chance to shoot him. We prepared for our expedition and started to walk toward the enemy line. At first, I was frightened, but the sergeant's capability and experience put me at ease and it turned out that we were a good team. After crossing the Russian line, we spotted their tanks and directed the bombardment of German artillery and rocket launches and were basically credited with spoiling the enemy's attack and the destruction of their tanks. Our performance was repeated several times. One time we were ordered to hold an important strategic point to the last man so that the front line could be reestablished and the men had time to dig their holes. A silo on the outskirts of the village seemed to be the perfect place. We blew a large hold in the wall, stacked bags filled with grain in the opening, and mounted our MG42 machine guns which had a firepower of six thousand rounds per minute. The wall was watered down to prevent the dust from flying. As we nervously waited, our quiet time was suddenly interrupted by the first wave of assault forces. We realized that our position turned out to be superb. Our great overall view proved to be very deadly for the enemy and we remained undetectable. Sergeant Schroeder and I fought back wave after wave of Russian soldiers; it must have blown their mind. In the evening, the village received a barrage of rocket attacks which we called "music from the Stalin organ." The sound was scary, but the explosion was the same as that of a hand grenade. The next morning, the enemy tried the assault once more but experienced the same deadly result as on the previous day. Since our mission was accomplished, we retreated during the following night and rejoined our unit who had by now written us off.

The battles continued to be fierce. We were becoming more desperate but were holding our ground. Since we were deeply engaged in fighting and were still winning some battles, it did not occur to us that we might lose the war. We were so young and full of idealism. Not even the fact that many times there was a distance of a hundred yards between each soldier bothered us. One day after we had been without sleep for quite some time, my partner (who was in the hole next to me) and I dosed off. When I awoke, I noticed a group of Russian soldiers approaching us. Since I did not have time to alert him, I fired an anti-tank rocket at the Russians, which took care of the immediate problem. My partner awoke from the noise, jumped up, and was hit by an explosive bullet. His leg was ripped apart and bled profusely. I rendered first aid, but since he was in need of immediate medical attention, I took him to the first aid station. All medical officers, with the exception of one, and the equipment were moved to a new location. The officer took one look at my partner and told me that he could not save him and that I should place him among the dead. I pulled a hand grenade and told the officer to radio for an ambulance or I would make it easy on both of them. To avoid the latter, he called for help. As I was waiting, I dozed off again and missed my partner's departure. Five years later after my return from the prison camp, I received the good news that he was alive.

It was a rule that when the men stopped complaining, it was time to take them out of the front line for a rest. On one of these occasions, a very nice lady offered to take me into her home. She looked at me in disbelief, uttering the words, "Dead don't return" and told me that I looked almost like her fallen son. The following days were unforgettable. I became her son for a short time and was showered with tender loving care. In turn, I tried to help her find peace and solace. The farewell was very hard; both of us knew that we would probably never meet again.

NATIONAL ARCHIVES

Supreme German Commander Field Marshall Karl Von Runstedt signs the unconditional surrender of Germany.

Although I experienced much hardship and sadness during my fighting on the Eastern Front, I encountered a few incidents which were on the lighter side. Once when we returned from penetrating the Russian line, we discovered a pig tied to a tree in no-man's-land. It was too weak to stand on its feet. I immediately imagined what it would do to improve our diet. Sergeant Schroeder decided to take it along. We wrapped the section of a tent around the pig, fastened a leather belt to its rear legs, and pulled it behind us as we crawled back to our unit. The pig's squeaking noise alerted friend and foe alike. As a result, the sky lit up due to the many flares and machine gun fire from both sides. Since our daily rations were prepared from dry food, bringing home the bacon was very appreciated by our comrades.

The final months of the war seemed to be a paradox. No matter where we fought, we had the communist forces on the run, but the overall picture was not encouraging. Even the slogan "Faith in our leader will bring us victory" could not perform miracles and turn the tide. Since Germany

B. E. NELSON FILE

The aftermath of a bombing raid.

had few resources, we learned to live with fuel shortages. The continued bombing of the Rumanian oil fields and refineries, producing synthetic fuel, also hurt us very much. In addition, there was an ever increasing shortage of badly needed ammunition. We were ordered to fire at the enemy only when they were within thirty yards of us. This resulted in more hand-to-hand combat and made us eligible for infantry assault badges. When we were younger and very patriotic, we were very impressed when older men returned home and proudly displayed their medals. Now we were also in combat with the enemy, and it was our chance to earn as many medals as possible. Beset by these thoughts, we cared very little about our own lives and in blind ambition volunteered for the most dangerous missions. The majority of young men never had a chance; they either lost their life or ended up in the hospital. Since we were constantly moving around, it was hard for our families to stay in touch with us. We never received our mail or commendations for bravery. It is not surprising that we all felt cheated.

It finally happened. On May 8, 1945, the remains of our regiment gathered and the commanding officer announced that we had lost the war. On that day, Germany surrendered unconditionally. The officer's advice to us was to go home immediately and help with the rebuilding of a destroyed Germany. He cautioned us not to get involved in unnecessary fighting and bloodshed. It was a rude awakening for all of us. The once victorious army, who had occupied nations from the equator to the Arctic, was defeated. A strong feeling of despair overwhelmed us. Were all the suffering, destruction, and death senseless?

Radio Prague in Czechoslovakia announced that by 12 PM no German soldier was allowed to carry any kind of weapon. The houses and government buildings in Prague displayed red and white flags to welcome the Soviet Army. We mounted machine guns on our truck, disregarding the warning from the officer, and headed toward Germany. The Czechs, now being liberated, fired several rounds at us but were overwhelmed by our firepower. At last, we reached the German border. While we were driving over a small bridge, it collapsed and damaged our truck. We had to walk until we found a maintenance truck to continue our journey in a more comfortable manner. Luck was certainly not on our side. The engine began to overheat, and subsequently blew up. That night, we liberated horses from a Hungarian unit but soon found that we were no horsemen and that riding a horse required certain skills. We could not get used to the rhythm; when the horses' behinds went up, ours went down. After a few hours of trying to ride, we became extremely sore. Disgusted with ourselves and the horses, we asked a farmer to provide us with a good breakfast in exchange for the animals. This was the first decent meal we had eaten in many days. With full stomachs and lifted spirits, we continued to move by foot, bicycle, and motorcycle.

On May 13, 1945, we reached the American troops and surrendered. Our feeling of being safe was short lived since the Americans turned us over to the Russians who were busy collecting watches, rings, knives, and anything else of value. They looked like clowns with rings on every finger, watches up to their elbows, and gun-cleaning chains hanging around their necks. It was a ridiculous sight. For us the waiting game began. We did not know what the future had in store for us. One thing was certain; the food was awful and not enough. While waiting, I met an officer who was a captain in the pro-German Army consisting of Russian prisoners dissatisfied with the communist system and willing to fight for a better tomorrow. They had volunteered to fight the Soviets. However, after the collapse of the German Army, they were afraid for their lives. The officer confided in me and told me of his plan to escape during the night. So that his absence would not be noticed immediately, he asked me to accept his food at roll call. I adhered to his request and gave him the two hand grenades I had saved. With my good wishes, he disappeared the following night, and I hoped he would arrive safely at his destination.

All of us were kept in a camp. When the screening began, the Russian officers wanted to know in which branch of the armed forces we had served. They were especially interested in finding the men belonging to the Waffen SS, an elite fighting force one hundred percent committed to Hitler. We were stripped of our clothes, and the Russians looked for tattoos, which identified the SS, under our left arms.

The food was not even fit for animals. It consisted of fish meal made from ground bones and heads boiled with sugar beets and diluted with an enormous amount of water. The taste was beyond description.

The day arrived when we left the camp. Twenty men, side by side with locked arms, marched together. We were told that if anyone escaped, the remaining men would be shot. Marching through Dresden allowed us to view the horrible destruction which had occurred during the final days of the war. This city had been fire bombed and blown to pieces. In excess of 500,000 people lost their lives. As I was marching, I could not help but constantly wonder what the Russians would do with us. In my mind I painted the grim picture of being held in a Russian slave labor camp to rebuild their cities and factories. It was certainly nothing to look forward to. The Russians had promised to pay fifty rubles for every man associated with the Division of Hermann Goering, and it was smart on our part that, at the end of the war, we had removed all identification connecting us to that division.

During my conversation with the man walking next to me, we both decided that our only chance for going home was to escape, but we were highly concerned with the fate of the other eighteen men. After giving the idea of breaking away much thought, we remembered the saying "Every man for himself, God for us all" and laid out the plan. We knew that all apartment houses had basements enabling a person, in case of an emergency, to move from one basement to the other by breaking through a special section of the connecting wall. It was our plan to jump into a coal chute leading to a basement. We could stay there until darkness and then try to make our way home. As we marched, our eyes searched for a perfect place to hide. After spotting it, we took off racing towards the building and jumped into the coal chute only to discover that the basement had been damaged by the bombs and had totally collapsed. The screaming and hollering of the remaining eighteen men, who feared for their lives, summoned one of the guards. They pulled us out of the hole, tied our hands together, and secured us to one of the horses. It was quite a task keeping up with the animals. As punishment we were deprived of food and water, which made our ordeal almost unbearable. Hearing American planes flying overhead rekindled my hope that they might rescue us, but it was only wishful thinking. My body finally gave up and I

THREE AGAINST HITLER

During the summer of 1941, the sudden appearance of anti-Nazi propaganda in Hamburg baffled the local Gestapo. As more and more leaflets and full-page articles began to appear all over the city, an all-out investigation began to determine the culprits and to break what was thought to be a large underground movement. Unbeknownst to them, a young Aaronic priesthood holder, Helmuth Huebner, from the St. Georg branch of the Church, had become disenchanted with the Nazi government, and particularly the treatment of the Jews, even in his own branch where a young Jewish convert, Solomon Schwartz, had been banned from attending meetings.

Using a short-wave radio brought home by his brother from France, the sixteen-year-old had begun listening to the BBC London's German news broadcasts. As a secretary to the branch president, he had been given access to the church's typewriter and had taken it home. Armed with paper, his typewriter, and an official party stamp from his work in the Civil Service office, Helmuth began writing the news in the hopes that he might be able to give his fellow Germans the truth. To help distribute his leaflets, he enlisted the help of his two friends from the branch, Karl-Heinz Schnibbe, 17, and Rudi Wobbe, 15.

While attempting to find help to translate their leaflets into French, the group was turned into the Gestapo. In February 1942, the three teenagers were arrested and brutally beaten and interrogated for five months. Local officials could not believe that the group had only consisted of the three young men, and no adults had been involved. After months of incarceration, the three teenagers were brought before the Blood Tribunal, the highest court in Germany. Their trial was quick, and biased, and the three were sentenced. Helmuth Huebner was to be immediately executed by beheading. Rudi Wobbe received ten years imprisonment, and Karl-Heinz Schnibbe five years. When asked if they wished to address the court, only Helmuth elected to speak. His words were spoken with power: "I have to die now for no crime at all, but your turn is next." Then, turning to his friends and embracing them for the last time, Helmuth spoke to Karl-Heinz with tears in his eyes. "I hope you have a better life and a better Germany."

On August 11, 1942, Helmuth Huebener was beheaded by guillotine in Berlin. Before his death, he had been allowed to write three letters, one to his mother, one to his grandparents, and one to his friend and surrogate mother, Marie Sommerfeld. His final words to his friends were words of testimony:

When you read this letter I will be dead. . . . Please remember me kindly. I am very thankful to my Heavenly Father that this agonizing life is coming to an end this evening. I could not stand it any longer anyway! My Father in Heaven knows that I have done nothing wrong. . . . I know that God lives and that He will be the proper judge of this matter. Until our happy reunion in that better world, I remain, Your Friend and brother in the gospel, Helmuth.

Source: *Three Against Hitler* (American Fork, UT: Covenant Communications, 2002).

passed out. I did not regain consciousness until several days later. They had stripped me of my boots, leather jacket, and pants. The only thing in my possession was a tunic with an officer insignia and some medals. My captain had given it to me, to protect me from the cold. In my misfortune, I was still the luckiest man and happy to be alive. Judged by my uniform, the Russians were under the impression that I was an officer. This saved my life because anyone of lower rank was viewed as a burden and shot and dumped by the wayside. In retrospect I must have been quite a sight without pants and shoes and wearing only long johns and the tunic. We arrived at a former French prison camp with three thousand beds. By this time, almost twenty thousand prisoners were housed in this camp. Since not enough beds were available, we slept side by side on the bare floor and had to turn upon command. The Russians continued to search for jewelry and other valuable items. I had in my possession a wristwatch given to me by my father, who was deceased. It had sentimental value and I was very proud of it. Whenever we were searched, I hid the watch between my buttocks until one day I unraveled an old wool sock and used the watch as the core to wrap the wool around. I thought the watch was safe but soon discovered that a fellow prisoner had stolen it while I was asleep. The time in this camp turned out to be a waiting period for us. We were only interrupted to be searched and interrogated. Shortly after our arrival at the camp, the Russians delivered a truckload of sand. To stay fit, we filled our metal dishes with sand and carried them back and forth from one side of the camp to the other.

The day arrived when we were shipped by train to Frankfurt on the Oder River. We were housed in a former German garrison and told we would go home in the near future; only my home was not located in the eastern direction. The Russians lied to us again. On one of our stops, I noticed a German soldier sitting on a small platform with wheels attached to it. His legs were missing, and in order to get around he had to move the platform with his hands. This sight convinced me that years of internment were by far better than that soldier's misfortune. Our journey into the unknown was uncomfortable, degrading, and inhumane. Since one boxcar did not hold the ninety prisoners assigned to it, the car was divided into a three-story compartment, each accommodating thirty men. The car had two small windows covered with wire. The doors were locked at all times. A square chute going to the outside served as a comfort station. After a few days, the smell became intolerable and the flies drove us crazy. We were not given any toilet paper or water; it was impossible to adhere to personal hygiene. Once a day the doors opened. We received dry bread and enough water to fill the cavities of our teeth. The men smoked anything that burned. The boredom and constant pounding of the tracks, as the wheels of the train moved over them, was enough to put everybody on edge and made us sick. Since I was one of the youngest prisoners, I was often stepped on and pushed around; after all, I was only seventeen years of age and did not command much respect. No one knew that I had served in one of the most elite divisions; nor were they aware of the many battles I had fought. But I stood my ground and showed them that I was no pushover.

It took weeks before we arrived in Brestlitowks, a former Polish city now occupied by the Russians. Our camp was located on the outskirts of the city and consisted of a bare field surrounded by a wire fence and four observation towers equipped with search lights and machine guns. For a place to sleep we dug holes, lined them with cement, and used burlap sacks as a cover. At the onset of winter, we were exposed to snow and ice which caused great misery. The kitchen was very primitive, but since our food did not require much preparation, it did not matter. Three times a day we received soup, or in other words, warm water and a slice of bread. If we would have found a mouse in the soup, it would have added at least some protein. The bread was handed out in loaves,

RICHARD BURT FILE

Captured soldiers board a train as POWs.

and it was up to us to cut and divide it. After the bread was sliced, a blindfolded person called out our names while someone else pointed to the bread. This was our way of making sure that no one would be short-changed; still everybody felt he had received the smallest portion and had been cheated. There was no trust among the men, and friend would turn against friend for a crumb of bread. Since the only water in the well was typhoid infested, it was off-limits. The Russians used this water only for the officers' laundry. Instead of water, the prisoners received coffee. Not knowing that the Russian people were tea drinkers, the Americans had shipped enormous amounts of coffee to Russia. To the delight of the prisoners, the coffee was a daily treat except for me. I was determined to adhere to the Word of Wisdom. At night, I filled my canteen with the contaminated water and put my trust in the Lord.

In preparation to ensure the smooth transfer of German spoil, Brestlitowks was designated as a point of entry. Prisoners of war and Russians alike erected a network of rails and loading docks. It was backbreaking work. We moved earth manually, and regardless of the weather conditions, had to be on the job in excess of twelve hours each day. The prisoners were divided into groups of twelve. Each group was called a brigade and headed by a former German sergeant or officer. We were assigned a certain amount of work each day. Only after completing the job were we permitted to return to the camp, or in other words, our designated holes in the ground. The work was very hard, the food just enough to stay alive, and the weather cold. By the middle of September 1945, we saw the first snowfall. Our clothing was insufficient. We were without coats, gloves, or hats. We wrapped paper and burlap sacks around our hands and feet and made masks to protect our faces. We checked each other for frostbite, and if the flesh turned white, rubbed that part of the body with snow. By December, five hundred of the one thousand prisoners had died. My weight dropped from 145 to 95 pounds. It was in my favor that I was young, tough, and endowed with a tremendous faith in God. My daily conversations with the Lord gave me great strength. Instead of quarrelling as most of the men did and doubting that there was a God in heaven who allowed such inequities, I thought of the Russian men who had spent years in German camps and of their struggle for survival. Each morning at roll call we were asked to report the number of prisoners who had died during the night. If the number was ten, the guards made the comment that it should have been twenty. I thought about my loved ones all the time and wondered if Mother and Wilma had survived the war since I did not know if they were alive. Unfortunately, my question was not answered until years later. I assumed that my brother was in a British prison camp and was assured by a Russian officer that Fritz was better off than me.

Our stomachs were growling, and our eyes constantly shifted around searching for food. It was common to see Russian women standing on the curb selling food on the black market. At times, some of the prisoners jumped at them and stole their goods. I thought it was terrible when members of the once proud and disciplined German Army turned into a bunch of common thieves with no respect for the women or themselves. Perhaps the conditions we were forced to live under dictated such behavior. In addition to not receiving a sufficient amount of food, the Russians also did not provide us with sanitary facilities. They did not give us any toilet paper, and I went without a bath for almost one year. Our bodies and clothes were full of lice; the head and other parts of our bodies that grew hair were shaved. In our spare time, we tried to kill the lice. I once counted five hundred lice before I decided to give up. In order to stay alive and nurture our minds, we would reminisce with thoughts of the good old days when food was plentiful and good. During these times food was an important topic of our conversations. We told exaggerated stories about the wonderful meals we used to eat at home. Being the youngest prisoner in my brigade soon proved to be a social disadvantage. At times, fellow prisoners envied the double rations of food the doctor had ordered since my weight was too low. The treatment I received from the other prisoners was nothing to brag about. They expected me to do all kinds of chores, and when I objected, pushed me around. I finally could not stand it any longer. When a former sergeant called me a "young punk" and ordered me to do work no one was willing to perform, I jumped on top of him and beat the living daylights out of him. The prison guard who had knowledge of the German language cheered me on and did not bother to stop the beating. This episode earned me respect. I told those "had been" officers that we were all prisoners, regardless of rank, and from that time forward they left me alone.

A prisoner by the name of August made history in his own way. The poor man had been captured by the Americans, processed, and released. When he arrived in his hometown, August waved to his wife as she looked out the window, and by the time she came out of the house to greet him, a Russian grabbed August and forced him to move along. The anticipated joyful reunion with his family never took place. August was sent to Russia. When he arrived in our camp, he was deeply depressed. He acted like an idiot and displayed all kinds of weird behavior. August did not work. Instead he fell on his knees and kissed the boots of the Russian officers. Judging by his behavior, we thought he was a clown. Since I knew what it was like to be pushed around, I began to look after August and shielded him from many abuses. It did not take long before the Russians figured out that he was useless. They were unable to reform him and felt that he was only a burden to them. The day arrived when August received word that he was going to be released. He took the news very calmly and assured the Russians that he would rather stay than go home. He realized that any excitement on his part would give his charade away. On the day of his departure, I shook August's hand and wished him good luck. I told him what great satisfaction it must be for him to know that the smart men had to stay behind, especially since he had been the target of all their ridicule and laughter. Now he was able to laugh all the way home. As he squeezed my hand, I saw a sparkle in his eyes revealing his true feelings. August was no dummy. In fact, he once confided in me that he owned and operated a large slaughter house and was very wealthy. Here was a man who, by playing stupid, had outsmarted his captors.

The Christmas season arrived and gave the

prisoners new hope for a better life. Our spirits were high, and the guards could not figure out what was going on and why we were so happy. We collected small shells and explained to the Russians that we would convert them into candles. We managed to drill holes into a stick and put tumbleweed serving as branches into the holes, and then fastened the rifle shells filled with oil to the branches and our tree was finished. On Christmas Eve, we gathered around the tree to celebrate our first Christmas in the prison camp by singing old familiar songs. With heavy hearts, we also thought about our families who were so far away. We wondered what their lives were like and if they also experienced hunger. Maybe for some of us it was better that we did not know. In 1945, Christmas was entirely different than in the previous years. There was little hope for the future. Our nation was destroyed and men were incarcerated in prison camps in Russia, America, and Great Britain. Gottlieb Winter, a native of Austria and good friend of mine, handed me a hand-carved wooden spoon as a Christmas present. In return, I gave him a week's ration of sugar consisting of exactly one spoonful. As we continued with our singing, we heard the harsh voices of the guards telling us to break up the celebration and get ready to go to work. However, this time it did not bother us as much since we were filled with the spirit of Christmas. During the following weeks, life seemed to be more joyous and was easier to handle. I was thankful for the spiritual uplift since the time ahead changed for the worse.

The daily work continued to be hard, the food scarce, and the cold almost intolerable. Once in a while, we received an assignment that provided us with the opportunity to find something to eat or items we could trade for food. Although the guards and Russian civilians were proud that they had won the war, instead of feeling envy, I could only pity them. I remembered the day when I was in school and had to view an exhibition called *The Soviet Paradise*. Propaganda Minister Joseph Goebbels tried to show the German people the conditions under which the communists lived. Weapons, tanks, and uniforms were displayed. He had also ordered a display of a model village depicting the poor lifestyles of the Russian people. At that time, I felt that it was merely propaganda. Now that I was living in Russia, I had to admit that Goebbels's attempt to inform the Germans of the poor living standards under communism was in vain. Nobody could have imagined the appalling conditions of the communist country.

It seemed that the cold winter would never end. We graded the land, laid railroad tracks, and built loading docks. The day finally arrived when the terminal was completed. The first train loaded with goods the Russians had pilfered from Germany rolled in. Everything was heavily guarded. Some cars were loaded with sugar, wheat, beans, rice, and potatoes; others filled with household items. My life started to improve. Whenever possible, I stole badly needed commodities. Our new assignment was to transfer the merchandise from German to Russian railroad cars. The work was not easy but paid off in the long run. The unloading of box cars was especially exhausting when heavy industrial equipment arrived. Everything had to be rigged and moved by manual labor since they would not furnish us with a crane. In the beginning, ten men were assigned to unload one car. The guard offered to take us back to the camp after we completed our task. It was very tempting since the temperature had fallen to 20 degrees below zero and we were freezing. I tried to tell the guys to be careful and not fall for the trick but I was outnumbered. Those fools worked like hell, and after a few hours, the guard took us home. This time I was proven wrong, however. During the following weeks fewer and fewer men were assigned to do the backbreaking job.

Due to my leadership abilities, I was chosen to be a brigadier. I surrounded myself with men who were professionals and were not used to manual labor. Other prisoners were laughing at my choices since the amount of food we received was based on the type of work assignments.

Instead of killing ourselves, my group decided to forgo the extra food. Our tactics were based on self-preservation. One example was the day when a train loaded with railroad ties rolled in. We were told that we had to stay on the job until it was finished, but disregarded the order. We built a fire in fifty-gallon drums, stayed warm, and did not worry about completing the job. Other leaders punished their workers like hell, forcing them to pry apart the frozen ties. After twenty-four hours, the Russians finally gave in and took us back to the camp. The other men were tired, cold, and worn out, but my guys were fine. Upon the arrival of a train loaded with passenger cars, we not only transferred them but added a handful of sand to the oil to make the Russians' driving more enjoyable. We scrutinized every incoming train, and according to its content, planned how to steal some of the goods. Jacob, our guard, had spent years in a German prison camp and knew what it was like to struggle in order to stay alive. He was very kind and did not care about our activities as long as we did not try to escape. We had enough sense not to be so foolish knowing that it was practically impossible to get across Poland and East Germany. Some prisoners had tried to leave but were apprehended and punished by the guards with severe beatings resulting in permanent injuries or death. The communists did not place a high value on human life, whether it was German or Russian. Only once did I hear of a successful escape. During the early months of internment, a former member of the SD (an organization like the CIA) left the camp at night looking for something to eat. On his way back, he was careless and was caught. The guard stuck him in a hole and poured water over him. Due to the freezing cold, it was impossible to survive more than a few hours under these conditions, so the prisoner knocked out the guard, put on his uniform, stuck him in the hole, and gave him the same treatment. We found the Russian dead the next morning and noticed that the prisoner had escaped. Several months later, we received the news from West Germany that he had arrived home.

During one of my adventures, I found a German officer's coat lined with fur and sporting a beautiful fur collar. I put it on and promenaded proudly around the railroad station to advertise the coat. It did not take long before someone spotted me and asked the price. I sold the coat for 450 rubles, which was a steal. I left and Jacob, our guard, cursed and went after the buyer to tell him that it was unlawful to purchase merchandise from a prisoner. He recovered the coat, met me, took one-half of the money, and I looked for a new sucker to strike another deal. Another time, on a very cold day, I saw a woman without a hat. I offered her one of my fur caps for a reasonable price. Excited over the bargain, she asked if I had other items for sale. Since it was unlawful to purchase anything from me, she invited me to her house. Upon arrival, I displayed my merchandise, quoted her the price, and in exchange, asked for food not only for me but also for my sick friend, Siegfried Schrumpf. We finalized the deal.

As I was sitting in a warm place enjoying the food and dreaming about a better life, the door opened and a high ranking officer of the KGB entered the room. I literally froze and imagined the worst. He pointed at my goods and asked me about their origin. In a calm voice, I answered that I had stolen them. He smiled and patted me on my shoulder saying, "You are OK. What else can you deliver?" My chilled blood started to flow again. From this time forward, I had access to a secure outlet, and during the following week, delivered a brand-new typewriter with a price tag of 15,000 rubles to him. I quoted him the price of 2,000 rubles, but he only wanted to pay 700. When I told him that the deal was unfair, he gave me the following explanation: "If I get caught I will be sent to Siberia for fifteen years. If you should have the misfortune, you will be transferred to a hard-labor camp which is under my jurisdiction." I realized that even communists believe in the old capitalistic idea that profit is associated with risk. I was in no position to argue; after all, he paid me promptly and his philosophy made sense. When I got hold of a set of beautiful red leather bound books containing the writings of Lenin, I thought they would be easy to sell. To my surprise, the Russians dismissed my offer with a smile and looked upon the books as being useless; but for Adolf Hitler's *Mein Kampf* they would pay top rubles.

During the time my enterprise was booming, I earned the name Specialist. When someone needed something, I was willing and able to deliver. A shipment of sewing machines arrived. At first, it did not excite my friends or I since the machines were too bulky and hard to steal. But when I realized that without needles and bobbins the machines were useless, I realized what I could do. We removed all of the needles and bobbins. Since the Russians who purchased the sewing machines were unable to use them, we subsequently sold the bobbins and needles to them for the same price we would have charged for the machines. Whenever loads of vodka were on the trains, the guards and prisoners got drunk. Because I did not drink, the sale of vodka turned out to be very profitable for me. Leather was another commodity high in demand, and fortunately, I was able to find an ample supply. When a German train would arrive at the station, I lay between the tracks and covered myself with snow. As the cars passed over me, I cut the generator belts, and my friends picked them up. During one of these activities, someone saw me and reported me to the authorities, who in turn, demanded a roll call. I had to leave my hiding place. I was recognized as the villain and pushed toward a Russian general. He demanded to know what I was doing under the train. I told him the truth, blaming hunger for my action. The general understood my predicament and felt pity. He said that if I had asked for food he would have gladly given it to me. To demonstrate his sincerity, he ordered a soldier to bring him bread, fish, and a piece of bacon and handed it to me. At the same time, the general ordered a young Mongolian soldier to punish me for my actions; his slanted eyes scared the hell out of me. He pushed me with his rifle and we left. After we were out of sight, the soldier asked me for my age. When I told him that I was eighteen, he looked at me, paused, and replied, "So am I. What in the hell are you doing here? We both should be home with Mama." I agreed wholeheartedly. He ordered me to scream and he started cursing. After a short time, he tapped me on the shoulder and told me that my screaming had sounded convincing. He wished me good luck and departed. At first, I was very scared but now was happy that I had received food and was able to keep the leather belts. Due to the loss of the belts, Marshall Zhukov, the number one Russian honcho, was forced to travel to Moscow by candlelight.

The will to survive was my daily companion. I became obsessed with the idea of outsmarting the Russians. Once when I saw another contingent of prisoners unloading beef, I joined with them to steal a side of beef. I was successful and took off at the right moment; unfortunately, I encountered the wrong guard who made me go back. After that incident, I was carefully watched, which made it impossible for me to remove any meat. Upon completion of the job, I returned empty-handed to my own place of work thinking that my endeavor had been a complete loss. To my great surprise and joy, I discovered in the center of a boxcar a bucket with choice cuts of beef and a storm lantern. I extinguished the flame, grabbed the lantern and bucket, and got lost in the darkness. I felt my efforts had been repaid.

Once we discovered a train full of silverware which was in high demand. Unfortunately, our usually clear thinking was blurred by greed. As we hustled from boxcar to boxcar, we were caught. Everyone received a shovel and was instructed to dig a hole several feet deep and large enough to accommodate our bodies. We were overcome with great fear. Our digging progressed very slowly, and stalling only increased our fear. The officer finally said that the hole was deep enough. He ordered us to take off our shirts, marked our chests, and asked if we wanted to be blindfolded. When everyone agreed that we would rather face our executioners, he assembled a firing squad, lined us up in front of the holes which were to be our graves, and gave orders to shoot. As the shots rang out, we fell into the holes, and after a few frightened and heart stopping moments, realized that we were the victims of a cruel hoax. I thanked God that my life had been spared. This experience was enough to slow my activities for a short time.

Not long after this incident, I was invited to a cookout. As I was eating and enjoying the meat, I noticed cuts and bruises on the body of one man. I asked him how he had received the injuries. He told me that he was caught and dragged along by a passing train. It was not until the next day that I found out the truth. The bruises were inflicted by the dog he had killed; subsequently, I realized that I had consumed dog meat.

When a shipment of badly needed construction staples arrived, my friends and I made it our business to hide huge amounts of the staples in an underground tunnel. To the surprise of the other prisoners, I requested that my men and I work as blacksmiths making staples. Everybody thought we had lost our marbles. We were the talk and laughter of the day. Other crews consisting of highly qualified men had been assigned to that job and were never able to produce 250 staples in one day to obtain the extra 300 grams of bread. The equipment was outdated. One can visualize a fire fanned by an old blow bag dating back to the time of the Czar. Considering these conditions, the production of 150 staples was in itself an accomplishment; no one could understand why we wanted the job, especially since none of us had any experience. Some of my men did not even know how to hold a hammer. No outsider knew what we were up to. We slept at the workplace while the other prisoners stayed in the camp. The accommodations were filthy but warm. During the night, we slipped out and searched for potatoes and anything else that was edible. The fire was at full blast, but instead of heating steel we were cooking food. We rigged the hammer and without any great effort it hit the anvil and bounced back. The rhythm convinced the Russians that we were working. At the end of the day, we turned in 250 staples which had been retrieved from the tunnel. In order to keep up our supply and meet the quota, we picked the lock of the warehouse where the staples were stored and stole the previously delivered staples. Life was better during the following months. During the spring of 1947, we were accustomed to the easy life but now were concerned that the supply of staples was getting low. To our delight, our predecessors demanded their jobs back. They were convinced that if flunkies like us could produce the required quota they should be able to do the same. No one ever realized how we outsmarted the system. The other men were never able to match our record in producing staples. They also could never figure out how we gained the extra weight. Well fed and in high spirits, my men and I looked forward to our next assignment.

The communists were no longer satisfied with looting German homes and factories and now began converting East Germany's multitrack railway system to a single system. Train loads of rails arrived and during the night we had to transfer them by hand to a Russian boxcar. The Russians transferred the rails during the day and were able to use an overhead crane. Our work was very hard until I managed to hotwire the crane. We made use of it and were back on easy street. The boxcars had to be modified so that they could be integrated into the Russian railway system. We did this by pressing the wheels apart and changing the position of the bearings. At first, this task was very difficult but after a few days we learned the tricks of the trade.

All boxcars were loaded with merchandise which was easy to sell on the black market. When a load of sugar or wheat arrived, we would drill a hole in the bottom of the car, enabling us to pierce the sacks with a sharp-edged pipe so that the contents could flow out easily. At other times, we carefully removed the seal from the doors of the boxcars, took some of the contents, and put the seal back on the doors. We also received train loads of V2 rockets and parts from Nordhausen. In their greed, the communists eventually removed the whole factory including toilet bowls and pictures of Adolf Hitler. During the unloading of these shipments, we were carefully watched and every move was scrutinized by the guards. By this time, we were also facing meager times. Our only activity consisted of making bundles of firewood to be sold or traded for food. Since railroad cars were furnished with potbelly stoves, firewood was always in demand during the cold weather. My buddy Siegfried and I made our rounds peddling wood and bags of coal. We met a Russian officer who at first agreed to our terms but then pulled his pistol and demanded the goods without compensating us. Siegfried disregarded his demand, started laughing, and stuck out his hand requesting something in return. I was getting worried and was almost ready to give the merchandise to the Russian, but Siegfried was adamant about payment. The officer finally gave us the food and we handed him the heating materials. After feeling relieved and out of danger, I asked Siegfried how he could have been so bold. He smiled and told me that the Russian forgot to release the safety lock on his gun. My friend was certainly more observant than I.

Another time, while canvassing the station, we met a guard who had been incarcerated in a German prison camp near Nordhausen. He had known Siegfried's father, who was the boss in a plant employing prisoners. The guard stated that the Russians in that factory were always treated in a humane manner. He was very appreciative of the good treatment he had received and tried to reciprocate. While the train was held up, the guard invited Siegfried to be his guest. The cargo on the train consisted of fifty-gallon drums filled with a substance used to manufacture synthetic rubber. It had to be kept at a certain temperature. A stove in every car, with an ample supply of coal, did the job. My buddies and I could not control ourselves, and while Siegfried was being fed we ransacked the cars and helped ourselves to some of the coal.

Our next assignment was to work as lumberjacks. We thoroughly enjoyed the fresh air and freedom. After a few days, we became very efficient not only in cutting down the trees but also in raiding nearby potato and cabbage fields.

When I returned to my camp, I asked myself why I was obtaining all the extra food when in reality it was only lengthening my stay. It was then that I decided to lose enough weight so that I would have to be sent home. By not indulging in extra food and sometimes throwing away my rations, my weight dropped rapidly. In a short period of time, I was skin and bones again. During the following health inspection, I was singled out and pronounced undernourished and unfit to work. The process for my release began. When the long awaited day arrived, I was in good spirits. My hopes were high and I saw myself already crossing the West German border. Other prisoners, also ready for release, and I said goodbye to our friends and promised them to notify their families. We left the camp and marched to the railroad station where we were assigned to different boxcars. It was a wonderful feeling to dwell on the thoughts of going home and at last being free, but then the unexpected happened. A Russian officer called out my name. I had to exit the boxcar and remain behind. No one ever gave me a reason for this action, but I knew that someone I had trusted must have revealed to the Russians that I had been affiliated with the Division of Hermann Goering. I regretted punishing my body by losing all that weight. Back at the camp, my friends were surprised to see me again, and some felt very badly about my misfortune.

I had no time to feel sorry for myself. Life went on, and staying in a depressed state of mind could be devastating. I resumed my former activities. While at the station, I talked to a German railroad worker and asked him to bring back all the flints and empty glass tubes he could find on his next trip. I gave him an advance in rubles. Upon his return, he delivered the merchandise, and I was ready for the next kill. My friends and I cut aluminum wire the same size as the flints. In each glass tube we placed three fakes and one real flint. Many Russians had returned from Germany with a lighter and never gave any thought to the day when the worn off flints had to be replaced. The moment our flints hit the market, they were an instant sellout. To reduce the odds of dissatisfied customers, we peddled the flints only to Russians traveling through our area. One day at the railroad station and to our great surprise, we heard quite a few people speaking our native language. Family members of German scientists who had been kept in Russia for missile research and production were being given a chance to reunite. It felt so good to talk with them.

Aside from working many hours during the day, we also spent time building a nice camp for ourselves. The housing was located underground and was hard to detect. It was a beautiful place and kept us cool in the summer and warm in the winter. Everything was finished and comfortable. Approximately eighteen months after its completion, we were evicted and the camp was turned into an army garrison. This experience taught me never to trust the Russian communists. They were full of unkept promises.

Once again the Russians told us that we were being sent home. The train again moved in the eastern direction, but this time the ride was more humane. The doors were kept open, and when the train stopped we were allowed to step out. It was a long trip. After weeks and much speculation, we finally arrived in New Gorlovka located in the Ukraine. Blocks of ruins surrounded by wire fences turned out to be our new homestead. Again we were enticed to build (of course after work) a camp from the ruins to keep us warm during the next winter. Our daily job consisted of rebuilding a chemical factory. At the advance of the German Army, the equipment and machinery had been removed and shipped to a location in the Ural Mountains. It was up to us and a Russian civilian work force to put the machines back together and get the plant ready for production. But prior to that task, miles of pipelines had to be installed. We had quite a job ahead of us and to our despair not enough tools. Most of the missing parts were not available and had to be hand made. It was an interesting undertaking. All of us learned something which would eventually help us in the years to come. First, we completed the pipeline. It was brought to our attention that the line would be filled with water and put under pressure to detect possible leaks. As we were talking about the inspection, we smiled, hoping that the inspector brought an umbrella and galoshes. There was never enough time or the right material to do a perfect job. Not to be embarrassed, we blocked off the line after the first few hundred feet, passed the inspection with flying colors and gave the Russians a severe headache when at a later date actual production started.

Putting the machines together and in place turned out to be a job in itself. During one of my endeavors, after assembling the equipment and putting it on the line, the noise of the mismatched gears was unbelievable. As time went on, the living and working conditions improved. We had transformed the ruins into decent living quarters with a bed to sleep in and at last something to come home to in the evening. For the first time during our imprisonment we had a kitchen with an adjacent mess hall. In the mornings and evenings we sat down, relaxed, and ate our meager meals. On weekends, it was our responsibility to completely clean the place. Everybody knew that as prisoners we lived in a better environment than the natives. Sometimes we even received Sundays off. We formed a band with musicians from the prison camp. The Russians furnished the instruments. On some Sundays, we were privileged to listen to good music. Even our personal hygiene had improved. Once a month our clothing was deloused and we were able to shower. This was a great luxury even though the water was cold. To entice us to greater productivity, we were told that anything earned above the 275 rubles for our room and board would be paid to us. This looked great on paper and sounded terrific, but after the earnings were averaged out we would have only received five rubles. It was not even enough to purchase a handful of sunflower seeds.

Even though I was hungry most of the time, I enjoyed good health until I was struck with diarrhea. The illness was so persistent that I had to be admitted to a hospital. This turned out to be a blessing from heaven because I was not subjected to another cold winter. The conditions in the hospital were horrible. Five people shared two beds. The sanitary conditions were beyond description and the food was bad. The Russian doctors were unfit to treat horses. As patients died, new ones took their place. I managed to hold my own and after a few weeks began to enjoy my confinement. I started to feel better, and the thought of being released and having to battle the cold weather worried me a great deal. When I found some stale water, I took a little sip and the runs returned. Drinking this contaminated water once in a while secured my hospital stay until spring. The doctors could not understand why after having been ill for such a long period of time, I was able to stay alive. I knew why; my exercises during times when I was alone helped me stay in shape. When the sun melted the snow, I realized that it was time for me to get well and move on. The doctors asked me what it would take to cure me. I answered, "Plenty of food." My request was granted and my health improved rapidly. After a few days, I was discharged.

Upon my return to the camp, I was assigned to a construction crew responsible for building an officers' club. I became aware that this so-called "classless society" had greater divisions than any other I was acquainted with. The work was very easy; yet, none of the Russians really knew what they were doing. It was, more or less, in the hands of the prisoners to build the club. Sometimes we rode a hundred miles on trucks to pick up the food supplies. Potatoes and cabbage were the main staples. These trips usually turned out to be rewarding. Since there were no gasoline stations on the way, we carried a fifty-gallon drum of diesel fuel. It did not take us very long to realize that we possessed a hot item. Farmers, who did not have the luxury of electricity, used diesel fuel in their lamps and were willing to trade anything for this precious liquid. They gave us butter, milk, ham, and eggs in exchange for the fuel. It blew the guards' minds when they saw and smelled our cooking. They could not figure out how the prisoners were able to live so high on the hog. We did not reveal our source but invited the guards to help themselves to some of the food; after all, they were the ones who ran out of fuel on later trips.

We finally received word that, according to the agreement of the allies, by the end of 1948 all prisoners were to be released. This news was invigorating. It gave us new hope and made us forget the broken promises. We went to work smiling, and the thought of being released replaced the terrible depression and our abrasive behavior. We looked forward to a new life and made plans for the future. The men talked about pursuing job training or perhaps enrolling in school. Even tender thoughts surfaced, some prisoners wondering if their former girlfriends were still waiting or thought about finding new loves. Since our spirits were high, time went by much faster. The constant reassurance that we would be home by the end of 1948 had its effect. Work that was disliked and had been a drag became easier and our production increased. At times we even had kind thoughts for the Russians, especially when we noticed that the quality of food had slightly improved. September 1948 came and went, but we still did not see any signs of an impending release. Our high hopes during the past months were slowly replaced with suspicion. The warm sunshine gave way to cold and cloudy days. Snow began to fall, and once more we had to prepare for a bitter cold winter. Groups of prisoners stood around debating why the Russians were not keeping their frequently made promises and sending us home. Angry and disgusted with their lying and conniving, our production sank to an all-time low. As we dragged our feet, we produced sloppy work which would cause the Russians problems during later months. Loose electrical connections and barely insulated wire above ground and underground were doomed for failure. Other crews saw to it that the welding was done poorly. Teams working in the mechanical field also did their part to make the communists pay for the broken promises.

During the last weeks of the year, our attitude changed from bad to worse. The prisoners now refused to work. At noon, when the food was ready to be served, we tipped over the fifty-gallon drums and let the soup run into the gutter. The word *Slythe* was on everyone's lips and painted on every wall. (*Slythe* is an old army expression which was used when everybody was totally dissatisfied and wanted to call it quits.) The civilians and military men alike were surprised at our behavior. Never before had they witnessed such total defiance toward their system. When word of our disobedience spread, a commission came from Moscow to investigate the situation, and if necessary, recommend swift action. They did not want the Russian people to know of our disregard for the established rules. It would have undermined their authority. When members of the commission asked us the reason for our dissatisfaction, we let them know that we were tired of the constant lies. We also told them that we basically adhered to the teachings of Marx, Engels, and Lenin, who had preached to the proletariat, "Strike and revolt." By nightfall, trucks lined up outside our camp. We were frisked; our few belongings searched, put on the trucks and hauled off in different directions to begin an uncomfortable journey into the unknown. The camp was dissolved in a matter of a few hours.

We finally stopped in the city of Kremlitowsk located in the Ukraine, and our contingent was integrated into one of the existing prisoner of war camps. The industrial plants were located on the outskirts of the city. Heavy fighting during the war had left most of them in total ruins. It would take an enormous effort to rebuild and repair the factories. Since they were used in the making of tanks and heavy artillery, it was the Russians' foremost interest to begin production as soon as possible.

Our work day consisted of eight hours from Monday through Saturday. We were off on Sundays. We were housed in a huge building that had been restored by the prisoners. It was surrounded by an eight-foot wire fence, and observation towers were located on every corner. We had cold running water and were able to shower once a week. The Russians gave us one set of underwear and clothing. The shoes were made of canvas and had heavy wooden soles. A barbershop employing several barbers kept our hair trimmed for one ruble. There was even a doctor and dentist available. The Soviet paradise was on the upswing. I also have not forgotten the room I shared with sixteen men and the army of bedbugs attacking me at night. I tried to combat those intruders by putting the iron legs of the bed into cans of water, thereby sending the bugs to an early grave. This worked for a while until the bugs decided to attack me from the air. They climbed to the ceiling and descended upon me like *Stukas* (German bombers). My blood must have been on the bedbugs' most-wanted list. It seemed as if I was always the target because I woke up in the morning with itching boils all over my body. I also became acquainted with the dentist. He extracted two teeth. This procedure was very painful; to this day I am fearful of the dentist.

Generally, the conditions of prison life changed for the better. The communists tried to convert us to their way of thinking, i.e. sell us on communism, etc. Twice a week we received political instructions; the evils of capitalism and Christianity were also pointed out to us. They told us that during the past two thousand years the result of Christianity was wars, destruction, dead, and exploitation of the masses. Communism would give the people a new and everlasting order to bring peace, freedom, and prosperity to all mankind. On the days that we were instructed, the food was much better and more plentiful. The Russians knew that an empty stomach would have a counter-productive effect on us. The food and some of the newly given freedom was worth the lip service and we encouraged the communists to keep up the good work.

I didn't have scriptures, but I had my daily prayers, and when I was in the camp, on Sundays, I got away from the rest of the prisoners, and in my mind, worked over a Sunday school lesson. Though I wasn't much of a singer, I more or less memorized some of the songs and had my own little service.

By mid-1949, we received the news that we were to wind down our projects, and once again were told that it was time for us to be released. We thought it was another one of the communists' tricks to increase our production. Because we did not want to be disappointed again, we paid little attention to the rumor. The officers put pressure on us to complete our tasks but only received the same reaction—no improvement in productivity. The Russians were getting desperate and established completion dates. This turned the doubtful prisoners into partial believers. Hopeful, we once again gave it a try, worked steady and made good progress. During the excitement and anticipation of going home, the rumor spread that the thirty-two prisoners who had previously belonged to certain blacklisted units would not be released. I was sure that I was one of them and did not want to nurture false hope. The cleanup started and the large building we had restored was soon to be occupied by the army.

The beginning of September 1949 marked the day of our departure. After an early morning roll call, we marched to the railroad depot to board a train. It was hard to believe that we were moving in a westward direction. The doors were left open. During the many stops we were able to get off and mingle with the Russian people. Most of the prisoners were finally convinced that the communists were serious about our release. My skepticism grew with every mile I traveled, although I heard news that due to the intervention of our camp commandant, everybody was to be released. The commandant, a lieutenant colonel, and hero of the Soviet Union, was the first Russian soldier who rode his tank into Berlin. He had promised the prisoners of war that everybody would be eventually released and intended to keep his word. The train moved very slowly and finally arrived at Brestlitowsk, the city where approximately four and one-half years previously we had built our first prison camp. All prisoners had to get off and enter nearby barracks. We were ordered to disrobe, leave our belongings behind, cross a hallway, and enter another room to receive new clothing. The communists were not interested in whether we looked nice and clean upon our arrival in Germany; they wanted to make sure that we did not take any lists containing the names of prisoners who had died in captivity or anything else that might be of interest to the western nations.

My return to Brestlitowsk brought back bitter memories. Hundreds of fellow prisoners were buried here; I thanked the Lord that I was not one of them. As I waited to board the connecting train, one of the Russians with whom I had previously worked recognized me and told his companions that the Specialist (the name given to me when I was dealing in stolen commodities) was back. To me it all seemed like a dream. I could not believe my eyes when I saw people I had known

My return to Brestlitowsk brought back bitter memories. Hundreds of fellow prisoners were buried here; I thanked the Lord that I was not one of them.

and worked with coming to shake my hand, bid me farewell, and wish me luck—the latter I really needed. Since I had been disappointed many times before, the doubt of going home was still lingering. The train made its way through Poland and stopped in Warsaw. I was amazed at the friendliness of the Poles. During the past years, they must have realized that Stalin was more of a tyrant than a liberator.

At the next stop, Frankfurt on the Oder River, we finally set foot on German soil. It was here that I sent a telegram to my family letting them know that I was on my way home. As a reminder of the wonderful treatment given to us by the communists, we received better food. Because the German Army brought death and destruction to the people of the Soviet Union, we were forced to sign a document stating we would never again raise arms against the Soviet people. The trip through East Germany was an education in itself. I did not see any signs of prosperity. At the train station in Leipzig, we were approached by children begging for food. Since all of us had experienced the pain of hunger, we gladly gave them our food. The children's eyes sparkled, and it felt good to see smiles on their faces; it was too bad that their joy was short lived. The East German People's Police took the food away from the children and threw it onto the railroad tracks. We could not let them get away with their actions and jumped out of the compartments to beat the heartless East German police officers. Soldiers of the Red Army came to their aid and wanted to know who had instigated the riot. They also said that unless this person identified himself, all of us would be sent back to the USSR. This was the first time that all the prisoners displayed a unified front; no one stepped forward to squeal. Although we had been threatened that we would be sent back to our camp, at that moment nobody cared. We told the Russian officer that we would rather go back than approve of the East German conduct. None of the officers could comprehend what they heard. They finally gave up and let the train continue its move toward the west.

As we crossed East Germany, we saw many people without smiles on their faces. The cities were destroyed; nothing had been done to erase the scars of war. The train stopped for the last time near the West German border. After receiving one more pep talk from the communists, we marched toward the fine line dividing freedom from communist tyranny. We ran the last hundred yards, and after crossing the border into West Germany, our joy was beyond description. Bur for some of the prisoners the day of reckoning had arrived. The guys that had collaborated with the Russians and had been instrumental in making their fellow prisoners' lives miserable, and practically unbearable, were now without protection. These turncoats were beaten and kicked by those men who had suffered because of their actions.

A much more pleasant sight was the Salvation Army's food service truck. It was specifically set up to welcome the prisoners of war. The aroma of coffee, hot chocolate, and the sight of fresh fruit and sandwiches made us realize that we had escaped hell and had entered paradise. My taste buds jumped for joy as I gulped down the good food that I had dreamed of during the past years of imprisonment. Since our stomachs were not accustomed to rich meals, we were cautioned to be careful and were told not to overeat. Buses transported us to the Friedland Dismissal Camp, where we received more good nourishment and a physical checkup. We were also interrogated by members of a British intelligence unit and received our discharge documents, some money, and food stamps.

For the last time we boarded a flower-draped train, and at every stop received a hero's welcome. We were greeted by choirs of school children handing us flowers. Women with baskets of food, soft drinks, and milk came to serve us. It was wonderful to realize that we had not been forgotten by the people of our homeland.

My testimony had grown. I had faced a lot of temptation and withstood it all. I had promised the Lord, "If I ever get out of prison camp, I'm never going to miss a meeting." And now I could keep that promise. There was nothing better to me than the Church. I wouldn't have been there if not for the Church.

The train finally arrived in Essen, my hometown. I had waited almost four and one-half years for this moment. Mr. Nigemann, a former schoolteacher, in the company of his students had come to the station to greet the prisoners of war. I also saw my brother, Fritz, his wife, Else, and other friends from the LDS Church. I noticed right away that my mother and sister were missing. My brother took me aside and informed me that Wilma had married and was living in the United States. I was also told that the most influential and loving person in my life was terminally ill and was waiting for me at home.

When I finally saw my mother, I hardly recognized her. She had always been a person of full vitality and now was a barely a shadow of herself. The faith and hope to welcome me home had kept her alive. Neither the printed message from the Red Cross, the announcement in the newspaper stating that I was killed in action, or the many years of my absence without any news, could convince her that I was dead. The realization that my mother's time was running out was extremely hard on me and almost impossible to bear.

On the evening of November 26, 1949, she got worse and I knew that the hour of her death was approaching. My brother, his wife, and I gathered around the sofa on which Mother was resting. Holding her hands and keeping back our tears, we tried to make her departure as easy as possible. When she stopped breathing and closed her eyes, we panicked and tried to wake her. Mother opened her eyes and in a weak, sorrowful voice asked, "Why did you call me back? It was so peaceful and beautiful on the other side." Shortly thereafter, she closed her eyes again. This time we were calm and thankful for the privilege of having the kindest, most wonderful mother who had ever walked the face of this earth.

Oskar Helmut Starke

Oskar Helmut Starke was born May 5, 1919, in Plauen, Germany, to Richard Oskar Schneider and Alma Elise Starke. His father, a railway employee, had died just months earlier at the end of World War I. Alone with a new baby, Alma moved in with her parents so she could work, and Oskar was raised by his grandparents. When Oskar was five, his mother had to leave Plauen and work in the city of Chemnitz for a time. While there, she lived with an aunt and was introduced to The Church of Jesus Christ of Latter-day Saints. When she returned to Plauen, she and Oskar began attending the small branch consisting of mostly women and children.

Oskar's childhood was not a pleasant one. His health was not good, and he had been told at a young age that he would never live to the age of sixteen. Because of that, he was not allowed to play sports or participate with other children in their outdoor activities. In addition, the family was very poor, which limited his education. Participation in Church activities became a highlight for Oskar, and he was excited when he was finally given permission from his grandparents to be baptized at the age of ten.

When Hitler came to power, things for Oskar began to change. With the many new programs instituted by the Nazi Party, the economic burdens that had plagued the family began to ease, and Oskar's educational opportunities began to expand. Though he was interested in aeronautics and wanted to study in a technical field, tradition dictated that his parents were to determine his career. Because of the economic uncertainty that existed, it was decided that Oskar would become a civil servant. He began work as a legal assistant and also began studying at a local trade college.

In 1934 my mother's feelings were hurt, and she felt offended and insulted by a lady member of the Church with whom she had been a close friend for many years. She took that very hard, and as a result my mother and I became inactive and stayed away from the Church for twelve years.

Because of my interest in flying, I joined the Deutsche Luftsport Verband at age seventeen, a club of flight enthusiasts engaged in constructing and flying gliders and sailplanes. In the summer during weekends, we hitched a trailer to an old car which carried a folded glider and headed for the mountains. I was finally cleared to sit behind the controls of one of those gadgets for my first experience off the ground and in the air. I was very proud of it. All of these activities would soon come to an end. Politically Hitler's party was now well established in all branches of the government. In defying international treaties, military service once again became a requirement in Germany in connection with a feverish buildup of the armed forces.

Hatred against the Jews and other non-Aryans flared up, and the inner political as well as the world situation in general deteriorated to a point that I lost interest in being a civil servant in support of a government that became more and more aggressive and violent. I began to concentrate on accounting as a possible future profession.

As required by law, I had to serve from October 1938 through March 1939 in the *Reichsarbeitsdienst* in Schwarzenberg im Erzgebirge, a premilitary organization that performed work on construction and other public projects. After a few weeks of basic training, boot camp style, we were assigned to build a drainage system into a rocky mountain area. It was very hard work and, as winter set in, became almost intolerable. However, I was fortunate. After two months, the commanding officer needed someone with a special talent for drafting. I volunteered and ended up through the rest of the winter sitting in a nice, warm office, drawing organization plans and doing statistical and general office work. The pay was not very good; we received fifty cents a day. However, I found a girlfriend that took care of the expenses when we went to a dance or restaurant.

In April 1939 I was drafted into the German armed forces and, because of my interest in airplanes, ended up in the German Air Force, which took me away from home for over seven years and through the Second World War.

During all the years Church members had been counseled to be good citizens, to support the government, and to obey the law of the land. Looking back, I now question the universal validity of the twelfth Article of Faith and the related section of the Doctrine and Covenants. In my opinion, these revelations were given exclusively for the benefit of the American people; to be otherwise would justify support for a government which commits crimes against humanity. Case in point: the German Saints. As I learned many years later, sometime shortly before the beginning of World War II, a letter from the Brethren of the Church was read from the pulpit. It said in essence that dark clouds of trouble were hanging over the world and war seemed to be inevitable. Saints everywhere were encouraged "to give allegiance to their sovereign and render loyal service when called thereto. When, therefore, constitutional laws would call the manhood of the Church into the armed services of any country to which they owe allegiance, their highest civic duty required that they meet that call, *regardless on which side.*" However, when it was all over, the German brethren were harshly criticized by many for having been a Nazi soldier, a stigma they carried for the rest of their lives. How could you support and render service to such a government? Why did you not kill your leaders? we were asked.

On April 18, 1939, I found myself together with approximately six hundred other young men of my age standing and waiting in a large hall at the main railroad station in Weimar, Thuringia. It was cold and drafty, and we were pushed around by some nasty sergeants. Toward the end of the day, we were transported to the brand new Weimar-Nohra base of the German Air Force, Flieger Ausbildungs Regiment 51. It consisted of two parts. The recruit training center was beautifully located in a pine forest with stone buildings amid trees and landscaped area; it looked more like a resort hotel complex. The other part across the highway to Erfurt was an open airfield complete with hangars, tarmacs, and technical support structures for flight training.

Military boot camp is not an enjoyable experience even in pleasant surroundings. It is depressing to be constantly harassed by screaming drill sergeants who generally were sadistic in nature, uneducated, and in my opinion unqualified for more sophisticated lifestyles. A certain Sergeant Schmidt comes to mind. He was so nasty, had he led us into combat, he would not have survived. I found some comfort in the fact that boot camp in the air force lasted only three months and was not quite as rough as in the army and that I was not alone. Some good friendships developed, and there was even time for practical jokes. I was usually quite tired at the end of a day and slept very well. One night I had the pleasant sensation that my bed was softly swinging back and forth. When I finally woke up, I found that six guys had carried it with me from the second floor down to the main hall. They had a good laugh watching me take the bed apart and carry everything back upstairs to my room. I really could not get mad at them because I participated in similar pranks.

Since I had fairly good learning abilities, it was not difficult for me to understand and follow instructions. I scored some points and in turn earned some privileges. One was a four-day pass to visit my folks back home.

While we did not have much time to follow the daily news, the few things we heard and read were disturbing. During the summer of 1939, the European political situation had turned from bad to worse. Hitler had made demands on neighboring countries that could not possibly be fulfilled without the risk of confrontation. At the end of July, I graduated from boot camp. At that time all the recruits had to take aptitude tests and undergo physical examinations which would determine that person's future in the air force. If I ever had hoped to work with airplanes, or even to fly, that dream was shattered. I was found not to be physically in the best condition or mechanically trained for such an assignment. In view of my previous administrative work experience, I ended up in the company office. Just out of boot camp, I rated the lowest among the low and was mainly used to do errands for the higher-ranking officials. Several times during the week I was called upon to do chores for the commanding officer who resided in the city of Weimar. That gave me a chance to get away and out of the compound for a few hours. I met a girl in town and was able to spend some time with her. All in all those days were a short and rather uneventful period of time, an uneasy quiet before the storm.

WILHELM KRISCH FILE

German troops prepare to assault a Russian position.

In the early morning hours of September 1, 1939, the whole regiment was called up to assemble on the parade grounds. We could hear Hitler's harsh voice over the radio announce that the German armed forces had attacked Poland that morning under what was later found to be false pretense. Although we had been aware of the political tension that had built up during the past months, the news came as a shock to all of us. The Second World War had begun.

During the following night, I found no sleep, trying to comprehend what had happened and how it would affect not only my life but also the lives of millions of others. I came to the conclusion that this was not a just war. A power-hungry despot who wanted to rule the world had provoked it. It was then that I resolved to do everything possible to stay out of confrontations. I strongly believed that any blood spilled during that conflict, whether mine or that of an enemy soldier, was not justified. Regardless of the situation, I would not kill or harm any human being.

Within a few days, England and France declared war on Germany in support of Poland without taking immediate action. The German armed forces overran Poland and hacked it to pieces. Under an apparent prearranged agreement, the Soviet Union took possession of the eastern part and Germany occupied the rest. Poland had ceased to exist. Even though the German war propaganda machine ran full steam celebrating the "victories," an eerie silence settled over the rest of Europe.

So far all of this had not affected our regiment. However, at the end of October 1939, we received marching orders and were transferred to the city of Koenigsberg in East Prussia, near the Baltic Sea, close to the Soviet border. The transfer took place by rail. On the way, we passed through parts of war-torn Poland and could see firsthand the destruction and horrible devastation brought upon that country and people.

In Koenigsberg we were housed in the Boelcke Kaserne, a fairly new facility on the eastern outskirts of town. The winters in East Prussia were very cold, with much snow and ice. We appreciated our comfortable quarters. Something happened in the first few days of February 1940 that had a dramatic effect on my life during the war years. It also proved the importance of "being at the right time in the right place and being able to do something that others could not."

It was a quiet Sunday afternoon. I had been assigned to duty at the company office. There was nothing to do. The office manager, a sergeant, and two assistants were sitting at their desks, chatting leisurely. Being the lowest rank, I sat at a small table in the corner, wearing worn-out work clothes. The door opened and a middle-aged gentleman in civilian clothing entered, wearing an overcoat and a hat and carrying a walking cane. Neither the sergeant nor the other two paid any attention to him. They continued their idle talk and let him just stand there. To them a civilian was not considered to be important. As the minutes went by, I somehow sensed a sharp increase in tension in the room. Suddenly the gentleman slammed his cane on the nearest desk and yelled, "I am Colonel Hartung, your new commanding officer! I will not tolerate the way you treat people who come to this office!" Everyone jumped up, snapped to attention, and there they stood with pale faces, dumbfounded and wondering what to expect next. And then with a thundering voice the colonel gave them a lecture on military discipline and behavior. I stood there with the rest of them, but as the lowest in rank I had nothing to fear; in fact, I must confess that I enjoyed the situation. The other guys had treated me like dirt, and I felt they deserved being chastised.

After his outburst, the colonel went to his private office and slammed the door shut. First there was silence among the three men; they just looked at each other in embarrassment and then tried to put the blame on each other.

I should mention that a buzzer had been installed from the commanding officer's desk to the outer office. The buzzer sounded; the sergeant jumped up and went into the colonel's office. After a minute or two we heard the colonel yelling again and out came the sergeant, red-faced, and sent the next guy in. After a minute the same thing happened until all three had their turn. From their conversation I gathered that the colonel wanted someone to take dictation in shorthand and to type some letters, and apparently none of them could do that. In those days there were no ladies employed in the German armed forces.

As a former law student, I had a lot of practice in shorthand and typing; in fact, I was quite good at it and had received awards in competitions. Of course, the others did not know that; nobody had asked me about it.

We could hear the colonel mumble in his office. After a while he came out, gave the sergeant another lecture about the incompetence of his office personnel. Then his eyes fell on me. He looked with disgust at my shabby work clothes and said, "Who are you?" I answered with my rank and name and he asked, "Can you take dictation in shorthand and type?" I said, "Yes, sir!" He snapped at the sergeant, "Why didn't you tell me that?" and ordered me to follow him into his office. He had me sit down at the side of his desk, gave me some paper and a pencil, and proceeded to dictate a short letter. He watched me, but he spoke slowly and I had no problem following him. He asked me to read the letter back to him, which I did. Then he dictated another letter. By that time the tension was gone; he became quite friendly and told me how he wanted it done and that he did not want any errors, corrections, or erasures in those letters. I learned later that in civilian life he had been an executive in a large corporation and that he expected much from his office personnel.

I went back to the outer office. All of a sudden the other three guys were very friendly and accommodating. They wanted to know how things went with "him." I told them that I was getting along with him just fine. I proceeded to type the letters just as he wanted and returned to his office. He looked at the letters, held them against the light to check for erasures. There were none. He signed the letters and thanked me for my work. Then he went with me back into the outer office and said, addressing the sergeant and the others, "From now on, this man (he pointed at me) will exclusively work for me. No other assignments will be given to him. He will receive a decent uniform and be put into quarters where I can reach him any time. Do you understand that?" The sergeant clicked his heels and shouted, "Yes, sir!" And so it was. I had reached a turning point. Colonel Gunther Hartung had entered into my life. I became his private secretary and in time his confidant, something not found very often in military service considering our difference in rank. I was placed in new, more comfortable quarters, received a new uniform and was on twenty-four-hour call. The colonel was very demanding, often dictating for hours. I did errands for him and his family. His wife and two small children lived nearby. Sometimes, when he could not sleep, he would call me at two o'clock in the morning and I would sit in my pajamas taking dictation over the telephone for two or three hours. Then he was gone for several days, and I had plenty of time to catch up. I obtained special privileges. According to military rules, one could leave the compound only with a pass that had to be returned after use. Time was restricted. Only officers had unlimited passes. Sergeants had to be back at 6:00 AM, noncommissioned officers had until 2:00 AM, ordinary soldiers could stay until midnight. Colonel Hartung issued me an unlimited special privilege (so-called red) pass, which I carried all the time. I once was arrested by the military police at 3:00 AM; they assumed that I, as a private, not being entitled to a red pass, might have acquired it illegally. It took a phone call to the colonel to correct that situation.

From my work with Colonel Hartung, I learned that he had been assigned to set up and organize a school with three-month courses to train noncommissioned air force officers, which later was expanded to include newly appointed officers. All the typing I had done pertained to organization, curriculum, finding a location, and making acquisitions for housing and maintenance. It was decided to start the school in Pillau, a port city on the Baltic Sea, fifty kilometers from Koenigsberg. It was a beautiful setting in a wooded area on a small peninsula across from the harbor, right on the beach. I was responsible to make sure that the administrative part of the unit was ready for operation on June 1, 1940. The colonel had promoted me to a private first class on

April 1. The base commander on location was a captain which made it difficult for me at times to get what I needed. The German military was very rank conscious.

My boss knew that he was very demanding. Sometimes he would say, "Starke, you look overworked. Take the rest of the day off and go over to the beach." Or he suggested getting out of town for a few days. Without question he would sign travel papers and would say, "Wherever you go, tell me about it. I may want to take my family there." So I used some of my spare time to see and explore as much as I could and visited many places of interest. I had a chance to travel along the Baltic Sea coast from Danzig to Memel. The colonel also saw to it that the men under his command had the opportunity to go home occasionally, especially around Christmas, if wartime conditions would allow.

On his desk was a picture of a good-looking young woman. I asked him about it, and he told me that the young lady was his daughter from his first wife, who was Jewish and died in the late 1920s, before Hitler came to power. The daughter (about two years younger than I) therefore was half-Jewish, something that was not acceptable in Nazi Germany. She was not permitted to attend public schools and was educated in private institutions. She had no social life; she was a "non-person," pretty much confined to their living quarters in Berlin. That troubled the colonel very much. The fact that he had been married to a Jewish woman, even though she had died, also affected his military career in Nazi Germany. He retained his rank only because, like many others, he had been a decorated officer during the First World War, and his experiences were desperately needed during this time.

Earlier in 1940 the German forces had marched into France, Belgium, and the Netherlands. By the end of that year they were sitting at the English Channel and had occupied much of Western Europe. Being stationed in East Prussia, we did not become involved in those actions. However, British bombers now began to appear over German cities, and the war moved closer to home.

—•—

Christmas 1940 was another significant milestone in my life. I had two weeks' furlough and visited my family in our hometown, Plauen. Since there was not much to do for me, I was sitting around the house bored. My mother suggested that I go to a dance. I did not like the idea too much, but I went to the best place in town, *Tromels*, an elegant restaurant, where among other things mouthwatering homemade pastries were served. There were also two dance floors. When it came to girls, I was quite shy; I did not know what to say. There were three young ladies sitting at a nearby table; two of them wore identical dresses. I finally mustered the courage to ask one of them to dance and then took the other one a few times. At the end of the dance, I asked what seemed to be the older one if I could escort her home. Her name was Anni Piering. She happened to live way out on the edge of town. She had told the other two that she would get rid of me as soon as possible and they would then go home together. Well, that did not happen! I took her home, and she agreed to see me again. That was the beginning of a courtship that ended in marriage.

In spring of 1941 Colonel Hartung promoted me to the rank of corporal. Our school was doing quite well. My involvement with it was a great experience for me, and I learned much from my boss. He was a very effective teacher, methodical, well-organized, and able to hold the attention of the students. He gave me chances to teach. Even today, after more than fifty years, I am still using some of the techniques I learned during that time.

There was another chance to go home, and on June 1, 1941, Anni and I were engaged. It turned out that the other young lady in the same dress at the dance was her sister. She also had a brother and two wonderful parents. I felt right at home with her family. In midsummer of 1941, after things settled down in Western Europe, Hitler decided to take on the Soviet Union. The war began on the Eastern Front, unprovoked, sacrificing millions of people in what proved to be the beginning of the bitter end for Germany. The war had now moved to our doorsteps, because the border of the Soviet Union was only about eighty kilometers from our present location in Pillau. We woke up one morning with Soviet aircraft bombing the neighborhood. Colonel Hartung had what I call a sixth sense, probably from his World War I experiences. He sensed danger and did something about it. Having been with him for most of the war years, I witnessed him saving not only his life, but also the lives of the men who were with him, including myself.

As soon as the war started with the Soviet Union, the colonel ordered the school with all the personnel to be transferred to Western Europe, away from the Eastern Front. In late June, we loaded up and moved to the small town of Maubeuge in Northern France. For about four weeks we tried to settle down, but the facilities were not what we expected. The colonel went away for a few days. He called me and told me to stop all proceedings and said that we would relocate to the city of Reims, France. He also told me that he would not return to Maubeuge and ordered me to clean out his desk and to pack all of his personal belongings and see to it that the transfer went smoothly.

While cleaning out his drawers, something fell out of my hand and flipped open. It was Colonel Hartung's personal journal. Perhaps it was not right for me to look into that small book, but the colonel had become a father figure to me, although I was smart enough not to misuse the trust he placed in me and lose the special privileges I had. In every respect, he was the colonel and I was a soldier. In private conversations we were quite open about the political situation in Germany and the war. I had traveled for him as a personal courier and had carried personal messages to his family and letters for his Jewish in-laws in Switzerland. I met the other members of his family, including his daughter. I had not yet told him that I was engaged to Anni.

Looking into his journal, I saw my name mentioned, and then something that shocked me. He had expressed feelings about his daughter from his first marriage and her troubles of being half-Jewish and what to do about it. His desire was to meet a young man whom he could trust and who shared his political views. He would promote him into the officer ranks and would groom him, to fit into his world and society. He wanted to bring him together with his daughter, hoping that there could be a marriage which would free his daughter from the stigma that had troubled her so much and hopefully in a post-war, different form of society, she would be able to live a normal life. It dawned upon me that I was that young man.

Now I began to understand why after a humble beginning he had shown so much interest in me, promoted me, was so concerned for my well-being and had been a father figure. And I had just become engaged to Anni! It took some time for me to comprehend and digest what I had seen, and try to figure out how to react.

We completed the move to Reims in August of 1941, and I stayed there for more than a year. I never told the colonel what happened with the journal. Only Anni knew.

The school was located at the airport. We were quite happy with the facility. The colonel was in good spirits; he promoted me to sergeant and ordered me to eat with him in the officers' mess hall, in preparation for becoming an officer. Everything went along fine, except that Anni and I planned to be married sometime in 1942. For that I needed the signature of Colonel Hartung under our marriage license. After several attempts, in a quiet moment, I mustered the courage to tell him about our plans. It was apparent that it irritated him. After a few tense moments, he became very angry and upset, even though he tried to control himself. He told me that I did not know what I was doing. He gave me a lecture about the significance of marriage and how important it was to think about all the ramifications before making such a decision. The outburst lasted for about an hour. He refused to sign and threw the marriage license on the floor. For seven days I went into his office with the license; each time he refused, until finally he calmed down and gave in. I had a signed marriage license, but our relationship had gone sour. I made every effort to do my best, to do my duty and avoid confrontation. In time things went somewhat back to normal.

By the end of March 1942, I had a nervous breakdown. Overworked and worried about our future, I cracked up. Colonel Hartung, in a conciliatory gesture, secured a place for me for six weeks in a military convalescence hospital in Bad Brambach, close to our hometown. Anni could visit me, and we prepared for our upcoming wedding.

After my release from the hospital, I went to Plauen and on May 9, 1942, married Anni Helene Piering.

We had met Christmas 1940. We had seen each other daily for about seven days and then I had to leave. In our first letters we had already mentioned the engagement rings. For the next year and half until the time we married, we had actually seen each other in person less than thirty days. We had bonded through correspondence. According to law, the marriage ceremony was performed by the state at the city hall. It was done around 10:00 AM; the reception took place at the home of Anni's parents and lasted the rest of the day. Since food was rationed during the war, the meals were not elaborate, but excellent. There was not much time for a honeymoon as I had to return to my unit within three days.

After I resumed my duties at the school, the colonel and I were successful in restoring the close relationship that we had before. He began taking interest in my marriage and saw to it that my salary was increased. I now had a wedding picture on my desk. He still wanted me to become an officer, but I did not share that desire. Under the political situation and the possibility of a lost war, being an officer did not interest me. Besides, most of the younger officers were arrogant snobs.

In December 1941 the United States had entered the war, and it had become ugly. German cities were bombed, the Eastern Front had stalled, and the Soviets had made significant gains. It seemed that Hitler's fortunes had reached a turning point. It became more and more apparent that Germany could not win the war.

In September 1942 the school was closed. Colonel Hartung was sent to Italy on special assignment, and I was attached to Flieger Ausbildungs Regiment 21 in Reims. After two months we were transferred to a large military training center in Grossborn in northern Germany. In spite of travel difficulties caused by heavy bombings and military restrictions, Anni took the risk and visited me there for a few days. As newlyweds, we tried everything to find a chance to be together.

Then I received orders to attend a course at the air force officers' school in Czestochowa, Poland. Those who made it to graduation would be commissioned as second lieutenants and immediately sent to the Russian front. I had no desire to end up there. I faked a physical and mental breakdown and was referred to a specialist in a general (non-military) hospital. It did not take long for the doctor to find out that I had faked the whole thing, but he was sympathetic and, based on my high blood pressure and general condition, recommended my dismissal from the officers' school. That was what I wanted. I returned to Czestochowa, was released from the school, and ordered back to my original military unit, the Flieger Ausbildungs Regiment 21 which, in the meantime, had become part of the Sixth Air Force Field Division (6. Luftwaffen Feld Division). I had a certificate from that doctor that I was not fit for combat and should be used for administrative duties only. In the process I lost contact with Colonel Hartung.

It took three days to travel back to Grossborn in northern Germany. Upon arrival, I learned that the whole division had just been shipped out to the Eastern Front in the Soviet Union. A small staff remained to take care of the continued flow of supplies. I was attached to that staff. The assignment lasted only two months. On February 12, 1943, I was ordered with eight others to accompany a trainload of supplies to the headquarters of the Sixth Air Force Field Division, located in the northern part of the Russian Front, east of Vitebsk. February is the worst month for travel in that part of Russia. Subzero temperatures and deep snow everywhere made life miserable. Our journey took five days. Because I had been classified as "home front use only," I hoped they would send me right back after delivering the load. But there was a shortage of manpower, and I was ordered to stay. Although I was assigned to do mainly office work, we became involved in heavy fighting in the battles around Nevel and the Upper Dvina River. We were still air force personnel but were used as infantry for which we were not trained, and we had heavy losses. One day during a break I walked together with a fellow sergeant, a friend, across an opening in the forest. Suddenly we heard the sound of approaching aircraft. Seconds later one of the low-flying Soviet attack planes came "tree-hopping" right at us and released a number of small, high-explosive bombs. Instinctively, I jumped into a nearby ditch. My friend stumbled and did not make it. All that was left of him were some bloody ribs, a gruesome and grim reminder of the unmerciful, pitiless, relentless reality of war.

The countryside consisted of endless forests, rolling hills, and rivers, and was sparsely populated. The summers were short with millions of mosquitoes. We could sleep only when covered with a mosquito net. The few highways were unpaved and either muddy or dusty. We became forest dwellers, living in small huts or dugouts among trees. The division commander was General von Heyking, an acquaintance of Colonel Hartung. That did not help me at the moment. I was in a tough spot and had to make the best of it. There were some bright moments, though, as part of my assignment involved contact with people who lived in the area. I developed a close friendship with a young Russian peasant from a nearby village. His wife had taught German as a schoolteacher before the war, which enabled us to communicate. In the harsh winter months, during a lull in the fighting, he came to me with a wooden narrow sleigh and his *Panye* horse. At below-zero temperatures, the two of us wrapped in warm clothing and blankets, lying flat on the sleigh on our stomachs, would race over the frozen rivers through the endless forests laden with snow, the little horse running and running with great endurance all day long. Occasionally we would stop at a hidden village for something to eat. Although I found myself as an "enemy" soldier, in enemy territory, without a weapon, alone with a native who was stronger than I, I was not afraid; we had become close friends. My German comrades thought I was crazy to endanger my life, but I enjoyed it tremendously.

—•—

The other bright spot came in November 1943 when I was able to get a three-week furlough and go home. I had not seen Anni for more than a year, and I wanted very much to be with her and the rest of our families. Unfortunately, good times seem to go by much faster. The war had taken its toll. Food was scarce. The people lived in constant fear of air raids. So far our hometown had been spared. Too soon came the time to say good-bye. It became harder and harder to take leave from each other, not knowing what the future would bring, sensing there would be a catastrophe at the end. When I left, Anni was pregnant.

Upon my return to Russia, I found that my unit had been moved, and it took a while to find the new location. In that process, I had also lost my Russian friend. Together with seven other

NATIONAL ARCHIVES

German officers prepare for a troop review.

divisions, my unit was now stuck in the woods east of Gorodock, almost encircled by Russian forces. With great effort and heavy losses we managed to slip away and establish a new base. It did not last long, and we were on the move again. The German armies were in retreat! During the first two months of 1944 I was able to make contact again with Colonel Hartung. He had reestablished the school, this time near Nancy in eastern France. He wrote that he was unhappy with his personnel and wanted me back under his command. From his end he initiated a transfer for me, which got stuck in the endless channels of military bureaucracy.

Then in March I heard of an order from the Air Force High Command that on a voluntary basis a limited number of soldiers could be transferred back to the air force. I was the first one to apply. Led by a captain with a group of twenty-five men, among them my buddy Sergeant Heinz Michel, we left the Eastern Front for good. We had to report to a reserve battalion in Posen, Poland. We arrived there on April 7. Now I could get in touch with Colonel Hartung again and received word that my transfer to him had been approved. However, it took another three months before I got the marching orders.

I had no special assignment in Posen. I had time to recuperate from the Russian front. Together with Sergeant Michel I explored the beautiful city of Posen, not yet devastated by the war. There was a large opera house, and we had the opportunity to see several productions. There was also access to a public swimming pool, and most important of all, we could go to a dentist. It had been years of unattended dental hygiene, and I had lost several teeth because of it.

From April 21 through May 3, Sergeant Michel and I volunteered to lead a group of soldiers to Verona and Mantova in Italy, under the supervision of an officer. We traveled through the countries of Eastern Europe, then into Austria and Italy. It was a relaxing trip with much to see. On the way back we talked the accompanying officer into changing our travel papers also so that each of us could stop in our hometown for two days. Anni was in her seventh month of pregnancy.

Back in Posen I had to wait two more months until my transfer became effective and I could go back to Colonel Hartung and the school. In the evening of June 6, rumors began to circulate that the allied forces had attempted an invasion at the English Channel. It took several more days before we heard officially that something was happening in the west. That, of course, was of interest to me because soon I would be on my way to France. Official reports from a new Western Front were vague, only "that the victorious German Armies were taking care of the invasion."

On July 17, 1944, I left Posen. My trip took me through Dresden and, as prearranged, our hometown, Plauen. On July 18, I made an unauthorized stop to see Anni. That triggered something. In the morning of July 19, I had to rush her to a clinic and at 1:20 PM, our son Dietmar was born. Just when the doctor brought him to me, the air raid sirens sounded. I grabbed Anni out of bed into my arms, put the newborn on top, and raced to the air raid shelter in the basement. I could not hear any bombs falling. After a short while, I stepped outside and saw above in the clear blue sky a seemingly endless parade of shiny American B-17 bombers flying in formation over the city, a beautiful picture. No harm was done at that time. The next day, July 20, news came over the radio of an assassination attempt on Hitler. My father-in-law excitingly said, "If Hitler is dead, you don't have to leave." Well, Hitler survived and I continued my trip to Nancy and on to Pont-a-Mousson, where I reunited with Colonel Hartung and the school. He promoted me to master sergeant, and I was again his office manager and secretary. One afternoon the colonel surprised me by showing up with two special guests. One of them was General von Heyking, who had been the commander of the Sixth Air Force Field Division when I was in Russia, serving on his staff. He made it out of there and was now on the run again because Allied forces had taken large portions of Western Europe. They had just liberated Paris, the general's headquarters. By the end of August we were also on the run again. As a school, we were not a combat unit, and Colonel Hartung made sure that we did not get involved. We loaded up and moved through the province of Lorraine, the Saarland, and into Germany. We were directed to head toward Holland. We traveled by train. At one time the engineer got the wrong signal, and we almost went straight into the approaching American lines. We ended up in Nijmegen, Holland, and had just settled down when, one morning, American paratroopers jumped into the outskirts of the city, trying to secure the bridges over the two arms of the Rhine River at Nijmegen and Arnhem.

Again we were able to get away during the night. By mid-September, we ended up in Gustrow in the province of Mecklenburg in Germany, trying to set up the school. By now it was obvious that this school was Colonel Hartung's obsession. There were not many more officers to train. To him it became the means to avoid combat and to make it through to the bitter end alive. I agreed with that philosophy. We could stay only two weeks in Gustrow and moved on to Quedlinburg in the Harz Mountains. We noted the arrival of a political (Gestapo) officer as a member of the staff who shadowed the colonel.

The school was in operation for one month and then transferred to Goslar am Harz. Travel had become extremely difficult because of the heavy bombings of tracks and moving stock. On the first of December 1944, the colonel gave me permission to visit my family. After a few days I received a telegram to return to the unit immediately. My assistant informed me that Colonel Hartung had been relieved of his duty and his whereabouts were unknown. It was later learned that the colonel (as well as many other officers) had been under suspicion by the Gestapo in connection with the assassination attempt on Hitler. Even though nothing could be proven, the colonel had been sent on a suicide mission to the Eastern Front, a location that had already been conquered by the Soviets. There he disappeared.

A new commanding officer was assigned and the school transferred to Berlin. We were housed at the Tempelhof Airport. The new boss was very nasty, the complete opposite of Colonel Hartung. During Christmas and the New Year 1945, we suffered heavy bombings with no chance to operate the school. It became obvious that Germany was now in a state of utter confusion. Destruction was everywhere. Ordinary people spent more time in air raid shelters than in their homes.

One more attempt was made to keep the school alive by moving to Braunschweig. In the midst of an air raid at the end of January 1945, we gathered what was left of personnel and equipment (leaving the nasty commander behind) and packed it into a railcar that was sitting in a rail-switching yard. There was no train available to hook onto. In the middle of the night, a large locomotive stopped at a signal on an adjacent track. We asked the engineer where he was going. He said, "Hannover." That was our direction. By hand we pushed our loaded railcar to a nearby switch, moved it over to the other track behind the locomotive, and hooked it up. Within a few minutes that engine took off and we were going full speed, with bombs falling around us, through the outskirts of Berlin. After a while things calmed down. We were very tired and must have dozed off. In the early morning hours, we were awakened by an unusual quiet. No rattling or swaying back and forth; our railcar stood still. In the early daylight we found that we were standing on a side track in a small train station out in nowhere. The engineer must have dropped us off during the night. Nearby was the small house of a rail linesman. We learned that we were actually quite close to our destination, and a telephone call arranged transportation into the city of Braunschweig.

For three more months the school was set up again. We carried on in the tradition of Colonel Hartung, even though on a very limited scale. It became now our obsession. Another commander arrived, General von Buch. He was a very pleasant old gentleman, and I became his secretary. I had Sergeant Usko and Sergeant Schmidt on the staff. Both were residents of Braunschweig and had their wives living there. Mrs. Usko was pregnant; her own family lived in Berlin. The war situation went from bad to worse. We spent much of our time in shelters in one air raid after another, but our facility was not damaged.

After crossing the Rhine River, the Western Allies in March 1945 approached the area of Hannover/Braunschweig. By mid-April we received orders to close the school, and all personnel had to move back to Berlin to "defend the German Capital City" against the onslaught of the Soviets. We left Braunschweig hastily in the morning of April 11 by special train. As far as we knew, the Americans were entering the city from the other side. General von Buch (74 years old) told me that he was going into retirement and went home. Sergeant Schmidt had also informed me that he was not coming with us; he went home also, clearly an act of desertion. Under the circumstances, I kept my mouth shut.

We arrived in Berlin on the thirteenth of April. As the first matter of business, the leading officer held a court martial and sentenced Sergeant Schmidt to death for desertion. Of course that had no effect on Schmidt; by now he was safe behind American lines.

We were placed with other units in the villages of Liebenwalde and Hammer on the northern ring of defense of Berlin. We had several encounters with Soviet forces, sitting on the other side of a canal. We were able to hold our positions. Sergeant Usko had secretly brought his wife along. She wanted to check on her folks in Berlin. In an unbelievable act of courage, in her pregnant condition, she went alone through the Russian lines to their home and back again through the Russian lines to our command post in two days. In the morning of April 22, I looked out of the window of our sleeping quarters and thought I had a vision. I could not believe my eyes. Out there talking with another officer stood Colonel Hartung! I ran outside and we greeted each other. There was no time for idle talk. He took me aside and told me how he had survived his ordeal and said, "Starke, it is all over, the war is lost. Get out of here and try to make it home safely!"

I took this as an order. During the day everything fell apart. Our commander was wounded and the Russians moved forward, cutting off large sections of the defensive ring. At night Sergeant Usko with his wife, two privates, and I requisitioned a truck. We took off into the northern forest. We knew that the Russians were in part of the woods so we just took a chance. It was the only way to get out or risk ending up in a Siberian prison camp.

We drove on a forest road with the lights turned off, hoping for the best. After two hours we turned west and connected to a road leading into Mecklenburg. We wanted to get away from the Soviets as far as possible and into the area of the advancing western allies. We could move only by night; during the day there were constant air attacks.

By April 26, we reached the small town of Rehna near Lubeck on the Baltic Sea. We ran out of fuel and needed some rest to plan our next move. The whole German population seemed to be on the run, including scattered units of the armed forces, civilians pushing handcarts with their belongings, and refugees from the eastern provinces now in Russian hands.

PRESIDENT MONSON'S POST-WAR MINISTRY AMONG THE GERMAN SAINTS

The stories of the sorrows and the joys of the German Saints during the decades which followed the end of the war in 1945 are remarkable and heart-stirring. In many cases there were modern miracles which allowed the Church to prosper during such challenging times. Many of the memorable moments during this era occurred as part of the ministry of President Thomas S. Monson.

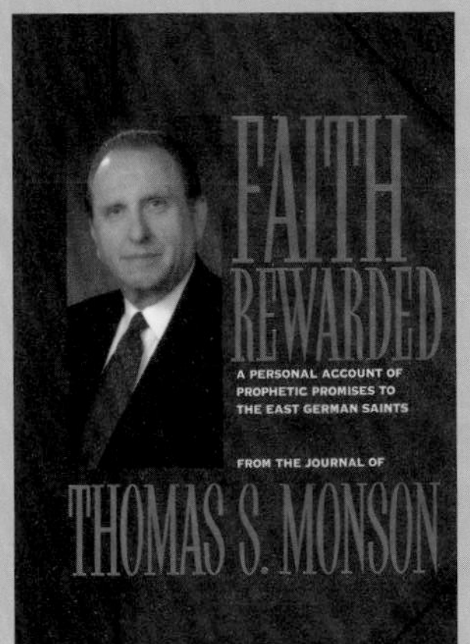

In his capacity as a member of the Quorum of the Twelve Apostles, Elder Monson labored among the German Saints during the period of 1968–1989. Again and again, Elder Monson visited the German Saints, inspiring them to remain dedicated to the gospel in spite of substantial obstacles.

President Monson's work during that period is the subject of the volume, *Faith Rewarded: A Personal Account of the Prophetic Promises to the East German Saints* (Deseret Book, 1996). The book includes excerpts from the personal journals of President Monson and provides vivid details about this important period.

We decided to move into the northern end of Germany, into Schleswig Holstein, close to the border to Denmark, assuming that the British army would take that area. Sergeant Usko's wife decided to leave our group and try to make her way back to their home in Braunschweig. The driver of our truck wanted to stay with the vehicle in Rehna; he had found a girlfriend there. The rest of us, Sergeant Usko, a private, and myself were now without transportation. The British were fast approaching. The mayor of the town and the town council were quarrelling with each other, whether to fight or to surrender. On April 30 the news came over the radio that Hitler was dead. That produced a sigh of relief!

The next evening we observed a column of about twenty-five brand new German trucks, covered with tarps, with a small group of drivers and maintenance personnel, led by a major. They had stopped to take a break. It seemed they were heading north. I asked the officer if we could hitch a ride with them to wherever they were going. The officer smiled and agreed. We got into the back of one of the trucks. In the darkness of the night we moved along slowly. I must have dozed off for a while, when suddenly I noticed that the column of trucks had stopped on the road. I looked outside and saw that daylight was just coming on. My first thought was that we need to get out of here. If we stayed there in daylight on the open road, the British air force would blow us to pieces. Just as I was waking up the others, I saw a jeep approaching, and riding in it were a British officer, two British soldiers, and the German officer, the commander of the trucks. During the night the unit had quietly and unnoticed crossed the British lines and under a prearranged agreement surrendered.

The day was May 2, 1945. We moved on into a small town. The British soldiers gave the German truck drivers a different uniform and they went right back into service, now for the British Army. The rest of us were advised just to walk down the road, which we happily did. We knew we would be prisoners of war and the future was uncertain, but it was like a ton lifted off our shoulders and minds. No more hiding, no more shooting, no more bombs. The war was over.

We walked along that road. British troops were everywhere; they did not pay any attention to us. We came through a village and were able to obtain some food and drink. Eventually other German soldiers, also walking along the roads, joined us. At some point we were gathered, loaded into trucks, and transported through Ratzeburg and Luneburg to Muensterlager, a former German Army training center in Luneburger Heide. Within a few days there were thousands of German POWs.

On May 8, 1945, we received word that Germany had officially surrendered. The war in Europe was now over. We were housed in old barracks with broken windows and organized into groups of eighty men. I became a group leader of one of those units. The German soldiers, after almost six years of war, were not an easy bunch to control. All military order had broken down and morale was at an all-time low. The British made sure that there was some degree of discipline. We had one watery meal a day with some crackers and lost quite a bit of weight.

After a few weeks, the guards announced that they wanted a group of prisoners for a work detail. Since I had the advantage of speaking some English, I sensed that there might be a chance to improve our situation. I talked to my men, but hardly anybody was willing to get up and voluntarily "work." No chance! I finally was able to talk about twenty-five men into accepting that assignment. The next morning we were picked up by a truck and brought to the British headquarters. Some were assigned to work in the officers' lounge and kitchen, and others did some cleanup work in the buildings and on the grounds. A British sergeant took me to his quarters behind the kitchen and indicated that as an equal rank I did not have to work. He had me sit down and let me have a gorgeous meal, leftovers from the officers' mess hall. That was the first decent meal I had eaten in months. I noticed that my men had also been well fed. When in the late afternoon we were taken back to the camp, most of them carried some container with leftover food. We made sure that there would be another request for a work detail.

The next morning, suddenly half of the camp population volunteered for work. Because of my knowledge of English (even though it was far from perfect), I was assigned to work at the office of the German camp commander. By mid-June the British began procedures for the release of prisoners, first those whose homes were in the British occupation zone of Germany, meaning the northwest sector. I had learned that my hometown of Plauen had been conquered by the Americans, only to hear later that they had retreated and allowed the Soviet Army to move in and take over. That was a most devastating blow.

I applied for release to the city of Braunschweig, where I had been a few months before as a German soldier and which was part of the British occupation zone. It was also the hometown of my buddy Usko, who also applied. On July 4, 1945, I was released as a prisoner of war and was moved by truck with a group of others to Braunschweig. After years of Nazi dictatorship, of military service and almost six years of war, we had our first taste of freedom!